Acknowledgements

KV-013-252

This book has its roots in my earlier collaborative work with Professor Bill Merrilees, where we emphasised the role and nature of best practices in retailing. Our later research and teaching in retailing, branding and innovation convinced us that it was timely to present a new approach to retail marketing, which was published by Tilde in 2007. This 2008 edition continues that tradition. I am pleased that the vision of an accessible and innovative retailing book that Professor Merrilees and I shared, has been realised through the ongoing partnership with Tilde University Press. Rick Ryan, who concurred with our vision, and Sally Keohane and Alison Besley in the editorial team at Tilde University Press all gave invaluable support in bringing this book to you, the reader.

Most importantly, I want to recognise the role of Professor Merrilees who continues to act as an Editorial Advisor for this new book. We have been able to continue to enrich our work through the generosity of those retailers, suppliers and consumers who have willingly participated in our research projects and those retailers who granted permission for photographs and illustrations.

I would like to recognise both my current students, who ask challenging and interesting questions, and my former students, who contribute to retail innovation and branding on a daily basis. My local and international colleagues continue to inspire, Grete Birtwistle, Brent McKenzie, Harry Timmermans, Charles Dennis, Gill Maxwell and Judy Faraday. Two remarkable archivists, Barbara Horton of David Jones Limited and Bev Brereton at The University of Western Ontario, continue to give very professional, unstinting support and valuable insights to my various archival research projects on retail branding and innovation, and to reaffirm my belief that we can learn from the entrepreneurship of past retailers as we try to meet contemporary challenges. Special encouragement and inspiration have come from Lynda Miller, Karina McKenzie, Susan Taylor, Sarah Gregory and Diane Ripley.

Finally, I wish to dedicate this book to the children of the 21st century, including Sienna Jean Davidson, Nixon Miller Pitham, Tomson McKenzie, William McKenzie, Brittany Jade Merrilees, Will Merrilees and Bree Merrilees. They are our future!

Retail Marketing:
A Branding and Innovation Approach

1st edition

Dale Miller

Department of Marketing
Griffith University
Queensland Australia

Retail Marketing: A Branding and Innovation Approach
1st edition, 2nd printing.

Author
Dale Miller

Cover designer
Christopher Besley, Besley Design.

ISBN-13: 978-0-7346-1058-4

Published in Australia by:
Tilde University Press
PO Box 72
Prahran VIC 3181 Australia
www.tup.net.au

TUP-RetailMktg-1e2p

About the author

Dr Dale Miller PhD *Newcastle*, MBA *Sth Australia*, B. App. Sc (OccThy) *LaTrobe*

Dr Miller is one of Australia's leading retailing academics particularly in retail innovation and branding, retail history and archival research. Her extensive work covers Australian and international research, consultancies, postgraduate and undergraduate teaching and the supervision of research higher degrees. She lectures in retail branding and innovation, retail marketing, shopping mall marketing and management, e-retailing and marketing channels and retail supply chains in the Department of Marketing, Griffith University, Gold Coast in Queensland, Australia.

Her research focuses on retail and distribution innovation and branding, cross-cultural retailing, branding communities and retail business history. Her research has been published in various international scholarly journals including the *Journal of Business Research, Long Range Planning, The Service Industries Journal, International Journal of Retail and Distribution Management, Journal of Retailing and Consumer Services, Canadian Market Research Journal*. Dr Miller was a recent joint Guest Editor of a Special Issue of the *Journal of Retailing and Consumer Services*. She co-authored *Retailing Management a Best Practice Approach* and has authored or co-authored other books, book chapters and case studies. Dr Miller also researches student focussed marketing and retailing education and her most recent work appears in *Assessment and Evaluation in Higher Education*.

Preface

Welcome to the dynamic world of retail marketing. The aim is to take you, the reader, on an exciting and enjoyable journey through the major aspects of retail marketing – particularly in the Australian and New Zealand environments. Just as travel is said to broaden the mind, I hope you will experience new perspectives along the way and complete your journey with a thirst for more.

Rationale for the book

The retailing world continues to change dramatically and irrevocably. Greater domestic and international competition, new government policies and laws, greater concern for ecological and economic sustainability, and more demanding and assertive consumers contribute to a volatile and challenging business environment. Intensifying competition means that a retailer must deal with more that just a similar competitor. Increasingly, retailers must compete with entirely new formats such as a superstore in yet another retail category, or new channels of distribution such as e-retailing. Retailers not only compete for customers but also for suppliers to help create a differentiated offer and build a unique retailer brand. Arguably, the best way for a retailer to succeed in such a turbulent context is to have sharper and more purposeful retail strategies that are underpinned by retailer branding and innovation.

Structure of the book

The book uses a strategic planning framework. **Part A** presents an introduction to retailing and sets out the context for contemporary retailing. Retail strategy formulation is contingent on developing a differentiated retail offer, and retail concept and retail personality help to contribute to a unique retailer brand. This part of the book explores the cutting-edge nature of retailer branding and innovation, and aspects of market-sensing and understanding. **Part B** elaborates on the key elements of the retail mix, the components of which contribute to a unique retail strategy and feature in the day-to-day running of a retail business. **Part C** discusses retail operations and the critical contributions of performance management systems. **Part D** examines retail challenges and opportunities – particularly retail innovation and sustainability.

Innovative features

The book thoroughly discusses the cutting-edge concept of retailer branding and fundamental types of innovation in the Australian and New Zealand retailing contexts, acknowledging some unique aspects of retailing in these countries as well as transnational influences.

The book's research-led approach to teaching and learning incorporates the latest available research and encourages readers to conduct their own research. For example, unobtrusive observational research, case studies and the gathering of business intelligence are powerful means of identifying current practices. The reader can then theorise these practices using the theoretical content of the book (Doty and Glick 1994; Eisenhardt 1989; Patton 2002; Yin 2004).[1]

Some suggested further reading supports the research-led approach. The proliferation of databases, email journal contents alerts and authoritative online resources – such as those offered by the American Marketing Association – are just a few 'clicks' away for many readers. We encourage you to delve into the wealth of literature available, as well as reading the business press and trade magazines.

Concepts such as 'the total shopping experience', the 'customer-merchandise interaction', the three way branding choice model and the interactive model of locational choice – all of which I introduced in earlier work – are retained because of their continuing relevance and usefulness.

Other innovative features include:

- the explicit recognition of the role of objectives in all components of the retail mix, and particularly for location where multiple stakeholders influence the location decision outcomes;

- elaboration on the contribution of retail marketing to retail success;

- the introduction of superstore interactivity as a new self-service paradigm of retail service;

- the exploration of innovation and strategy in the Australian supermarket industry;

- the incorporation of e-retailing;

- the identification of the substantial role of shopping centres as community hubs;

- the treatment of small- and medium-sized retailers as well as franchising; and

- coverage of the retailing of goods and services.

Many practical examples and illustrations demonstrate the retail principles discussed as they apply to small, medium and large retailing business. Uniquely, we also include not-for-profit retailing and many other forms of non-store retailing.

---

[1] For more information about further reading, refer to the list of relevant titles at the ends of chapters.

The inclusion of selected illustrative websites indicates the 'state of the art' at the time of publication. As firms update their websites, readers can view the latest developments in retailing in those businesses. Websites for various government agencies and business and consumer organisations are also indicated.

Using a Tilde publication

The following features can be found throughout this Tilde publication.

Take notice – a noteworthy point.

Example - an example of how a topic may be applied within the industry.

Vignette – a case example to illustrate a particular retail marketing application.

Conclusions – a review of the content discussed within this chapter.

Review and applications – questions to prompt review and examination of your understanding of each chapter, and your ability to apply theory to practice.

Website references – an indicative list of websites to explore for information relevant to this chapter.

References – references for the current chapter.

Advanced reading - a list of sources from which you can gain additional knowledge on the subject area.

Teaching and learning philosophy

This book is the successor to my earlier book, written with Professor Bill Merrilees - *Retailing Management: A Best Practice Approach* – which was Australia's first retail management textbook that explicitly featured a best practice approach. We believe in an integrated learning model that combines **theory**, **past experience**, **experimenting** (doing, action, practice), and **reflection**.

Each chapter embraces the first two learning methods by structuring the principles of retailing and illustrating the practices with branding and innovation vignettes. Readers can experiment by using the exercises and questions the end of chapters. **Reflection** pulls together the other three forms of learning. Previous users of our work have commended the integration of theory and practice, and I have continued this approach. In many cases, practices precede theory. Researchers investigate particular practices to help develop conceptual understanding and predictive models to contribute to practices that are more effective.

The platform of branding and innovation

The first proper text on retailing was Paul Nystrom's *Economics of Retailing* in 1915. Nystrom, an economics professor, developed a comprehensive set of principles for effective retailing in the early part of the 20th century. Much of Nystrom's work still stands up to scrutiny. The *Journal of Retailing* was founded in 1925, well before the *Journal of Marketing* in 1936.

Over the years, many researchers have addressed corporate reputation, and more pointedly retail image (for example Martineau 1958). In 1988, Norman Berry turned to examining how to revitalise brands. However, it was only in the early 1990s that the idea of a retailer brand – as opposed to a product brand – was canvassed. Davies (1992) questioned whether retailers could be brands, and since then a dynamic literature has been evolving traversing service brand equity (Berry 2000; de Chernatony, Drury & Segal-Horn 2005; de Chernatony & Segal-Horn 2003), corporate branding (Balmer 2003; Balmer & Greyser 2002; Merrilees & Fry 2002), corporate re-branding (Daly & Moloney 2004), brand evolution (Merrilees 2005) and brand renewal.

The emphasis in the book on branding and innovation is relevant to firms of any size, anywhere in the retail supply chain. The challenge is to add value at every stage.

In summary, I urge all current and future retailers to treat the new retailing environment as one of excitement and opportunity rather than one of despair. This book is offered as a support to help meet this challenge.

Dale Miller
February 2008

Table of Contents

Table of Figures

Table of Tables

Table of Vignettes

The Context of Retailing

**An introduction
to retailing**

Introduction

Retailing influences most things that we do each day of our lives. What we eat, where we eat, how we eat it, even disposing of leftovers – retailing is there to either respond to consumer needs or, in some cases, to mould the range of choices available. The same is true for our clothing, our residence and its household effects, our transport and our leisure activities. Major retail categories have developed to help meet consumers' needs. This book is about the processes that retailers need to embrace for sustained success in a dynamic and turbulent context.

The nature of retailing and its role in the distribution channel

Retailing is the provision of goods and services to final consumers. As such, it includes all the traditional retail formats such as supermarkets, butcher shops and department stores. In fact, most of what we regard as traditional retailers are primarily merchandise retailers – this is, goods retailers. This is also the emphasis given by most Australian and other national bureaux of statistics classifications. However, this taxonomy understates the total importance of retailing, which includes the often-neglected sector known as services retailing. **Services retailing** is defined as services supplied to final consumers and includes hairdressers, plumbers, real estate agents, dentists, physiotherapists, and house cleaning and maintenance services. Often, the Australian Bureau of Statistics (ABS) classifies services retailing as personal services, community services or business services. The reality is that most of these organisations are retailers in that they sell goods and/or services to final consumers. Some, such as banks, actually refer to some of their networks as retail banking networks. Others, such as hairdressers and veterinary practices, have an explicit over-the-counter merchandising component of their business – in the order of 10 to 30 per cent of sales. The scope of this book covers both merchandise retailing and services retailing.

The nature of retailing can also be clarified by identifying its role in the distribution channel. The **channel of distribution** is the process whereby goods or services journey from raw materials or raw knowledge, go through various intermediate transformation stages, and then end their journey as retailed goods or services. The intermediate stages include multiple stages of manufacturing, transportation and wholesaling. Each stage adds value to the previous stage, with the distribution channel also referred to as the **value chain** (see Porter 1985).

The conventional channel of distribution moves from primary producer to manufacturer to wholesaler to retailer, and then on to the final consumer. Retailing is thus the final link in the channel of distribution, that is, the *process* by which goods and services ultimately become available to final consumers. This notion suggests that the main focus of retailers is meeting the needs of final consumers. However, the ability of retailers to do so is dependant upon a well-functioning link between the retailers and the earlier stages of the distribution channel – particularly the manufacturers and wholesalers. This relationship between retailers and suppliers is vital in helping retailers provide good service and meet customer needs. An obvious example is the fresh produce retailer who depends on timely distribution from suppliers.

How do retailers add value to wholesalers and manufacturers? Essentially, retailers provide a number of services more effectively than can be provided by manufacturers dealing directly with the public. This is not to say that manufacturers do not sometimes provide services directly to the public themselves – which for those sales would make them a retailer – including some shops attached, literally, to clothing factories as well as separate factory outlet stores. Retailers provide a service to the final consumer by providing a greater range of goods in one location than any one manufacturer could provide. The result is dramatic savings in shopping time for the consumer. At the same time, the manufacturer saves on the expense of having to set up numerous retail outlets to display their products. Thus, the main function of retailers is to provide convenience to the consumer.

The consumer is also able to buy goods in small parcels, i.e. a single shirt or one pair of shoes. Manufacturers usually insist that buyers purchase a minimum-sized parcel, for example 20 shirts, which would be impractical for most consumers. This function of retailers is referred to as **breaking bulk**. Retailers usually design and achieve convenience by having suitable goods available on display, ready for purchase at a convenient location with adequate access measures including parking, public transport and sufficient store opening hours. Additional services are provided through personal services, credit, lay-bys, wrapping, alterations, warranties and delivery.

What the above conveys is the role of retailing in a *conventional* distribution channel where manufacturers, wholesalers and retailers are separate entities – usually under separate ownership – with distinct functions. This configuration is still a widespread method of retail distribution. However, another type of distribution channel – vertical marketing systems – has become very common in recent decades. **Vertical marketing systems** comprise various ways for the one company to be involved in more than one stage of the distribution channel. For example, many retailers own manufacturing business units. Some retailers, for example Metcash Trading, have strong wholesaling operations, while some manufacturers handle their own wholesaling. Some retailers have also integrated in a forward sense and run their own credit and transport operations rather than using specialist firms for these services.

A vertical marketing system does not necessarily require one organisation to have cross-ownership over more than one component of the distribution channel. A vertical marketing system can also arise from coordination *across* components of the distribution channel, e.g. co-operative buying groups such as Mensland which assist a grouping of independent retailers. Co-ordination can also come from retail co-operatives (for example, the Newcastle Co-operative Store was one of the largest retail co-operatives in the southern hemisphere until its closure), from franchises between manufacturer-suppliers and retailers (for example, Capt'n Snooze, Wendy's and McDonalds among many others), and from franchises between suppliers and wholesalers (for example, Coco-Cola and distributors or Shell and distributors.

The development of **franchises** has made a particularly big impact on trans-forming distribution systems from conventional to vertical marketing systems. Franchises are a very efficient way for suppliers to have considerable control over a retailing network without having to outlay vast amounts of capital finance. Reference to franchising systems is integrated throughout this book rather than being treated in a distinct, separate chapter. This approach recognises the importance of franchising in contemporary retailing in many countries.

The conventional distribution channel makes sense for manufacturers and retailers who can specialise, as well as for consumers who can shop more effectively. However, it does have one major drawback – namely that it is difficult for manufacturers to *control* how their merchandise is offered to the public. To this day, manufacturers of major branded goods such as Coca-Cola and Reebok are always concerned that retailers are going to excessively discount their brands – for example, as 'loss leaders' as discussed in *Chapter 8 – Retail pricing* – and thereby reduce the perceived value of their brand's goodwill. Retailers in turn do not fully trust manufacturers. These dynamics set the stage for what is called 'conflict in the channel' and a potential power struggle between manufacturers and retailers.

Initially, manufacturers seemed to have the upper hand in this power struggle – particularly through branded goods – giving them influence over consumers and therefore respect from retailers. However, major retailers such as Wal-Mart and Carrefour in numerous countries – and Woolworths and Bunnings in Australia have become very large organisations with powerful distribution channels. An early manifestation of the shift in power from the manufacturer to the retailer occurred with bread; as the retailers gained more power they put more demands on the manufacturer, including making them deliver more frequently, providing price-tags, and even stacking the bread and collecting old stock. This shift in power consequently transferred profitability from the manufacturer to the retailer. Franchises and other forms of vertical marketing systems, in contrast, are an attempt by suppliers to reverse such power by controlling the retail network.

Is conflict inevitable in the conventional distribution channel? Although the possibility for conflict exists because each party has its vested interests, there is the opportunity for co-operation between retailers and suppliers. Indeed, co-operation is fundamental to the pursuit of **benchmarking** and other components of **best practice retailing**. At a broader level, there is scope for strategic alliances between retailers and a wide range of other parties involved in the distribution channel.

A profile of retail categories

Because retailing is a major contributor to national economies, national authorities monitor retailing activity closely. In Australia, for example, the Australian Bureau of Statistics (ABS) conducts a Retailing Census periodically as well as frequently producing regular reports. Check the ABS website for the latest figures. It is notable that retail establishments employ more than one million people and contribute significantly to the economy.

The ABS statistics can be summarised as follows:

- The most common retail establishments are takeaway food retailers, hairdressers and beauty salons, clothing retailers, cafes and restaurants, and automotive repair and maintenance services.

- The retailers with the largest total floor space are supermarkets and grocery stores, cafes and restaurants, clothing retailers, furniture retailers, and automotive fuel retailing.

- The retailers with the largest sales turnover are supermarkets and grocery stores, car dealers, automotive fuel retailers, department stores, clothing retailers, and takeaway food retailers.

These comprehensive retail surveys provide a fascinating dissection of the Australian retail industry and should be perused in detail by all retailing students, managers and owners. Such studies provide a first basis for planning retail strategy by exploring the broad range of choices available to an actual or potential retailing business. Each retail category – from the smallest to the largest – needs to be examined on its own merits. For example, even the relatively small retail category of flower retailing employs thousands of people.

Some retail categories are extremely economical in terms of space as measured by the **turnover to floor space ratio**. Some examples are photographic equipment retailers, liquor retailers and jewellers. Other retail categories have high productivity as measured by the **ratio of turnover to persons employed**. Such categories include car retailers, liquor stores, automotive fuel retailers and domestic appliance retailers.

The ABS reports are useful because they clearly classify retail activity into retail categories according to the type of retailing merchandise or service. This next section considers the ongoing evolution of the main retail categories, drawn in part from ACRS (1992).

Automobiles, automotive parts, servicing and repairs

Apart from buying a house, the next most expensive purchase most people make is a car. Car ownership is high in Australia. Dealers who represent the major brands of cars, are the main retailer of automobiles. A relatively recent trend is the emergence of multi-brand dealerships. Intense competition results in quite low margins per new car sold. Consequently, many dealers also emphasise separate used car sales and auto servicing. As well, a highly competitive automotive aftermarket sector exists which sells parts, servicing and auto repairs. Consumers frequently use the internet to compare prices across brands, dealers and outlets.

The Grand Motors Dealership on the Gold Coast has managed multiple dealerships for forty years. They currently have Mercedes-Benz, Toyota and Smart. Interestingly, their website homepage invites visitors to choose a dealership, each of which is self-contained, rather than having an integrated site.

Supermarkets and grocery stores

From the 1970s until the early 2000s, the big three – namely Woolworths, Coles (including Bi-Lo) and Franklins – dominated the *grocery retailing* category in Australia with about 1,500 supermarkets and about 70 per cent of the market, until Franklins effectively left the market. Currently, in 2008, the major players are now Woolworths and Coles – which converted 129 of its Bi-Lo banner stores to Coles Supermarkets as part of the Coles Group's rebranding and refocussing since it sold its Myer department store chain in 2006. As an aside, Coles itself was subsequently acquired by Wesfarmers in 2007. In 1994, the then Prime Minister – Paul Keating – warned the two leading retailers at the 1994 Supermarket Show that further moves to dominate the Australian market were likely to be met by Trade Practices Commission action. He suggested that they should look at expanding into Asia rather than fighting harder for ever-diminishing gains in market share at home (Dodd 1994). Check the Woolworths websites in Australia and New Zealand to investigate their long-term presence and their recent expansion in New Zealand.

The second tier chains – including Metcash Trading Ltd – have strong wholesalers as well as retailers. The second tier also includes various buying groups that represent the large number of independent grocers, also referred to as 'corner stores'. Most independent supermarkets or foodstores operate under banner-group trade names such as IGA and Foodworks. Foodworks, for example, has more than 700 stores. (See the Foodworks and IGA websites.) The wholesaler's role is to co-ordinate the buying and marketing functions on behalf of the independent retailers. Over the years, the second tier firms have gone through considerable merger or aborted merger activity – controlled by the Australian Competition and Consumer Commission (the ACCC) and its predecessor the Trade Practices Commission.

In 2001, another entrant into the Australia grocery scene was the international German retailer ALDI, which commenced by developing supplier relationships, building a strategically located major warehouse in outer suburban Sydney, and then opening its first store in Yagoona. By late 2007, ALDI had 150 stores in New South Wales, Queensland, Victoria and the Australian Capital Territory (see the ALDI website).

Whether or not another force emerges, the small independent grocery retailers continue to lose market share to the big supermarkets – but also increasingly to convenience stores as described below – since peaking in the late 1950s. More recently, the de-regulation of shopping hours has accelerated this trend – late shopping hours had been one of the last bastions of convenience advantage that small grocery retailers enjoyed relative to the larger chains. This is an important contextual issue as different regions have different regulations for shopping hours. The remaining independents are now fighting for survival, mainly through their buying groups but in some cases also through more attention to retail branding, refurbished premises, better stock presentation, and even through the provision of new services such as dry-cleaning, roast dinners, petrol discounts and other promotions.

Convenience stores

Convenience stores carry groceries, some takeaway food and other merchandise and generally use a self-service, 24-hour trading format. The main stores in this category are 7-Eleven (almost 400 stores in Australia) and BP Connect and the other stores attached to major petrol station chains (see the 7-Eleven website for a current profile). The central business districts (CBDs) of major Australasian cities are seeing a resurgence of extended trading by convenience stores as urban renewal increases and more people begin to reside within the city precincts.

Specialised food retailers

In contrast to the wide range and mass-merchandising approach of the supermarkets and to a lesser extent of the convenience stores, **specialist food retailers** such as butchers and takeaway stores focus on a very narrow product range. Within the specialist food retailer category, the different sub-categories adopt very different organisational approaches. For example, there is a major difference in emphasis between take-away food and liquor retailers on one hand, and what we term staple food retailers on the other hand.

The **takeaway food retailers** are dominated by large, often international and often franchised chains such as Pizza Hut, McDonalds, KFC, Red Rooster, Wendy's and Donut King. These chains typically have several hundred outlets each – KFC for example currently has about 600 outlets in Australia and New Zealand, while McDonalds has 730 outlets in Australia. Numerous independent takeaway shops also exist, but these are rapidly losing market share. A similar pattern relates to **liquor retailing**, with major chains Liquorland (previously owned by Coles Group Ltd and now part of Wesfarmers) and BWS (Woolworths Ltd) associated with the two major supermarket retailers.

In contrast, consider the **staple food retailers** within the specialist food retailer category. The term staple food retailer includes butchers, fresh seafood retailers, fruit and vegetable retailers, bakeries and delicatessens. Staple products refer to everyday necessities such as bread, meat, milk, and fruit and vegetables. Most staple food retailers are small independent stores (e.g. one or two butcher shops under the one owner), a single outlet patisserie, or a single outlet gourmet grocer. There are also a few chains within this category (i.e. Lenard's Poultry), but these represent a small market share within this category. Some independent butcher shops have recently banded together to sell 'branded meat', however the staple food retail category still remains dominated by the small independent store.

Department stores

Department stores are mass-merchandisers who highlight a quality image and high customer service. Increasingly, they feature soft goods such as clothing, homewares, soft furnishings and manchester. In Australia, two chains – Myer and David Jones – dominate the department store market, having taken over most competitors during the period 1950 to 1980 (see Vignette 1.1). Coles Myer sold its Myer department store chain in 2006 for $6 billion to a private consortium (and the remaining Coles Group has since been acquired by Wesfarmers).

The last independent Queensland department store, McDonnell and East, closed in 1994 (O'Meara 1994) which further increased concentration in the sector. The only significant offset to this trend was the entry of the Japanese department store Daimaru to Melbourne in 1991, and to the Gold Coast in 1998. However, Daimaru struggled and did not expand into other states as initially envisaged (Clarke and Rimmer 1997), and by 2002 had closed all its Australian outlets.

Discount department stores

Discount department stores are large mass merchandisers with an emphasis on self-service and low prices. Compared to department stores, discount department stores are more likely to have departments such as gardening, hardware, auto-parts, sporting goods and toys – that is, hard goods. Clothing is more likely to be at 'lower price points' (see *Chapter 8 – Retail pricing*). In 2008, Target currently dominates the Australian category with 260 stores compared with K-Mart's 168 stores and Big W's 142 stores. The big three discount department stores are essentially pitted against each other – although note that two competitors, K-Mart and Target, are now both owned by Wesfarmers – with no sign of major new competitors entering this retail category. A few smaller chains remain including Harris Scarfe (23 stores in South Australia, Victoria and Tasmania). In 2007, Harris Scarfe was bought for A$80 million by a consortium which included a Myer stake of 20% and a management stake of 15%. Elsewhere, however, just a few independent chains or single outlet discount department stores remain.

Other variety stores

In contrast to the discount department store category, new competitors positioned as chains of **low price variety merchandise** have emerged. These chains include The Reject Shop, Go-Lo, The Liquidators, Priceline, and Dollars & Sense. These stores are not unlike the original discount Coles and Woolworths variety stores with the emphasis on *absolute* low prices – that is most items are under $10 – although with a somewhat smaller product range than the original discount variety chains. These outlets are often, but not always, smaller with a considerably smaller product range than discount department stores – although some of them in fact occupy the space previously used by Coles and Woolworths variety stores.

Specialty stores

Compared to the mass-merchandising approach of department stores and discount departments stores, specialist stores focus on a narrow range of merchandise, but with a greater depth of offering. **Specialist stores** cover an extensive range of the retail categories (see the ABS website). Florists, toy shops, stationery, pharmacies, video hire, optical dispensers, stationers, books, gift shops, travel agents, jewellers, music shops, antique shops, furniture shops, newsagents, nurseries and photographic equipment retailers are just some of the many types of specialist retailers.

Most of the specialist retail categories are strongly influenced – although not necessarily dominated – by national chains including:

- in clothing – Just Jeans, Jeans West, Sportsgirl, Katies, Lowes, Rockmans, Sussan, Suzanne Grae, Fletcher Jones, Esprit, Sportsgirl and Tie Rack;

- in footwear – Williams The Shoeman, The Athletes Foot;

- in hardware – Bunnings, Mitre 10;

- in furniture – Harvey Norman, IKEA, Freedom, Oz Furniture;

- in mufflers and automotive aftermarket – Midas;

- in computers – Harvey Norman;

- in books – Angus & Robertson, Borders;

- in recorded music – HMV, Sanity;

- in electrical – Retravision;

- in electronics – Dick Smith, Tandy; and

- in jewellers – Prouds, Wallace Bishop, Michael Hill.

In some cases, the market leaders in selected retail categories are not simply leading specialist retailers but are super-specialists – or what are now known as category killers. **Category killers** are specialist retailers who provide extremely deep product ranges within a narrowly-specified product line, that is lots of choice in variety and types, sizes, styles and colours within a narrowly-specified product line, sometimes at lower than usual prices and through larger than usual sized outlets. (See below under Superstores.)

Regardless of whether certain chains are termed category killers or not, we note that the chains operate under various legal arrangements, including company owned branches (e.g. IKEA), franchises (e.g. Video Ezy, Shell, BP, Holden and Ford), or are linked through buying or marketing groups (e.g. Retravision and Mitre 10). Moreover, many specialist retailers are still small independent retailers. Collectively, small independent retailers may represent 50 per cent of the market share in some of the specialist retail categories, including florists, hairdressers and nurseries. This is similar to the situation in the US where a Dun and Bradstreet study found that small retailers of women's accessories, jewellery, sporting goods, musical instruments, children's clothing and other items still accounted for more than half of employment in their respective categories (Bloomberg 1994).

Superstores

Superstores, also known as **category killers**, are a retailing phenomenon that first entered the Australian market with any strength in the early 1990s. In 1997,

Merrilees and Miller surveyed the success of this format and differentiated the characteristics of superstores from those of stores that were merely large in physical dimensions. Moreover, they found that superstores in different categories required a different scale of operations to qualify as superstores. Another point to note is that just because a retailer is a self-styled 'superstore', that retailer does not necessarily fulfil the technical criteria advanced by Merrilees and Miller (1997). Part of the dramatic impact of superstores arises from the fact that they are market *drivers* rather than being market *driven*. Although, of course, superstore retailers recognise the importance of consumer needs and wants, they have actually led the market by presenting a new way of conceptualising merchandise selection. Thus, they are driving the market – hence **market driving**, a term discussed by Kumar (1997) – and breaking with the approach of being responsive only to existing *identified* needs and wants.

It is a matter of conjecture as to which of the major national chains of specialist stores are category killers and which are simply major specialist stores. However, in the Australian context there is likely to be agreement in the following categories:

- in toys – Toys 'R' Us;
- in recorded music – HMV, Sanity;
- in hardware – Bunnings;
- in car dealers – Holden, Ford, Toyota;
- in computers – Harvey Norman;
- in stationery – Officeworks;
- in sporting goods – Rebel Sport; and
- in furniture – IKEA, Freedom, Harvey Norman.

Where do people shop?

Many geographic dimensions contribute to answering the question of where people shop. *Chapter 6 - Location* addresses this question in more detail. Here, however, two fundamental choices facing the consumer are highlighted. First, there is the need to choose between shopfront retailers on one hand, and home shopping and other direct shopping mechanisms on the other. Advocates of the information superhighway suggest that home shopping may surge in the next decade.

Second, within shopfront retail shopping, the consumer must choose between the central business district (CBD) – also know as downtown, city centre or high street – regional shopping centres, community shopping centres, and freestanding sites including strip shopping and markets. With the exception of Brisbane, Melbourne and Sydney, some CBDs and neighbourhood shopping centres seem to be losing ground, with regional and community shopping centres continuing to expand. There is also renewed interest in freestanding sites. The latter include growing interest in markets for clothing, crafts and fresh food as well as growing interest in stand-alone sites for superstores, i.e. the IKEA store on the Pacific Highway, Logan in southeast Queensland (see the IKEA website). Some supermarket chains, such as Woolworths, are also looking favourably at freestanding sites.

From shopping basket to green trolleys and online malls: The transformation of Australian retailing 1946-2008

The 60-plus years since the end of World War II have seen a dramatic transformation in Australian retailing. Understanding this history can provide insight into future retailing directions, though we are hampered somewhat by the paucity of historical analyses, and especially analysis by retail marketing researchers. Historical studies in retailing can inform the development of new theories as well as and the strategies and practices of current retailers (Alexander 1997; Hollander 1986; Savitt 1989). Two of the few social and historic discourses about major aspects of Australian retailing are from Reekie (1993) and Kingston (1994). Even celebratory histories of Australian and New Zealand department stores are scarce, with some notable exceptions (Brash, Burke and Hoeben 1985; Millen 2000).

To begin, Kingston (1994, ch. 3 and ch. 4) notes that, prior to the 1920s period, the retailing emphasis had been narrowly focused on a small wealthy class market. Kingston characterises the 1920s and 1930s as the period of modernisation for Australian retailing. The emphasis shifted to the growing middle class market and the use of mass-merchandising techniques including catalogue retailing. The proliferation of branded goods and the use of mass media reinforced these trends. Apart from newspapers and then later radio, a further fillip came with the launch of the *Australian Women's Weekly* in 1933. During this period, most of Sydney's department store retailers modernised their premises. More use was made of lighting and visual merchandising (Reekie 1993). Coles consolidated their variety store operations, focusing on all items under a shilling, that is 10 cents in decimal currency, which was revised upwards by 1918 to two shillings and six pence, that is 25 cents. In 1923, Grace Bros introduced 'cash and carry' as a novelty in their grocery department. They also established a self-service cafeteria. In 1924, the first Woolworths store – based on low prices, easily-carried merchandise and a money-back guarantee – was opened.

The 1940s, in contrast, was a much more sombre and austere period characterised by wartime rationing, merchandise shortages, energy shortages and restricted advertising. Petrol shortages made deliveries difficult. The Ministry of Munitions took over the David Jones Ltd Market Street store just prior to Christmas 1942 (Kingston 1994). Consider the impact on the retailer when its newest store, opened just four years earlier, was forcibly withdrawn from the firm's property portfolio until the late 1940s.

Some rationing continued after the cessation of World War II, but by the late 1940s, the pre-war modernisation process recommenced. However, by today's standards many retailing formats looked radically different. Kingston paints a vivid picture for us by describing the typical grocery store in the 1940s as follows:

> ...(It) still had two counters: one for groceries, one for provisions, which was covered with the washable surface such as linoleum, marble, tiles or glass, with a cutting board. There might be wall fittings for display and show cases and aisle tables if there was plenty of room, but access to the counters was not to be obstructed, nor should anything be displayed which would put a premium on theft. Bacon was still sliced, butter and sugar weighed, and most stock kept in the storeroom where a cat was recommended to keep down the rats and mice. (Kingston 1994, p. 86.)

By the late 1950s, there had been some conversion of groceries to self-service, including Murray Bros of Parramatta in 1953. The first modern supermarkets did not appear until 1960. However, Kingston's description of a grocery store in the late 1940s remained the norm until at least the mid-1950s. Check with older acquaintances who may still vividly remember as youngsters buying sugar or biscuits at the local grocery store – retailer grocers literally were breaking bulk – taking the product from bulk packages (e.g. tins, Hessian sugar bags), and then weighing and packaging the sugar or biscuits in front of the customer. At that time there were no modern supermarkets, no category killer superstores and no regional shopping centres. Rather, the CBD was the pre-eminent shopping area, with many shoppers – who were mostly women at the time – dressing up to shop there. However, despite the change in details, a very strong relationship between shopping, leisure and entertainment continues to this day.

Local neighbourhood shopping centres were the dominant type of shopping centre. The first planned community shopping centre development did not open until 1957 when Chermside, a Brisbane centre, opened with a department store and 24 lock up shops (Kingston 1994, p. 96). Very few electrical appliance stores existed until television was introduced in 1956 in time for the Melbourne Olympics; home entertainment appliances had previously been basic radios (i.e. the wireless) and record players – or radiograms, which so modernly combined the two. Basic white goods had not fully penetrated the market, and the prevalence of clothes dryers, microwave ovens and an almost inexhaustible variety of kitchen and household appliances was still decades away.

Small independent shops dominated the staple product retail categories, including limited range grocery shops, butchers, fruit and vegetable shops, fish mongers, chemists, milk bars and delicatessens – alias 'ham and beef' shops. There were also numerous home vendors of milk, bread, ice, fruit and vegetables, soft drinks, and meat such as rabbits – exemplified in the famous Rabbito Man and his horse and cart in Leichhardt in the early 1950s.

From the 1960s, Australian retailing underwent a dramatic transformation. Regional and community shopping centres begin to take ascendancy over both the CBD and neighbourhood shopping centres.

The growth of modern supermarkets and the associated growth of supermarket national chains was clearly the dominant force of the 1960-2008 period. Supermarket chains displaced small independent grocery stores, and also gained market share by drawing from the full suite of specialist staple product retailers, including the retail categories of butcher shops, fishmongers, milk bars, chemists, fruit and vegetable shops, and delicatessens. All retailers in this group have declined in relative terms and in some cases in absolute terms. To this day, this group is prominent in rearguard political action against the major retailers to protest 'unfair competition' arising, for example, from extended shopping hours and 'liberal' development licences.

The small specialist staple product retailers have not been the only group to lose retail market share over the past 50 years. Department stores, too, have lost relative share, mainly due to competition from discount department stores but also increasingly from specialist stores – particularly in hardware, gardening, sports equipment, electrical appliances and toys. One response by department stores to this increased competition has been to shed some of these departments, particularly hardware and gardening.

Most recently, the superstore specialist retailers – often referred to as category killers – have been appearing in an increasing number of categories, including recorded music (Sanity), hardware, (Bunnings), computers (Harvey Norman), furniture (IKEA; Harvey Norman, Freedom), stationery (Officeworks) and toys (Toys 'R' Us).

What has contributed to this major transformation of Australian retailing? The retailing transformation is, in fact, largely a transformation of Australian society. Australia has experienced six decades of prosperity – save for intermittent periods of high cyclical unemployment. There have been major changes in the profile of the workforce, particularly more white-collar service jobs, more working women, and indeed more men with family responsibilities. There has also been a large increase in the age at which the average student leaves secondary school, and a considerable increase in students attending tertiary education.

The widespread ownership of motor vehicles has facilitated the development of community and regional shopping centres, as well as fostering a large retail category of car dealers and repair centres. The car also created a more acceptable image and means for men to do the shopping, which in turn stimulated the liberalisation of shopping hours.

The introduction of black and white television in 1956 and its rapid household penetration during the 1960s and 1970s accelerated the consumerism movement, with its emphasis on spending on discretionary goods – particularly consumer durables – as well as non-durable goods. Television is a powerful medium, arguably the most creative and influential of the mass media, and in particular it stimulates the demand for packaged, low-cost, branded goods typically found in supermarkets. Therefore, advertising helps create the critical mass (referred to as the **size of the trading area** in *Chapter 6 – Location*) necessary for large, modern supermarkets to be viable, ably supported in this role by the motor vehicle. Apart from advertising on television, the actual content of programs also stimulates consumer interests. In the early days of television, and without the benefit of easy access to international travel, television programs gave many Australians their first glimpse of lifestyles in other countries. As noted above, the advent of television spawned the growth of specialist electrical appliance stores, which was further reinforced by the introduction of colour television to Australia in 1976.

The 1960s was also a period of rapid household penetration of white goods, including refrigerators with freezers and twin-tub automatic washing machines. More sophisticated refrigerators enabled consumers to buy larger amounts of merchandise at more infrequent intervals. This provided a stimulus for community and regional shopping centres, and helped generate a wide range of merchandise suited for refrigeration – including frozen vegetables, frozen meat, ice cream and bread stored in a freezer. In turn, these new products accelerated the switch from small, independent specialist staple product retailers to supermarkets.

Another contributing force during this period was the new development and widespread use of new forms of **packaging**, including new configurations of tin, cardboard, glass, and plastic. These new forms of packaging accompanied new types of merchandise, especially frozen goods, and hence they have supported the changing trend towards both dry and frozen groceries. This trend also diminished the importance of small staple retailers and related home vendors positioned as *fresh* food providers, as meat and bread could now be frozen and one could now buy tinned and frozen vegetables and fish. These choices had not been plentifully available in the 1950s.

Innovative retail formats and the ever-changing nature of retail competition

The previous section highlighted the social and institutional changes that have contributed to the transformation of Australian retailing over the past 60 years. These have made the world of retailing both exciting and dynamic, and have contributed to the development of innovative retail formats – including the re-emergence of older formats with slight design modifications. Superstores are a good example of the former while hot bread shops are a good example of the latter.

In the late 1950s and early 1960s, the main retail innovation was the rapid spread of the **self-service grocery**, falling short, however, of conversion to a modern supermarket format. Thus, by 1961-62 there were fewer than 200 supermarkets in Australia. However, more significant at the time, 5,000 of the 33,000 grocery retailers were using a self-service format, which represented about 60 per cent of total grocery sales in Australia. Victoria and Western Australia in particular led the other states in this conversion to a self-service format (see ABS 1964, p. 1244).

During the 1960s, the main development in grocery retailing was the rapid expansion of the modern supermarket format, so that by 1968-69 there were 650 supermarkets that accounted for about one-third of total grocery sales. By the mid 1970s, the number of supermarkets reached the 1,000 mark and accounted for about 50 per cent of grocery sales. Thirty years later, in 2007, supermarkets' share of the market exceeds 95 per cent.

During the 1975-85 period, supermarkets continued to expand but made only minor gains in market share. The explanation for this conundrum is the rapid growth of a major new competitor – the ubiquitous **takeaway retailer**. The growth of takeaway retailing in the period was dramatic and can be clearly described as a highly innovative development – albeit following overseas trends. After 1985, the growth of takeaway retailing subsided but still remains above the rate of growth for overall retailing.

From the mid 1980s, one particular and significant trend occurs that has not been fully recognised in retailing analysis or in the academic literature. This is the trend to fresh, healthy and varied natural food. Such a trend emanates from changes in community tastes and concerns for a healthy lifestyle – including food intake – and can be termed the **fresh food revolution**. This trend is different, although related, to a simultaneous concern for a healthy global environment – the so-called **green revolution**.

From an Australian retailing perspective, the first manifestation of the fresh food revolution was the rapid 1985/86 to 1991/92 increase in the constant price turnover of **specialty fruit and vegetable retailing**. This development represented a reversal of a product life cycle in which this category of retailing had peaked 30 years earlier and had declined gradually since then. The only major supermarket retailer to respond quickly to the fresh food revolution was Woolworths, who made 'The Fresh Food People' a major positioning statement and promotional campaign. Franklins 'No Frills' was the slowest major supermarket chain to respond to the fresh food revolution because its initial product range deliberately excluded fresh goods. Franklins was forced to start afresh, as it were, and introduced a new retail format 'Big Fresh' in 1992.

The Big Fresh format in Australia was derived from New Zealand. The first New Zealand Big Fresh commenced at Mt Wellington in 1988. Both the Australian and New Zealand companies had a common owner, the Hong Kong based Dairy Farm company. In 1995, two of the New Zealand Big Fresh supermarkets – Mt Wellington and Glenfield – were refurbished into a second generation format (see *Supermarketing* 1995). Consistent with the turbulence in the sector, the Big Fresh format peaked and then disappeared with changes in ownership.

Another staple retail category to join the fresh food revolution was **bread and cake retailers**. By the late 1980s, a surge started with hot bread shops, which almost doubled in the number of outlets over the 1985/86 to 1991/92 period. As with specialist fruit and vegetable retailers, the specialist bread and cake retailers reversed a product life cycle decline of 30 years' duration. Two of the major bakery chains are Brumby's and Baker's Delight. Supermarkets belatedly followed the trend by refurbishing instore bakeries. Apart from changing community tastes towards fresh (hot) bread, the shift to bread and cake retailing was no doubt supported by the contribution of people who migrated to Australia, bringing specialised pastry and baking knowledge and skills. Most recently, **fruit juice drink** retailers such as Boost Juice (from 2000) have revolutionised this niche, adding many fruit varieties and introducing combinations such as 'smoothies'.

The **fashion competitive cluster** incorporates competition between department stores, discount department stores, and specialist clothing and footwear stores. Over the 1985-2006 period, the clear winner has been the specialist clothing and footwear stores – especially the national chains – with department stores the main losers in terms of market share.

The various **hard goods specialist categories** – such as toys, furniture, hardware and computers – can be seen as a battle between category killers, other national chains and small independent retailers. Although these competitive 'wars' are at an early stage, it seems as if the category killers are getting the upper hand with the small independent stores being the main losers.

The final major competitive cluster is that of **leisure and personal service retail categories** such as video hire outlets, travel agents, photographic processors, hairdressers, cinema and restaurants. These categories may seem unrelated, but in fact compete against each other in that they all compete for limited consumer budgets for leisure and entertainment. Travel, health and restaurants seem to have been the biggest winners in recent years based on ABS consumer expenditure figures.

Analysis of the retailing environment

Australian firms are conducting their businesses in turbulent times. Analyses of both an organisation's internal and external environments provide the retailing firm with essential information which will influence the long-term and short-term strategies of the firm. Apart from the **external influences** on contemporary retailing, there are megatrends potentially affecting all retailers and their retailing strategies. The external forces are diverse. They include local, regional and global, and span political, legal, economic, environmental, socio-cultural and technological influences. The **internal influences** relate to organisational capability. **Organisational capabilities** refer to people, finance, physical location, plant, equipment and inventory as well as to intangibles such as goodwill, intellectual property, retailer brand equity, and own brands – sometimes referred to as private labels. Success-orientated retailers must recognise and manage the potential impacts of these complex forces.

Environmental scanning is one of several tools which retail managers can use for recognising and assessing influences. The available tools are neither mutually exclusive nor exhaustive. The tools that focus on external influences include: PEST, opportunities and threats, business intelligence systems, external organisational research and competitor analysis. The tools that focus more on the internal influences include: retail audit, SWOT, internal organisational research and value chain analysis. Impact analysis is a tool common to evaluating both internal *and* external influences. Retailers must choose the assortment of tools that meet their needs and that will help them formulate retail strategies that acknowledge internal and external forces in the context of the firm. Retailers also must evaluate the organisation's capacity to implement the desired strategy.

Being either too internally or too externally focused will give the manager a distorted view. A balanced and multi-dimensional approach is vital for success. Managers must scan the environment. They must assess not only the key forces which are influencing the firm currently, but also those forces which will have a critical impact on the firm and its competitors in the longer term. The environmental scanning approach is applicable to any size retailing enterprise. What will alter is the *degree* of sophistication relative to the size of the organisation. What will not alter is the need for environmental scanning and evaluation to be a *process* rather than a one-off *snapshot.*

Megatrends relevant to retailing

What are the overreaching trends which are relevant to retailing in Australia and New Zealand? What are these trends which are likely to have a critical impact on the retailing firm and its competitors in the longer term?

Globally, changing political boundaries and relationships can affect trade, including imports and exports. Illustrative examples include: the political changes in the early 1990s in Eastern Europe, the first free elections in South Africa in 1994, and the ending of economic sanctions against South Africa. Other examples include the North American Free Trade Agreement (NAFTA), the replacement of the General Agreement on Trade Tariffs (GATT) by the World Trade Organisation (WTO), the evolution and continuing expansion of the European Union, and the formation of APEC and ASEAN. Trading blocs generally emerge with a regional focus, such as southeast Asia, or the western or eastern Pacific Rim – which includes Canada and South America.

The continued emergence of global strategic alliances and networks will be enhanced by improved telecommunications and the increasing ease of international travel. These enhancements will be both in terms of technology, transport and transport schedules, and in terms of governments facilitating inter-country business travel. These global relationships are enriched by international tourism, particularly coupled with major events such as the Melbourne Commonwealth Games in 2006, the Sydney Olympic Games in 2000, New Zealand's defence of the America's Cup in 1999-2000, and the annual Indy Carnival on the Gold Coast.

Retailing, as noted elsewhere, is a people-intensive service industry, and within Australia and New Zealand there is a rapidly changing employment relations environment. At the Australian federal and state government levels, the dynamic environment is highlighted by the shift to enterprise-based bargaining. This shift has the potential for negative effects for some retail employees who have not been empowered to participate in the bargaining processes. Significant changes in government policy related to superannuation, retirement and training continue to occur.

There are paradoxical trends, such as an increased emphasis on career paths for employees, and concomitantly much of the organisational theory literature is advocating 'flatter structures' which inherently mean less vertical advancement. The trend to flatter organisational structures is often coupled in larger firms with the centralising of various functions, for example merchandising may be managed centrally by national retailing chains. Aspects of human resource management may be centralised or outsourced, for example pay administration and industrial relations may be centralised in the state headquarters of a large retailer, or outsourced to retail support services for either large or small retailers. Centralising or outsourcing functions reduce the career opportunities available at the local or branch level. These career-related trends signal significant challenges to the retailing industry.

The career paths thrust is supported by what we term **the gentle professionalising** of retailing – that is, retailing will increasingly be seen as a career choice. Traineeships and courses in retailing are well established in the Technical and Further Education (TAFE) sector. Retailing-focused courses are poised to become boutique or niche courses in universities too. Currently, government policy seems to favour areas like biotechnology, medicine and some sciences above business. There is the potential for retailing specialisation in undergraduate programs in business, commerce and economics as well as in postgraduate programs. However, universities tend to resile from such innovations. Moreover, postgraduate researchers have written some excellent doctoral theses recently. This emerging trend will inspire greater academic research into retailing and stronger partnerships between management education, research and business. Over time, greater resources must be allocated to retailing, marketing and management research.

A contemporaneous trend will be towards greater **training** for all staff – not only for full time staff. The training will start with better designed and implemented orientation and induction programs, and an explanation of the retailer's brand, and must be supported by suitable performance management and reward systems.

There is an emerging inclination by governments to acknowledge the existing and potential roles of small- and medium-enterprises (SMEs) in the Australian economy. Hence, governments are ostensibly giving some more support in this area, with possible one-stop access to government enterprise improvement programs and services.

Another trend allied to career paths and career redirection is emerging. Some people are self-selecting a career change into retailing. This change is often predicated on the receipt of a substantial redundancy package which can provide the capital necessary to establish a new business – frequently in the realm of retailing. One can surmise that such people will predominantly be males with long service to one employer, and therefore *may* lack the entrepreneurial spirit, breadth of experience, skills and drive required to establish a new business. They may be better suited to partnerships with existing retailers, to buying existing successful businesses, or to entering into franchises.

If governments were indeed serious about increasing the number of SMEs, including retail SMEs, there would be more sensible, sensitive, responsive and efficient administration policies and practices. Dissemination of policies and information about programs would be targeted and streamlined. There would be a deliberate change from a *compliance* approach adopted by government agencies – especially taxation and revenue agencies – to an *enabling* approach with a resultant decrease in barriers to accessing information. Equally, if the federal government were serious, there would be equitable funding for best practice programs within SMEs, and these would include retailing. The funding would need to be commensurate with that devoted primarily to manufacturing in the early and mid 1990s, and more recently to the health and human services sector.

What other megatrends are relevant? Changing *modes* of shopping and changing *characteristics* of shoppers are of particular interest. Other trends that will have impacts on retailing are environmentalism – which includes environmental awareness and a demand for environmentally friendly goods – as well as demands imposed by government regulations. These factors create demand for what we term **green retailing**, which includes a reduction in the use of plastic bags along with the introduction of viable alternatives.

There is a demand for **locally owned and produced goods and services** as evidenced in the various 'Buy Australian' campaigns, and the not-unrelated movement towards republicanism in Australia. There is a push for educated and ethical management and the rise of consumerism – that is an educated and aware clientele together with improved consumer protection.

Another significant trend is the shift to more flexible shopping hours. This trend has triggered a major debate between small and large retailers, with a variety of responses. Shopping hours are, however, under the jurisdiction of state governments, which accounts for differences in adjacent cities like Tweed Heads in NSW and Coolangatta in Queensland. Another state matter that affects these particular adjacent cites is daylight saving time, which is still not in use in Queensland.

The diversity of relevant trends underlines the importance of retailers being aware of the scope of trends that can affect them and their business.

Print media can be useful sources of information about retailing. Frequent analyses of reported earnings by publicly listed companies, evaluations of retailers' public announcements, and notices of product recalls all inform the astute reader. Policy announcements on interest rates and the reporting of economic and social indicators add texture. Finally, each retailer's advertising indicates the firm's emphasis, for example whether it is on promotional pricing and growth through new locations or online shopping, or perhaps on sustainability, fair trade or community engagement.

e-Retailing

The innovations that created the possibility of e-retailing were based on the concepts of real-time 24/7 shopping using virtual shopping environments spanning individual specialist outlets, virtual department stores, auction sites and online malls. Some retailers – such as amazon.com – commenced business as 'pure' e-retailers, that is, the firm did not have a conventional 'bricks and mortar' store where customers would physically and personally enter and complete their shopping transactions. The 'clicks' retailer was a type of late 20th century counterpart both to the highly descriptive, informative and customer service oriented catalogues of early department stores in various countries, and to mail order retailers such as Sears Roebuck and Montgomery Ward. One appeal of online shopping for consumers is the lack of borders and time constraints. e-Retailers have tried to emulate some of the excitement of in-store retailing through the design and operation of their websites, so that consumers develop an emotional association (Merrilees and Miller 2005) and can find their way around the site (Dennis, Fenech and Merrilees 2004). However, the delivery of products still relies heavily on conventional routes such as postal services or couriers.

Product categories that are most amenable to online purchase are those where the consumer is confident or experienced. Therefore, the purchase of books and music tends to be less problematic than the purchase of perishable food, which is vulnerable to climate, and some types of clothing – especially where fit and fabric are critical to the customer. The purchasing of services such as travel and entertainment seems relatively easy and straightforward, and many consumers are comfortable here.

Conclusions

Retailing is a major sector of the economy, representing more than seven per cent of gross national product (GNP) and employing more than a million people in Australia. This represents at least one in seven persons employed, and wholesaling contributes nearly half as many again.

Despite the significance of retailing, it has been neglected in many respects. Historical treatises of the Australian economy usually feature manufacturing (e.g. steel and aluminium), or primary industries (e.g. example wool, wheat or coal) with scant regard for retailing. The official factual history, the *Australian Year Book* and related ABS publications, are written in the same vein. Government grants for research and development, tariffs, export incentives and best practice demonstration programs – among others – follow the same favoured treatment for manufacturing in particular. Let this textbook be a call that the emphasis must change! Retailing should be treated on an equal footing with other sectors, as the economic and social significance of retailing must be recognised. Certainly, the talents of some great retailers like Paul Simons have helped to turn this image around.

A useful way of conceptualising retailers in the first instance is in terms of retail categories. This assumption underpins this entire book. Retail categories provide an initial reference frame which can be used to then clarify different market positions and the strategies of different retailers within that retail category, and to clarify possible competition across retail categories.

The schema and preliminary description of retail categories provided here are built on and further develop the ABS classification. Some conventional ABS groupings such as supermarkets are used, and new clusters have been added for convenience, variety and specialist staple food retailers. The wider umbrella of services retailing is advocated, and thus the new classifications are:

- supermarket and grocery retailers;
- convenience stores;
- specialist food retailers including takeaway retailers and specialist staple food retailers;
- department stores;
- discount department stores;
- variety stores; and
- specialist merchandise and service stores, including category killers.

This chapter has flagged the important issue of *where* people shop, which is taken up in other chapters. For example, will CBDs continue to decline in importance? Will the information superhighway become the dominant form of shopping? Will planned shopping centres be community hubs in modern societies, or will they be superseded by virtual shopping malls and communities of interest?

The brief historical synopsis of retailing in Australia helps to situate contemporary retailing. The full story has not yet been written, but the changes which have occurred in Australian retailing between the 1950s and the 21st century are nothing short of revolutionary (see Vignette 1.1.) It is hard to imagine the 1950s world - a world without supermarkets – with a dominant role for the local corner grocer, an eminent role for CBD shopping, no community or regional shopping centres (at least until the end of that decade), and many home vendors.

Retailers are much more than product providers. By focusing on corporate social responsibility, by encouraging environmentally-friendly products, practices and stores, and by thinking about sustainability, retailers can be positive contributors in their own contexts and communities. With piercing insight, Professor Stanley Hollander (2002, p.514) explains:

> *We live in materialistic cultures and the materials retailers bring us tend to shape who we are and who we think we are. This impact goes well beyond product assortment.*

As a reader, you are invited to take a journey into the history of retailing through the historical works about particular retailers such as Gowings (Gowing 1993, Miller and Merrilees 2000) and Soul Pattinson (Shand 1993), or into a broader academic analysis or retailing through the work of writers such as Game and Pringle (1983), Reekie (1993) and Kingston (1994). Such a journey might suggest three key epochs in Australian retailing history: the 1880s and 1890s where retailing narrowly focused on a small, wealthy market with a major emphasis on personal service; the 1920s and 1930s where the emphasis shifted to the growing middle-class market with mass-merchandising techniques and more in-store visual merchandising becoming the vogue; and the period 1970 to the present where we see self-service as the norm with personal service used more selectively.

While history provides insights into the dramatic structural changes which have transformed retailing, this chapter also explored the new retail formats that have emerged over recent decades – partly driven by intense competition within retail categories and between retail categories. In particular, we illustrated these issues by referring to the competitive cluster incorporating the big two supermarket chains, second tier grocery chains, convenience food stores, takeaway retailers and specialist food retailers. This cluster has seen the different players jockeying for position and making major moves to best meet the changing needs of society. To survive in this competitive foray it is necessary for retailers to adopt best practice retailing methods and to build strong retailer brand images that contribute to a sustainable competitive advantage. This book is a guide for how to achieve this based on modern retailing theory and practice.

Review and applications

1. Discuss how retailing contributes to the economy.

2. Explain the contributions of retailing to society.

3. How can retailing contribute to the image and well-being of a city or region?

4. Discuss the concept of the shopping centre as a community hub.

5. Compare and contrast department store retailing and supermarket retailing. Explore the scope for retail innovation in both categories.

6. Research the origins of the term 'manchester' as an identifier of both a product and a store department.

7. Research the term 'mercery', and discuss the product innovation it represents.

8. Search through company reports and websites to identify how retailers position their firms. Will customers perceive the same retailer brand image?

Website references

7-Eleven: <www.7eleven.com.au>.

ALDI: <www.aldi.com.au>.

Australasian Association of Convenience Stores: <www.aacs.org.au>.

Australian Bureau of Statistics (ABS): <www.abs.gov.au>.

Australian Competition and Consumer Commission (ACCC): <www.accc.gov.au>.

Foodworks: <www.foodworks.com.au>.

Grand Motors: <www.grandmotors.com.au>

IKEA: <www.ikea.com.au>.

Independent Grocers of Australia (IGA): <www.iga.net.au>.

Shopping Centre Council of Australia: <www.scca.org.au>.

Woolworths Ltd: <www.woolworths.com.au> and <www.woolworths.com.nz>.

References

Aaker, J 1997, 'Dimensions of Brand Personality', *Journal of Marketing Research*, vol. 34 (August), pp. 347-356.

Alexander, N 1997, 'Objectives in the Rearview Mirror May Appear Closer Than They Are', *The International Review of Retail, Distribution and Consumer Research*, vol. 7, no. 4, pp. 383-403.

Alexander, N & Akehurst, G 1999, *The Emergence of Modern Retailing 1750-1950,* Antony Rose Ltd, Chippenham, Wilts.

Australian Bureau of Statistics (ABS) 1964, *Australian Official Year Book*, no. 50, ABS (1993), *Retailing in Australia*, Catalogue no. 8613.

Australian Centre for Retail Studies (ACRS) 1992, *The Australian Retail Industry: Potential for Entering Overseas Markets,* Report No. 9, Service Industries Research Program, DITAC, Canberra.

Barney, N 1995, 'Scott the busy draper', in the *Newcastle Herald*, 8 February.

Bloomberg 1994, 'Small retailers thriving', the *Australian Financial Review*, 20 September, p. 32.

Brash, N, Burke, A & Hoeben, C 1985, *The Model Store 1885-1985, Grace Bros: 100 Years Serving Sydney*, Kevin Weldon, Sydney.

Clarke, IC & Rimmer, P 1997, 'The Anatomy of Retail Internationalisation: Daimaru's Decision to Invest in Melbourne, Australia', *The Service Industries Journal*, vol. 17, no. 3 (July), pp. 361-382.

Davies, G 1992, 'The Two Ways in Which Retailers can be Brands', *International Journal of Retail & Distribution Management*, vol. 20, no. 2, pp. 24-35.

Dennis, C, Fenech, T and Merrilees, B 2004, *e-retailing*, Routledge, London.

Dodd, T 1994, 'Keating threatens the retail giants', the *Australian Financial Review,* 4 October, pp. 1, 8.

Game, A & Pringle, R 1983, *Gender at Work,* Allen & Unwin, Sydney.

Gowing, S 1993, *Gone to Gowings,* State Library of New South Wales, Sydney.

Hollander, Stanley 1986, 'A Rearview Mirror Might Help Us Drive Forward - A Call for More Historical Studies in Retailing: Guest Editorial', *Journal of Retailing*, vol. 62, no. 1, pp. 7-10.

Hollander, S. 2002, 'Retailers as creatures and creators of social order', *International Journal of Retail &Distribution Management*, vol. 30, no. 11, pp. 514-517.

Jones, M 1995, 'Convenience sells well', the *Sydney Morning Herald*, 20 April, p. 34.

Kingston, B 1994, *Basket, Bag and Trolley: A History of Shopping in Australia*, Oxford University Press, Melbourne.

Koehn, N 2001, *Brand New: How Entrepreneurs Earned Consumers' Trust from Wedgwood to Dell*, Harvard Business School Press, Boston.

Kumar, N 1997, 'The Revolution in Retailing: from Market Driven to Market Driving', *Long Range Planning*, vol. 30, no. 6, pp. 830-835.

Merrilees, B & Miller, D 1997, 'The Superstore Format in Australia: Opportunities and Limitations', *Long Range Planning*, vol. 30, no. 6, pp. 899-905.

Merrilees, B & Miller, D 2005, 'Emotional Brand Associations: a New KPI for e-Retailers', *International Journal of Internet Marketing and Advertising*, vol. 2, no. 3, pp. 206-218.

Millen, Julia 2000, *Kirkcaldie & Stains: a Wellington Story*, Bridget Williams Books, Wellington (New Zealand).

Miller, D & Merrilees, B 2000, 'Gone to Gowings – An Analysis of Success Factors in Retail Longevity: Gowings of Sydney', *The Service Industry Journal*, vol. 20, no. 1, pp. 61-85.

O'Meara, M 1994, 'End near for retailing icon', the *Australian Financial Review*, Weekend Review, 25 February, p. 2.

Porter, M 1985, *Competitive Advantage*, Free Press, New York.

Reekie, G 1993, *Temptations: Sex, Selling and the Department Store*, Allen & Unwin, Sydney.

Savitt, R 1989, 'Looking Back to See Ahead: Writing the History of American Retailing', *Journal of Retailing*, vol. 65, no. 3, pp. 326-355.

Shand, K (ed.) 1993, *A Singular Success: Washington H. Soul Pattinson 1872-1993*, Focus, Sydney.

Supermarketing 1995, 'Second Big Fresh refurbishment complete', *Supermarketing*, National Business Review Publications, 27 March, pp. 1 – 2.

Advanced reading

Ailawadi, K & Keller, K 2004, 'Understanding retail branding: conceptual insights and priorities', *Journal of Retailing*, vol. 80, pp. 331-342.

Arnold, MJ & Reynolds, KE 2003, 'Hedonic shopping motivations', *Journal of Retailing*, vol. 79, pp. 77-95.

Baker, M (ed.) 2000, *Downtown London: Layers of Time*, especially pp. 80 & 85, Second Revised edition, The City of London and London Regional Art and Historical Museum, London, Ontario.

Balmer, J (ed.) 2003, 'Special issue: Corporate and service brands', *European Journal of Marketing*, vol. 40, nos. 7 & 8.

Berry, L 2000, 'Cultivating service brand equity', *Journal of the Academy of Marketing Science*, vol. 28, no. 1, pp.128-137.

Berry, N 1988, 'Revitalizing brands', *Journal of Consumer Marketing*, vol. 5, no. 3, pp. 15-20.

Birtwistle, G & Freathy, P 1998, 'More than just a name above the shop: a comparison of the branding strategies of two UK fashion retailers', *International Journal of Retail and Distribution Management*, vol. 26, no. 8, pp. 318-323.

Burt, S & Sparks, L 2002, 'Corporate branding, retailing, and retail internationalization', *Corporate Reputation Review*, vol. 5, nos. 2 & 3, pp. 194-212.

Crossick, G & Jaumain, S 1999, *Cathedrals of Consumption, The European Department Store 1850-1939*, Ashgate Publishing Ltd, England.

Hellegers, J 1987, *Against the Current: The Story of Adeline Keating*, Dent, Melbourne.

Jamal, A 2003, 'Retailing in a multicultural world: the interplay of retailing, ethnic identity and consumption', *Journal of Retailing and Consumer Services*, vol. 10, pp. 1-11.

Jones, K & Doucet, M 2000, 'Big-box retailing and the urban retail structure: the case of the Toronto area', *Journal of Retailing and Consumer Services*, vol. 7, pp. 233-247.

Kaufman-Scarborough, C 1999, 'Reasonable Access for Mobility-Disabled Persons is More Than Widening the Door', *Journal of Retailing*, vol. 75, no. 4, pp. 479-508.

Laidler, N 2004, 'A future of tradition: How does Canada's longest-operating department store continue to prosper?', *Business London*, July, pp. 18-22.

Margo, J 2000, *Frank Lowy: pushing the limits*, Harper Collins, Sydney, pp. 76-77.

McBride, H 1997, *Our Store: 75 Years of Canadians and Canadian Tire*, Quantum, Toronto.

Merrilees, B 2005, 'Radical brand evolution: a case-based framework', *Journal of Advertising Research*, vol. 45, no. 2 (June), pp. 201-210.

Merrilees, B & Fry, M 2002, 'Corporate branding: a framework for e-retailers', *Corporate Reputation Review*, vol. 5, nos. 2 & 3, pp. 213-225.

Miller, D 2005, 'Diverse Transnational Influences and Department Stores: Australian Evidence from the 1870s-1950s', *Jahrbuch Fur Wirtschaftsgeschichte: From Department Store to Shopping Mall: Transnational History/ Vom Warenhaus zur Shopping Mall: Einzelhandel transnational [Economic History Yearbook]*, A. Sedlmaier (ed.), pp. 17-40, Akademie Verlag, Berlin.

Miller, D 2006, 'Strategic human resource management in department stores: an historical perspective', *Journal of Retailing and Consumer Services*, vol. 13, no. 2, pp. 99-109.

Miller, D & Merrilees, B 2000, 'Gone to Gowings – An Analysis of Success Factors in Retail Longevity: Gowings of Sydney', *The Service Industry Journal*, vol. 20, no. 1, pp. 61-85.

Miller, D & Merrilees, B 2004, 'Fashion and commerce: a historical perspective on Australian fashion retailing 1880-1920', *International Journal of Retail & Distribution Management*, vol. 32, no. 8, pp 394-402.

Nasmith, G 1923, *Timothy Eaton*, McClelland & Stewart, Toronto.

Nesbitt, R 1993, *At Arnotts of Dublin, 1843-1993*, A & A Farmar, Dublin.

Nystrom, P 1915, *The Economics of Retailing*, 1919 edn, The Ronald Press, New York.

Pasdermadjian, H 1954, *The Department Store, its Origins, Evolution and Economics*, Newman Books, London.

Phenix, P 2002, *Eatonians: The Story of the Family Behind the Family*, McClelland & Stewart, Toronto.

Rex, D, & Blair, A 2003, 'Unjust des(s)erts: Food retailing and neighbourhood health in Sandwell', *International Journal of Retailing and Distribution Management*, vol. 31, no. 9, pp. 459-465.

Roberts, E 2003, 'Don't sell things, sell effects: Overseas influences in New Zealand department stores, 1909-1956', *Business History Review*, vol. 77, no. 2, pp. 265-289.

Santink, J 1990, *Timothy Eaton and the Rise of his Department Store*, University of Toronto Press, Toronto.

Svennson, G 2001, 'Glocalization of business activities: a 'glocal' strategy', *Management Decision*, vol. 39, no. 1, 6-18.

The Scribe (1919), *Golden Jubilee 1869-1919: a Book to Commemorate the Fiftieths Anniversary of T Eaton Co Ltd*, T Eaton Co Ltd, Toronto.

Warnaby, G, Bennison, D, Davies, BJ & Hughes, H 2002, 'Marketing UK towns and cities as shopping destinations', *Journal of Marketing Management*, vol. 18, nos. 9/10, pp. 877-904.

Webber, K & Hoskins, I 2003, *What's in Store? A History of Retailing in Australia*, Powerhouse Publishing, Sydney.

Vignette 1.1

Longevity of a retail icon

David Jones Ltd is the most enduring department store in Australia – and arguably the world. It is positioned as a premier department store, and apart from flagship stores in capital cities it has stores in suburban and regional areas, with more than 35 stores.

The roots of the business go back to the Welsh-born founder David Jones, who set up a drapery business in George Street, Sydney in 1838. To trade successfully, he maintained strong links with London, and had trusted people buying on his account to ensure that he could supply goods which were suitable to the climatic, economic and social conditions of the developing colony. His letters show an astute understanding of the business and the ingredients of successful merchandising. The 1840s diary of his daughter, Jane, highlights a trip they took together to England, Wales and Europe. They renewed family acquaintances and, importantly from a business perspective, David Jones observed the latest developments in retailing and manufacturing.

By 1887, Edward Lloyd Jones I was presiding over the opening of an opulent and fully-fledged department store, the design of which was inspired by William Whiteley's department store in Westbourne Grove, London. Edward's diaries from his overseas trips show a keen appreciation of the explosion of retailing forms and practices. Like his father, he was keen to bring the best to Australia and, to the extent necessary, adapt to local needs – a very early example of 'glocalization' (Miller 2005; Svennson 2001).

Changes in legislation and the scale of the business meant that incorporation in 1906 was a logical step in the expansion of the business and the development of more sophisticated business strategies and processes – including an extensive mail order business. Edward Lloyd Jones II was now Chairman, and one of his brothers, Charles Lloyd Jones, was on the Board and was quite active in the firm. The opening of a huge manufacturing facility in 1914 was a strategic support, and proved to be critical to the store's continued success when supply chains were disrupted during World War I.

Charles became Chairman in 1920, and 1927 saw the grand opening the magnificent flagship store in Elizabeth Street – still the pre-eminent store for the firm. Despite the economic crisis of the Great Depression, the business continued to be successful – paying a dividend to shareholders each year and increasing profits. This remarkable success was achieved by modifying the merchandise mix and appointing associate buyers with specialised skills and roles. In 1935, the 1887 store was refurbished and refocussed, and in 1938, the modern and beautiful Market Street store was opened.

With the declaration of World War II, the firm again adjusted to its context, increasing its manufacturing capacity away from the state capital and winning contracts for military supplies. After the war, a renewed focus on fashion led to a surge in fashion shows and visits by designers including Christian Dior.

Other changes in the 1950s include the expansion of the business through regional acquisitions of existing department stores. This growth strategy was in contrast to retailers like Grace Bros (Sydney) who built new suburban stores from the 1930s.

The firm continued to grow and respond to changes such as the advent of planned shopping centres (i.e. malls). The tumultuous last two decades of the 20th century brought many challenges and changes in competition. Many direct competitors had ceased trading as department stores – and new forms such as superstores and e-retailing – were emerging.

The 21st century now sees David Jones with a justified new confidence, reasserting its positioning and branding.

The threads which weave together the successful longevity of the retailing icon are: entrepreneurial marketing, innovation*, branding (i.e. harnessing heritage and proactive strategies), being market driven *and* market driving, and continuing to understand the dynamic context for retailing.

*Miller and Merrilees 2004.

See also <www.davidjones.com>.

Retail strategy, branding and innovation

Introduction

The development of retail strategy gives the retailer a unique opportunity to assess the roles and purposes of the firm. The strategy development process helps the retailer determine what is important to the business both in current and projected contexts, and what resources – including leadership and intangibles – are either available or required to achieve the desired outcomes.

This chapter explains how retailers can use a strategic planning framework to create a sound retail strategy that recognises the firm's vision and history. The strategy should have built-in flexibility so that the retailer can respond to surprises in the external environment such as changes in legislation, taxation, the value of the dollar, inflation, or indeed natural disasters or even shifts in world affairs.

A sound retail strategy is critical to business success because it defines the scope and purpose of the business as well as establishing the retail brand, retail concept and retail personality. It must also define both the target market and key offerings relative to competitors, that is, what is the **unique retail offer**. Furthermore, the strategy must also mould the integration and the co-ordination of the **retail mix** in support of the strategy.

The keys to an effective retail strategy are simplicity and focus. If the strategy is too complex or too confusing, it is unlikely to be successful. **Branding** offers a tool to integrate the strategy in such a way that all aspects of the business can mutually reinforce it. For example, all employees of Virgin understand the essence of the brand which helps them perform their daily tasks.

Branding can be used to drive a retail strategy (see Vignette 2.1). It is important to differentiate between the retailer brand – that is, the **corporate brand** - and **product brands** offered by the retailer. Davies (1992) drew attention to the two ways in which retailers could be brands – in part highlighting the corporate brand – as well as own brand products. Own brand products are discussed more in *Chapter 4 - Merchandising*. Academic researchers refer to brand-based strategy as **brand orientation,** which "…becomes the driving force for firms that consider branding a significant issue in business decisions and directions" (Wong & Merrilees 2007, p. 447). For Urde (1999, p. 117), brand orientation is "an approach in which the processes of the organisation revolve around the creation, development, and protection of brand identity in an ongoing interaction with target customers with the aim of achieving lasting competitive advantages in the form of brands".

Branding and innovation are strongly connected. Even for a retailer to maintain the status quo, revitalisation and refreshment of the retailer brand is necessary, and this is usually achieved by innovation, that is retail innovation.

Retail innovation is essential for creating a distinctive retail business. Overarching concepts or retail innovation include: convenience; loyalty (see *Chapter 3 – Market sensing and understanding*), and store atmosphere (see *Chapter 5 – Store design*). In the e-retailing channel, all these factors are important but must be adapted to the online medium (see Dennis, Fenech and Merrilees 2004).

Vignette 2.1

Retail strategy: a branding approach

The leaders of a firm must have a definite retail concept and a clear and synergistic vision so that they can work together to create a retail strategy. The directors of a small regional shoe chain worked with a branding consultant as a step towards reinvigorating their business. Initially, each director saw the firm's focus individually and differently. There was no unity of vision, although all directors were keen to achieve business success.

For your consideration:

- What methods could be used to help a retailer clarify the firm's concept and brand?

The development of retail strategy

The retail strategy of a retailing business is critical to the success of that business. It defines the essence of the retailer, the scope and purpose of the business, the retail category, the target market, the key offerings in the market place relative to competitors, and the integration and co-ordination of the retail mix to support this strategy (see Figure 2.1). The preferred framework for formulating retail strategy is the strategic planning framework.

Figure 2.1 Schematic representation of retail strategy and the retail mix

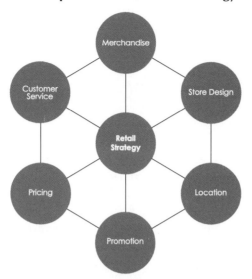

The major elements of a **strategic planning framework** are:

- the mission of the retail organisation;

- identification of the retail concept;

- identification of the desired retailer brand image (see Davies 1992);

- identification of the desired retailer personality (see Aaker 1997);

- strategic opportunities;

- alternatives;

- objectives and resources;

- the retail mix: overall, including competitive positioning;

- the retail mix: the detailed components;

- implementation through the scope of retail operations; and

- evaluation and performance management.

What are the benefits of a clearly defined retail strategy? In summary, a clearly defined retail strategy:

1. **highlights** the essential features;

2. **guides** the organisational direction & resource allocation, that is, it helps to determine priorities;

3. **facilitates** communication within the firm *and* with suppliers and customers; and

4. **facilitates** achievement of common goals.

*The espoused strategies of **public companies** are evident in their annual reports, which are official company documents. The difficulty with annual reports is that much of the material is retrospective. Even more difficult is the fact that **private retailers** do not lodge publicly available annual reports, although they often use public relations to highlight the firm's strategy (e.g. see media announcements by Myer in 2007). Therefore, the external analyst needs to draw on media releases, company websites, the firm's promotions, investor reports, industry analyses, media analysis and astute observation to infer the current strategy.*

The development of retail strategy takes place in the retailer's specific context, which has two facets – the external context and the internal context. The *external context* consists of factors which influence the business, yet over which the retailer has little if any control. These influences are often referred to by the acronym **PEST** – **P**olitical, **E**conomic, **S**ocial and **T**echnological. Retailers also have an *internal context* which brings together organisational capabilities – that is financial, physical, people and intangible – to develop and implement strategy. The internal context also encompasses organisational culture, heritage, traditions and internal stakeholder **buy-in** to the retail brand.

A basic way of bringing the external and internal influences together is through a SWOT analysis. A **SWOT** analysis (i.e. **S**trengths, **W**eaknesses, **O**pportunities and **T**hreats), is useful because it helps the retailer to disaggregate the aspects of each of these factors. And, an effective SWOT analysis also **weights** each aspect for importance and performance, and then ends with an evaluative summary.

The idea of weighing the factors in the SWOT analysis helps to enrich the value of the analysis. For example, a firm may have a perceived strength or weakness that is not very important for its future directions. As a result, the firm will probably choose not to invest any further in this aspect. Conversely, a perceived weakness may be critically important to future success. Recognising this importance allows the firm to make meaningful and relevant decisions about the allocation of resources to overcome this weakness. For example, a retailer may have a perceived weakness (i.e. poor performance) in e-retailing, which it identifies as very important for the future. With this knowledge, the firm can then either buy-in or outsource appropriate skills, technologies and processes.

A SWOT analysis is much more than a list of bullet points. A successful and therefore useful analysis will be the result of experience, observation, reflection and critical thinking. Many firms will need to conduct extensive research on: the external context (both current and predicted), the competition, trends, and the resource capacity of the business. The final evaluative summary then brings together the analysis.

The **retail mission** refers to "…what the firm plans to accomplish in the markets in which it competes for the customers it wants to serve…" (Mason & Mayer 1987). To define the mission further, retailers can identify the mission's scope which will cover: the retail category (see *Chapter 1 – An introduction to retailing*), market segments (see *Chapter 3 – Market sensing and understanding*), geography (see *Chapter 6 - Location*), size, for example sales, outlets, employees, and vertical scope, that is the extent to which retailers produce their own supplies. Kotler (1994) suggests that the choice of mission will be influenced by: history, owner and management preferences, market environment, resources and disincentive competencies. Furthermore, the retailer must balance these influences. The first three factors (history, preferences and market environment) shape what is *desired* for a mission, whereas the last two (resources and distinctive competencies) shape what is *feasible*. Once articulated, the mission becomes a working tool for the company because it guides and motivates staff and management. A well-designed and clearly expressed mission facilitates communication with customers, suppliers and the community.

Tools to assist strategy development and evaluation

The following tools are briefly looked at below to assist with strategy development and evaluation: **organisational research methods**, a **business intelligence system**, the **value chain**, and the **retail audit**.

Organisational research methods

Organisational research methods are part of the retailer's **business environmental scanning** capability. They can be used for research and can be either internal or external to the firm. A variety of research resources and tools are available to retailers to assist decision-making. The selection of methods will depend on the objectives of that research.

Retailers may decide to access existing research from external resources, such as the Australia Bureau of Statistics and Statistics New Zealand, the Business Council of Australia, the Australian Institute of Management, retail traders associations, the Shopping Centre Council, shopping centre management, local government, and federal and state government agencies. There are academic centres such as the Australian Centre of Retailing Studies at Monash University in Melbourne, and academics at Griffith University to name some institutions where there is particular interest and expertise. Other centres include the European Institute of Retailing and Service Studies (EIRASS) at Eindhoven in The Netherlands, and the Institute for Retail Studies at the University of Stirling in Scotland.

Retailers may decide to commission specific research conducted by either internal or external researchers. Research may survey areas of market research such as: the competition, suppliers, customer satisfaction, customer buying behaviour, or product and service innovations. Other areas of research interest are staff related and can focus on employee satisfaction, turnover, absenteeism, tenure, overtime, workforce composition, training needs analysis or skills audits.

Small retailers must not resile from participating in or initiating organisational research. Specifically commissioned research using well-briefed consultants, using the consultancy services of the Australian Bureau of Statistics or Statistics New Zealand, or employing a partnership with the tertiary education sector may be a cost-effective solution for the small retailing firm.

A business intelligence system

No matter the size of the retailing firm, there is always a need for a business intelligence system. The sophistication of such a system generally depends on the size of the organisation. Being a small firm does *not* negate the need for a business intelligence system; what varies is the degree of sophistication and automation required, and the availability of resources. The approach to business intelligence proposed here is an ethical one – we are not proponents of commercial espionage! Notwithstanding, there is a wealth of information readily available to retailers of large and small firms. Tyson (1986) has written cogently about both the need for and methods of acquiring business intelligence. His work focused on businesses in the 1990s, yet it is just as applicable to businesses in the 21st century.

Business intelligence makes its greatest contribution to retail strategy if it is seen as a planning tool rather than as research for the sake of research. Every person in the organisation can contribute to its collection. Thus, business intelligence can be gathered both internally and externally to the organisation. Retailers need to create a comprehensive framework that enables ongoing monitoring, staff involvement and recognition, and appropriate analysis and dissemination.

The general components of a business intelligence system are: market, competitor, product, customer and technological information (Tyson 1986). For the retailing industry, we would add **retailing industry** intelligence and **public policy** information as well as benchmarking and best practice information across the service and manufacturing sectors, and all aspects of the retail mix. Critically, large or small, any retailing firm must be alert to the diverse influences that can have an affect on its retail strategy, retail mix and organisational capabilities.

Business intelligence is not an event, it is a *process*. In its simplest form, it combines data collection and analysis which leads to retail strategy development or adjustment. The issues for firms to consider are:

- the capability for business intelligence;
- the strategy for business intelligence collection, analysis and dissemination;
- the implementation and evaluation of the business intelligence system; and
- the designation of a responsible business intelligence manager or co-ordinator.

Furthermore, there should be an analysis of the costs and benefits of such a system. Certainly, it must be a value-adding activity for the firm. Precursors to the successful implementation of a business intelligence system include: the development of a supportive organisation culture; the acquisition of appropriate skills; the development of internal communication systems to support data collection, analysis and dissemination; and the creation of an information security system.

Resources available to retailers include: **scanning** the print and electronic media such as business sections in newspapers, business magazines and business and documentary programs on television and DVDs; media clipping services and other information services and databases; libraries; directories such as Telstra's *White Pages*, *Yellow Pages* and the *National Business Directory*; and publications and research facilities from Statistics New Zealand and the Australian Bureau of Statistics. As well, the staff of the firm can also be a key resource in this area – not only are they staff, but they are also customers of a range of *other* retailers. This potentially potent source of information should not be neglected.

The value chain as an analytical tool

The **value chain**, proposed by Michael Porter, is another useful tool "for relating an organisation's resource profile to its strategic performance" (Johnson and Scholes 1993, p. 120). We believe this constructive approach presents medium and larger retailers with another way of evaluating organisational capability. The value chain analysis underscores the value relationships between resources – either owned or accessible – and activities, rather than merely identifying resources.

The retail audit: An overview

A key tool for retailers is the **retail audit**, which should analyse and evaluate the retail strategy including the retail mix and the extent of fit with the organisational capabilities of the firm. The retail audit is discussed *Chapter 10 – Retail operations, performance management and support systems*. The benefit of the retail audit is that it is designed to enable the retailer to systematically review the retail strategy overall, particular components of the retail strategy, and particular retail functions.

The nature and sources of sustainable competitive advantage

What is the *nature* of competitive advantage? We can think of **competitive advantage** as a strength that a firm has relative to its competitors, and which is important to its customers (Merrilees 1992). And what are the sources of competitive advantage in retailing? Every aspect of organisational capability can be a potential source of competitive advantage.

A useful way of incorporating advantage into retail strategy is to first identify the nature of the retail offer which will give a retailer an edge in the market. For example, this may be in terms of product range, quality of merchandise, EFTPOS payment facilities, or a loyalty program. The second stage is for the retailer to ensure that they have the skills and capabilities to support the chosen retail offer. This will generally mean putting more emphasis on backstage activities such as market research, business intelligence, technology, employee training and motivation, management training, and vendor selection. These skills and capabilities may need to either be developed in-house or acquired externally.

Retailer brand

One of the most exciting conceptual breakthroughs in the retailing literature has been the development of the concept of retailer – as opposed to product – branding. Although store image was discussed in the literature previously, the 1990s saw the advent of conceptual papers and empirical studies on **retailer brand** – also termed **retail image** or **retailer brand image** (Davies 1992) – and **retailer personality** (Aaker 1997). By the mid 1990s, major retailers like Wal-Mart and Gap were discussing the value and meaning of their retail brands in their annual reports. Ten years on, it is now common practice for retailers to be very conscious of building their retail brand and valuing it as an intangible asset. They achieve this in part by appointing brand managers.

Retailer branding is analogous to product branding in that it is unique and has an underlying concept. Product brands are also thought to have a personality, and advertising has been used extensively to create awareness. More recently, work has examined brand relationships. The translation to retailer branding is relatively easy – the retailer brand should express the total benefits on offer to the customer; it should have a unique identity based on an underlying concept and a brand personality (hard to do but achievable); advertising is important but effective public relations is also vital; and finally, retailer brand relationship management is essential.

In summary: a strong retail brand is well known; all stakeholders know what the brand represents; it is very special or distinctive; it is consistent; and it has high credibility or authenticity. It is probably the leader in its category, although there is scope for niche retailers to build strong brands quite locally. For small or niche retailers, brand relationship management and positive work of mouth will be essential.

Brand positioning

Brand positioning, like its close counterpart market positioning, is a relative term. That is, the positioning of a particular retailer is *relative* to its competitors. A two-step process can be envisaged to develop brand positioning. The first step is to clarify the target market, often in terms of low, medium or high pricing. For example, North America's largest clothing retailer, GAP, has three major retailer brands: Old Navy – low priced; GAP - mid priced; and Banana Republic –

premium priced. The second step requires fine-tuning of the position to reflect the desired unique brand. For example, the original Old Navy concept was a 'high value, down to earth, basic needs' brand concept. However, an alternative brand conceptualisation is possible, and in 2007 the brand was reformulated to include a greater fashion emphasis and a new stylised name 'ON' – initially linking to the retailer's heritage but with a planned disconnection over time. Whether this repositioning is successful remains to be seen.

Research and review the changes in the brand positionings of Abercrombie & Fitch, and Topshop.

Designing the retail mix

Retailers formulate the retail mix by taking a comprehensive approach to ensure that all components work together synergistically to achieve the retail strategy (see Figure 2.1). The **retail mix** is the total package of goods, services and messages that a retailer offers to a customer. The main components of the retail mix are:

- **merchandise selection**, which embraces product assortment and sourcing;

- **store design**, which brings together store infrastructure, store layout, merchandise spatial planning and visual merchandising;

- **location**, which covers macro and micro decisions;

- **promotion**, which integrates all forms of advertising, in-store promotion, special events, public relations , sponsorships and community partnerships;

- **pricing**, which is critical to the retailer's brand and financial success; and

- **customer service**, which includes customer service elements such as retail selling, and elements designed to achieve customer loyalty.

Product is critical to the retail mix – as are service type, quality and range. Price and store design are also very important, as are promotion, customer service, location, selling and distribution. All of these components represent points of contact between the retailer and its potential or actual customers.

The overall objectives of the retailer in general – and the positioning statement in particular – guide the formulation of the optimal retail mix. The retailer must shape the retail mix to achieve the desired competitive positioning by creating a unique retailer brand image. Chapters 4-9 discuss elements of the retail mix in greater depth.

The retail mix provides tools for strategy development and the translation of strategy into practice. Synergies between components are essential when creating a coherent retailer brand.

The implementation and evaluation of retail strategy

Much waste occurs when a well-formulated retail strategy is imperfectly implemented. The best retailers consider formulation and implementation as an integrated strategy package. Later chapters highlight some of the implementation and evaluation issues as do the chapters on the elements of the retail mix.

Many firms develop potentially successful retail strategies, which fail because the retailer fails to manage the implementation cost-effectively. The Coles Group 2007 Annual Report notes problems with the implementation of a turnaround strategy, which included rebadging Bi-Lo stores to Coles. After changing 129 stores, management stopped the process, leaving 71 Bi-Lo stores, and some confused and angry customers. [See Coles Group Annual Report 2007, pp. 2-12]

Investing in the strategy

Successful strategies require major investments by the firm. By assessing the requirements of the strategy and the current organisational capabilities, the retailer can determine which existing resources can be allocation to the strategy, what further investment is needed, and the likelihood of making that investment. For example, a retailer may decide to change the store design of current stores as part of a major makeover strategy to sharpen the retailer's brand. This strategy is likely to be expensive, and require store design expertise; possible changes to infrastructure, store layout and merchandise spatial planning; redesign of visual displays, and potentially slightly different merchandise mix that is consistent with the refreshed store image. If the retailer has a chain of stores, a planned rollout of the makeover will be important for managing the financial investment, as well as the allocation of expertise. As well, the retailer will need to plan internal marketing so that employees understand the proposed changes and the ramifications during implementation and beyond. Some retailers will have the required resources available 'in-house' or will have the financial capability to 'buy' the expertise, materials, and systems needed. Other retailers will need to raise the required capital.

No matter the size of the retailer, priorities must be set based on what is feasible and what is desirable. The overall test is the extent to which investing in the strategy is consistent with the overall directions and retailer brand.

Not only must a retailer have a sound strategy and brand concept, they must have suitable people to drive the retail brand. Ulrich and Smallwood (2007, p. 93) claim that "You want your leaders to be the kind of people who embody the promises your company makes to its customers".

Internal branding

How does a firm manage internal branding? The aim is to achieve **buy-in** by employees so that they understand and trust the brand, and feel committed to the corporate strategy. The leadership of the firm can create a culture of excellence consistent with the firm's goals by managing the internal relationships.

Other stakeholders – including suppliers – can be considered internal to the firm for the purposes of implementation. The customer sees very few of a firm's employees – this is the **frontstage** which, like a theatre or live performance, has some actors or performers. However, for the performance to take place successfully, many people **backstage** must also work together behind the scenes to ensure a smooth and timely performance.

Gapp and Merrilees (2006) examine how to achieve internal branding in a health care setting. Their findings can be adapted to the equally complex retail setting. In each case, people are at the heart of the matter.

Retail operations

The roles of retail operations are twofold. First, retail operations are the means of implementing or translating major strategies into action. Second, cost-effective retail operations facilitate the day-to-day management of the **retail mix**. Retail operations are discussed in *Chapter 10 – Retail operations, performance management and support systems*.

Performance management systems

The leaders of the retail firm must be committed to managing performance. This commitment needs to be supported by a performance management strategy and by performance management systems which incorporate **key performance indicators** (**KPIs**). There has been a significant shift recently from performance *measurement* to performance *management*. That shift suggests that it is insufficient to simply *measure* performance. Rather, we must develop suitable systems, measure appropriate key performance indicators using suitable tools, and then take the necessary management action to adjust performance-to-date in line with the current retail strategy or, if necessary, adjust the strategy so that it is more closely aligned with organisational capabilities.

Special issues

Retail format development

Offering a new retail format to existing customers is known as **retail format development** (discussed in *Chapter 5 – Store design*). Retailers may introduce these changes with little substantial change to the range of products and services offered. However, implementation must take account of resources needed for consistency with the desired retail brand.

Strategy revision

The context in which retailers operate is dynamic, and retailing strategy needs to be closely monitored and adjusted as required. Ideally, major changes will not be required more often than every two to three years. Unanticipated factors may make it necessary to adjust the strategy more frequently. The most obvious trigger for reviewing the strategy is any plan to add or reduce outlets, and applies particularly to franchising groups, to single company chains, and to conglomerates with multiple retail brands. The most common reasons for strategy revision may stem from changes in **consumer demand** patterns, changes in **competition**, or a deliberate decision to **revitalise** or **reposition** a company.

Revitalisation

Every retailer has the scope to conduct a serious review of its strategy from time to time. Few retailers have thoroughly researched their target market or fully assessed their position in the market. Many retailers could pay more attention to ensuring that all components of the retail mix are properly formulated and implemented. Evaluation may show that the retailer could improve some **key performance indicators** (**KPIs**), such as customer service ratings, percentage of loyal customers, or asset productivity. Considerations about revitalising the firm may result in a decision to **rebrand** the firm.

Corporate rebranding: The great opportunity

Corporate rebranding is a relatively new area of research and practice overall, and it recognises business lifecycles and dynamic contexts. An even newer area is rebranding in the retailing context (Merrilees 2005; Muzellec and Lambkin 2006). Proactive retailers will seek the means of differentiation and sustainable competitive advantage, and corporate rebranding is a potentially cost-effective approach to use. Corporate rebranding can be successfully undertaken by any sized retailer. Larger scale retailers, of course, have to grapple with much more complexity in the planning and execution of corporate rebranding.

Retail innovation and its role in rebranding

Existing theories of long-term retail success have a common ingredient and that is, not surprisingly, innovation. Some theories have covered retailing innovation in a narrow way, such as improved inventory management (Savitt 1999) or innovative human resource management (Miller 2006). Other research has a broader focus, highlighting the role of modernisation (innovation) together with astute retail mix management over time (Miller and Merrilees 2000). **Retail innovation** can be classified as retail marketing innovation, organisational process innovations, people management/relationship innovations and techno-logical innovations. Achieving innovation depends on creating a corporate culture that fosters innovation, tying innovation to strategy and the retail brand, offering incentives, and most importantly meeting customer needs either directly or indirectly. See *Chapter 11 – Retail innovation and sustainable retailing*.

Sustainable retailing

Increasing demands for sustainable retailing are coming from all stakeholders, albeit with fairly quiet voices at present. Many public retail companies are now producing statements on corporate governance, environmental issues and fair-trading. The term **sustainable retailing** can incorporate all these dimensions and more. The business itself must be sustainable, so that customers, suppliers, employees and other stakeholders can depend on the continuity of the business. Proactive retailers, large and small, can aim for sustainable retailing by:

- creating a sustainable competitive advantage;

- using ethical practices;

- exercising corporate social responsibility;

- minimising the firm's environmental footprint; and

- introducing innovative practices that enable customers to co-produce aspects of sustainable retailing.

Astute retailers, of any scale, recognise that sustainable retailing is central to business durability. Chapter 11 – Retail innovation and sustainable retailing *discusses this topic further.*

Conclusions

Retail strategy has its roots in early calls for more systematic approaches to retailing. A retail vision or concept is an important staring point, however, as shown by successful retailers, a more comprehensive and sensitive approach will help to design and implement a retail strategy that delivers and supports the unique retailer brand – for all stakeholders including customers, employees, suppliers, shareholders and the community. The burgeoning academic and business literatures offer many ideas for retailers to consider when developing retail strategy and their retailer brands. Understanding the essence of the retailer's business is very important, as are the differences and similarities between retailer and product branding. To create a sustainable competitive advantage, a retailer must have a sound strategy and invest appropriately in that strategy.

In an increasingly competitive environment, retailers must be proactive increasing sound strategies. In the past in growing markets, retailers could at times achieve success, even without strategic strengths, however that era is past and every retailer must be on their mettle. A clearly defined retail strategy which meets the needs of a well-defined target group, and which the retailer supports with organisational capabilities and the necessary investment, is the core that unifies both this book and exceptional retailing.

Review and applications

1. Discuss the processes retailers could use for strategy development:

   - for large retailers with multiple store types and names;

   - for small retail chains of up to five outlets; and

   - for a retailer who plans to add online shopping (e-retailing) to the business which has one 'bricks and mortar' store.

2. Explain the differences and similarities between retailer branding and product branding.

3. Discuss how consumers use retailer brands.

4. Develop a retail strategy and implementation program for a niche retailer specialising in shoes for people with 'hard to fit feet'.

5. Choose a small retail business and evaluate the external influences and internal contexts. Identify the strongest and most important factors. Explain how the firm can use this analysis.

6. Discuss how a firm can achieve employee buy-in for its retail strategy and implementation.

7. Explain how not-for-profit retailers like charity retail chains can develop unique and successful retailer brands.

8. Choose a long-existing retailer. Examine the factors that have contributed to the longevity of this firm.

9. Choose a recent retailing takeover or merger. Evaluate the impacts on the retailer brands concerned and make recommendations for corporate rebranding.

10. Identify a retailer whose current positioning requires adjustment. Make recommendations for corporate rebranding.

Website references

http://www.insideretailing.com.au/default.aspx.

References

Aaker, D 1991, *Managing Brand Equity*, The Free Press, New York.

Aaker, D 1996, *Building Strong Brands*, The Free Press, New York.

Aaker, J 1997, 'Dimensions of Brand Personality', *Journal of Marketing Research*, vol. 34 (August), pp. 347-356.

Ailawadi, K & Keller, KL 2004, 'Review: Understanding retail branding: conceptual insights and research priorities', *Journal of Retailing*, vol. 80, pp. 331-342.

Alexander, N 1997, 'Objectives in the Rearview Mirror May Appear Closer Than They Are', *The International Review of Retail, Distribution and Consumer Research*, vol. 7, no. 4, pp. 383-403.

Balmer, J (ed.) 2003, 'Special issue: Corporate and service brands', *European Journal of Marketing*, vol. 40, nos. 7 & 8.

Berry, L 2000, 'Cultivating service brand equity', *Journal of Academy of Marketing Science*, vol. 28, no. 1, pp. 128-137.

Berry, N 1988, 'Revitalizing brands', *Journal of Consumer Marketing*, vol. 5, no. 3, pp. 15-20.

Birtwistle, G & Freathy, P 1998, 'More than just a name above the shop: a comparison of the branding strategies of two UK fashion retailers', *International Journal of Retail and Distribution Management*, vol. 26, no. 8, pp. 318-323.

Burt, S & Sparks, L 2002, 'Corporate branding, retailing, and retail internationalization', *Corporate Reputation Review*, vol. 5, nos. 2 & 3, pp. 194-212.

Carlson, CR & Wilmot, WW 2006, *Innovation: The Five Disciplines for Creating What Customers Want*, Crown Business, New York.

Carpenter, J, Moore, M & Fairhurst, A 2005, 'Consumer shopping value for retail brands', *Journal of Fashion Marketing and Management*, vol. 9, no. 1, pp. 43-53.

Davies, G 1992, 'The two ways in which retailers can be brands', *International Journal of Retail & Distribution Management*, vol. 20, no. 2, pp. 24-34.

Davies, G & Chun, R 2002, 'Gaps between the internal and external perceptions of the corporate brand', *Corporate Reputation Review*, vol. 5, nos. 2/3, pp. 144-158.

de Chernatony, L & McDonald, M H B 1998, *Creating Powerful Brands in Consumer, Service and Industrial Markets*. Oxford: Butterworth-Heinemann.

de Chernatony, L 2002, 'Would a brand smell any sweeter by a corporate name?', *Corporate Reputation Review*, vol. 5, nos. 2/3, pp. 114-132.

Delgado-Ballester, E & Munuera-Aleman, J 2001, 'Brand trust in the context of consumer loyalty', *European Journal of Marketing*, vol. 35, nos. 11/12, pp. 1238-1258.

Dennis, C, Fenech, T, Merrilees, B 2004, *e-Retailing*, Routledge, London.

Koehn, N 2001, *Brand New: How Entrepreneurs Earned Consumers' Trust from Wedgwood to Dell*, Harvard Business School Press, Boston.

Low, G, Lamb, C 2000, 'The measurement and dimensionality of brand associations', *The Journal of Product and Brand Management*, 2000; 9 (6): 350-368.

Low, G & Mohr, J 2000, 'Advertising vs. sales promotion: A brand management perspective', *Journal of Product & Brand Management*, vol. 9, no. 6, pp. 389-414.

Martineau, P 1958, 'The personality of the retail store', *Harvard Business School Press*, January/February, pp. 47-55.

Maver, K 1990, 'A marriage of traditionalism with a progressive management style are rings of success for Kingsmill's', *London Business Monthly Magazine*, July, pp. 31-36.

Merrilees, B 2005) 'Radical brand evolution: a case-based framework', *Journal of Advertising Research*, vol. 45, no. 2 (June), pp. 201-210.

Merrilees, B & Fry, M-L 2002, 'Corporate branding: a framework for e-retailers', *Corporate Reputation Review*, vol. 5, nos. 2/3, pp. 213-225.

Merrilees, B & Miller, D 2005, 'Emotional Brand Associations: a New KPI for e-Retailers', *International Journal of Internet Marketing and Advertising*, vol. 2, no. 3, pp. 206-218.

Miller, D & Merrilees, B 2000, 'Gone to Gowings – An analysis of success factors in retail longevity: Gowings of Sydney', *The Services Industry Journal*, vol. 20, no. 1, pp. 61-85.

Moore, C 1995, 'From rags to riches – creating and benefiting from the fashion own-brand', *International Journal of Retail & Distribution Management*, vol. 23, no. 9, pp. 19-27.

Muzellec, L & Lambkin, M 2006, 'Corporate rebranding: destroying, transferring or creating brand equity?', *European Journal of Marketing*, vol. 40, no. 7/8, pp. 803-824.

Olins, W 1978, *The Corporate Personality: an Inquiry into the Nature of Corporate Identity*, Mayflower Books, New York.

Oliverio, M 1989, 'The implementation of a code of ethics: the early efforts of one entrepreneur', *Journal of Business Ethics*, vol. 8, pp. 367-374.

Selnes, F 1993, 'An examination of the effect of product performance on brand reputation, satisfaction and loyalty', *European Journal of Marketing*, vol. 27, no. 9, pp. 19-35.

Spector, R & McCarthy, PD 2000, *The Nordstrom Way: The Inside Story Of America's #1 Customer Service Company*, John Wiley, New York.

Svennson, G 2001, 'Glocalization of business activities: a 'glocal' strategy', *Management Decision*, vol. 39, no. 1, 6-18.

Traub, M & Teicholz, T 1993, *Like no other store... : the Bloomingdale's legend and the revolution in American marketing*, Times Books, New York.

Wong, H Y & Merrilees, B 2007, 'Closing the marketing strategy to performance gap: the role of brand orientation', *Journal of Strategic Marketing,* vol. 15 (December), pp. 443-458.

Advanced reading

Balmer, J, Mukherjee, A, Greyser, S & Jenster, P (eds) 2006, 'Corporate marketing: integrating corporate identity, corporate branding, corporate communications, corporate image and corporate reputation', *European Journal of Marketing*, vol. 40, nos. 7 & 8.

Birtwistle, G & Freathy, P 1998, 'More than just a name above the shop: a comparison of the branding strategies of two UK fashion retailers', *International Journal of Retail and Distribution Management*, vol. 26, no. 8, pp. 318-323.

Burt, S & Sparks, L 2002, 'Corporate branding, retailing, and retail internationalization', *Corporate Reputation Review*, vol. 5, nos. 2 & 3, pp. 194-212.

Christensen, C 1997, *The Innovator's Dilemma*, New York, Harper Collins.

Davies, G & Chun, R 2002, 'Gaps between the internal and external perceptions of the corporate brand', *Corporate Reputation Review*, vol. 5, nos. 2 & 3, pp. 144-158.

de Chernatony, L 2006, *From Brand Vision to Brand Evaluation: The Strategic Process of Growing and Strengthening Brands,* 2nd ed., Oxford, Elsevier.

de Chernatony, L & Dall'Olmo Riley, F 1998, 'Modelling the components of the brand', *European Journal of Marketing*, vol. 32, nos. 11 & 12, pp. 1070-1090.

de Chernatony, L, Drury, S & Segal-Horn, S 2005, 'Using triangulation to assess and identify successful services brands', *The Services Industries Journal*, vol. 25, no. 1, pp. 5-21.

de Chernatony, L & Segal-Horn, S 2003, 'The criteria for successful services brands', *European Journal of Marketing*, vol. 37, nos. 7 & 8, pp. 1095-1118.

Ewing, M, Fowlds, D & Shepherd, I 1995, 'Renaissance: a case study in brand revitalization and strategic realignment', *Journal of Product & Brand Management*, vol. 4, no. 3, pp. 19-26.

Gapp, R & Merrilees, B 2006, 'Important factors to consider when using internal branding as a management strategy: a healthcare case study', *Journal of Brand Management*, vol. 14, nos. 1 & 2 (Sept/Nov).

Hatch, M & Schultz, M 2003, 'Bringing the corporation into corporate branding', *European Journal of Marketing*, vol. 37, nos. 7 & 8, pp. 1041-1064.

Ind, N 2004, *Living the Brand: How to Transform Every Member of your Organization into a Brand Champion*, 2nd ed., London, Kogan Page.

Kaikati, J 2003, 'Lessons from Accenture's 3Rs: rebranding, restructuring and repositioning', *Journal of Product & Brand Ma*nagement, vol. 12, no. 7, pp. 477-490.

Kapferer, J-N 1997, *Strategic Brand Management: Creating and Sustaining Brand Equity Long Term*, London, Kogan Page.

Karmark, E 2005, in Schultz, M, Antorini, Y & Csaba, F (eds) 2005, *Towards the Second Wave of Corporate Branding: Corporate Branding Purpose/People/Process*, Copenhagen Business School, Chapter 5 (Living the Brand), pp. 103-124.

Keller, K 2003, *Strategic Brand Management: Building, Measuring and Managing Brand Equity*, Upper Saddle River, Prentice Hall.

Knox, S & Bickerton, D 2003, 'The six conventions of corporate branding', *European Journal of Marketing*, vol. 37, nos. 7 & 8, pp. 998-1016.

Kohli, A & Jaworksi, B 1990, 'Market orientation: the construct, research propositions, and managerial implications', *Journal of Marketing*, vol. 54, no. 2 (April), pp. 1-18.

Lindström, M & Andersen, T 1999, *Brand Building on the Internet*, Melbourne, Hardie Grant Books.

McEnally, M & de Chernatony, L 1999, 'The evolving nature of branding: consumer and managerial considerations', *Academy of Marketing Science Review*, vol. 1999, no. 02, pp. 1-25.

Muzellec, L, Doogan, M & Lambkin, M 2003, 'Corporate rebranding – an exploratory review', *Irish Marketing Review*, vol. 16, no. 2, pp. 31-40.

Olins, W 2003, *On Brand*, London, Thames & Hudson.

Schroeder, J & Salzer-Morling, M (eds) 2006, *Brand Culture*, Milton Park, Routledge.

Schultz, M & de Chernatony, L (eds) 2002, 'Introduction to Special Issue on Corporate Branding', *Corporate Reputation Review*, vol. 5, nos. 2 & 3, pp. 105-112.

Schultz, M, Antorini, Y & Csaba, F (eds) 2005, *Towards the Second Wave of Corporate Branding: Corporate Branding Purpose/People/Process*, Copenhagen Business School.

Schultz, M & Hatch, M 2003, 'The cycles of corporate branding', *California Management Review*, vol. 46, no. 1 (Fall), pp.6-26.

Stuart, H & Muzellec, L 2004, 'Corporate makeovers: can a hyena be rebranded?' *Journal of Brand Management*, vol. 11, no. 6, pp. 472-482.

Urde, M 1999, 'Brand orientation: a mindset for building brands into strategic resources', *Journal of Marketing Management*, vol. 15, nos. 1-3, pp. 117-133.

Urde, M 2003, 'Core value-based corporate brand building', *European Journal of Marketing*, vol. 37, nos. 7 & 8, pp. 1017-1040.

Vallaster, C & de Chernatony, L 2006, 'Internal branding building and structuration: the role of leadership', *European Journal of Marketing*, vol. 40, nos. 7 & 8, pp. 761-784.

Wong, H & Merrilees, B 200), 'A brand orientation typology for SMEs: a case research approach', *Journal of Product & Brand Management*, vol. 14, no. 3, pp. 155-162.

Market sensing and understanding

Introduction

The final aspect of the context of retailing is the market. Fundamental to good retail practice is an understanding of the market where the retailer operates. Engaging with the market requires an ability to *sense* the idiosyncrasies and nuances of a given market. For example, Virgin Airlines understands that customers need reassurance and diversion. It provides a genuine rapport with customers by offering value for money airline flights and a quirky friendly on-board service. The challenge facing all retailers is how to **market sense** *and* leverage this market sensing with a genuine **understanding** of consumers.

Retailers continue to attempt to predict trends and to forecast consumer needs and wants. In the Harvard Business Review, Paul Saffo (2007) declares: "The goal of forecasting is not to predict the future but to tell you what you need to know to take meaningful action in the present." How, then, can retailers create the processes, resources and tools to sense and understand the market?

How does a retailer know when to introduce greener options for customers? How does a retailer sense and understand that customers want innovations that will lead to sustainable consumption? See Vignette 3.1.

The platform for this chapter – and in fact for the entire book – is that the role of retailers is to facilitate the choice process for consumers and not to force sales unfairly on consumers. That is, an **ethical approach** to all facets of retailing and the supply chain should be the basis for the exchange between retailer and customer. Therefore, it is incumbent on the retailer to assist the customer to make **informed choices**, with retailers adding real value to the decision process.

Retailers can use many factors to help customers make an informed choice. Product labelling, explanations of features and benefits, adequate and accurate descriptions, and opportunities for sampling or trialling products are all important. Retailers should provide sufficient information so that customers can make meaningful comparisons quite easily. Governments also have a part to play, for example, with regulating for unit pricing, and meaningful nutritional information on food products' labels.

Vignette 3.1

Woolworths senses the market

How important is sensing the market and understanding the customer to Australia's largest retailer largest, Woolworths Limited? The firm also uses internal marketing through its staff newsletter, Woolies News, to communicate brand values and to show the firm understands its customers. In the words of the newsletter (Winter 2007):

"Our shoppers are so important to our business that we have formed a new team to help serve them better – The Customer Engagement Team.

We know that in our fast moving industry it is important to adapt our business to respond to industry changes, major new trends and even the behaviour of our individual shoppers. Our shoppers are so important to our business that we have formed a new team to help serve them better – The Customer Engagement Team.

Based ... in Sydney, [they] are developing new techniques to understand our customers better. "The trick is to pick up on the trends quicker than our competition, and then turn that learning into action – fast", commented Richard Umbers, General Manager – Customer Engagement.

The team are drawing heavily on the knowledge of experts from across the business. ... The project employs some of the latest technology and analysis techniques, but the outcomes of the project are down-to-earth and practical. It will give the company the ability, for example, to adapt our range to cater for ever-changing customer trends and to target our promotions to those who will benefit from them.

It's all about one of the retail basics – serving the customer better. Follow the shopper!"

Sources:
Woolworths Limited: 2006 Annual Report and Woolworths news Winter 2007, Woolworths Corporate Social Responsibility Report 2005 (released 2006) available at <www.woolworthslimited.com.au>.

Most of the theories presented in this chapter were selected for their simplicity, in that they provide as much insight into consumer behaviour as possible using quite general assumptions about the way consumers behave. Please do not believe that these models *precisely* predict what people are likely to buy over, for example, a monthly period. Most people are not that predictable. Many of the models seem to assume very rational behaviours. Rarely can people be easily modelled as *individuals*. However, budding researchers have much scope to develop better models, which explain more of consumers' *actual* behaviour. Nevertheless, retailers require some broad insights into the ways consumers behave.

At a more detailed level, retailers want to know the **sequence** consumers use to make merchandise/service and store decisions – that is which comes first? This chapter also explores the implications of consumer behaviour for retailing decisions about which **market segments** to target, and the effect of the **promotion mix** and other elements of the retail mix. The chapter then discusses the role of **market research** in ascertaining actual customer needs.

Retail customers

Retailing is a people-focused business. In retailing, it is critical to develop an understanding of retail customers, their motives for shopping and their methods for deciding what to buy and where to buy it. This corresponds to the field of investigation called consumer behaviour. Retailers are particularly interested in the reasons *why* consumers shop at one store rather than another. It is also necessary to obtain an understanding of the reasons consumers choose certain brands of goods and not others. The matter of product brand choices is pertinent especially in the grocery sector where major retailers are introducing a much greater percentage of own or private brands.

Classification of merchandise

To consumers, some shopping decisions are more important than others and may require more planning and consideration of the options. We can look at classifications in two ways. The first way is a classification based on the complexity of the decision; the second is a classification based on the merchandise type.

Classification based on the complexity of decision

One classification of decisions is that by Howard and Sheth (1969) which distinguishes routine decisions from limited problem solving and extensive problem solving.

Routine decisions are those that rely on habit and experience, and that consumers make quickly and with very little deliberation. Many of the items that consumers buy regularly a supermarket would fall into this category. **Limited problem solving** describes the situation where a medium level of time and deliberation are taken to make a decision. This may be the case when a new brand enters the market. A consumer may be familiar with the product but not with a new brand, and may therefore undertake some effort to assess it. **Extended problem solving** refers to the situation where considerable time and effort are spent in evaluating a good or brand. This may be because of the large amount of money involved, or because a new product – such as a plasma television set or a mobile phone – is introduced into the market.

Classification based on the merchandise type

Another useful way of classifying merchandise is to use the four main merchandise (including services) types: **convenience goods**, **preference goods**, **shopping goods** and **specialty goods** (Figure 3.1). This classification of merchandise can be thought of as a two-by-two matrix, where each element depends on the degree of involvement or shopping effort by the consumer, and the degree of clarity and confidence that the consumer has about the attributes of the good being bought. The degree of clarity is often referred to as the **degree of complexity** in retail and marketing literature.

Convenience goods refers to those goods where the consumer is confident about their attributes and only wants to spend a minimal amount of shopping effort on them. These goods typically include everyday items such as milk, bread, newspapers, toilet paper, paper towels, household cleaners, breakfast cereals, aluminium foil, and tinned fruit and vegetables. These items are typically bought on a regular basis from a supermarket or convenience store and are relatively inexpensive. There is also a relatively low brand loyalty.

Preference goods refers to those goods where the consumer is not fully confident about the desired and actual attributes, but only wants to spend a minimal amount of shopping effort on them. These goods typically include such merchandise as instant coffee, deodorants and shampoos. Consumers generally buy these items at a supermarket or convenience store. They are relatively inexpensive, and have relatively high brand loyalty.

Shopping goods refers to those goods where the consumer is fairly confident about the desired and actual attributes, and wants to be highly involved in the decision. Therefore, they are prepared to expend a high amount of shopping effort on them. These goods include cars and other motor vehicles, boats, major appliances, and health insurance. These items are often bought at exclusive outlets of specialist retailers, are expensive, and may have low to medium brand loyalty.

Specialty goods refers to those goods for which the consumer is not confident about the desired attributes, and wants to be involved in the decision. Therefore, consumers are prepared to spend a medium to high amount of shopping effort on them. These goods include cameras, perfume, DVD players and sporting goods. These items are often bought at selective outlets of specialist retailers, are fairly expensive, and have the potential for medium to high brand loyalty.

This classification of goods suggests broad tendencies. In practice, it can vary from individual to individual. For example, someone who is extremely self-confident and knows what is fashionable may regard boutique clothes as a shopping good, whereas someone who is not as confident may regard boutique clothes as a specialty good.

From a retailer's perspective, the retailing strategy could alter depending on the type of goods or services offered. **Convenience goods** require a wide distribution of outlets and therefore focus on instore promotion at eye-level. **Preference goods** rely on branding and mass advertising to build up the image of the merchandise. **Shopping goods** – such as those sold through car dealers – do not require as many outlets as convenience goods because the shopper is willing to search for what is wanted. Suitable locations near target customers are still important. However, retailers would be wise to have a reasonable range of the merchandise to aid comparisons by the shopper. **Specialty goods** also do not need too many outlets. The retailer would emphasise instore advice by expert sales persons because of the consumer's lack of knowledge or confidence of what, for example, represents a good tennis racquet.

Figure 3.1 Classification of merchandise

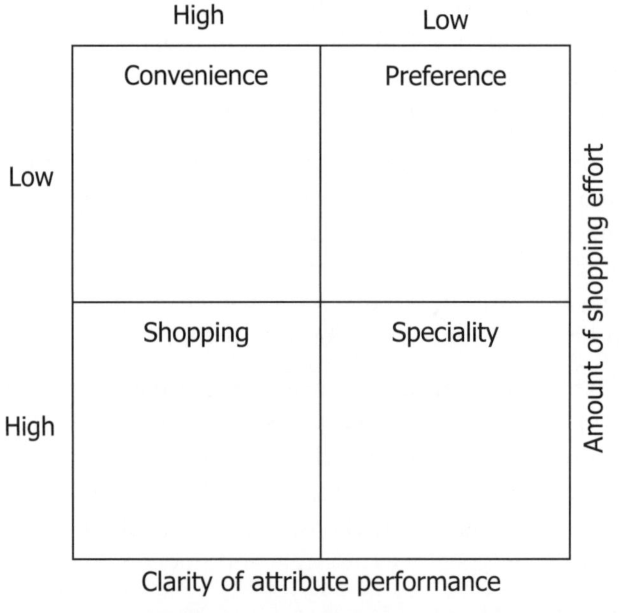

	High	Low	
Low	Convenience	Preference	Amount of shopping effort
High	Shopping	Speciality	

Clarity of attribute performance

Note: Each element depends on the degree of involvement or shopping effort by the consumer and the clarity about the attributes of the goods purchased. Shopping effort means willingness to spend time and cost in searching for desired goods. Clarity means certainty or understanding about what the good is and what it can do.

Motives for shopping

People have a variety of reasons for shopping. Many shoppers have sophisticated, complex and often-subconscious motivations. Shopping can be an essential chore, or a creative or sensory stimulus. It can be a physical activity; a diversion from one's daily routine; relaxing, fun and entertaining; or social (Fiske, Hodge & Turner 1987; Reekie 1993; Kingston 1994). Some people go shopping without any particular need in mind. However, they are ready to buy and, as a result, it is the excitement of the search, the power of the choice and the satisfaction of the purchase that all ultimately make this activity a positive experience.

The reasons for shopping will differ across consumers, across retail categories and across time. Individual shopping motivations will vary with context and purpose. For example, a British study found that grocery shopping was seen more as a chore than clothes shopping, which in turn was more of a chore than shopping for household items (Mintel 1986). In contrast, about a quarter of buyers of clothes and household items saw it as fun, compared to only 4 per cent of grocery buyers. If nothing else, these figures suggest a big opportunity for supermarket chains to make grocery shopping more fun and enjoyable.

Shopping cannot be equated with simply buying merchandise (see Tauber 1972). Rather than simply buying merchandise, most consumers are seeking what Merrilees and Miller (1996) term the **total shopping experience**. The core component of a total shopping experience is the merchandise itself. However, consumers also seek a number of **peripheral components**, including convenience, price, store atmosphere and service. As well as the core and peripheral components, the total shopping experience also requires another dimension – the **dynamics of the experiential shopping process**. Some of the peripheral components – such as store atmosphere, music and interaction with employees – double up here, but these forces vary for each retail encounter between the customer and the store. The dynamics of the experiential shopping process will be more important if the motive for shopping is one of diversion, creative or sensory stimulation, fun, building self-esteem or socialising.

Retailers are gradually recognising the importance of the shopping experience, although the experiential aspects can be developed further. For example, the Coles Group says:

> *"As well as enhancing our merchandise offer, we have undertaken significant work to improve our customers' in-store shopping experience, by introducing our ambience program. ... Looking ahead, we will continue to open new stores and improve the shopping experience in our existing store network." (Coles Group Ltd Annual Report 2007, p. 10)*

The consumer decision process: merchandise choice

The traditional decision model developed by Engel *et al.* in the 1960s suggests that consumers progress through a number of well-defined steps when they make decisions about what to buy. These steps are summarised in Table 3.1. Note that this model applies to both goods and services. The main difference between these two categories is that consumers often have less objective information with which to make choices about services.

This fairly elaborate process could be more relevant for limited or extensive problem-solving rather than routine decisions. The **five step consumer decision process** is more relevant for shopping goods and specialty goods. However, the model might still be applicable for less expensive convenience or preference goods, although here the consumer may move through each stage very quickly. For some consumers, the stages may follow a different pattern to that proposed in the model.

Table 3.1 Five step consumer decision process

- Problem recognition
- Information search
- Evaluation of alternatives
- Decision
- Post-purchase evaluation

Source: See Engel, Kollat & Blackwell 1968.

The first stage of the consumer decision process is **problem recognition**. This occurs when a consumer becomes aware of certain unmet needs and seeks to meet those needs. It may be the need for a new tube of toothpaste, or a new washing machine because the old one has broken down, or an extension to the house as the family has grown in number.

An **information search** may take place if the consumer has to find out more information about the good or brand, or the location of a suitable outlet to purchase it from. We have already foreshadowed that the amount of search is likely to be greater for shopping goods and specialty goods than for convenience goods and preference goods. At the level of the individual, some people – particularly those with more education and higher incomes – better appreciate the benefits of an information search and may therefore be more likely to search. However, the benefits of an information search have to be compared with the costs and time of additional searching.

Another way of defining the dimensions of classification of merchandise is in terms of **financial, psychological and social risks** on the vertical axis and **performance risks** on the horizontal axis. Thus, cars have well-identified performance risks on the horizontal axis, and high financial and social risks if something goes wrong. The consumer search process is to consult with friends and across outlets until the perceived risks of buying a good are reduced to an acceptable level.

Manufacturers assist consumers by **branding** many of their goods. Branding has the effect of reducing both the risks of variable product performance, that is performance risk, and any adverse impact on the ego, that is psychological and social risk (the latter is achieved through image building advertising and other measures to develop greater perceived value). The Australian legal system also helps the consumer through implied warranties and other forms of consumer protection (see Merrilees & Cotman 1976). Manufacturers and retailers add to this protection through extended warranties, merchandise exchange and refund policies. The net impact of all these devices – from branding to refund policies – is to reduce the need for the consumer to search as much as they would otherwise need to do.

To the extent that consumers do search for information, there is a hierarchy of credibility of the sources of information. Heading credibility is the consumer's own knowledge and understanding about the product. Next comes friends and relatives, followed by independent experts such as *Choice* magazine, automobile associations, for example RACV, RACQ or NRMA, and perhaps journalists. The next most credible sources are testimonies from customers and in-house, partisan experts. The least credible seems to be advertising, where the source has a clear stake in the way the information is framed.

In general, having appropriate information is important if consumers are to make what we called an **informed choice** – that is, having sufficient information from labelling and other sources to make a decision that is in the perceived best interests of the consumer.

Once consumers have information, how do they compare or evaluate alternatives? An important concept in consumer behaviour is that of the evoked set. The concept of the **evoked set** indicates that a consumer generally chooses one brand from a small group of brands that are all broadly acceptable to the consumer. This set evolves over time through consumer experience and learning about various brands. An Australian study shows that the majority of consumers have an evoked set of up to four brands in relation to coffee, toilet paper and laundry detergent. The set is smallest for coffee, indicating relatively greater brand loyalty, and is largest for laundry detergent, indicating less brand loyalty (Bednall, Walker & Grant 1995).

The actual selection of the particular brand is influenced by what is called the **evaluative criteria**, that is, the basis upon which a consumer evaluates the alternatives. There are various types of evaluative criteria. They share the feature that consumers conceptualise a product into various **attributes** and are able to rate each attribute for each brand in the evoked set. By attributes, we mean characteristics or features. For example, a stove may have optional features such as a fan-forced oven rather than a conventional oven, a lift-up lid for easy cleaning, an integrated unit, a ceramic hot plate, and a lift-off oven door. While these additional features may provide quicker cooking, better cooking, more energy efficiency and make the product easier to clean, consumers have to decide if the benefits are worth the additional cost.

The best known evaluative criteria is the Fishbein (1967) model which multiplies the **consumer's importance weighting** for each attribute by the **consumer's rating score** for that attribute for a particular brand, and then adds up these sums for each brand separately. The buying decision of the consumer depends on the evaluative criteria chosen. If the Fishbein model is used, either explicitly or implicitly, then the brand which receives the highest score across all of the attributes is chosen. The Fishbein model may be seen as too elaborate or sophisticated for many of the hundreds of consumer decisions that are made weekly.

Some of the simpler evaluative criteria include the **conjunctive model**, where the brand that first satisfies a minimum standard for each attribute is chosen. An even simpler model is the **disjunctive model**, where a brand is chosen based on the highest rating in one key attribute. There are also other more unusual criteria such as the **scenario model**, where consumers choose a brand based on a more holistic image of the composite of attributes. A possible example of the scenario model is the way consumers choose a travel holiday – assuming that they somehow compare different 'packages' of holidays.

After consumers make their buying decision, they proceed to make a **post-purchase evaluation**. Did I buy the right make of car? Did I buy the right model? Should I have bought power steering? These questions represent a form of **post-purchase dissonance** in which doubts may arise as to whether the right decision was made. In recent years, car manufacturers have responded to the need to reassure buyers, partly by continuing advertising and partly by writing to them and saying: 'Dear Valued Customer … Congratulations on the purchase of your new … '. To this end, some manufacturers offer extended warranties for three to five years, while others offer 24-hour roadside assistance.

The consumer decision process: store choice

The five-step model of the consumer decision process from Table 3.1, which was applied to merchandise in the previous section, can also be applied to **store choice**. Problem recognition is not confined to merchandise choice but can relate to the broader motives of shopping. The search process now is explicitly for an appropriate outlet, although direct marketing and e-retailing options also need to be considered.

The alternatives are distinct stores that differ on attributes such as price, convenience, product range, quality, store atmosphere, customer service and location. Note that, as shown in *Chapter 2 – Retail strategy, branding and innovation*, the branding concept applies to stores as well as merchandise. Stores have certain overall images that are the sum of specific attributes or are in a bundled, scenario-type form. For example, David Jones has an overall upmarket image. The evoked set concept is also relevant to stores since many consumers only shop at a distinct group of stores, depending on their price range, merchandise selection and image. **Store loyalty**, namely the extent to which a consumer is loyal to a store, is generally shared across the evoked set rather than being limited to one particular store.

Store image is particularly important because it conveys to customers the key attributes that they may be seeking. Different retail categories emphasise different attributes. For example, mail-order retailers emphasise shopping time saved, price discounts and guarantees. Supermarkets and discount stores highlight price, range and convenience. Department stores and many specialty stores are prominent with quality, service and selected range. Within each category, different retailers will be attempting to convey their own specific image as part of the inter-brand competition across retailers. Mass media advertising is particularly important in communicating these specific images, but ultimately *all* components of the retail mix contribute to image.

Figure 3.2 External and instore influences that affect purchase choice

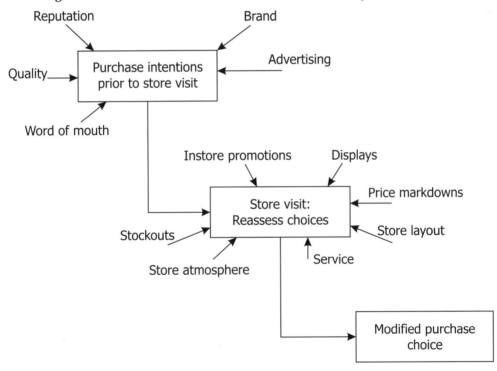

The consumer decision process: instore choices

Many consumer decisions are not made until the consumer is in the store, with some studies showing that two-thirds of brand decisions for supermarket items were made in the store (Agnew 1987, McIntyre 1995*)*. This is particularly the case for supermarket purchases, but also applies to other retail categories. The importance of **instore decisions** means that it is useful for the retailer to have an understanding of factors that influence instore decisions (Figure 3.2). **Stockouts** are situations where the brand that the customer wants is out of stock. The customer must decide between choosing an alternative, visiting a different store in the hope of finding that product, or making no purchase.

One Australian supermarket selected at random had stockout signs for 60 items on one particular day.

The retailer can use various techniques to influence last minute decisions by consumers when they are in the store. For example, flashing lights and other specials, displays and helpful sales personnel can attract customers. It is important to see instore promotion as part of an **integrated marketing communication strategy** in which all components of promotion are integrated and linked. The negative impacts of ineffective linking can be quite serious.

In a recent supermarket experience, the 'narrow-casting' instore announcement of a reduced price for potatoes was not communicated effectively to the checkout person, who then did not know about the price change. Rather than wait several minutes to resolve the price difference, the customer simply left the potatoes at the checkout.

Similarly, instore promotion needs to be linked with concurrent mass media promotion which includes television and press advertising, current catalogues and flyers delivered directly to households, and online promotions.

Staff at Big W spend time 'tying up the ad', that is, modifying shelf-talkers to reflect the mass media advertised sale and promotions.

The choice sequence between merchandise, store and shopping centre

There is debate as to what comes first:

- Do consumers choose the specific brand of merchandise, and then the store? ~or~

- Do consumers choose the store first, and then the merchandise?

The answer greatly influences the type of promotion needed and by whom. For example, if the second sequence were more common, the importance of promotion by retailers compared to manufacturers would be increased and would favour point-of-purchase promotion. Given that many consumers are influenced by instore stimuli, this suggests that, for many individuals, the relevant sequence is 'store first, merchandise second'.

The author suggests that, for some merchandise types – such as perfume – the relevant sequence is 'merchandise first, outlet second'. Perfumes have very strong brand images and high perceived value, leading to clear preferences across most consumers. Rather than trying to counter this, image retailers such as David Jones emphasise **co-operative advertising** with the manufacturers of selected brands. The advertisements tend to highlight both David Jones and one particular leading perfume brand.

Arguably for some retail categories such as supermarkets and boutique clothing shops and perhaps category killers such as Bunnings (hardware category) and Toys 'R' Us (toys category), the **dominant sequence** is likely to be 'outlet first, merchandise second'. For boutique clothing stores, the store name and the designer labels are likely to be entwined, with customers attracted to particular stores such as Liz Davenport and then choosing from the selection therein. For supermarkets, convenience and prices are likely to be major influences on consumer choice. The fact that the major supermarket chains advertise specials on branded goods does not contradict our indicated sequence. This type of advertising is intended to build up an overall low price image, with overall store choice as the main objective and the selection of particular brands as a secondary consideration.

For some individuals, the above sequences could be reversed. For other individuals the decisions of merchandise and outlet could be simultaneous. For some retail categories, such as car dealers, there could be a strong mix of both sequences. If the consumer does not know much about cars, they may emphasise the outlet-merchandise sequence and use the dealer as one of their advisers in making a choice. If more is known about cars, the consumer may decide the make and model, and then shop around the dealers for the best deal.

There is still only limited research as to the dominant sequence between merchandise and outlet choices as well as the possibility of simultaneous choice for some consumers. These patterns are not known for most retail categories, although indicative factors which might influence the sequence have been suggested here.

The above gap in knowledge is further complicated. There is a *third* major decision which needs to be brought into consideration, namely the **choice of shopping centre** (Finn, McQuitty & Rigby 1994). This choice is explored in more detail in Chapters 4 and 6. Note for now that some shoppers choose a centre, then a variety of outlets, and then relevant merchandise. Other shoppers may use different patterns. This **three way choice model** between centre, outlets and merchandise, as shown in Figure 3.3, has yet to receive serious extensive attention by researchers. However, it does quickly open up the need for shopping centres to market themselves *vis-à-vis* other competing centres. This issue is being explored by researchers and shopping centre managers, including those in some central business districts.

Figure 3.3 Sequential relationships between shopping centre, store and brand of merchandise – the three way choice model

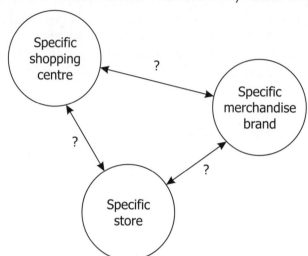

Market segmentation for retailers

An important practical tool that can be used by all retailers is the notion of market segment. A **market segment** is a particular cluster of consumers in a market which have fairly similar needs but whose needs differ from consumers in other market segments. One of the easiest divisions of the market is by income group, for example high, middle and low. Each retailer needs to identify which of these three groups it wishes to target, because the retailing strategy could be radically different depending on which target markets are chosen. Other segments could be based on age, gender, region or lifestyle. More generally, the four main bases for segmentation are given in Table 3.2, and three of them are discussed in more detail here. Note, however, that there may be advantages in using *combinations* of bases rather than just a single base.

Table 3.2 Major bases for market segmentation

Geographic	Country, state, city, suburb.
Demographic	Age, gender, marital status, family size, income, education, occupation.
Psychographic	Lifestyle, personality, social status.
Behavioural	Use situation: occasion, importance of purchase, prior experience with product or service, user status.
	Buyer's needs and preferences: benefits sought, quality, proneness to make a deal, brand preference, brand loyalty.
	Purchase behaviour: size of purchase, frequency of purchase.

Demographic and regional segmentation bases

Demographic and regional data are usually the easiest to collect or discern, and tend to be the most commonly used. The data closely correspond to the questions asked in the five-yearly Census of Population, and hence Australian Bureau of Statistics (ABS) figures can be used as a benchmark. Note that the ABS figures may not be in the detail required by the retailer, but they may still be useful as a guide. Age and gender are common in the examples given in Table 3.3. Age is particularly important in differentiating the retail strategies of various clothing retailers.

Jeans West caters for a slightly younger age group than Just Jeans, and this is reflected in merchandise styles and store atmosphere including music, lighting and displays.

Table 3.3 Australian examples of special interest market segments

The 18-39 year age group	Shoebridge 1995
'Thirtysomethings' age group in the magazine industry	Burbury 1993
'Twentysomethings' age group	Wynhausen 1995
The over-50s age group buying financial services	Fox 1993
Unattached professional women buying property	Moodie 1995
Loyal customers	Canu 1994 Howarth 1994 Mitchell 1994 Dowling 1994 Burbury 1995b
Gays and lesbians	Burbury 1994a Burbury 1994b
New 'brands' of men buying supermarket products	Windsor & Foreshew 1994
Demographic groups which control the household purse strings, budgeting and financial decision making	Burbury 1995a
Different buying segments in four different types of retail wine shops	Lockshin & Spawton 1995
Mavens, that is, innovative or pioneer consumers	Nicholson 1995

Psychographic segmentation bases

Psychographic data are more subjective than demographic data, and therefore need to be specially designed and collected by the user. These features make it less likely that retailers would use this approach compared to demographic and regional bases. Nonetheless, there are examples in Table 3.3 which have a lifestyle characteristic. Some categories, such as the maven segment, are essentially combinations of a psychographic and behavioural approach. Some other categories, such as Generation X, are essentially combinations of psychographic and demographic approaches. In Australia, an important study of lifestyle segments was carried out by Horizons in conjunction with Roy Morgan Research. They developed ten lifestyle categories and sampled the proportion of the Australian population in each group. They also studied the shopping behaviour and brand loyalty of the different groups.

Behavioural segmentation bases

The final market segmentation base classified in Table 3.2 is the behavioural approach, that is, the actual consumer behaviour of the shopper. This behaviour has been divided into the use situation of the potential purchase, the buyer's needs or preferences, and purchasing behaviour (Cravens 1994). One example of this approach to supermarket shoppers is given in Table 3.4.

Table 3.4 Classification of supermarket customers

Avid shoppers	Traditional supermarket customers who cook most family meals, shop frequently, and look for bargains (about 25 per cent of the US sample).
Kitchen strangers	Childless men and women who find cooking an inconvenience and rely instead on takeaway food and restaurants (about 20 per cent).
Constrained shoppers	Low income families and individuals who buy little but basic food needs (less than 20 per cent).
Hurried shoppers	Busy people who mostly eat at home, but look for shopping and cooking shortcuts (less than 20 per cent).
Unfettered shoppers	Primarily older working people whose children have flown the nest, leaving them with more disposable income to spend on food (about 13 per cent of total).
Kitchen birds	Mainly older people who are light eaters (about 6 per cent of total).

Source: Based on a study for the Coca-Cola Retailing Research Council (Otten 1989) and reproduced in Cravens (1994, p. 163).

From a marketing perspective, this final segmentation base is particularly attractive as it is reasonably objective and gets to the heart and mind of shopping decisions. A useful summary of alternative studies of segmentation analyses of shoppers in terms of their motivation for shopping is given by Westbrook and Black (1985) and shown in Table 3.5.

Table 3.5 identifies a range of shopper types, which vary by retail category and by research methodology. Westbrook and Black (1985) in their own study define department store shopping around seven motivations aligned with evaluating options and acquiring the product, engaging in the sales process, and gaining stimulation and affiliation through the retail environment. A useful Australian extension of the Westbrook and Black model is that by Jarratt (1995). Jarratt's work uses cluster analysis in three regional cities to confirm the importance of three broad aspects of shopping to segment shoppers:

- variables that reflect the **shopping offer**;

- variables that reflect the **shopping environment**; and

- variables that reflect, specifically, the **service** part of the shopping offer.

Jarratt's work is more general than Westbrook and Black's because it applies to *all* retail categories. Furthermore, her six clusters or segments seem better defined. The six segments are itemised in Table 3.6 and provide a useful profile of different types of shoppers.

Table 3.5 Previous shopper typologies

Reference	Shopper population	Sample size	Measurement basis	Shopper types
Stone 1954	Female department store shoppers	124	Depth interview	1 Economic 2 Personalising 3 Ethical 4 Apathetic
Chicago Tribune 1955	Female department store shoppers	50	Depth interview	1 Dependent 2 Compulsive 3 Individualistic
Stephenson and Willet 1969	Adult buyers of apparel, shoes and toys	315	Number of stores shopped and patronised	1 Store loyal 2 Compulsive/ recreational 3 Convenience 4 Price/bargain conscious
Darden and Reynolds 1971	Female heads of households	167	AIO statements	1 Economic[a] 2 Personalising 3 Moralistic 4 Apathetic

(Table continued overleaf.)

Table 3.5 continued

Reference	Shopper population	Sample size	Measurement basis	Shopper types
Darden and Reynolds 1971	Female supermarket shoppers	116	Store attribute preferences	1 Quality orientated 2 Fastidious 3 Convenience 4 Demanding 5 Stamp collectors 6 Stamp avoiders 7 Apathetic
Moschis 1976	Cosmetic buyers	206	AIO statements	1 Store loyal 2 Brand loyal 3 Specials shopper 4 Psychosocialising 5 Name conscious 6 Problem solving
Williams, Painter and Nichols 1978	Adult grocery shoppers	298	Store image semantic differentials	1 Low price 2 Convenience 3 Involved 4 Apathetic
Bellenger and Korgaonkar 1980	Adult shoppers	324	Single item shopping enjoyment	1 Recreational 2 Economic

[a] Shopping orientations rather than discrete shopper types
Source: Westbrook and Black 1985, pp. 80-1; reproduced in Jarratt 1995.

Apart from general classifications of market segments, retailers may take a special interest in a *particular* market segment to the extent of carrying out detailed market research into that segment. In the Australian context, there has been interest in various groups, including those listed in Table 3.3. Many of the above groups have been 'invented' by advertising agencies for the purpose of helping their clients – including retailers – better target their marketing activities. This highlights the importance of *creative skills* in identifying market segments, which need to be combined with good *analytical skills*. In some cases, companies have explicitly featured the profiles of different segments as the basis of their advertisements.

The AMP describes the profiles of five different types of investors, including the Swiss low risk investor, the Boston conservative investor, the London balanced investor, the New York growth investor and the Asian tiger aggressive investor, and suggests investment plans for each (AMP 1994).

Table 3.6 Australian shopper types classified by shopping motivation

The *apathetic* or *'have to'* shopper	Low scores on all three dimensions of offer, shopping environment and service.
The *'moderate'* shopper	Moderate scores on all three dimensions.
The *'service'* shopper	Moderate scores on the importance of offer and environment and high score on service.
The *'experimental'* shopper	High scores on all three dimensions.
The *'practical'* shopper	Moderate scores on importance of offer and service and low score on importance of shopping environment.
The *'product focused'* shopper	Moderate score on offer and low scores on the importance of service and environment.

Source: Jarratt 1995.

Evaluation of customer needs, market research and customer satisfaction

Theoretical insight is useful, but retailers need more than this. They need some practical method of estimating their customers' needs. This requires some form of **market research**. Many of the smaller retailers do little serious, formal market research, while some of the larger retailers are heavily involved in formal market research.

Before embarking on market research, it helps if the retailer is aware of the market research process, for which an Australian market research text such as Kinnear, Taylor, Johnson and Armstrong (1993) can be of immense help. This text – and others – places high value on the company first clarifying its **research objectives**. For instance, is the retailer trying to understand why consumers come to the store? Or is the objective something else? The key stages of the market research process are given in Table 3.7.

Retailers can facilitate the research process if they maintain good links with their suppliers, who may be able to advise on broader trends in the industry and changing consumer patterns. Another useful route into market research is simply talking to customers about their needs. Those retailers emphasising special orders from their customers can use this connection to identify new trends in the market.

Table 3.7 Stages in the process of market research

1. Identify the nature of the retail problem or opportunity.
2. Develop research objectives.
3. Develop the research design, including the way in which the data is to be collected and analysed.
4. Develop the sampling plan.
5. Plan and conduct the field work, both pre-testing and final survey.
6. Code and process the data.
7. Analyse the data.
8. Write up final report.
9. Apply the findings to retail planning and operations.

One small clothing retailer uses a group of customers to pre-test seasonal new offers. A chain of Asian food restaurants has a panel of tasters for proposed menu changes. Members of the panel commit to four tastings in a year.

Another vehicle to evaluate customer needs is through some form of database marketing built up from customer data (Merrilees 1994).

A number of retailers – for example Katies, Telstra, ANZ, GM, Westpac and the FlyBuys companies – have introduced clubs or loyalty programs. A key objective of these programs is to develop customer loyalty and greater customer satisfaction. For these retailers, and others, it is important to monitor customer satisfaction over time to ensure that customer needs are being met. This can be done through customer surveys and customer focus groups. Any problems identified can then be resolved through variations in the retail mix.

In summary, market research is a powerful tool to promote the use of best practices by retailers. Some initiatives by retailers to better understand the needs of their customers and to increase customer satisfaction have been illustrated here. In practice, market research has many applications, as further illustrated in Table 3.8. Moreover, retailers have many methods to choose from, including:

- focus groups to test the new season range;
- mystery shopper evaluations;
- simple customer evaluation forms asking the customer, for example, to rate service, speed of checkout, store cleanliness, pricing and quality of various departments; and
- major surveys using incentives for respondents.

Table 3.8 Examples of Australian retail market research

Area	Study	See reference
Consumer behaviour	Role of women in household expenditure decisions.	Burbury 1995a
	Outshopper behaviour.	Jarratt & Polonsky 1993
	Evoked sets and brand and store loyalty.	Walker & Grant 1995
Market segmentation	Wine store segments.	Lockshin & Spawton 1995
	Other segmentation studies.	Jarrett 1995, Table 3.3.
Suppliers researching retailers	BIS Shrapnel interviewed executives in 200 whitegoods retail stores seeking their perceptions of supplier's marketing service factors, such as product quality, breadth of product range and pricing policies.	Green 1995
Franchising	Franchise satisfaction among Australian restaurant franchises	Hing 1995
Retail strategy	Barry's The Home Improvement Specialists spent $200,000-$300,000 in research which led to its new name and positioning in the market.	Clout 1994
	Linking retail strategy to organisational capabilities.	Merrilees & Miller 1995a
Location	The State Bank of NSW used demographic mapping techniques to rationalise their banking network.	Hogan 1994
	Location research by the Pen Shop.	Robertson 1995
	Location research by the Australian Gold Exchange.	Pickering 1994
Store design	Wendy's carried out research in the early 1990s which led it to lower the height of its window displays to be more accessible to children.	
Merchandising	For various examples of retailers using market research to guide new product development and changes in product range, see *Chapter 4 - Merchandising*.	
Pricing	The effect of price on value and willingness to buy in an electrical appliance store.	Soutar, Sweeney & Johnson 1995

(Table continued overleaf.)

Table 3.8 continued

Area	Study	See reference
Promotion	Integrated marketing communication in clothing stores.	Fam & Merrilees 1995
	Database marketing in clothing stores.	Merrilees 1994
Customer service	Customer service in clothing stores.	Merrilees & Miller 1994a
		Dapiran & Grant 1994
Selling	The greeting stage of selling in clothing stores.	Merrilees & Miller 1995b
	Car salesmen.	Lynch 1994
	Personal service in clothing stores.	Merrilees & Miller 1996
Human resource management	National Australia Bank conducts annual opinion surveys of its employees to ascertain job satisfaction and attitudes on related matters.	Boyd 1995
	Human resource management in hair-dressing services retailing	Merrilees & Miller 1994b
Financial management		Kent 1993
		McDowell 1995

Relatively absent in Table 3.8 is reference to environmentally friendly segments. Certainly, Australian, New Zealand and overseas retailers are responding to this challenge through the use of recyclable shopping bags for example (Vignette 3.1). Woolworths and Coles both sell reusable bags which are a distinctive green colour, alluding to environmental responsibility. Interestingly, consumers appear to use these bags for many carrying tasks. However, the surge of retailer interest is quite recent (see Vignette 3.2 and 3.3). The opportunity exists for selective retailers to make their mark in this domain, creating both a benefit to society and a potential competitive advantage for the retailer.

Annual Reports are publicly available documents and indicate a firm's policies, practices and performance. Woolworths Limited discusses their initiatives in responsible retailing in their 2006 Annual Report and includes comment on plastic bag usage, which is "(T)he annualised rate of plastic checkout bags issued, as a member of the Australian National Retailers Association (ANRA). We have also established a Plastic Bags Task Force with the Federal Department of the Environment and representatives from other state Governments and industry bodies to seek to identify environmentally sound and commercially feasible degradable alternatives to the current high density polyethylene bags used by supermarkets across Australia." (Woolworths Ltd 2006, Being Responsible, pp. 32-33)

Vignette 3.2

Sensing the green environment:

Wal-Mart innovates and recruits environmentalists & Tesco engages with customers in Greener Living

How does the world's largest retailer show customers that it senses the green environment issues?

Such a large organisation has many opportunities for backstage and frontstage green initiatives. Backstage Wal-Mart is working with suppliers to reduce packaging, an exercise which requires product innovation, for example, when introducing concentrated laundry detergents as reported by Fishman (2007, p. 78).

One initiative undertaken at the store level has been to recycle waste, which means a reduction in garbage (with its associated costs) and value being derived from recycling. Wal-Mart points out: "If everything in our store could have extra value as recyclable, it would be good for our customers as well as the world".*

A clever feature of the way Wal-Mart has developed its green policies is the co-opting of two well-known environmentalists, Adam Werbach, President of the Sierra Club, and David Suzuki. According to some reports, each has received negative feedback because they have joined forces with Wal-Mart to help it pursue its objective to "… redefine itself as environmentally progressive" (Saks 2007, pp. 74-81).

Check out the Tesco website for information about their innovative Greener Living initiative. Tesco has appointed a green category director and introduced a Greener Living product range and related website, which explains what Tesco is doing and what customers can do too, as well as providing a Green Glossary and Tips. Tesco is thus engaging customers both in co-production of greener shopping and in a green virtual community.

Contributed by Professor Bill Merrilees.

Sources:
Fishman, L. 2007, "How green is Wal-Mart?", Fast Money Company, September, p. 78.
MacQueen, K. 2007, "The trials of Saint Suzuki", Maclean's, November 5, pp. 66-73.
Saks D. 2007," Working with the enemy", Fast Money Company, September, pp. 74-81.
Wal-Mart: <www.walmartstores.com>; <walmart.ca>

*<www.walmartstores.com/ GlobalWMStoresWeb/navigate.do?catg=346>, 2007 Nov.

For your consideration:

- What can smaller retailers learn from such initiatives?

- How can smaller retailers have a 'green relationship' with their customers?

Vignette 3.3

Woolworths reinforcing brand values by going greener

In 2007, Woolworths celebrated 20 years as 'The Fresh Food People'. However, apart from its supermarket offerings, the firm has other significant retailer brands. The parent company, Woolworths Limited, is emphasising transparency in all aspects of its business, and the 2006 Annual Report explains that the first Corporate Social Responsibility Report is one of its initiatives. By placing this and other materials on their website, Woolworths Limited positions itself as open to scrutiny and public accountability, and reinforces the values of the Woolworths brand.

To reduce their 'environmental footprint', Woolworths Limited has implemented many backstage policies and practices. In the 2005 Corporate Social Responsibility Report, Roger Corbett, CEO at the time, noted that the firm's aim was to be practical and down-to-earth, and that while some improvements could be readily made, others were more complex. In Corbett's own words, "For example, how far do we reduce food packaging without compromising food safety?"

Sources:
Woolworths Limited: 2006 Annual Report, Corporate Social Responsibility Report 2005 (released 2006) available at <www.woolworthslimited.com.au>.

For your consideration:

- How can a retailer identify customers' predisposition to 'reduce, reuse, recycle'?

- How can retailers educate customers about green consumption?

Conclusions

This chapter has presented a framework for sensing and understanding the market. Retailers can gain insight about what motivates customers and what factors influence their spending decisions. They can then see the possible roles of: the quality of merchandise, a wide range of merchandise, low or high prices, customer service and promotion. Promotion could be singled out by retailers because promotion influences the information search by consumers, and it is readily linked to the models of consumer behaviour discussed in this chapter.

Note that all components of the retail mix are potentially important to consumers when they evaluate their choices of store outlet and shopping centre. Similarly, in e-retailing retailers need to understand how consumers choose e-retail sites – do they choose a 'bricks and mortar and clicks' retailer first, a purely online retailer (such as amazon.com) or do they use a search engine or an online mall?

The chapter highlights some useful concepts including informed choice, evoked set, evaluative criteria, specific models of evaluative criteria, store image, store loyalty, and the total shopping experience. All of these concepts contribute to understanding consumer behaviour and the way consumers decide between stores. As noted, store image and instore promotions affect consumer choices and thus should be given priority in retail strategy. In both of these areas, the consumer is seeking some guidance from retailers. Store image emphasises the way the retail is perceived externally in comparison to competing retailers, whereas instore promotion emphasises the flow of information to the consumer internally within the store environment.

The concept of the total shopping experience highlights the notion that shopping has many motives beyond simply buying merchandise. The dynamics of the experiential shopping process need to be explored by both retailers and researchers. A range of methodologies could be used to explore aspects of the shopping experience, depending on the specific research question.

There is still much to be learnt about making shopping more enjoyable. Retailers and shopping mall developers could learn from the early department stores which provided extensive facilities for shoppers. For example, the provision of adequate comfortable seating, washrooms, lounges and quiet zones would help shoppers who need to rest or refresh during their shopping expedition. Much more research and related innovation are needed to make shopping more fun.

Some ways of contributing to the experiences of enjoyment and fun are discussed in Chapter 5 – Store design and Chapter 7 – Retail promotion.

While entertainment of various types has been added – echoing again the early department stores and later the first decade of shopping malls – there is scope for further innovation. One approach is to apply the store-as-theatre concept:

> *The stage and its set have but one mission: to support the show (merchandise) and make it the centre of attraction. The set creates an environment for the*

merchandise, which enhances and complements it rather than competing with it; at the same time, it creates atmosphere, making customers feel comfortable and motivating them to buy.

Levy and Weitz 1992, p. 664.

Additional literature which is relevant here is the work by Deighton (1994), who analysed performance as a process. It is also relevant that the services marketing literature has little to say about how to manage a good 'show' (p. 123). Deighton presents a model of different types of performances which generate different expectations in consumers. He also presents a useful framework for managing performance in terms of actions which amplify an event's meaning and which intensify involvement with the event.

Finally, the chapter has underscored the importance of market research to ascertain consumer needs and to monitor retailers' performance in achieving customer satisfaction. Market research is vital for identifying and measuring the importance of market segments.

Market sensing and understanding are the foundation of best practice retailing, providing conceptual insight and empirical knowledge of the motivation and behaviour of consumers in all retailing contexts. With this understanding, retailers can enhance the formulation of their strategy and brand by identifying which market segments to target. Then they can design the synergistic components of the retail mix, especially store design and retail promotion.

Review and applications

1. Discuss how small- and medium-sized retailers can use market sensing activities.

2. Explain some cost effective market research strategies for SME retailers.

3. Develop a market research process for a not-for-profit retailer.

4. Explain how shopping centres can encourage customers to choose the centre first for their shopping needs.

5. Explain how cities and regions can use market sensing to create shopping destinations.

6. Explore how a retailer could interpret and respond to the surge in interest in environmentally-friendly products.

7. Discuss how a retailer can research and respond to the needs and wants of the 'baby boomer' segment.

8. What types of questions could retailers ask their suppliers in order to identify changing consumer patterns in their retail category? Explain *how* the retailer would ask these questions.

9. Discuss what is meant by the 'total shopping experience', and explain the relevance of this concept to the consumer and the retailer.

10. Explain how the classification of goods matrix (Figure 3.1) can shed light on the competition between Target and Big W.

Website references

Harvey Norman: <www.harverynorman.com.au>.

Just Jeans: <www.justjeans.com.au>.

Jeans West: <www.jeanswest.com.au>.

Tesco: <www.tesco.com/greenerliving>.

Woolworths Ltd: <www.woolworthslimited.com.au>.

References

Agnew, J 1987, 'P-O-P displays are becoming a matter of consumer convenience', *Marketing News*, 9 October, p. 14.

Alexander, N & Akehurst, G (eds) 1999, *The Emergence of Modern Retailing 1750-1950*, Frank Cass, London.

Australian Mutual Provident Society (AMP) 1994, Advertisement, the *Australian Financial Review*, 17 August, p. 9.

Bednall, D, Walker, I & Grant, P 1995, `Impact of values and demographic data in accounting for patterns of brand and store loyalty', *World Marketing Congress Proceedings*, vol. VII-I, pp. 3-25 to 3-40.

Boyd, A 1995, `And the morale of NAB's success story: Get staffed', the *Australian Financial Review*, 21 April, pp. 1, 46.

Burbury, R 1993, `Thirtysomethings targeted', the *Sydney Morning Herald*, 2 September, p. 34.

Burbury, R 1994a, `How to chase those plentiful pink dollars', the *Sydney Morning Herald*, 28 April, p. 32.

Burbury, R 1994b, `Gays show high brand loyalty', the *Sydney Morning Herald*, 28 July, p. 32.

Burbury, R 1994c, `Disney moves into shopping centres', the *Sydney Morning Herald*, 11 August, p. 32.

Burbury, R 1995a, `Women control the finances', the *Sydney Morning Herald*, 11 May, p. 34.

Burbury, R 1995b, `Branding together in pursuit of loyalty', the *Sydney Morning Herald*, 18 May, p. 34.

Canu, S 1994, 'Loyalty is Bankcard buzz word', the *Australian Financial Review*, 7 October, p. 43.

Clout, J 1994, `Mad Barry's seeks quality image', the *Australian Financial Review*, 25 October, p. 29.

Coombes, P 1995, `How to survive in the retail jungle', the *Sydney Morning Herald*, 12 September, p. 29.

Cravens, D 1994, *Strategic Marketing*, 4th edn, Irwin, Sydney.

Dapiran, G & Grant, K 1994, *A Comparison of the Status of Customer Service in Australian Retail and Manufacturing Companies*, Paper presented to the First Joint European Institute of Retailing and Services Studies (EIRASS) and Canadian Institute of Retailing and Services

Studies (CIRASS) Conference, Recent Advances in Retailing and Services Science, Banff, Alberta, Canada, May.

Deighton, J 1994, `Managing services when the service is a performance' in Rust, R & Oliver, L (eds), *Service Quality,* Sage, Thousand Oaks, California, pp. 123-38.

Dowling, G 1994, `Pros and costs on loyalty ladder', the *Australian Financial Review,* 2 September, p. 55.

Engel, J, Kollat, D & Blackwell, R 1968, *Consumer Behaviour,* 1st edn, Holt, Rinehart & Winston, Chicago.

Fam, K & Merrilees, B 1995, `The extent, nature and benefits of integrated marketing communications', University of Newcastle Working Paper, August.

Finn, A, McQuitty, S & Rigby, J 1994, `Residents' acceptance and use of a mega-multi-mall: West Edmonton Mall evidence', *International Journal of Research In Marketing,* vol. 11, pp. 127-44.

Fishbein, M 1967, `Attitudes and prediction of behaviour' in Fishbein, M (ed.), *Readings in Attitude Theory and Measurement,* John Wiley, New York, pp. 477-92.

Fiske, J, Hodge, B & Turner, G 1987, *Myths of Oz: Reading Australian Popular Culture,* Allen & Unwin, St Leonards, NSW.

Fox, C 1993, `Reading the Mature Market', the *Australian Financial Review,* 7 December, p. 39.

Green, J 1995, 'F&P marketing detail pays off', the *Australian Financial Review,* 6 June, p. 20.

Hawkins, D, Best, R & Coney, K 1992, *Consumer Behaviour,* Irwin, Homewood Illinois.

Hing, N 1995, `Franchisee satisfaction: Contributors and consequences', *Journal of Small Business Management,* vol. 33, no. 2 (April), pp. 12-25.

Hogan, R 1994, `Demographic mapping plots a new course for branch networks', the *Australian Financial Review,* 23 December, p. 26.

Howard, J & Sheth, J 1969, *The Theory Of Buying Behaviour,* Wiley, New York.

Howarth, I 1994, `Shell's secret strategy: Frequent buyers', the *Australian Financial Review,* 8 April, pp. 1, 34.

Jarratt, D 1996, `A shopper taxonomy for retail strategy development', *International Review Of Retail, Distribution And Consumer Research,* vol. 6, no. 2, pp. 196-215.

Jarratt, D & Polonsky, M 1993, `Causal linkages between psychographic and demographic determinants of outshopping behaviour', *International Review Of Retail, Distribution And Consumer Research,* vol. 3, no. 3 (July), pp. 303-19.

Kent, P 1993, `Supply of management advisory services from accounting practices: A model, small enterprise research', the *Journal of SEAANZ,* vol. 2, no. 2, pp. 73-83.

Kingston, B 1994, *Basket, Bag and Trolley: A history of shopping in Australia,* Oxford University Press, Oxford.

Kinnear, T, Taylor, J, Johnson, L & Armstrong, R 1993, *Australian Marketing Research,* McGraw Hill, Sydney.

Levy, M & Weitz, B 1992, *Retailing Management,* Irwin, Homewood, Illinois.

Lockshin, L & Spawton, A 1995, *The Role Of Product And Situational Involvement In Segmenting Retail Customers For Individualised Database Marketing,* Paper presented to the Second Joint EIRASS and CIRASS Conference, Recent Advances in Retailing and Services Science, Gold Coast, Australia, July.

Lynch, M 1994, `New-car salesmen give women raw end of the deal', the *Australian Financial Review,* 25 May, p. 5.

McDowell, C 1995, `Small business objectives: An exploratory study of NSW retailers, small enterprise research', the *Journal of SEAANZ,* vol. 3, nos. 1-2, pp. 65-83.

McIntyre, P 1995, `Brand loyalty continues to slide', the *Australian Financial Review,* 3 October, p. 38.

Merrilees, B 1994, `Database marketing: Tailor made for clothing retailers', *Database Marketing Magazine,* December, no. 7, p. 44.

Merrilees, B & Cotman, N 1976, `An Economic Analysis of Consumer Protection Law', the *Australian Quarterly,* March, pp. 79-95.

Merrilees, B & Miller, D 1994a, *Retail Customer Service and Organisational Capability,* Paper presented to the First Joint EIRASS and CIRASS Conference, Recent Advances in Retailing and Services Science, Banff, Alberta, Canada.

Merrilees, B & Miller, D 1994b, `The people factor: The key to differentiating small services enterprises' in Ryan, J & Gibson, B (eds), *The People Factor In Small Enterprises,* no. 22 in the conference series of the Institute of Industrial Economics.

Merrilees, B & Miller, D 1995a, `The nexus between marketing strategy and organisational capability', *World Marketing Congress Proceedings,* vol. WI-III, pp. 15-88 to 15-94.

Merrilees, B & Miller, D 1995b, *The Retail Greeting: A Neglected Dimension of the Service Encounter,* Paper presented to the Second Joint EIRASS and CIRASS Conference, Recent Advances in Retailing and Services Science, Gold Coast, Australia, July.

Merrilees, B & Miller, D 1997, `The nexus between human resource capabilities and a competitive advantage in retail personal service', *Journal of Customer Service in Marketing & Management,* vol. 3, no. 1, pp. 19-29.

Mintel 1986, `Is shopping fun?', *Mintel Leisure Intelligence (UK),* vol. 16, pp. 45-75.

Mitchell, S 1994, `Lift-off for Frequent Buyer program', the *Australian Financial Review,* 12 July, p. 28.

Moodie, A-M 1995, `Home aloners important segment of main market', the *Weekend Australian,* Property Section, 11-12 March, p. 5.

Nicholson, V 1995, `The mavens are here', *Australian Professional Marketing,* April, pp. 17-19.

Often, A 1989, `People patterns', the *Wall Street Journal,* 13 June.

Pickering, M 1994, `Ringing the changes lifts sales', the *Australian,* 16 November, p. 50.

Reekie, G 1993, *Temptations: Sex, Selling and the Department Store,* Allen & Unwin, St Leonards, NSW.

Robertson, R 1995, `The Pen Shop gets it write', the *Australian Financial Review,* 14 February, p. 24.

Saffo, P 2007, 'Six rules for effective forecasting', *Harvard Business Review,* July-August, pp. 122-131.

Soutar, G, Sweeney, J & Johnson, L 1995, *The Influence Of Retail Service Quality On Perceived Value,* Paper presented to the Second Joint EIRASS and CIRASS Conference, Recent Advances in Retailing and Services Science, Gold Coast, Australia, July.

Shoebridge, N 1995, `Young adults are the new conservatives', *Business Review Weekly,* 18 September, pp. 64-7.

Sydney Morning Herald 1994, 24 November.

Tauber, E 1972, `Why do people shop?', *Journal of Marketing,* vol. 36, no. 4, pp. 46-9.

Westbrook, R & Black, W 1985, `A motivation-based shopper typology', *Journal of Retailing,* vol. 61 Spring, pp. 78-103.

Windsor, G & Foreshew, J 1994, `Ad agencies advised to target new brand of men', the *Australian,* 3 August, p. 3.

Wynhausen, E 1995, `Generation EX', the *Weekend Australian,* Review section, 18-19 February, p. 3.

Advanced reading

Arnold, MJ & Reynolds, KE 2003, 'Hedonic shopping motivations', *Journal of Retailing*, vol. 79, pp. 77-95.

Carlson, CR & Wilmot, WW 2006, *Innovation: The Five Disciplines for Creating What Customers Want*, Crown Business, New York.

Carpenter, J, Moore, M & Fairhurst, A 2005, 'Consumer shopping value for retail brands', *Journal of Fashion Marketing and Management*, vol. 9, no. 1, pp. 43-53.

Delgado-Ballester, E & Munuera-Aleman, J 2001, 'Brand trust in the context of consumer loyalty', *European Journal of Marketing*, vol. 35, nos. 11/12, pp. 1238-1258.

Eagle, L, Hawkins, J, Kitchen, P, Rose, L 2005, 'Brand sickness and health following major product withdrawals', *Journal of Product & Brand Management*, vol. 14, no. 5, pp. 310-321.

Eisenhardt, K 1989, 'Building theories from case study research', *Academy of Management Review*, vol. 14, no. 4, pp. 532-550.

Jamal, A 2003, 'Retailing in a multicultural world: the interplay of retailing, ethnic identity and consumption', *Journal of Retailing and Consumer Services*, vol. 10, pp. 1-11.

Kaufman-Scarborough, C 1999, 'Reasonable Access for Mobility-Disabled Persons is More Than Widening the Door', *Journal of Retailing*, vol. 75, no. 4, pp. 479-508.

Kim, S & Jin B, 'Validating the Retail Service Quality Scale for US and Korean customers of discount stores: an exploratory study', *The Journal of Services Marketing* 2002; 16 (2/3): 223-237.

Loker, S, Good, L, Huddleston, P 1994, 'Entering Eastern European Markets: lessons from Kmart', *Journal of Retailing and Consumer Services 1994*; 1 (2): 101-106.

Merrilees, B, Miller, D, McKenzie, B 2001, 'Cross-Cultural Retailing Research: A Comparison of Shopping Experiences in Estonia and Canada', *Journal of East-West Business 2001*; 7(1): 83-100.

Merrilees, B, Serenty, M 2000, 'Strategic marketing by change agents in Poland: The case of domestic marketing consulting firms', *Marketing Intelligence and Planning 2000*; 18 (5): 247-255.

Miller, D 2006, 'Marketing perspectives on the value and conduct of archival research', *Canadian Journal of Marketing Research*, vol. 23, no. 1, pp. 47-55.

O'Connor, P 2005, 'Local Embeddedness in a Global World: Young People's Accounts', *Nordic Journal of Youth Research 2005*; 13 (1): 9-26.

Patton, MQ 2002, *Qualitative Research and Evaluation Methods*, Sage, Thousand Oaks.

Rex, D, & Blair, A 2003, 'Unjust des(s)erts: Food retailing and neighbourhood health in Sandwell', *International Journal of Retailing and Distribution Management*, vol. 31, no. 9, pp. 459-465.

Rinne, H, Swinyard, W 1995, 'Segmenting the Discount Store Market: The Domination of the 'Difficult Discounter Core'', *The International Review of Retail Distribution and Consumer Research 1995*; 30 (2): 123-145.

Roberts, E 2003, 'Don't sell things, sell effects: Overseas influences in New Zealand department stores, 1909-1956', *Business History Review*, vol. 77, no. 2, pp. 265-289.

Saunders, J & Lee, N 2005, 'Guest Editorial: Whither research in marketing?', *European Journal of Marketing*, vol. 39, nos. 3/4, pp. 245-260.

Welch, C 2000, 'The archaeology of business networks: the use of archival research in case studies', *The Journal of Strategic Marketing*, vol. 8, pp. 197-208.

Yin, R 2004, *Case Study Research: Design and Methods*, 3rd ed., Sage, Thousand Oaks.

Designing the Retail Mix

Merchandising

Introduction

The products and services that a retailer chooses to sell to customers are central both to the retail offer and to positioning the retailer. By **merchandise** we mean the tangible products of the retailer. **Merchandising** refers to the management of the value chain – from identifying appropriate merchandise which meets customer needs, to sourcing this merchandise, to nurturing suppliers, and to making stock available to consumers when required. Each element is part of the merchandise buying process which is summarised in Figure 4.1. Merchandising is the first component of the retail mix that is addressed in this book because it is fundamental to the retailer's brand and to the retail offer. However, it interacts with all other components, especially store design (see *Chapter 5 – Store design*) and pricing (see *Chapter 8 – Retail pricing*) (see Vignette 4.2).

Government regulations, for example product safety requirements, contribute to the context for merchandising (see the ACCC website). In the fresh food category, natural disasters – such as the ongoing drought in eastern Australia, the 2007-2008 floods and Cyclone Larry in early 2006 in North Queensland which effectively eliminated the banana crop – affect not only the price of food items but also the availability of produce.

Emerging issues in merchandising include the rise of **aspirational consumers** who seek specific product characteristics, and **concerned consumers** using their power to resist products produced in sweatshops, animal products such as fur, or genetically modified foods. Other issues take in supply chain management approaches, and include **fast fashion** (Bruce & Daly 2006), **quick response** (Birtwistle, Siddiqui & Fiorito 2003), **category management** (Dewsnap & Hart 2004), and **auto-replenishment** (Dandeo, Fiorito, Giunipero & Pearcy 2004). Two mounting concerns are the recycling, salvaging or disposal of used products such as mobile phones, computers, textiles, and fashion and the recycling, disposal or reduction of packaging such as excessive cardboard, paper, metal and plastic bags.

The characteristics of merchandise itself are clearly important for merchandise retailing. For most retailers, the cost of merchandise sold is the largest single cost item, so it is not surprising that an American study found that the more successful, best practice retailers were those that made merchandising a core part of their business (Aufreiter, Karch & Smith Shi 1993). A study of Australian clothing retailers found that quality merchandise was the second most important component of the retail mix – second only to customer service (Merrilees & Miller 1994). Similarly, in services retailing – such as restaurants, hairdressing and car maintenance – there can be significant merchandise components.

There are many dimensions to merchandising. The core need is for the retailer to select a particular *category* of merchandise within a particular **price** and **quality** band. Relatedly, the retailer must select the **breadth** and **depth** of the product range. These merchandising decisions are critical to the overall retail strategy and are strongly influenced by competitor activity. These decisions should be considered interdependently with other key components of the retail mix (see *Chapter 2 – Retail strategy, branding and innovation*) as retailers are urged to take an integrated approach to merchandising.

It is essential for a retailer to focus on the **quality** and **range** of merchandise that meets customer needs, but it is also necessary to look vertically backwards in terms of managing suppliers appropriately. If this is not done, then it becomes very difficult to provide the right merchandise at the right time and at the right price to the consumer. The price issue is important because distribution logistics can be an expensive process. That is, in services marketing terminology **backstage** operations are important for **frontstage** (customer interface) performance.

The early sections of this chapter are organised as a sequential elaboration of each element in the **merchandise buying process**, predicated on the specification of the retail strategy and on forecasting based on an understanding of the nature and magnitude of future consumer demand. It should be noted that the order of the stages may vary slightly, for example some retailers may select a supplier first and specify the merchandise later. An iterative rather than linear process is the best way to conceptualise these stages.

The essence of best practice merchandising is achieved by emphasising the importance of perceiving the merchandise buying decision as a *process* and by thoroughly understanding each sub-process. In addition to discussing each element of the merchandise buying process, there are separate sections dealing with special issues in merchandise buying. These sections are particularly important for arriving at a best practice approach to merchandising and include:

- managing the merchandise brand portfolio;

- the role of information systems in aiding merchandise decisions;

- the role of budgeting and financial management as an aid to merchandise decisions;

- the need to integrate merchandise decisions with other components of the retail mix, particularly pricing, promotion and store design, especially merchandise spatial planning;

- the role of a relationship marketing framework to improve the quality of the relationship between retailers and vendors (suppliers);

- additional value added benefits, especially to smaller retailers, from a good relationship with vendors ;

- socially responsible merchandise buying including sourcing from fair trade suppliers; and

- explicit models of best practice merchandising.

Figure 4.1 The merchandise buying process

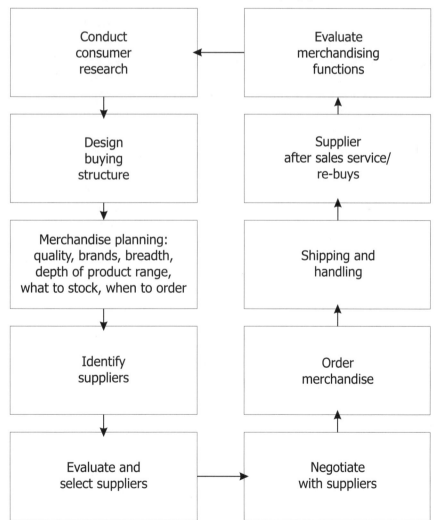

To comprehend all of the above is challenging, but the rewards and opportunities are considerable given that there are relatively few Australian retailers who have really made a mark in merchandising.

Vignette 4.1

Merchandising & innovation:
Sustained innovation in supermarkets

Some consumers find supermarkets boring and find shopping there a not particularly exciting chore. Yet from an industry perspective, supermarkets are at the forefront of innovation. They are one of the most dynamic retailing categories in Australia. The innovations include: self-service (from the 1950s); low price formats (1960s to 1980s); the fresh food revolution (late 1980s); larger, more modern units and instore bakeries (1990s); and superstores, instore banking and e-groceries (mid-1990s to 2000s). Behind the scenes there have been further innovations, including e-procurement and a supply chain management revolution. For example, supermarkets work with growers to develop specific fresh food offerings. Fruit images can be scanned at the farm gate and supplies could be rejected if they do not conform with prescribed colour, shape and appearance.

Different supermarket chains have taken the lead in innovation at various times. Coles and Franklins were early innovators, while Woolworths has been the main pioneer in the past 10 to 15 years. ALDI uses an innovative merchandise mix that includes very few manufacturer brands, with newly designed private label products and weekly 'surprise buys' to totally differentiate its offerings from other supermarkets.

Related reading

Merrilees, B & Miller, D 2001, Innovation and Strategy in the Australian Supermarket Industry, *Journal of Food Products Marketing*, vol. 7, no. 4, pp. 3-18.

Setting the scene: Retail strategy and future consumer demand

Future consumer demand is never fully predictable and is subject to whims and fads. New products and services can and do emerge, and need to be factored into merchandising plans. Sometimes the new products are quite radical. Some new products will be designed and introduced by the *retailer*, while other new products may result from *manufacturer* initiatives. From time to time, new products and services may be associated with new retail formats (see Vignette 4.1).

Retail strategies and the retailer brand need to be kept firmly in mind when developing **merchandise plans** – also referred to as **stock plans**. Retailers using a low price, average quality, self-service format will need to have different merchandise plans to upmarket retailers who emphasise quality and service. Thus, merchandise tactics should support and reinforce the relevant retail strategy.

Another key element which underlies each aspect of the merchandise buying process is an understanding of the nature and likely magnitude of future consumer demand. Retailers need to first understand and forecast likely trends in the patterns of consumer demand, and then decide how they should respond to them. In *Chapter 3 – Market sensing and understanding*, both the notion of market segments and the role of market research to help identify and quantify these segments were highlighted. The targeting of particular segments is an integral part of retail strategy. The same market research can also assist with the details of merchandise planning. Retailers can use all types of market research – including surveys and focus groups – to help project future consumer demand.

 A small clothing retailer can test out the reactions of selected customers to new seasonal lines before introducing the lines to the broader market.

Retail staff can be trained to monitor customer attitudes to existing and new products, and to report their observations. This is in line with a continuous improvement approach and with performance management systems.

Product lines with a fad component such as novelties or gifts are the most difficult to predict for future consumer demand. Merchandisers of lines such as Spiderman or Superman products operate with considerable uncertainty. In product lines with a fashion or seasonal component, it is also difficult to predict future consumer demand. Inevitably there are risks in forecasting any product line, although the use of market research can help reduce these risks. Another tool which can be used to assist in forecasting demand and can speed up the re-ordering process is regular analysis of sales data through online computer access. Again, this tool can reduce – but not eliminate – the risks of errors in forecasting demand. **Shelf-space management** software systems, for example, perform a similar function.

Successful forecasting also depends on understanding trends including new products, new materials, availability, and new styles, shapes, designs and colours in the product category (see the Fashion Forecast Services website as well as The Committee for Colour & Trends website).

If retailers do not forecast well, they may pay a penalty in terms of dissatisfied customers who cannot get what they want (Vignette 4.2). This can result in lower future store patronage or in excessive price markdowns which can quickly erode the bottom line. On a more positive note, a well-considered approach to demand forecasts sets the stage for each component of the merchandise buying process (Figure 4.1).

> ## Vignette 4.2
> ### Forecasting what the customer wants
>
> Apparently-strategic decisions can backfire if the retailer has not accurately forecast what the customer wants. Sometimes, assortment decisions such as reducing the number of SKUs (stock keeping units) are based on what the retailer perceives will be efficiencies.
>
> FoodweekOnline reported on the problems faced by Carrefour, the multinational retailer, when dramatically adjusting their product brand portfolio (04 July 2007):
>
> "The global grocery retailing trend of cutting back the range on offer does not serve customers' expectations. ... The chairman of Carrefour's management board, Jose Luis Duran ... admitted the giant France-based multinational made a mistake when it culled its supermarket product ranges. ... Culling ranges ... reflected a lack of respect for the customer. In a message relevant to retailers all over the world, Duran said the company was now undoing the damage, expanding its range by 15% annually, with *an even balance of branded and house brand products.*"
>
> Reporter: Robert Stockdill. See <www.foodweek.com.au>.
>
> ### For your consideration:
>
> Can you suggest innovative ways that independent retailers in the fresh food sector can use to identify what customers want?

Establishing an appropriate buying organisation

In smaller retailing organisations, the owner is likely to be the main **buyer**, whereas larger retailing organisations are likely to employ specialist buyers. In some cases the buying is conducted centrally, for example Target and Kmart discount department stores, and in other cases buying is conducted at a decentralised level. Similarly, Woolworths uses a more decentralised buying system than Coles, although Coles supermarkets did move towards a **store micro marketing**, that is decentralised promotions, approach (see McIntyre 1995). The advantages of the centralised approach include: greater financial negotiating power and greater control over the type and image of merchandise bought, whereas the advantages of the decentralised approach include flexibility and a greater capacity to meet the needs of the local area. Some retailers have attempted to combine the best of both approaches through a combination of central group buying discounts and local flexibility in selecting the mix of merchandise.

The functions of the buyer may also be team based. These functions include: identifying and analysing customer needs, translating those needs into product specifications, evaluating merchandise trends and options, and evaluating the sources of the merchandise. The buyers at Sportsgirl, for example, go overseas to research fashion possibilities. When they return, they give elaborate post-trip briefings to other team members in the design and marketing areas (Video Education Australia 1992).

In carrying out their functions, buyers need to ensure that they work according to a suitable code of conduct. Codes of conduct are often used as part of the retail selling process. Buyers also need a **code of conduct** to ensure that their behaviour is ethical. Major retailers establish **vendor guides** as a framework for buyers and vendors.

 Navigate to the Woolworths website, then click through to the vendor guide to review its contents.

There has been a public debate about the allegedly unethical practices of some of the buyers of a major Australian retail chain, a debate sufficiently heated for the company to appoint an ex-police officer to audit these activities.

The necessary functions of buyers lead to a need for certain skills. These skills include:

- the ability to conduct or organise and then interpret market research;
- being able to compare both merchandise and suppliers;
- financial, marketing and people management skills;
- the ability to act ethically; and
- having an overall sensitivity both to customer needs as well as to organisational capability.

In short, the buyer has to be able to see the issues from the customer's perspective, and not just from their own personal tastes or from the retailer's view point.

The necessary skills of a good buyer increasingly require a holistic approach to managing the buying process. Some companies have used drastic measures to change the culture of their buyers. For example, in the early 1990s the newly appointed CEO of David Jones briefed his marketing manager to take control of marketing at their subsidiary called 'Georges'. Previously, the buyers at Georges were known "to have a glorious lifestyle and little budgeting control" (Stretton 1994, p. 13). Under the new management, buyers were asked to work the floor and become more responsible. Problems with the buying process may have been a contributing factor in the 1995 decision to close the two remaining Georges stores. In general, the buying function needs to be integrated into the entire retail strategy and buyers must fully comprehend the retailer's brand.

Apart from centralised versus decentralised buying systems, there are other ways of organising the buying function. Some retailers may be part of franchising chains which perform these functions (see *Chapter 2 – Retail strategy, branding and innovation*). Other retailers may be part of co-operative buying groups, for example Chem-Mart, Mensland or QIW, where they can gain some buying **economies of scale** without sacrificing their independence.

Merchandise planning

Selecting a particular category of merchandise is the precursor to all merchandising decisions. At this point we assume that an appropriate buying structure is in place and that the retailer has forecast some estimation of the future pattern and the future magnitude of consumer demand, both of which are discussed in greater detail later.

Merchandise planning activity includes the following decisions:

- the quality of the merchandise, including brands and private brands;
- the breadth and depth (assortment) of the product range;
- additions and deletions to the product range;
- how much merchandise to stock; and
- when to order.

Each of these components of merchandise planning is discussed in turn below to show the contributions they make to a unique merchandise plan.

Quality of merchandise

After a merchandise category is selected, it is necessary to specify the desired quality level. In some cases the quality and branding decisions are inter-related. In other words, by aiming to sell particular brands or labels, retailers are positioning themselves in a particular quality band. Related to the quality decision is the need to select price lines for the merchandise. Price lines are ranges of prices, for example from $10 to $20, which help define the target customer. See *Chapter 8 – Retail pricing* for more discussion of price lines and related pricing issues.

The quality, branding and price line decisions are closely linked with the target market the retailer is aiming for. This is an essential part of the overall retail strategy. Branding decisions can include: the extent of emphasis on specific **national, manufacturer** or **designer** brands to help identify the store image; the use of **exclusive brands** which may tie a retailer to a supplier; or the possible use of **private**, that is own-label, **brands**. Private labels are often pitched at low to mid price points, although in some cases they are presented as premium priced.

Department stores and upmarket specialty stores usually focus on a small to medium range of high quality brands – usually national brands. Good examples would be well-known national cosmetic brands, for example Clarins and Estee Lauder, that are typically handled by department stores. Mid-market specialty stores may also have a strong national brand emphasis in their offerings, although some of these retailers may be willing to switch brands and therefore possibly suppliers if the trade terms are better.

Vignette 4.3

Merchandising & innovation:
The development of a product brand portfolio and co-operating with suppliers

Putting together the optimal product brand portfolio is a great challenge for retailers. What is the ideal combination of national (manufacturer), and own brands? The answer will depend very much on context, the retailer's strategy, consumer research and supplier relations.

In the 1930s, Canadian Tire Corporation was operating in a context of economic depression, where car owners were often keen to maintain and repair their vehicles rather than replace them. In addition, the automobile was a relatively recent innovation and did not come with many of the accessories that we now consider standard. Many customers owned their first car and were less confident consumers than most car owners are today. The firm used an integrated branding strategy to reassure customers about the values of the business overall and about **product integrity** through product range, product branding using own brands and national brands, and product sourcing. In addition, the firm augmented the product offering with customer education, warranties and guarantees, and add-on services such as installation.

Several own brands including Motormaster and Mastercraft, that the firm applied to various product lines in the 1930s are still major **own brands** today.

Check out the Canadian Tire website: <canadiantire.ca>.

For your consideration:

What factors can contribute to **enduring** own brands?

Another group of retailers, for example The Body Shop, make use of **own-label** or **private brands**. In some cases these private brands may be combined with national brands in a product portfolio. This is a well-established practice in supermarkets, for example at the end of 1994 Coles supermarkets carried 720 Farmland products and had plans to expand the range further. Coles also introduced a major house brand, Australia's Choice, into Kmart (Fox 1994). In the ensuing decade, Coles and other supermarkets continued to develop their private-label offerings. The major supermarkets are reportedly expecting to expand to 60 per cent of own brands in some product categories. This combination approach is now spreading to other retail categories including chemists and department stores. However some retailers, such as Woolworths, use a policy of discounting leading national brands (Fox 1993) as well as developing house brands. Generally, the use of private labels contributes to differentiating the retail offer and gives the retailer more discretion over where to source merchandise. National brands must, of course, be sourced from specific companies, whereas private brands can be sourced from a number of suppliers (see Vignette 4.3). Notwithstanding, sometimes the private brand retailers have their own manufacturing base, for example most factory outlet clothing retailers.

Specifying the merchandise in more detail is often done by: viewing the stock in showrooms or at trade shows, through sales representatives' demonstrations, or from product catalogues.

Breadth and depth (assortment) of product range

The **product range** is such an important part of merchandising that it warrants listing as a separate part of the retail mix. By **breadth of product range** we refer to the number of product lines carried, whereas **depth of product range**, that is, **assortment**, refers to the models, styles, brands, price lines, colours and sizes within each product line.

The breadth and depth of product range even help to characterise the type of retailer. **Department stores**, discount department stores and supermarkets have a very wide and fairly deep product range. **Convenience stores** – such as 'corner' grocers, petrol food stores like Shell Coles Express, chemists and news-agents – tend to have both a narrow and shallow product range. **Specialty stores** tend to be narrow and deep in their product range, with the extreme case – the **category killers** – tending to be narrow and very deep in their range.

The product range decision has had a major bearing on Australian retailers' strategy changes. In supermarkets, for example, Woolworths made a major move in 1986 to add more depth to their fresh food lines. Coles supermarkets attempted to follow that move. The eventually unsuccessful Franklins also followed, but in a different way. It added breadth – in the form of fresh food – as part of a new 'Big Fresh' format, which added items not included in their 'No Frills' format. By way of contrast, the most recent entry to the Australian grocery category is ALDI, which has a relatively narrow and focused product range (see Vignette 4.4).

In another example, toys have seen the emergence of category killers since 1993. Previously, small specialist stores were almost a match in terms of depth of range against discount department stores, and offered customer service as a trade-off to the lower prices of the discount department stores. The current major competitor is the superstore Toys 'R' Us which has a major focus on a very deep product range. Also, the product range dimension has featured in developments in other industries, including newsagents, chemists/pharmacies and petrol stations. In general, there has been a trend towards **scrambled merchandising**, with an increase in the breadth of product range – often in unrelated areas.

Vignette 4.4

Merchandising & branding: Revamping own brands to strengthen competitive position

The turmoil in the supermarket industry has challenged the major players to review their product brand portfolios. In Australia, supermarket own brands tended to be at the lower price points and carried names to reinforce that image, for example Savings or Home Brand.

The demise of Franklins and the entry of ALDI into Australia in 2001 signalled increased competition in the private label domain. ALDI offers a much shallower assortment based on the premise of 'everyday groceries of the highest quality at very low prices' (see the ALDI website). Most products are ALDI own brands.

In response, Coles and Woolworths have undertaken extensive repositioning, rebranding and repackaging in their private label offerings (see the Coles and Woolworths websites). Recently, Coles introduced 'You'll love Coles' as an own brand. It remains to be seen if consumers will accept such a name for generic products.

Franklins has returned, although not in as big a way. Both Woolworths and Coles have recently also introduced their new ranges of Woolworths and Coles-branded products which aren't the same as the home brands of the past.

Additions and deletions to the product range

Consistent with their overall retail strategy there is an ongoing need for retailers to review their product range as part of periodic performance reviews. In response to this review process, retailers may add lines and assortments while deleting others. Additionally, new products are always coming on to the market, and retailers have to decide which – if any – of each year's new products will be ordered. Essentially retailers' needs for particular merchandise are likely to be based on their estimation of their customers' needs and demands.

Additional lines are more likely if these lines are:

- expected to be profitable – primarily by adding to consumer value relative to cost;

- consistent with the store image and retail strategy;

- offered to the retailer on good terms and conditions; and

- backed up by supplier reliability and dependability.

One Australian electronics supplier, Pioneer, has noted that more retailers – both mass merchandisers and specialists – are demanding commitment regarding the future of suppliers. This is because the retailers' customers – that is the public – are seeking a similar commitment from the retailer regarding quality and availability of parts (Cornell 1994). This highlights the role of the fourth criterion for new product selection given above, namely supplier reliability.

The risks in adding new products to the range of retailers can be reduced firstly through market research, and secondly through the active involvement of the retailer in the new product development process. Regarding the latter, good suppliers should be seeking this anyway, although this should not preclude any retailer-led initiatives. A special case is the development of private brands, where retailers are inextricably involved in the design of new products, including product specification and packaging.

Deleted lines should be treated in a similar way to added lines, using the same four criteria as above, except in negative rather than positive terms. For example, this could lead to some lines being dropped if they were inconsistent with the desired store image. In practice, organisations are less likely to use formal processes for product deletions compared to additions. Sometimes there may be emotional attachment to certain lines, and sometimes it is simple inertia – with either reason contributing to a line being kept on beyond its useful life. An additional consequence of this asymmetry between additions and deletions is that the net breadth of the product range can creep up without it being a conscious part of the retail strategy. Whatever the underlying cause, it is important that decisions to delete products should be subject to the same rigour, analysis and formal procedures as decisions to add new products.

How much merchandise to stock?

The amount of merchandise stocked is related to both the product range decisions and the estimates of future consumer demand for each item. This information forms the basis of a stock plan which sets the desired stock levels of merchandise classified by the product line in the first instance. Then, estimates for each line are broken down by models, styles, brands, price lines, designs, sizes and colours. The stock plan would be lengthy for mass merchandisers with a large number of lines and a deep assortment, and relatively short for specialist retailers with narrow lines and a medium to deep assortment. The stock plan can be used as the basis of initial purchases as well as subsequent purchases, known as **re-buys**. Merchandise budgeting, that is controlling the dollars expended, as well as estimating quantities are the two key elements of the merchandise plan.

When should merchandise be ordered?

The timing of merchandise purchases is critical. It is important to have the stock available when it is needed by customers. Seasonal demand is particularly difficult to predict. This difficulty is compounded by interstate and intrastate differences. **Seasonality** is partly related to the four seasons but also varies depending on particular festivals, such as Christmas or Mother's Day, and on the specific weather.

A cold snap in spring could delay the purchase of new summer stock by customers.

This aspect is further complicated by Australia's seasons being the opposite to those occurring in the Northern Hemisphere, and by geographic dispersion within the country, for example there can be a heatwave in Queensland while there is snow in Tasmania. Designers from the Northern Hemisphere are one influence – although possibly a declining one – on some of our fashions. The issue is also confused by retailers trying to gain an edge on their competitors by introducing some lines earlier and earlier in the season. This sometimes confuses the consumer as well as other retailers, and can make seasonal patterns even more unpredictable.

In general, categories with **high stock turnover** should be ordered more frequently than those with low stock turnover. The frequency of purchase is closely related to the buying cycle of consumers and the need to keep merchandise fresh. Much of the re-ordering – or re-buys – of high stock turnover merchandise is a matter of routine. However, even these items can be reviewed from time to time, and the review results may influence the size and timing of purchases in the future.

In the case of low stock turnover merchandise, the ability of retailers to control the timing of purchases may be constrained by the use of minimum size orders by suppliers. Therefore, retailers have to wait until they are sure there is sufficient demand before they can place a reasonably-sized order. This builds in a delay factor, which is further exacerbated by the fact that suppliers may need weeks – or possibly months – before they can respond to the retailer's order. These factors reinforce the importance both of accurate consumer demand forecasts when retailers place the initial orders, and of good relationships with suppliers for re-buys – as well as a capacity to manage cash flow and customer satisfaction.

Identifying alternative suppliers

Retailers, like consumers, tend to choose from an **evoked set of suppliers**, that is, from a small to medium number of preferred suppliers. Newly-established retailers may have a fairly large evoked set of suppliers based on Yellow Pages business directory advertisements, trade lists, other advertising, and word-of-mouth recommendations. As retailers gain more experience with both suppliers and with merchandise, they tend to gradually reduce the size of their evoked set.

Although most retailers prefer to work with a small- to medium-sized evoked set of suppliers, the actual set can change over time. Moreover there is the need to seek other suppliers if the main supplier experiences production problems. New suppliers are always emerging and they often have innovative products. Retailers need to decide whether to add these new items to their shelves. They have to be disciplined in not adding too many low volume lines. This means that small manufacturers or suppliers may find it difficult to launch their innovative products, or at least they may have to pay a premium for shelf space. The social risk in this arrangement is that Australia may have a lower rate of product innovation than would be the case if retailers took a more liberal approach to experimenting with innovative suppliers.

Another perspective is that smaller manufacturers or suppliers who do not have a close relationship with retailers will be at a disadvantage until they too develop close relationships. Some small suppliers may even go a step further and develop innovative niche marketing strategies targeted at small retailers.

Evaluation and selection of suppliers

The evaluation and selection of suppliers requires the retailer to determine key selection criteria for choosing a supplier. The retailer has to weigh the relative importance of: the quality of the merchandise, price, delivery service, terms of payment, returns policy, flexibility, and the overall quality of the retailer-supplier relationship. Theoretically, this can be a complicated process depending on the 'model' used. For example, variations of the Fishbein (1967) model could be used (where the *consumer's importance weighting* for each attribute is multiplied by the *consumer's rating score* for that attribute for a particular brand). In practice, retailers are more likely to emphasise two or three selection criteria and compare vendors on that basis.

In terms of the criteria used by retailers to select suppliers, there will always be a focus on price and service quality. In recent years, some suppliers have provided superior service quality through advanced technology such as electronic data interchange (EDI). In the future, the vendor-retailer relationship may emerge as an additional explicit supplier selection – and retention – criterion.

As with staff performance, vendor performance should be evaluated. The retail audit protocol and the principles of best practice alliances can both contribute to the processes retailers use to evaluate vendor performance.

Negotiating with suppliers

One of the inherent merchandising interactions is the retailer-supplier negotiation. There is scope for negotiations between retailers and suppliers over price, credit, terms of payment, product features, barcodes or RFID (radio frequency identification devices), exclusive lines, size of order, provision of display materials, installation and arrangement of displays, consultants, demonstrators, support advertising, scope of sales territory, software support, ordering systems, and all aspects of delivery and back-up service.

If the relationship between the retailer and supplier is undeveloped or underdeveloped, there is a possible focus on win-lose negotiations. Suppliers and manufacturers too have a need to better understand their customers, that is the retailers, and to better negotiate deals. To illustrate this issue, a survey discovered that less than five per cent of all **point-of-sale** material supplied by manufacturers was actually displayed. The rest was thrown away or returned unused to its source. Most success with these materials came when it was in 'spectacular' form and only used in the store for a short period of time, such as the week before Easter (Lloyd 1992).

The notion of win-win negotiations has supplanted the former traditional approach to negotiation, which was confrontational and adversarial. In that approach, the desired outcome was deemed to be a win at the expense of the other party, hence the term win-lose. Conversely, win-win suggests that both parties benefit (Cornelius & Faire 1989/1992).

In a critique of win-win, Albrecht and Albrecht recognised that a genuine win-win approach to negotiating is quite rare, and indeed is "often…used fraudulently in business" (Albrecht & Albrecht 1993, p. 20). Notwithstanding, they stress that win-win is achievable provided there is the right "combination of attitudes, values, self-esteem, and assertiveness" (Albrecht & Albrecht 1993, p. 20). They propose that added-value negotiating is true win-win negotiating, founded on a philosophy which espouses co-operation in a shared "search for value in the deal" (Albrecht & Albrecht 1993, p. 35).

Negotiations with suppliers are more likely to take on a different meaning if there is a long-term, mutual relationship. There is likely to be less haggling over small details such as price and terms of payment, and a more holistic approach to developing parcels of financial and other mutual benefits of the exchange.

There is no point jeopardising a particular contract worth a million dollars over a five year period because of a dispute worth a hundred dollars.

Big deals can still be lost with long-term partners over small issues if the parties' separate needs are not recognised and understood. A genuine win-win approach to negotiations is more likely to prevail, and the changing industrial relations context in Australia parallels this aim of a consultative approach with a win-win outcome for employees and employers.

How does the retailer go about the task of negotiating? The framework for best practice retailer-supplier negotiations is shown in Table 4.1. It is noteworthy that all aspects of retail marketing can use this approach.

Managers – and indeed all staff – can benefit from developing their negotiation skills through formal training courses, in-house training, in-house discussions and reflection on performance. The caveat is that formal courses should be firmly based on a best practice approach emphasising genuine win-win and value-adding negotiation principles and practices.

As shown in Table 4.1, negotiations should result in mutual benefits to the parties, and should be formalised in a lucidly written agreement or contract. The contract should include an agreed dispute resolution process. Any contract must be legally constructed for it to be binding on the parties. Small retailers may need to seek external legal advice, whereas larger retailers may have in-house expertise. Employer and industry associations can also be useful in this regard.

The need to review the negotiation process – including its outcomes – is emphasised in Table 4.1. That is, the negotiation process is not complete until it has been subjected to evaluation and follow-up management action. This pro-active approach presents exciting opportunities for building effective and mutually beneficial retailer-supplier relationships, based on an ethical approach to business.

The ordering process

It is useful for retailers to fully assess their **ordering process** to ensure that it is effectively contributing to the merchandising function. Often the method by which retailers place orders emanates from suppliers (see the Logistics Association of Australia website, the Efficient Consumer Response Australasia website and the SAP for Retail website). Suppliers use their sales representatives, written and faxed order forms, telephone order systems (both incoming and outgoing), and EDI order systems in various combinations to facilitate the placement of orders by retailers. The better suppliers will *involve* their customers – including the retailers – in adapting these order systems to suit their customers' needs. Some retailers could benefit by being more pro-active in ensuring that the ordering systems – which vary across suppliers – suit the retailer's own needs.

Shipping and handling

The role of **shipping and handling** is to support the retail strategy by making products available to customers. Shipping and handling includes the physical movement of goods and information to and from warehouses, in and out of the store, and around the store. Apart from receiving shipments, stacking shelves, replenishing stock and delivering stock, ancillary activities include arranging merchandise for display purposes, placing price information, and the preparation and cleaning of the merchandise. Thus, shipping and handling must be consistent with the merchandise plan.

Table 4.1 Retailer- supplier negotiations – a best practice framework

The principles	Negotiation should be based on: • an ethical approach; • fairness, equity and consistency; • a willingness to co-operate; • achieving mutual gain and value; • shared values; and • a desire to maintain effective working relationships.
The method	Effective negotiation is a process which includes: • building a credible relationship based on trust, honesty and an ethical approach to business; • recognising the needs of the retailer, the supplier and other significant stakeholders; • developing options which can be thought of as parcels of benefits; • creating opportunities for mutual benefit; • agreeing on the most feasible and desirable option; then • jointly writing a plain language agreement – in the form of a formal contract where appropriate. The process is not complete until: • the agreement has been implemented; • the negotiation process has been reviewed; • the negotiation outcomes have been assessed and reviewed; • the effectiveness of the retailer-supplier relationship has been reviewed; and • the outcomes of the review are transformed into management action.

Successful shipping and handling will require that staff be provided with and trained in the firm's policies and procedures. More radically but consistent with best practice, staff should be consulted in the development of these policies and the procedures as they need to understand how their work contributes to the success of the retail firm and how it relates to other functions in the business.

The process must be designed to maximise security so that **stock shrinkage** (stock loss at any point in the supply chain) is prevented. Also, the ergonomics of handling consignment pallets and packages must be designed to minimise **occupational health and safety (OH&S) hazards**. This may mean giving special attention to store design and the provision of specialised equipment for accessing and transporting stock. This approach will promote best practice OH&S for all staff involved in handling merchandise, provided it is supported by proper staff training and performance management systems.

Particular attention must be given to ensure staff receive effective training and performance feedback so that they are able to fulfil their roles safely and with job satisfaction. Comprehensive orientation programs, refresher training, job rotation programs and staff forums all contribute to well-skilled staff working effectively and safely.

Supplier after sales service and re-buying merchandise

Supplier after sales service includes: the delivery of the merchandise; assistance with providing merchandise display materials; helping arrange displays; correcting mistakes in delivery; invoicing; and giving further advice if needed, including product recalls. This can be seen as part of the ongoing relationship between retailers and suppliers, which in turn encourages a straight forward re-buy decision to replace stock from the *same* suppliers rather than seeking new suppliers. This arrangement means that the re-buy situation is simpler for both parties, which may enable the supplier to pass on some of these savings to the retailer in the form of a more favourable discount. Note that re-buy decisions can also benefit from more sophisticated computerised ordering systems because the order can be placed more quickly and with less chance of error in transmission.

A relationship approach to vendors is likely to increase the importance attached to after sales service. A close relationship is likely to increase the chance of re-buy purchases. For the retailer, this has the added benefits of better knowing the stock when re-ordering, and in simplifying and economising on the ordering process.

Special issues in merchandise buying

In addition to the various elements of the merchandise buying process, there are also special issues in merchandise buying which are particularly important for arriving at a best practice approach to merchandising. These are discussed in more detail below.

Managing a merchandise brand portfolio

Retailers can deal with the matters raised about merchandise planning by developing a **merchandise brand portfolio** (see Table 4.2). As shown earlier, Vignette 4.4 presents some current examples of retailers repositioning their total merchandise offer. As in any system, a change in one part of the portfolio will affect other parts. The merchandise brand portfolio approach helps the retailer to manage the combinations of product brands systematically and holistically, rather than in a piecemeal way where the focus would be at the individual product brand level. Larger retailers appoint product or category managers to co-ordinate elements of the merchandise brand portfolio. These managers generally report to a senior merchandise manager who is responsible for the overall synergies within the portfolio and for ensuring that the portfolio is consistent with the retailer strategy.

Table 4.2 Simple schematic representation of a merchandise brand portfolio

Type of brand	Product line 1	Product line 2	Product line 3
Manufacturer brand 1	Yes	Yes	No
Manufacturer brand 2	Yes	Yes	No
Manufacturer brand - exclusive	No	No	Yes
Own brand - Level 1 (low price)	No	Yes	No
Own brand - Level 2 (mid price)	Yes	Yes	Yes
Own brand -Level 3 (higher price, high quality)	No	No	Yes

The role of information systems in merchandise decisions

Retailers can use various technologies to assist with their merchandise decisions. These technologies include: the use of bar code scanners, RFID, EDI, executive information systems (EIS), stock ordering systems, automated warehouses, computerised relational databases, and expert systems. The key issue for most retailers is how to choose an appropriate *supplier* of these technologies, although in a few selective cases the retailer may take a more pro-active role in attempting to lead the application of new technologies.

These information systems provide the software and the data to develop, implement, monitor and adjust the merchandise plan. Analysing changes in inventory levels, evaluating the product mix and evaluating the product range are three specific financial applications to merchandising using information systems.

Another application, shelf space management – and in particular **merchandise spatial planning** – looks at the location of merchandise groupings through departments (if relevant) as well as the location of merchandise within each department. Some important concepts in merchandise spatial planning include the notion of **anchor departments** or products, **drawing power**, and **synergies** across departments or products.

The management of existing shelf space, which is part of merchandise spatial planning, is now analysed at a more detailed level – namely the use of specific models which can guide the re-allocation of shelf space. This detailed store level shelf management is sometimes referred to as **micro merchandising**. A number of the earlier models are reviewed by McGoldrick (1990), with Greenland and McGoldrick (1994) providing another perspective on related issues.

In Australia, the APOLLO software packages have been commonly used for shelf space management. These packages are used and controlled by suppliers in specific categories, for example Mars in confectionery and Uncle Ben's in pet foods. Supermarket retailers supply scanner sales data and cost data to the suppliers who enter the information in their APOLLO systems. One of the outputs of the APOLLO systems, and of related systems, is a computer printout of **planograms**, that is maps that illustrate the ideal location and space of all stock items throughout the store. This data can then be compared to maps showing the *actual* allocation of stock. Based on their computer analyses, suppliers can then provide periodic suggestions to retailers for changing shelf space allocations. Until recently, the main retailers using such systems were Woolworths, Coles and the larger independents.

To understand the size of the benefits from using optimising micro merchandising models and associated information systems, consider the single store study of Dreze, Hoch and Purk (1994). Essentially, their model relates sales to a wide number of spatial and control variables, and measures the effect of each variable. Their study indicated that retailers could increase both sales and profits by better managing shelf space. The model suggests a possible boost to sales of up to 15 per cent by re-allocating space as directed. However, in practice it is suggested that the increase might be closer to four or five per cent. The lower figure in practice occurs, first, because retailers may not have sufficient people to manage store planograms in more than a handful of the 300-plus categories that they carry and, second, because the model does not allow for new product introductions or for changes in the demand for individual brands, sizes and flavours. That is, these changes would outdate the optimal shelf set before it could be fully implemented.

More detailed findings by Dreze, Hoch and Purk (1994) found that the majority of products were actually over-allocated in terms of shelf space. Furthermore, the number of **facings**, contrary to popular belief, was not very important. The benefits of additional facings, beyond a threshold level, declined very quickly. *Position* was seen as more important than the number of facings. In fact, a couple of facings at eye level did more for a product than five facings on the bottom shelf. Generally, but not universally, two positions were favoured in vertical terms: the well in refrigerated sections and slightly below eye level in the other categories. Horizontally, the categories themselves were equally favoured between the centre of the aisle or the edges as being the best locations.

Budgeting & financial management in merchandise decisions

Given that merchandise is the largest cost item for most retailers, it is prudent that an appropriate merchandise budgeting system is put in place. This encompasses both the total merchandising budget and the detailed components classified by product line and assortment. The **merchandising budget** is a planning tool to assist in the ordering of merchandise, with cash flow requirements, and to monitor spending as the year progresses.

Recall that the criticism of the Georges store buyers included the comment that they had a poor merchandise budgeting discipline.

In addition to merchandise budgeting, there are a number of other financial management tools – many of which utilise the information systems – which can be used to improve the efficiency and effectiveness of merchandising. These tools include the monitoring of **stock turnover ratios** and **profitability calculations** for the different product lines and assortment types. Financial management tools need to be used: to evaluate changing inventory levels, to evaluate the product mix, and to evaluate the product range.

Integrating merchandise decisions with the retail mix

Merchandise decisions need to be tightly linked with the overall retail strategy and specific components of the retail mix (see Vignette 4.5). The decisions need to be supported by external promotion activity. External advertising and promotion help to create the desired image and demand for merchandise. If there is too little promotion, the merchandise may not sell in the quantities predicted by the stock plan. If external promotion is too great, it can create problems through **stockouts** and frustrated customers. Similarly, **visual merchandising** and **instore promotion** need to support the selected merchandise. This introduces the concept of **customer-merchandise interaction** (**CMI**) where the merchandise *itself* has a role in communicating with the customer. This role supplements the support given by employees as well as other methods of providing service to the customer.

Pricing is another component of the retail mix which needs to be integrated with the merchandising. Pricing has several linkages. First, if the initial price is either too high or too low, it will create problems similar to what would result if the promotional effort were too little or too great. Second, the merchandise plan should ideally plan for staged price markdowns to clear future unsold stock.

With fashion goods, it is not uncommon for about one third of the stock to be sold at marked down prices.

If the markdowns are built into the initial merchandise plan, then the retailer has more control over the best timing for the markdowns. The size of the percentage markdowns can be altered depending on the surplus stock situation. Thus, a second role of price is to help solve any future surplus or deficit stock problems that may arise from sales forecasting errors or supply shortages.

A relationship marketing framework

The role of a relationship marketing framework is to contribute to improving the quality of the relationship between retailers and vendors. The retailer-supplier (vendor) relationship can be considered in terms of a *process of staged relationship development* (Levy & Weitz 2007; Gross, Banting, Meredith & Ford 1993) where the relationship moves through five stages, namely: pre-relationship, early, developmental, long-term, and final stage (Gross, Banting, Meredith & Ford 1993). Or, alternatively, the retailer-supplier relationship can be viewed as consisting of *five stages of complexity* – moving from awareness through exploration, expansion, commitment and ultimately to dissolution – where with each successive stage the retailer-supplier relationship increases in complexity (Levy & Weitz 2007).

Vignette 4.5

Integrating merchandise decisions with the retail mix

The largest takeover in Australia's business history took place effective from 23 November 2007 – when Wesfarmers Ltd, the parent company of the home improvement and hardware retailer Bunnings – took control of the former Coles Group. With many challenges and opportunities ahead following the acquisition of businesses in additional retail categories, it is notable that the reported current success of the Wesfarmers Home Improvement category (Bunnings) recognised the strong relationship between context, and components of the retail mix:

"Positive external trading conditions, enhanced product ranges and well-presented stores all contributed to the strong result."

Richard Goyder, Managing Director, Wesfarmers Limited, Annual General Meeting – 15 November 2007 , Chairman's Address and Managing Director's Address.

See Wesfarmers website: <wesfarmers.com.au>.

For your consideration:

Can you suggest how a sportswear retailer could create synergies between the merchandise assortment and the store design? What role will the retailer's relationships with suppliers play?

Most models share a similar progression from a minimal relationship in the early phase – which has a very specific transaction orientation – to a highly developed relationship where each party is an explicit stakeholder in the other party's business – becoming business partners in spirit if not in contract.

These models suggest that the relationship development process is linear and can be understood in terms of the often used 'marriage' metaphor. Of itself that metaphor should suggest an iterative and thus dynamic process rather than a linear or mechanistic one. Indeed, Wilkinson and Young (1994) offered an alternative metaphor – the dancing analogy – as a basis for considering the richness and diversity of inter-firm relations.

All of these process models provide insight into how both retailers and suppliers can develop their mutual relationship. The models also help both parties focus on the relative strengths as well as actual and potential benefits of the relationship. The models often take the perspective of larger retailers and small suppliers. In retailing, large retail chains – including category killers – are able to exert strong influence over smaller specialist suppliers. The literature generally emphasises the power of the large retailer over the less powerful, and thus more dependent, supplier (Atkinson 1993).

Even if a large retailer is in a dominant position *vis-a-vis* small suppliers, there are many benefits in nurturing suppliers. By supporting small suppliers, large retailers potentially gain more reliable and flexible deliveries, better quality merchandise, more innovative products, and more influence over new product development. The larger retailer can take the initiative by setting minimum quality and other standards, by accrediting suppliers, and by both disciplining and rewarding suppliers with certificates of competence and quality acknowledgement. Some of these issues are incorporated into total quality management (TQM) and just-in-time (JIT) inventory management approaches (Wong & Johansen 2006).

The existing literature on relationship marketing seems to assume that the retailer is usually in a position of strength; that is, the focus seems to be on large companies manipulating smaller suppliers. The literature has not afforded a view or window on the smaller, less powerful party's perspective.

What, then, of small retailers and larger or more powerful suppliers? It can be argued that there are many benefits for small retailers in fostering a positive relationship with larger suppliers. These benefits include: a higher quality delivery service, more flexible deliveries, access to co-operative advertising, a more positive response to special orders, and better access to supplies when there are supply shortages. In some cases, a further benefit could be the facilitating role of the supplier in transmitting marketing, technical and management skills and knowledge to the retailer.

Despite the potential benefits of small retailers fostering a positive relationship with large suppliers, it seems to be the exception rather than the rule. A study of small clothing retailers found that only about a quarter of the sample perceived that they had a special relationship with their suppliers (Miller & Merrilees 1995). Most of the sample of small clothing retailers seemed to perceive the vendor relationship in *transactional* rather than in *relationship* terms. In some cases, the supplier service was perceived to be very low, with the retailer being required to place orders of a minimum quantity and value. This may reflect a large supplier using the so called 80/20 rule, which indicates that 80 per cent of customers only generate 20 per cent of profits. In this light, small customers – such as small retailers – might be seen as uneconomic, somewhat akin to the commercial banks' current approach to small customers. Even if large suppliers wished to pursue this direction, it may be poor public relations to do it in the way the banks have. Moreover, there may be advantages in some suppliers' explicitly targeting and giving priority to the small retail sector by developing niche distribution channels. Some small retailers or their business associations may wish to foster this type of development.

This discussion adds insight into the behaviour of large suppliers giving allegedly poor service to small retailers. There are opportunities for large suppliers to initiate a more positive relationship with small retailers; equally, there is an opportunity for small retailers to target suppliers who are more responsive to a positive relationship. A minority of small retailers have taken up this challenge, though the vast majority have yet to seize the day (or *carpe diem* in Latin). Identifying the need for particular merchandise and then specifying that merchandise are tasks often jointly worked out between retail buyers and suppliers. The initiative could come from either party. Suppliers do not always have the time nor do they have the resources to present all of their offerings to all retailers. Choices are thus made as to which merchandise is relevant to a particular retailer. So, as a general conclusion we could say that the closer the relationship between the retailer and the supplier, the more effective will be the matching of merchandise to retailer.

Some broader benefits of good supplier relationships

A relationship between retailers and suppliers based on trust, mutual respect and information sharing can be highly beneficial in meeting customers needs (see Vignette 4.6). The role of suppliers in transmitting marketing, technical and management skills and knowledge to retailers is also worthy of further exploration. Marketing skills and knowledge include the setting up of displays, product pamphlets and brochures, and customer relations. Technical skills and knowledge include product knowledge and applications knowledge. Management skills and knowledge include recruitment and selection, training, financial management and business planning. This framework is further discussed in Miller and Merrilees (1995).

Apart from the posters and display stands themselves, some suppliers – for example china, porcelain and ceramic companies such as Villeroy and Boch –

actually assist in the setting up of the displays or in the training of retail staff to do the same. Sometimes these activities are linked to promotional campaigns conducted by the supplier. In either case, the supplier's activities augment the marketing skills of the retailer. More commonly, suppliers provide product knowledge – partly through product catalogues.

Additionally, suppliers often provide product knowledge through sales representative presentations, visits to manufacturing and wholesale establishments, hotlines, or supplier-arranged training.

Vignette 4.6

Merchandising & innovation:
Co-operating with suppliers

Retailers and suppliers can work together on product innovation in many ways. Leadership can come from large retailers, manufacturers, government authorities and industry bodies. Small retailers or small manufacturers may have innovative product ideas but may lack the resources to bring the product to market. Networking is one mechanism for developing synergies.

As the media release excerpt below shows from a 2007 initiative entitled "Competing in the global marketplace – developing innovative products that meet the needs of consumers", Canadian Tire Retail and the Ontario Ministry of Economic Development & Trade and the Ministry of Small Business & Entrepreneurship hosted 50 Ontario manufacturers at a jointly-sponsored Spirit of Innovation seminar in Toronto. The focus was to bring "industrial and product design experts, provincial business and trade representatives, and Canadian Tire innovation specialists and product buyers together with … manufacturers to share insights on how to develop new and innovative products that meet the needs of today's savvy consumer".

Check out the Canadian Tire website: <www.canadiantire.ca>.

In an Australian study of hairdressers, Merrilees and Miller (1994) found that some hairdressing managers were receiving some human resource management tools not through formal courses or management books – either popular or academic – but through product suppliers such as Schwarzkopf. Product suppliers in this industry are responsible for extensive training, particularly in technical areas. As well, and more unexpectedly, suppliers distribute recruitment and selection protocols, sample job application proformas, and performance appraisal ratings forms. Suppliers may also sponsor management training seminars that focus on business management, including staffing matters.

All of these value-adding activities by suppliers are fostered by strong, positive relationships between suppliers and retailers. Given that it takes a reasonable investment in time and energy, it is unlikely that all suppliers and all retailers will develop high quality relationships. Ultimately, each party must be selective regarding whom they want to form relationships with. However, the benefits that can accrue to retailers from investing in a positive, quality relationship with suppliers should not be underestimated.

Socially responsible merchandise buying

Protests and complaints abound in the media about retailers who source products manufactured in sweatshops, that use animal fur, or that are tested on animals. Other concerns centre on the extent of recent product recalls in many product categories. **Socially responsible merchandise buying** means sourcing products from ethical primary producers, manufacturers and wholesalers who comply with the legal context in which they operate.

Because different legal and ethical circumstances apply in various countries, Australian retailers need to consider not only Australian made or grown products, but also products made with imported components and with products sourced entirely outside Australia. Retailers in any country should address these matters in their own contexts.

Retailers can consider sourcing from fairtrade producers. Starbucks and Oxfam are examples of this approach. The retailer must also consider the legal and ethical aspects of the **vendor's manufacturing processes**. Questions can be asked about the sources of raw materials and the environmental sustainability of the manufacturing processes. Retailers will want to be sure that the manufacturer uses **best practice staff management** at least consistent with the country of origin if not the country where the retailer will be selling. The staff management practices should cover remuneration, training, non-discriminatory workplaces and occupational health, safety and welfare.

Regarding products, retailers need to make certain that the products comply legally with requirements such as electric voltage and safety devices, and that they are efficient, effective and environmentally friendly. As a final point, responsible retailers will also consider the potential for recycling of products after their useful life in their current forms (see Vignette 4.7 and *Chapter 11 – Retail innovation and sustainable retailing*).

Explicit models of best practice merchandising

Best practice merchandising emphasises the importance of perceiving the merchandise buying decision as a process, and of thoroughly understanding each sub-process. It is important to integrate the merchandise process with other components of the retail mix. And, the importance of a relationship marketing approach to the retailer's relationship with their vendors has been stressed, as well as the importance of using both information systems and budgeting and financial management tools. It is also important to ensure that staff roles are well-defined and that staff are involved in the development of merchandising.

Further insight into best practice merchandising comes from one of the few studies with an explicit best practice merchandising focus, namely a 1993 McKinsey study (Aufreiter, Karch & Smith Shi 1993). The McKinsey study attributes a large part of the superior profit performance of American retail market leaders – such as Nordstrom and Dillard's in department stores, Wal-Mart in discount stores, Gap in specialty stores, Home Depot among category killers and JC Penney among mass-merchants – to a superior merchandising approach that makes merchandising a core part of their businesses.

Vignette 4.7

Product innovation for sustainable retailing

Materials from renewable resources such as hemp, bamboo and cotton will have less environmental impact provided they are grown responsibly, and processed from raw material into yarn and fabric using as little energy as possible.

Clothing and accessories from these raw materials are slowly becoming available. However, it will take increased consumer demand to encourage retailers to work with manufacturers to develop, manufacture and stock such products.

Product innovation could be fostered by incentives offered by government, industry and educational institutions.

Further reading: Tamsin Blanchard, 2007, *Green is the new black*, Hodder & Stoughton, London.

First, one aspect of this more successful approach among market leaders is that the merchandising process is seen as more than just buying, and ideally is a cross-functional process across buying, distribution and selling. The **buying** function has mainly been discussed in this chapter. The **distribution** function includes the physical movement of goods and information to and from warehouses, in and out of the store, and around the store. The **selling** function of merchandising, according to the McKinsey study, includes aspects such as advertising, store staffing, instore promotion and space allocation. The integration of the buying, distribution and selling functions in a cross-functional manner is a useful ideal, and the importance of good information systems, internal communication and employee reward systems as a means of implementing cross-functional merchandising is critical (Aufreiter, Karch & Smith Shi 1993).

Second, Aufreiter, Karch and Smith Shi (1993) characterise best practice merchandising as one where the merchandise process is simplified wherever possible by reducing complexity. They provide some practical advice about how to reduce complexity in the merchandising process, partly through standardisation of store formats, narrowing the target market, and clarifying the scope of the tasks of different team members in the buying group.

Third, Aufreiter, Karch and Smith Shi (1993) advocate a relentless focus on assortment performance by involving suppliers in assortment development and tracking product performance on an ongoing basis, and particularly by pruning 'losers' and capitalising on winning items, quick responses to new opportunities, and a focus on local area needs.

The above findings are relevant to Australia, however the McKinsey study primarily emphasises the larger retailers. Therefore it is interesting to note that a study which advises smaller retailers on how to compete with retail giants also offers some of the same merchandising suggestions, such as getting rid of slow-moving merchandise and being customer focused (Stone 1995). By way of difference, Stone (1995) advises smaller retailers where possible: to offer different merchandise than larger retailers; to place more emphasis on fast-moving, convenience-oriented items; to offer to get out-of-stock merchandise for customers; and to seek special buys from suppliers. Compared to the McKinsey study, there is less emphasis on reducing complexity in merchandising, on information systems, and on cross-functional merchandising activities.

Conclusions

Merchandising is one of the most important aspects of merchandise retailing. This chapter has covered all the key elements of merchandising, starting with consumer demand forecasting, progressing through merchandise and supplier selection and ongoing management, and ending with after sales service. A strategic approach has been emphasised. This is reflected in the need to focus on merchandise which best meets the desires of the target market, and guides the selection both of appropriate national and private brands and of the optimal product range. The product range – both breadth and depth aspects – is becoming a more important component of the retail strategy, particularly with the emergence of superstores in more retail categories.

These issues relate mainly to the merchandise itself. Equally important is the sourcing of the merchandise, that is, the selection of and ongoing relationship with the suppliers. There is a major opportunity for retailers to obtain a competitive advantage by developing a special relationship with their supplier. The chapter has highlighted the importance of a relationship marketing framework to better understand merchandising. Retailers first have to come to terms with the need for close relationships with their suppliers, rather than relying on the win-lose basis of many current relationships. (See especially the principles of best practice negotiations in Table 4.1.) This opportunity is relevant to both large and small retailers, though the gap between best and actual retail practice on supplier relationships seems greater for small retailers. To illustrate, only about a quarter of an Australian sample of small clothing retailers claimed to have a special relationship with their suppliers (Miller & Merrilees 1995).

In advocating best practice merchandising, this chapter has emphasised the importance of perceiving the merchandise buying decision as a process, and understanding each sub-process thoroughly. The importance of integrating the merchandise process with other components of the retail mix has been stressed, and the importance of a relationship marketing approach to the retailer's relationship with vendors has also been highlighted. Merchandise planning and budgeting are extremely important and include the use of financial management tools to evaluate inventory levels, product-mix, product range and display space allocation across products. Information systems, such as computerised ordering systems and scanners, can help with each stage of the merchandise buying process.

Further insight into best practice merchandising comes from a dedicated McKinsey study (Aufreiter, Karch & Smith Shi 1993). This study indicates that best practice merchandising is based on three main factors:

- the reduction of complexity in all aspects of merchandising;

- an obsession with assortment performance; and

- a co-ordinated, cross-functional organisation of the merchandising activities across buying, distribution and selling.

Another study (Stone 1995) suggests somewhat different merchandising tactics for small retailers with a focus on differentiating the merchandise offer.

Both for large and small retailers there are exciting challenges and creative opportunities for developing excellence in the merchandising aspect of retailing. This is best achieved by the active involvement of customers, suppliers, managers and employees.

 # Review and applications

1. Are merchandising issues likely to be more important for certain retail categories? Discuss.

2. How would a retailer select the breadth and depth (assortment) of their product range? How would these decisions be altered by a high rate of new products being offered by suppliers?

3. On what basis should retailers choose suppliers? Should discount retailers use the same selection criteria as mid and upmarket retailers?

4. On what basis should suppliers choose retailers? Discuss. Why would your answer be useful to a retailer?

5. How can retailers improve their relationship marketing with suppliers?

6. Develop a best practice merchandise budget plan for a small retailer of your choice. Ensure that you relate the plan to organisation capability.

7. Develop an evaluation strategy for the previous question.

8. Research the legal and contractual aspects of buying for a small retailer. Specify the particular retailer or the retail category.

9. Assess the current impact of technology on the merchandising activities of a retailer of your selection. Explore the potential impacts over the next five to ten years.

10. Prepare a skills audit and training needs analysis for buyers in a specialist retail category. Identify the category which you have selected.

11. Examine the merchandise ordering and receiving processes for a medium-sized retailer. What advice would you give to the retailer to reduce shrinkage, and also to enhance occupational health and safety?

12. Discuss the importance of seasonality to both hardware retailers and to retail pharmacists.

13. Research career options and opportunities for retail buyers.

14. Advise a small retailer on negotiating with suppliers. Illustrate your answer with examples.

15. To what extent and why is there a difference between the best practice merchandising activities of large versus small retailers?

Website references

Retailers

ALDI: <www.ALDI.com.au>.

Canadian Tire Corporation: <www.canadiantire.ca>.

Coles: <www.coles.com.au>.

IKEA: <www.ikea.com>.

lululemon athletic, inc.: <www.lululemon.com>.

Oxfam: <www.oxfamshop.org.au>.

Woolworths Ltd: <www.woolworths.com.au>.

Associations and industry sources

Logistics Association of Australia: <www.laa.asn.au>.

Australian Competition and Consumer Commission (ACCC): <www.accc.gov.au>.

Efficient Consumer Response Australasia: <www.ecraustralasia.org.au>.

Fashion Forecast Services: <www.fashionforecastservices.com.au>.

Inside Retailing: <www.insideretailing.com.au>.

SAP for Retail: <www.sap.com/industries/retail/index.epx>.

The Committee for Colour & Trends: <www.colour-trends.com>.

The Fair Trade Association of Australia and New Zealand: <www.fta.org.au>.

References

Albrecht, K & Albrecht, S 1993, *Added Value Negotiating*, Business One, Irwin, Homewood Illinois.

Atkinson, G 1993, `The retail sector: Grocery store retailing' in de Silva, J, *Australian Industry Studies*, vol. 1: *Industry Study 6*, TAFE Publications, Collingwood.

Aufreiter, N, Karch, N & Smith Shi, C 1993, `The engine of success in retailing', *The McKinsey Quarterly*, no. 3, pp. 101-16.

Birtwistle, G, Siddiqui & Fiorito, SS 2003, 'Quick response: Perceptions of UK fashion retailers', *International Journal of Retail & Distribution Management*, vol. 31, no. 2, pp. 118-128.

Blanchard, T, 2007, *Green is the new black: How to change the world with style*, Hodder & Stoughton, London.

Burbury, R 1995, `World 4 Kids $9m account for review', the *Sydney Morning Herald*, 20 July, p. 34.

Cornelius, H & Faire, S 1989/1992, *Everyone Can Win: How to Resolve Conflict*, Simon Schuster, Sydney.

Cornell, A 1994, `Quality now sells: Pioneer', the *Australian Financial Review*, 23 November, p. 13.

Dandeo, LM, Fiorito, S, Giunipero, L & Pearcy, DH 2004, 'Determining retail buyers' negotiation willingness for automatic replenishment programs', *Journal of Fashion Marketing and Management*, vol. 8, no. 1 pp. 27-40.

Dreze, X, Hoch, S & Purk, M 1994, `Shelf management and space elasticity', *Journal of Retailing*, vol. 70, no. 4, pp. 301-26.

Fishbein, M 1967, 'Attitudes and prediction of behaviour' in Fishbein, M (ed.), *Readings in Attitude Theory and Measurement*, New York, John Wiley, pp. 477-402.

Fox, C 1993, `Category killers move in on department stores', the *Australian Financial Review*, 14 September, p. 52.

Fox, C 1994, `Eager Coles wakes up', the *Australian Financial Review*, 13 December, p. 31.

Greenland, S & McGoldrick, P 1994, `Atmospherics, attitudes and behaviour: Modelling the impact of designed space', *International Review of Retail, Distribution and Consumer Research*, vol. 4, no. 1, pp. 1-15.

Gross, A, Banting, P, Meredith, L & Ford, I 1993, *Business Marketing*, Houghton Mifflin Co., Boston.

Jones, M 1995, `Preference for private brands decline: Nielson survey', the *Sydney Morning Herald*, 25 May, p. 34.

Levy, M & Weitz, B 2007, *Retailing Management*, 6th edn Irwin, Homewood, Illinois.

Lloyd, S 1992, `Point-of-sale material fails to make an impact: Survey', the *Australian Financial Review*, 21 April, p. 30.

McGoldrick, P 1990, *Retail Marketing*, McGraw-Hill, London.

McIntyre, P 1995, `Coles seeks pitches for a new world', the *Australian Financial Review*, 31 January, p. 27.

Merrilees, B & Miller, D 1994, `The people factor: The key to differentiating small service enterprises' in Ryan, J and Gibson, B (eds), *The People Factor in Small Enterprise*, Proceedings of the Joint SEAANZ and IIE Small Enterprise Conference, Institute of Industrial Economics vol. 22, pp. 134-48.

Merrilees, B & Miller, D 2001, 'Innovation and Strategy in the Australian Supermarket Industry', *Journal of Food Products Marketing*, vol. 7, no. 4, pp. 3-18.

Miller, D & Merrilees, B 1995, *Small Retailers, Large Suppliers: The Unexplored Skills Nexus,* Paper presented to the ICSB 40th World Conference, Sydney, June.

Pollin, R, Burns, J & Heintz, J 2004, 'Global apparel production and sweatshop labour: can raising retail prices finance living wages?', *Cambridge Journal of Economics,* vol. 28, no. 2, pp. 153-171.

Stone, K 1995, *Competing With The Retail Giants,* Wiley, New York.

Stretton, R 1994, `Jacking up Georges', the *Australian Financial Review,* 21 December, p. 13.

Sydney Video Education Australasia 1992, *Behind the Seams No. 4: Creating Retail Fashion in Australia,* Bendigo.

Wilkinson, I & Young, L 1994, `Business dancing - the nature and role of interfirm relationships in business strategy', *Asia-Australia Marketing Journal,* vol. 2, no. 1 (August), pp. 67-79.

Wong, CY & Johansen, J 2006, 'Making JIT retail a success: the coordination journey', *International Journal of Physical Distribution and Logistics Management,* vol. 36, no. 2, pp. 112-126.

Advanced reading

Abelmajid, A & Cadenat, S 2003, 'Efficient retailer assortment: a consumer choice evaluation perspective', *International Journal of Retail & Distribution Management*, vol. 31, no. 10, pp. 486-497.

Adams, RJ 2002, 'Retail profitability and sweatshops: a global dilemma', *Journal of Retailing and Consumer Services,* vol. 9, pp. 147-153.

Anderson-Connell, LJ, Ulrich, PV & Brannon, EL 2002, 'A consumer-driven model for mass customization in the apparel market', *Journal of Fashion Marketing and Management,* vol. 6, no. 3, pp. 240-258.

Bamfield, J 2006, '*Sed quis custodiet?* Employee theft in UK retailing', *International Journal of Retail & Distribution Management*, vol. 34, no. 11, pp. 845-859.

Bandyopadhyay, S & Divakar, S 1999, 'Incorporating balance of power in channel decision structure: Theory and empirical application', *Journal of Retailing and Consumer Services,* vol. 6, no. 2, pp. 79-89.

Barnes, L & Lea-Greenwood, G 2006, 'Fast fashioning the supply chain: shaping the research agenda', *Journal of Fashion Marketing and Management,* vol. 10, no. 3, pp. 259-271.

Birtwistle, G, Fiorito, SS & Moore, C M 2006, 'Supplier perceptions of quick response systems', *Journal of Enterprise Information Management,* vol. 18, no. 3, pp. 334-345.

Birtwistle, G & Freathy P 1998, 'More than just a name above the shop: a comparison of the branding strategies of two UK fashion retailers', *International Journal of Retail & Distribution,* vol. 26, no. 8, p. 318.

Blatherwick, A 1998, 'Insights from industry vendor-managed inventory: fashion fad or important supply chain strategy?', *Supply Chain Management,* vol. 3, no. 1, pp. 10-11.

Boyaci, T & Gallego, G 2002, 'Coordinating pricing and inventory replenishment policies for one wholesaler and one or more geographically dispersed retailer', *International Journal of Production Economics,* vol. 77, no. 2, p. 95.

Brandes, D 2004, *Bare Essentials: The ALDI Way To Retail Success,* Cyan Campus, Frankfurt/Main.

Bruce, M & Daly L 2006, 'Buyer behaviour for fast fashion', *Journal of Fashion Marketing and Management,* vol. 10, no. 3, pp. 329-344.

Cadeaux, JM 1997, 'A closer look at the interface between the product lines of manufacturers and the assortments of retailers', *International Journal of Retail & Distribution Management*, vol. 25, no. 6, pp. 197-203.

Christopher, M, Lowson, R & Peck, H 2004, 'Creating agile supply chains in the fashion industry', *International Journal of Retail & Distribution Management*, vol. 32, no. 8, pp. 367-376.

Clarke, I & Rimmer P 1997, 'The Anatomy of Retail Internationalisation: Daimaru's Decision to Invest in Melbourne, Australia', *The Service Industries Journal*, vol. 17, no. 3 (July), pp. 361-382.

Cooper, R & Kleinschmidt, E 1986, 'An Investigation into the New Product Process: Steps, Deficiencies, Impact', *Journal of Product Innovation Management*, 3, 1986, 71-85;

Cooper, R & Kleinschmidt, E 1990,' New Product Success Factors: A Comparison of 'Kills' versus Successes and Failures', *R & D Management*, vol. 20, no. 1, 1-7.

Davies, G 1992, 'The Two ways in Which Retailers Can Be Brands', *International Journal of Retail & Distribution Management*, vol. 20, no. 2, pp. 24-35.

Davies, B & Ward P 2002, *Managing Retail Consumption*, John Wiley & Sons Ltd, West Sussex, England.

Dewsnap, B & Hart, C 2004, 'Category management: a new approach for fashion marketing?' *European Journal of Marketing*, vol. 38, no. 7, pp. 809-834.

Diamond, J & Pintel, G 1993, *Retail Buying*, 5th edn, Prentice Hall, New Jersey.

Doyle, SA, Moore, CM & Morgan, L 2006, 'Supplier management in fast moving fashion retailing', *Journal of Fashion Marketing and Management*, vol. 10, no. 3, pp. 272-281.

Editor 2005, 'How Zara fashions its supply chain', *Strategic Direction*, vol. 21, no. 10, pp. 28-31.

Ellram, LM, La Londe, BJ & Weber, MM 1999, 'Retail logistics', *International Journal of Physical Distribution & Logistics*, vol. 29, no. 7/8, pp. 477-494.

Emberson, C, Storey, J, Godsell, J & Harrison, A 2006, 'Managing the supply chain using in-store supplier employed merchandisers', *International Journal of Retail & Distribution Management*, vol. 34, no. 6, pp. 467-481.

Fearne, A, Duffy, R & Hornibrook, S 2005, 'Justice in UK supermarket buyer-supplier relationships: an empirical analysis', *International Journal of Retail & Distribution Management*, vol. 33, no. 3, pp. 570-582.

Fiorito, SS, Giunipero, LC & Yan, H 1998, 'Retail buyers' perceptions of quick response systems', *International Journal of Retail & Distribution Management*, vol. 26, no. 6, pp. 237-246.

Fowler, D & Clodfelter, R 2001, 'A comparison of apparel quality, Outlet stores versus department stores', *Journal of Fashion Marketing & Management*, vol. 5, no. 1, pp. 57-66.

Freathy, P & O'Connell F 1998, 'The role of the buying function in airport retailing', *International Journal of Retail & Distribution Management*', vol. 26, no. 6, pp. 247-256.

Gupta, Y, Sundararaghavan, PS & Ahmed, MU 2003, 'Ordering policies for items with seasonal demand', *International Journal of Physical Distribution & Logistics Management*, vol. 33, no. 6, pp. 500-518.

Halepete, J, Hathcote, J & Peters C 2005, 'A qualitative study of micromarketing merchandising in the US apparel retail industry', *Journal of Fashion Marketing and Management*, vol. 9, no. 1, pp. 71-82.

Hayes, SG & Jones, N 2006, 'Fast fashion: a financial snapshot', *Journal of Fashion Marketing and Management*, vol. 10, no. 3 pp. 282-300

Hogg, MK, Bruce, M & Hill, AJ 1998, 'Fashion brand preference among young consumers', *International Journal of Retail & Distribution Management*, vol. 26, no. 8, pp. 293-300.

Horne, S & Broadbridge, A 1995, 'Charity shops: a classification by merchandise mix', *International Journal of Retail & Distribution Management*, vol. 23, no. 7, pp. 17-23.

Howgego, C 2002, 'Maximising competitiveness through the supply chain', *International Journal of Retail & Distribution Management*, vol. 30, no. 12, pp. 603-605.

Juhl, HJ, Esbjerg, L, Grunert, KC, Bech-Larsen, T & Brunso, K 2005, 'The fight between store brands and national brads – What's the score?, *Journal of Retail and Consumer Services*, vol. 13, pp. 331-338.

Karkkainen, M 2003, 'Increasing efficiency in the supply chain for short shelf life goods using RFID tagging', *International Journal of Retail & Distribution Management*, vol. 31, no. 10, pp. 529-536.

Ko, E & Kincade, DH 1997, 'The impact of quick response technologies on retail store attributes', *International Journal of Retail & Distribution Management*, vol. 25, no. 2, pp. 90-98.

Lightfoot, W 2003, 'Multi-channel mistake: the demise of a successful retailer', *International Journal of Retail & Distribution Management*, vol. 31, no. 4, pp. 220-229.

Littrell, MA, Ma, YJ & Halepete, J 2005, 'Generation X, Baby Boomers, and Swing: marketing fair trade apparel', *Journal of Fashion Marketing and Management*, vol. 9, no. 4, pp. 407-419.

Manning, KC, Bearden, WO & Rose, RL 1998, 'Development of a Theory of Retailer Response to Manufacturers' Everyday Low Cost Programs', *Journal of Retailing*, vol. 74, no. 1, pp. 107-137.

McMichael, H, Mackay, D & Altmann, G 2000, 'Quick response in the Australian TCF industry', *International Journal of Physical Distribution & Logistics*, vol. 30, no. 7/8, pp. 611-626.

Miller, D & Merrilees, B 2004, 'Fashion and commerce: a historical perspective on Australian fashion retailing 1880-1920', *International Journal of Retail & Distribution Management*, vol. 32, no. 8, pp. 394-402.

Miranda, M & Joshi, M 2003, 'Australian retailers need to engage with private labels to achieve competitive difference', *Asia Pacific Journal of Marketing and Logistics*, vol. 15, no. 3, pp. 34-47.

Moore, CM & Birtwistle, G 2004, 'The Burberry business model: creating an international luxury fashion brand', *International Journal of Retail & Distribution Management*, vol. 32, no. 8, pp. 412-422.

Moore, CM, Birtwistle, B & Burt S 2004, 'Channel power, conflict and conflict resolution in international fashion retailing', *European Journal of Marketing*, vol. 38, no. 7, pp. 749-769.

Mumel, D & Prodnik, J 2005, 'Grey consumers are all the same, they even dress the same – myth or reality?', *Journal of Fashion Marketing and Management*, vol. 9, no. 4, pp. 434-499.

Pan, B & Holland, R 2006, 'A mass customised supply chain for the fashion system at the design-production interface', *Journal of Fashion Marketing and Management*, vol. 10, no. 3, pp. 345-359.

Pelton, LE, Strutton, D & Lumpkin, JR 2001, *Marketing Channels and Retail Supply Chains*, 2nd edn, McGraw Hill, Irwin.

Piron, F & Young, M 2001, 'Retail borrowing: definition and retailing implications', *Journal of Retailing and Consumer Services*, vol. 8, pp. 121-125.

Roth, E and Sneader, K 2006, 'Reinventing innovation at consumer goods companies', *The McKinsey Quarterly*, November.

Savitt, R 1999, 'Innovation in American retailing, 1919-39: improving inventory management', *The International Review of Retail, Distribution and Consumer Research*, vol. 9, no. 3, pp. 307-320.

Semeijn, J, Van Riel, ACR & Ambrosini, AB 2004, 'Consumer evaluation of store brands: effects of store image and product attributes', *Journal of Retailing and Consumer Services*, vol. 11, pp. 247-258.

Sheridan, M, Moore, C & Nobbs, K 2006, 'Fast fashion requires fast marketing: the role of category management in fast fashion positioning', *Journal of Fashion Marketing and Management*, vol. 10, no. 3, pp. 301-315.

Sheu, C, Yen, HR & Chae, B 2006, 'Determinants of supplier-retailer collaboration: evidence from an international study', *International Journal of Operations & Production Management,* vol. 26, no. 1, pp. 24-49.

Sohal, AS, Power & DJ, Terziovski, M 2002, 'Integrated supply chain management from the wholesaler's perspective: two Australian case studies', *'International Journal of Physical Distribution & Logistics Management,* vol. 32, no. 2, pp. 96-109.

Sparks, L & Wagner, BA 2003, 'Retail exchanges: a research agenda', *Supply Chain Management: An International Journal,* vol. 8, no. 1, pp. 17-25

Summer, TA, Belleau, BD & Xu, Y 2006, 'Predicting purchase intention of a controversial luxury apparel product', *Journal of Fashion Marketing and Management,* vol. 10, no. 4, pp. 405-419.

Thaver, I & Wilcock, A 2006, 'Identification of overseas vendor selection criteria used by Canadian apparel buyers', *Journal of Fashion Marketing and Management,* vol. 10, no. 1, pp. 56-70.

Tyler, D, Heeley, J & Bhamra, T 2006, 'Supply chain influences on new product development in fashion clothing', *Journal of Fashion Marketing and Management,* vol. 10, no. 3, pp. 316-328.

Vahie, A & Paswan, A 2006, 'Private label brand image: its relationship with store image and national brand', *International Journal of Retail & Distribution Management,* vol. 34, no. 1, pp. 67-84.

Varley, R 2006, *Retail Product Management,* 2nd edn, Routlege, Oxon.

Whiteoak, P 1999, 'The realities of quick response in the grocery sector: a supplier viewpoint', *International Journal of Physical Distribution and Logistics Management,* vol. 29, no. 7/8, pp. 508-519.

Wong, CY, Arlbjorn, JS & Johansen, J 2005, 'Supply chain management practices in toy supply chains', *Supply Chain Management: An International Journal,* vol. 10, no. 5 pp. 367-378.

Wu, J & Delong, M 2006, 'Chinese perceptions of western-branded denim jeans: a Shanghai case study', *Journal of Fashion Marketing and Management,* vol. 10, no.2, pp. 238-250.

Store design

Introduction

How does retail store design contribute to retailer branding? Store design is a critical element of the retail mix and of retail strategy. It is a major means of communicating to customers, staff, suppliers and other stakeholders. There is scope for innovation in store design to support the retailer's brand. One of the first things that a shopfront retailer has to do when commencing business is to 'fit out' the store. The cost of fitting out a store could range from $20,000 for a small 50 square metre handbag retailer in an outer suburb, to over $40 million for a large department store. **Fitting out** includes such activities as the design, purchase and installation of fixtures and fittings as well as of window displays. In turn, these activities are part of a broader set of activities called **store design.** To help understanding, we divide store design into four main categories:

- store infrastructure;
- store layout;
- merchandise spatial planning; and
- visual merchandising.

It is not easy to discuss these four categories separately as there are some interdependencies. In the final analysis, retailers need to resolve their store design components simultaneously so as to link them with their positioning and strategic retail direction. Initially, we deal with each factor separately in the first instance to ensure that all relevant issues are fully considered. The common design principles bind together the four store design categories. The separate issues, and the staff who may specialise in each area, are also brought together to discuss two generic store design issues, namely **refurbishments** (i.e. **makeovers**) and **new generation formats**, and **self-service formats**.

Broadly, the four categories of store design are discussed in ascending order by the ease in which they can be varied by the retailer. That is, we begin with that category which is least able to be varied by the retailer, that is store infrastructure. By ease of change we mean the cost to the retailer of changing retail store design. This cost includes the cost of new equipment, facilities and of staff time as well as the disruption of services to customers while renovations are under-taken. The ascending order reflects a sequence which deals with the broader considerations first and then progresses to the more detailed, micro aspects of merchandise display.

The concept of store organisation

Research suggests that an emerging segment of customers is very demanding in terms of how well a retail store is organised. So, what is store organisation? When asked, shoppers suggest that store organisation embraces: how things flow around the store; the ease of finding products and services; the availability of stock (i.e. the avoidance of **stockouts**); the smooth operation of the store; how efficiently everything is managed; safety; and the neatness, tidiness and cleanliness of the store and the stock. **Store organisation**, then, is a perception the consumer may have about how well the store is organised as a whole. That is, there is a **frontstage** impact that is part of the store brand. However, to manage store organisation there must also be a **backstage** approach.

How does store organisation fit into the store brand? Store organisation affects the consumer's overall perception of the store, and thus affects the perceived store brand. Like location, store organisation can play a minor or major role in the retail brand. So, when is store organisation very important? When should retailers give more prominence to store organisation?

With high fashion retailers, a messy store could destroy the image of the immaculate merchandise.

For low involvement shopping and for complex shopping, for example in supermarkets, consumers can easily become very frustrated if a store is not well organised.

What should retailers consider? The vital components of store organisation are store design, store layout and signage, shelf-filling and shelf-maintenance, the general tidiness and appearance of the store, payment systems, and the role of store organisation in maintaining security. What is required is the overall integration and co-ordination of the store's organisation factors. On a day-to-day basis, this role falls to the store manager who needs to include all staff to help maintain the desired levels of store organisation. The manager, as well, will need to conduct regular store organisation audits as part of ongoing performance management. However, at a strategy level, planners should incorporate these factors into the store design to facilitate ongoing retail operations.

The role of store design

Store design is part of the retail mix and contributes to the overall retail strategy. Together with location, most aspects of store design need to be considered before the store is opened as they become costly to change after that time. **Store design** shares another similarity with **location** in that jointly they can be considered as the **distribution component of the retail mix**. Jointly, they assist in making the merchandise available to the customer. Location is the distribution component which brings the customer to the store entrance. Store design then takes over the distribution function through the shop facade and window display to entice or invite the customer into the store. Shop design through store layout and visual merchandising – which includes store map guides – then helps the customer find and purchase the merchandise. In other words, store design is based on assisting the customer to move to appropriate parts of the store in order to meet their merchandise needs.

Store design should be evaluated by the extent to which it contributes to retail strategy and objectives, and the extent to which it has an impact on retail sales. As with store location, the objectives of store design can be summarised as follows:

- to generate store traffic;

- to enhance the overall image of the retailer; and

- to contribute to the convenience of customer shopping.

Objective 1 – Generating local traffic

The first objective of store design ties in with its logistic concern. This emphasises guiding **people traffic** around the store generally and to particular product groupings in particular. Store layout is important to this process, as is merchandise spatial planning.

Traffic control, however, is not a passive process. The retailer is aiming to ensure that the store's merchandise is noticed and that it is attractive and accessible to the consumer, with visual merchandising playing an important part in this process. The relationship between store design and sales may be direct. If customers cannot find a product, a sale may be lost. In other cases, the relation between store design and sales is more subtle.

Objective 2 – Enhancing the image of the retailer

Store design needs to contribute to the desired **brand image** of the retailer, and there are some retailers where **visual merchandising** is a major part of the retail strategy. The core of retail strategy is **competitive positioning**, and the following questions need to be considered:

- Is the retailer a discounter or a high image merchandiser?

- Is the emphasis modern or traditional?

- Is the retailer appealing to a particular market segment?

It is crucial that store design is aligned to the retailer's competitive position in the market.

While store design directly helps the right customers find the right merchandise, it also gives cues about the overall store image. Just Jeans is a good example with bright, colourful window displays which are unbacked so that the window display image extends to the rest of the store. Image, the second objective, requires further discussion. Retailing is a service industry, and physical **atmospherics** contribute to the cues that customers use to assess both the quality of the merchandise itself and the service they get from the retailer (Vignette 5.1). For example, expensive fittings and fixtures may reinforce the image of expensive merchandise and therefore make it easier to sell these high margin goods. Many city menswear retailers use this tactic. A growing number of studies demonstrate that shoppers' experience within the store can affect their purchases and therefore can affect retail performance (Dawson, Bloch & Ridgeway 1990; Swinyard 1993; Baker, Grewal & Parasuraman 1994; Greenland & McGoldrick 1994; Donovan, Rossiter, Marcoolyn and Nesdale 1994; Vazquez & Bruce 2002; Hu & Jasper 2006).

Vignette 5.1

Visual merchandising:
The case of BNT (formerly Bras 'n' Things)

In 1986, Brett Blundy launched the lingerie chain Bras 'n' Things. Bras 'n' Things (BNT) has since become Australia's largest lingerie chain with more than 150 BNT stores plus online selling as of 2006, and is now part of Brazin.

The original product concept for the store was itself highly visual, that is, 'for lingerie to become pretty and feminine and co-ordinated' (Burbury 1993, p. 34). Apparently, Mr Blundy also used his visual merchandising skills – using real models – to convince shopping centre executives to include lingerie in their tenant mix (Burbury 1993). Merchandise displays stand out in BNT outlets – with a good use of signage and a neat, orderly and colourful arrangement of merchandise. The author has used this store as a benchmark to compare the signage and display in other clothing stores.

In 2002, a rebranding strategy enabled the retailer to reposition its offerings to include younger customer segments.

See <www.bnt.com.au> and <www.bbretailcapital.com.au>.

Music is a special case of store atmosphere. Various studies show that background music can influence the behaviour of shoppers (see Milliman 1982; 1986). One of the more detailed studies of the influence of music on shopping is Brunner (1990) who classifies music in more detail than most other studies, namely in terms of the rhythm, tempo, staccato notes, pitch and texture of the music. He also investigated the role of specially developing music for the store. Generally, however, he emphasised the benefit of music familiar to the clientele. The important work of Vinovich (1975) demonstrates the usefulness of music generally. Vinovich showed that different musical moods produced different interpretations of the same video stimulus. Otherwise-ambiguous video images were made more cognitively predictable because of familiar music. This finding gives retailers some scope to risk-manage at least minor changes to their visual merchandising by supporting their visual merchandising with familiar and acceptable music.

Objective 3 – Contributing to convenience

With respect to the third objective, store design and image contribute to the convenience of shopping through good layout, physically accessible departments or sections, helpful customer services such as sales points or checkout facilities, and appropriate merchandise stock levels arranged in an eye-catching and accessible manner. **Infrastructure features** – such as wide entrances, easy open or automatic doors, and spacious fitting rooms – benefit shoppers who have mobility restrictions and need assistance by carers, or who have children in prams. Other components of infrastructure include easily-accessible toilets with carer-friendly facilities and adequate signage which means accuracy of directions, ease of reading and understanding, supported by pictographs and multi-lingual text where appropriate. The idea of **physical, visual, aural** and **psychic access** can contribute to the overall concept of convenience.

Compatibility with competitive strategy and the brand are the most useful ways of evaluating store design. Certainly costs have to be considered, as no retailer has an unlimited budget to provide high levels of store design. However, store design costs need to be regarded as part of a package when selecting a retail competitive position. There is generally no point having expensive, quality merchandise and then saying that the budget does not allow for appropriate fixtures, fittings and visual merchandising. Both aspects are needed unless it is a factory outlet type of operation – although even here there is a limit to how far store brand image can be sacrificed when economising on store design. All retailers need to assess the most cost-effective way of developing and maintaining the optimal level of store design – weighing up both the benefits and the costs. In this regard, retail store designers should factor in the use of **environmentally sustainable** materials and **low energy** usage features for ventilation, lighting, heating, cooling, and refrigeration for food. This approach contributes to environmental sustainability and has positive economic and social impacts for the retailer, the customer and other stakeholders.

Stores often go through either major or minor refits, which may be part of a retailer brand makeover. For example, Kmart is an Australian store which has gone through a number of major format changes and many more minor changes over the years. In the shopping centre (mall) context, retailers' leases may dictate how frequently they are required to refit the store. Note that even in the **e-retailing** domain, retailers revamp their virtual stores by making over their websites. Retailers who have both a storefront and virtual presence have to address congruence between the two.

Given the high costs involved, one major consideration is the *frequency* of changing store design. Modern or special theme designs may have more sales impact in some circumstances, but such designs generally have to be changed more frequently. The additional cost of more frequent special theme designs may outweigh the sales benefits of such designs. By contrast, traditional designs may only need to be changed every 10 to 15 years, although the store must be well maintained at all times.

The choice between modern and traditional store design is most likely to be influenced by the profile of the target market and by the retailer's competitive position in that market. Potential frequency of store design change needs to be kept in mind when formulating a retailer's competitive position.

Market research can assist when comparing store designs. For example, Ward and Eaton (1994) conducted an experimental study comparing modern and traditional designs for professional dental practices. They showed their respondents different pictures of dental waiting room environments, and then measured the different emotional responses. Generally, the traditional practice environment – with its warm colours, soft fabrics and wood rather than metal or glass fixtures, curved lines and use of decorations – evoked more positive emotions and, overall, a more positive attitude toward the practice.

This is only one of many techniques that retailers can use to evaluate store design, with other techniques including direct surveys of customers and staff, and observing customers as they move around the store. Staff and customer comfort, security, safety and convenience need to be built into the store design. Store design must also accommodate all the backstage functions that a retailer requires. These functions may include areas for switchboards, computing equipment, the storage of merchandise and visual display materials, the assembly of displays, and staff.

Most current categories of retailers, from supermarkets to takeaway stores, tend to use a modern store design. This style reflects the underlying needs of consumers for convenient, well displayed and well laid out store design. Studies of banking designs usually find that customers prefer the more modern designs that are well signed, open and accessible. Nonetheless, some categories – such as professional dental services as noted above – may do better to concentrate on more traditional store designs. However, there is also exciting scope for niche petrol stations or niche banks to go against the general trend and opt for a more traditional store design which can imbue reassurance and trust.

Regardless of the type of design – although this may be slightly more difficult for traditional designs – all retailers can minimise the cost of store redesign by building in as much flexibility as possible, such as by leasing fixtures and fittings where possible. Additionally, fixtures and fittings that are more detachable and mobile can be chosen. Some design suppliers have responded to retailers' needs for flexible designs by using materials and patterns which can suit a number of different store images.

Flexibility enables retailers to make at least minor adjustments to store design on an annual, seasonal, special event or even a daily basis. These adjustments are important, given the need for retailers to inject vitality into their stores and to prevent them from taking on a shabby, tired look.

Store design categories

There are four store design categories, and these will be explored in more detail below. They are:

- store infrastructure;
- store layout;
- merchandise spatial planning; and
- visual merchandising.

Store infrastructure

The term **store infrastructure** refers to those relatively fixed components of the store, and includes:

- the store façade and main entrance;
- external and natural lighting;
- artificial lighting;
- front windows and doors (automatic and manual);
- floors, ceilings and wall textures;
- fixtures and fittings including gondolas, 'rounders', four-way stands or hanging fixtures, shelves for folded or stack goods, tables, and cabinets that may be open, closed or locked glass (e.g. jewellery showcases);
- heated, cooled or refrigerated displays for food products;
- ventilation and fans for heating and cooling;

- facilities for customers and staff (toilets, fitting rooms, seating, refreshment, and play areas, first aid, cloak or parcel storage areas);

- facilities for storage on the shopping floor and at back of store;

- vertical and horizontal transport (lifts, stairs, escalators, ramps, railings, moving footways);

- direct sensory stimuli (lighting, sound, temperature, smell, colour);

- technology (transaction equipment, pneumatic tubes for shifting cash and dockets to a secure central area, sensor tags, in-house television or **captive audience network** or **CAN**);

- mobile customer service equipment (trolleys, baskets, bags, umbrellas, wheelchairs); and

- security lighting, security closed circuit television (CCTV), exit signage, structures (such as fire doors and fire escape stairs), fire and smoke alarms, sprinkler systems, fire hydrants, fire reels and fire extinguishers.

In some cases, such as the fragrant smell from hot bread shops, store infrastructure can be a key competitive advantage of the store. The store façade and window display can have an influence on whether some customers enter a shop at all. The main issues facing retailers are to ensure that they are conscious of all the components of store infrastructure and to treat their selection as a collective, coherent decision.

Retailers with small stores in shopping malls often have very limited window space, so they must make the entrance and the view into the store interactive and inviting.

The keys to formulating store design are the retail category and a store image consistent with competitive positioning. Retailers potentially use floor and wall textures, scents, and sounds, width of aisles and different quality fixtures and facilities to influence their store image. An upmarket retailer such as David Jones can use marble or parquet floors, panelled wood walls and counters, mirrors, subdued colours, natural wood smell, soft music, pleasant temperature, carpeted fitting rooms, comfortable seating and clean toilets to reinforce their image. These components of store infrastructure need to be fine-tuned to ensure they interface coherently in colour, texture and tone. In contrast, Myer has in recent times shifted to a starker, more minimalist approach emphasising white walls and columns.

Some upmarket retailers differ in their design approach. For example, in the planning for the now defunct Daimaru department store in Melbourne, the General Manager of Finance and Administration stated:

> *... Daimaru will have a casual, youthful look. It will not mimic the glass, brass and marble opulence of David Jones' flagship Sydney and Melbourne*

stores. Our research found that shoppers felt intimidated by swank department stores ... . (Shoebridge 1990)

The scope of store infrastructure also covers functional customer, staff and supplier use in the store environment. For example:

- How easy is it to find relevant merchandise?

- Does the scale of merchandise fit the scale of the store?

- Is an information desk needed? Or will some type of information kiosk suffice?

- How easy is it to move around from one part of the store to another?

- Can people with disabilities or mobility restrictions move around easily?

- How safe are the floor surfaces?

- How easy is it to reach and inspect merchandise?

- Can customers less than 155 centimetres in height reach all items?

- Are some items too low, requiring too much bending?

- Are there sufficient trolleys and/or baskets in which to put the merchandise?

- Are the aisles wide enough for two trolleys or for wheelchair access?

- How easy is it to obtain non-merchandise services such as rest rooms, credit, eating, entertainment, resting or calling a taxi?

Most of these issues apply with equal force to customers, staff and suppliers. Ease of activity, convenience, and safety of staff and suppliers need to be an integral part of store design. They are relevant to health and safety, and to security. Security systems and computer systems are also part of store infrastructure.

Many of these facilities and services contribute to **customer service**. We must recognise that customers see these facets as part of their **total shopping experience**. The better retailers will study which mix of customer services is appropriate for their customers. Low-service retailers generally see amenities, play areas and telephone areas as 'dead areas', that is, space for things other than merchandise. In contrast, high-service retailers see the same areas as 'live areas' (an expression coined by the author), that is, providing customer services which supplement and integrate with the merchandise function.

The situation for discount retailers is more complicated. One expects less trimmings in fixtures and fittings and fewer add-on services and facilities such as eating areas or rest rooms. However, how much of a reduction in customer service is optimal? Some stores, such as ALDI food stores, have turned stark store infrastructure into a competitive advantage (Vignette 5.2).

Vignette 5.2

Using store infrastructure for efficient operations: The case of ALDI

ALDI uses store infrastructure to contribute to efficient and effective retail operations. Much of the merchandise is displayed instore on pallets which are brought directly into the store so that the retailer doesn't have to transfer the stock onto shelves from the delivered pallets. The pallets are organised logically as if they *were* the permanent shelving, so that customer wayfinding is easy. This approach supports store design objectives by:

- **generating instore traffic** as most customers would walk throughout the store, and, as pallets are relatively low in height, customers can still see around the store and easily navigate the store to locate other retail offerings; and

- **enhancing the retailer's overall brand image** because pallets suggest lower prices since money has not been allocated to elaborate fixtures.

For your consideration:

Explain how successful negotiations with merchandise suppliers can contribute to effective instore presentation.

Nonetheless, sometimes this strategy may backfire in circumstances where stark store infrastructure is equated with poor quality merchandise. All discount retailers need to ensure that they present at least the minimum customer service offerings so that their customers can shop safely and efficiently. Some discounters will find it appropriate to increase some infrastructure customer service levels beyond the minimum, provided that these changes have no more than a minimal impact on their prices.

The Foodworks supermarket chain has successfully used this strategy, achieving noticeably less clutter, more friendly staff, and better signage than many of its competitors in the same price range. For intermediate retailers who are between upmarket and discounter, there is the need to find the appropriate colour, texture and tone of their store infrastructure, and the optimal level of facilities and customer services. A good example is the Ross Evans Nursery (see Vignette 5.3).

Store layout

Store layout refers to *where* both the merchandise and other structures and facilities are physically located, with the effect of creating a particular pattern of people traffic. It is like designing a road system where we also design the surrounding landscape; the landscape corresponds to what we call **store infrastructure**.

Vignette 5.3

Mixing colour, texture and tone with facilities and services:
The case of Ross Evans Nursery

The Ross Evans Nursery on the Gold Coast, Queensland, offers a comprehensive garden nursery, home accessories, and a bistro with meals and snacks available from breakfast until late afternoon – seven days a week.

The garden section draws on the natural attributes of the products by grouping them to highlight colours and textures. Accessories such as pots and garden sculptures reinforce the visual qualities of the plants. The colour and texture themes carry through into the bistro, which has several significant water features and associated sculptures as well as displays of plants, flowers and accessories. Showing the merchandise in use has the duel function of creating ambience and of suggesting to customers how the merchandise might be used in various settings.

Customer services include the provision of shade and umbrellas, and toilets that are well designed and co-ordinated in terms of décor with the adjacent bistro. Overall, the store design effectively incorporates colours, textures and tone into the facilities and services, and satisfies all of the three store design objectives.

For your consideration:

What lessons could big box (i.e. superstore) retailers learn from this example? Are the lessons similar or different for supermarkets?

When we walk into a store, we tend to travel subconsciously in a certain pattern. This pattern is not accidental, but has been deliberately controlled by the retailer. The flow of retail traffic follows what we call the **CRTW law of retail traffic.** CRTW is an acronym for 'cars rule the world'. If a country has a left side road system – for example the UK, Australia, New Zealand and parts of Asia – then generally pedestrian traffic and retail traffic follow the same pattern.

Observe this for yourself by standing in any street or retail outlet for a reasonable time. Given an equal choice, shoppers in Australia – but not in Canada, for example – start on the left side of an outlet. The author has tested this proposition with colleagues, retailers and students from a number of countries, including Australia, India, Indonesia, Sweden, Hong Kong, Canada, Estonia, Columbia and Finland. Of course, the physical shape of an outlet may force shoppers to the right. However, where retailers have a choice, they might consider using the CRTW law of retail traffic to achieve a more harmonious flow of retail traffic.

Once the shopper enters the road system, the CRTW law guides the shopper around the store. Customers follow the road system as it interacts with their motivation to get to a particular destination based on desired products. Retailers use store layout to map out routes whereby customers' attention will be drawn favourably to other merchandise that may either not be as high on their shopping lists or may not even be on their lists at all, that is, **unplanned items**.

Grid store layouts

This approach to store layout has been perfected by supermarkets that use a **grid store layout system.** The grid system has many parallel rows of shelving in a fairly repetitive pattern, supplemented by extensive wall shelving. Together with appropriate ceiling signs (similar to road signage), the customer is guided through most bays even though a customer may only want to buy a few items. Maximum exposure to products ensues. Convenience goods like milk and bread are placed generally in remote locations, with the result that the reluctant consumer is exposed to most of the store's wares before finally getting back to the checkout.

The key benefit of the grid system is that it effectively controls and speeds retail traffic as well as maximising storage display capacity and hence space productivity. **Space productivity** is defined as sales per square metre. The grid system is particularly suited to large volume, small 'per unit' item retailing that is common in shops such as supermarkets, hardware stores, newsagents, card shops and chemists. Yet the grid system seems to work better for some retail categories, for example supermarkets, than it does for others, for example hardware stores.

At the same time, the grid system has the potential to disadvantage customers who want only a few items. Special **fast checkout lanes** – such as '8 items or less' – help with these cases, although many of these shoppers often prefer to use convenience stores anyway. Retailers using multiple checkouts have been slow to develop queuing systems that customers deem fair. How frustrating is it to stand in a supermarket queue at one checkout only to have customers from the back of your queue redirected to a newly-opened checkout.

Free form systems

A second store layout approach is the **free form system**. This approach is popular in small specialty shops such as clothing and clothing accessories stores. The fixtures and aisles are arranged asymmetrically so that there is more scope for the consumer to focus on particular areas depending on their interest. There is still a broad road system in place, but there is less compulsion to take in all displays in the store. The environment is more relaxed and selective than the grid system. Retailers need to ensure that either cluttered merchandise or aggressive sales people do not counteract the free flow benefits – which rely on relaxation, enjoyment and enticement.

Boutique designs

A third store layout form is the **boutique design**. This is particularly relevant to department stores, for example Myer or David Jones, and discount department stores, for example Kmart or Big W. There are generally key departments – or hubs – that customers need to travel to, which are then linked to smaller departments – or spokes – through a series of loops.

Part of the design strategy of the boutique system is to ensure that each department does not have excessive sameness. Differentiation across departments is important to help customers identify certain merchandise and to arouse excitement in travelling across departments. This is where the term 'boutique' comes in – each department can be set up as a separate boutique to facilitate differentiation across departments. The boutique itself may actually resemble the 'free form' layout design common among stand-alone, small specialist retailers.

Some of the more upmarket department stores, particularly in Canada and the United States, have carried this to a stage where many of the boutique departments actually resemble separate shops with their own façades. Specifically, this scheme is used where certain boutiques are each dedicated to a specific designer label. In some cases, these separate shops are in fact managed individually as 'concessions', with the space rented from the host department store. In Australia, cosmetics and hairdressing products are often sold this way in department stores, as illustrated with the Karpati salons 'at selected David Jones stores'. In recent years a number of specialist clothing retailers (e.g. Table Eight), some jewellery retailers and other types of retailers including fresh fruit and flower retailers have also leased space in department stores.

Racecourse layouts

A fourth layout often referred to is the **racecourse layout**, which has many similarities to the boutique design.

Hybrid store layouts

A fifth layout, not often discussed in the literature, can be termed **hybrid store layout**. In one of the more interesting retailing developments in the past 15 years, the boutique or 'store-within-a-store' concept has been applied to supermarkets. This is shown, for example, in how Woolworths and Coles have both used the 'shop-within-a-shop' concept in various departments in combination with the classic grid system. Following on from the Franklins 'Big Fresh' format of the late 1990s, large supermarkets have moved towards this approach with a combination of boutique, free-form and grid systems. The **boutique** approach is shown with notionally separate 'stores' for delicatessen and seafood. The **free form** layout is used with bakery and smallgoods likes cheeses and dips set up on island fixtures, and the **classic grid** is used for staple items including fresh fruit and vegetables, breakfast foods, tea, coffee, biscuits, drinks, confectionery and snack foods, laundry and household cleaning products, personal hygiene products, and tinned and bottled produce.

Another important aspect of store layout is the arrangement of non-merchandise facilities so that they harmonise with the relevant 'road system'. As with navigating any road system, maps and map planners help. The store needs to ensure that customer service areas, including information centres, are conveniently located – perhaps on each floor. Some customer service facilities – such as refreshment areas and rest rooms – can be located in less immediate areas, although there is scope to explore new venues particularly for café areas (see the Ross Evans case in Vignette 5.3), rest areas and waiting areas. Parcel pickup, storage and docking areas, where relevant, need to be planned in relation to parking and delivery areas.

Technological factors also need to be planned. As a starting point, retailers need to consider the following questions:

- What computing resources will be required within the selling space?
- What **backstage** computing systems will be needed?
- What communication interfaces with suppliers will be needed?
- What types of cash registers and payment equipment are needed?
- Are product scanners needed? Are they for price checking or for checking out? Will staff use the scanners? Will customers use them for self-scanning?
- Are weighing scales required? Will they be self-service? Are they for checking by the customer, or for weighing, labelling and pricing by the customer? Do they need to be integrated with the cash register system?
- Are sensor gates or entrance/exit sensors to be used?
- Are **EFTPOS** facilities needed?
- Will pneumatic tube systems be used for transporting cash from the cash register to a central point?
- What telecommunications equipment will be needed? Is special electrical wiring or cabling needed?

- What use of technology is required for environmental monitoring (such as the efficiency and effectiveness of air-conditioning, water heating, smoke and fire alarms, and sprinkler systems)?

A special consideration is the placement of the checkout area. Should it be near the front, side, middle or back of the store? Generally the discount, large volume retail categories place the checkout area – including scanners and cash registers – near the front of the store. This approach fits in with a **self-service** format (discussed later in this chapter). Recently, a number of newsagents have been redesigning their store layouts by generally moving the checkout area to the front and side of their premises, reflecting a realisation that newsagents are large volume retailers who require a store layout that both saves space and maximises throughput. When the checkout area is positioned near the front of the store, taking a holistic approach is important.

For example, if the checkout is too close to the doors, there could be congestion with the mixing of exiting and entering customers. Another potential problem is related to the weather. If doors open automatically, continual draughts may affect checkout staff.

More upmarket boutiques tend to place the checkout facilities near the back of the store to avoid any unfavourable connotation that the main objective of the business is simply 'to get your money'. Also, if a small specialist retailer has a cash register near the front of the shop, it makes it more vulnerable to robbery. Having been robbed was enough to prompt one retailer in Sydney to move his cash register from the front to the back of the shop. An unintended bonus was that the image of the shop was enhanced. Thus, store security systems and policies must also be integrated with store design decisions.

Many of the key considerations which influence store layout decisions also influence merchandise spatial planning, and these are further explored in the following section.

Merchandise spatial planning

Physical spatial planning includes planning the location of store infrastructure and the store layout. In contrast, in this section we discuss *merchandise* **spatial planning** which includes the location of merchandise groupings through departments – if relevant – as well as the location of merchandise within each department.

The most fundamental aspect of merchandise spatial planning is to decide which departments or focus areas the store should have. This is a **product range** question, and the retailer's response must be closely allied to the store's retail strategy (see *Chapter 2 – Retail strategy, branding and innovation*). Astute retailers recognise the synergies in these two aspects of the retail mix, and they integrate merchandise spatial planning and merchandise assortment planning so that they know that the product range they buy will be displayed appropriately in the store.

Retailers can assess the roles of **anchor departments**, that is, departments that have greater drawing power than others. Then, if there *are* anchor departments, what are the implications for that particular store and what adjustments can or should be made.

This idea is analogous to the anchor stores in shopping centres, covered in Chapter 6 - Location.

For discount stores, department stores and supermarkets, the product range question is particularly important because of the many hundred product types they may carry. Generally speaking, the Australian trend has seen discount stores and department stores reducing their range, while in contrast supermarkets have been increasing their range. A similar trend has been observed for the United Kingdom (Hart 1994).

Department stores can be used to illustrate these issues. Australian department stores have followed a worldwide trend of contracting their lines to include little more than a core group consisting of clothing, soft fabrics, electronics, cosmetics and furniture. In the early 1990s, Grace Bros (Myer) in NSW phased out hardware as a department. Similarly, in the 18 months to June 1990, David Jones removed hardware, gardening products and sporting goods. Instead, they concentrated on home furnishings, designer labels, furniture and gourmet food. In the 2000s, department stores now generally focus on fashion and cosmetics, homewares, manchester, home accessories, electrical, some general merchandise, and seasonal offerings such as festive food and gifts in the lead-up to Christmas. At the same time, major reductions have been implemented in the furniture, fabrics and haberdashery offerings.

In the supermarket category, the most recent moves focus more emphasis on fresh fruit and vegetables, delicatessen products, and store-cooked fresh bread and bakery products. In some cases, new departments have been added or refurbished in existing stores.

Other retail categories have also been active in this area. Newsagents, convenience stores at petrol stations and pharmacists (chemists) have added more product groupings to their core businesses. These product lines are now so diverse that they can be referred to as **'scrambled merchandising'** or simply **generic convenience stores**. Petrol stations are a good example, with their longer trading hours and added emphasis on impulse and convenience lines, consistent with the making over of their store brands.

Two Australians who run a unique newsagency, The Source, in Melbourne have taken scrambled merchandise to a new level, and have developed a distinctive store design for their retail offer. They augment the usual newspapers and magazines with gourmet foods, fresh flowers, chocolates and homewares. The store is in a heritage building and the owners say that,

> *"[T]he interior is a combination of original fittings with contemporary flair. The lighting is bright, warm and inviting". (See Chris Black 2007,*

"Visual merchandising – it's a gift", Inside Retailing Online, July 09, <www.insideretailing.com.au>.)

What principles are there for placing departments within a store? The overall principles remain as before, namely: to enhance the overall store image, to maximise sales, to enhance customer service, to economise on space, to allow for interdependencies across departments, and to take advantage of retail traffic *en route* to moving to particular destinations. A useful aid is a classification of departments relating to different consumer behaviour characteristics linked to particular types of merchandise.

The **departmental classifications** given in Table 5.1 provide an initial guide to retailers for their merchandise spatial planning. To reinforce these concepts further, we can make use of the related concepts on retail location (see *Chapter 6 – Location).* Two very useful concepts are those of the anchor store and of drawing power. Instead of the anchor store, however, there is the **anchor department**, which would be represented by demand merchandise in Table 5.1. Anchor departments or demand merchandise are the reason the consumer comes into the store. **Drawing power** measures the strength of this effect. Other departments then rely more on impulse behaviour once the customer has been drawn into the store.

Retailers need to evaluate the suitability of their merchandise spatial plans regularly. As a starting point, the retailer evaluates the performance of each department. Market research can also help in this process. For example, the American company FJ Woolworths could not understand why its goods at the rear section of each shop lagged behind other sections. They subsequently hired a consumer research consultant who specialised in observing consumers and monitoring retail traffic. The consultant discovered that poorly-designed check-out areas created queues which prevented people getting to the back of the store. The checkout areas were then redesigned (Larson 1994). This is a case of two components of store design **interacting** where the evaluation of merchandise spatial planning led to a redesign of the store layout.

The principles and options for locating departments in a store have comparable principles for locating merchandise *within* a department. The department can be thought of as a mini-store, somewhat similar to the boutique concept of store layout. Within a department, there will be a front section for convenience or impulse items – sometimes in the form of sales or specials. There will also be space for **demand** and **comparison shopping** merchandise, which represent the core business and include anchor products. Synergies across merchandise can be featured, such as to display and sell a total outfit in clothing or alternatively a total dining room setting.

Freedom, IKEA and Country Road are good examples of **concept selling**. This means product lines which integrate an entire household – from bedroom furniture to lamps to dining ware, among others. Narrower versions are concept shops, which emphasise specific lifestyles or a major distinctive theme to their products. Such retailers include RM Williams, Ken Done, Billabong, and idiosyncratic clothing and variety shops such as Cartoon World. Retailers like Villeroy & Boch define themselves as concept shops. Concept shops generally give high priority to visual merchandising.

Table 5.1 Classification of departments as an aid to merchandise spatial planning

Type	Discussion
Convenience merchandise	These are departments in high traffic areas and which generally have **high space productivity**, defined as sales per square metre. A departmental store example would be cosmetics which are generally placed near the front of the store at street level for maximum convenience. A supermarket example would be magazines and confectionery which are placed near the checkout counters. Many of these purchases are based on impulse, made because of convenience, or even stimulated by the display itself. Also, as Reekie (1993, p. 84) observes historically, "The men's departments were usually located on the ground floor because a man preferred to do his shopping in the few minutes he has to spare on his way back to the office from lunch". In some ways, life has changed little over the past hundred years.
Demand merchandise	The consumer has come to the store deliberately to buy items or services such as furniture, sporting goods or hairdressing. Given the strong shopping motivation of the consumer, the retailer can place these items in more remote areas. Generally, the most bulky, space-demanding items, for example furniture, are located in the most remote areas.
Comparison shopping items	These are merchandise items where there is a greater emphasis on browsing and comparing items, with clothing being a classic example. Often, these departments are placed *between* convenience merchandise and demand merchandise. Often the clothing departments are near the elevator to arouse interest as shoppers move around the store. An exception to this pattern is more expensive, designer label boutiques which can be placed in more remote areas as they are more exclusive, require less traffic, and have their own brand loyal following as a motivator.
Interdependencies across departments	Some departments form natural **synergies** with each other. In clothing, many shoppers want a total outfit that may also include shoes and accessories. It is important that the key components of the total outfit be located as close as possible so informed choices can be made.

Tools which can help retailers with merchandise spatial planning are the classification of merchandise (Table 5.1), conducting a **merchandise spatial planning audit** (see *Chapter 10 – Retail operations, performance management and support systems*), observing and mapping traffic flows, and the use of **planograms** – which usually indicate the number of product facings, adjacencies and the physical positioning of products. Planograms can be very sophisticated when generated electronically and integrated with checkout and ordering data. However, depending on how they use input data, they may only reflect past sales. Ideally, they have predictive elements as well. Retailers, especially of chains, need to monitor adherence to planograms at the local level. Deviations or exceptions should be examined for factors which have not been incorporated in the planogram software system. More detailed merchandise spatial planning conveniently leads us to the next section, which deals with displays in particular and visual merchandising generally.

Visual merchandising

Visual merchandising includes window displays as well as wall, shelf and rack displays. It also includes the use of lighting, colour and signage. Visual merchandising is an important communication tool that can be used to enhance store image. It is designed to create a mood which excites and attracts the consumer. Some writers almost equate merchandising with visual merchandising (Banks 1993). However, the author sees the concept of merchandising as much broader than visual merchandising. Other writers – including the author – use the terms **visual merchandising** and **instore promotion** almost interchangeably. **Instore promotion** includes: signage, displays, samples, tastings, demonstrations, recipes, information sheets, store maps and guides, product packaging, brand names, aromas, trolley advertisements, and specials advertised over the store's public address system or on captive audience networks (CAN).

Historically, it seems that, at the start of the twentieth century in Australia:

> *...the main effort associated with store design had shifted from external cathedral architecture to the professional planning of interior store display and decoration...The showroom became bigger, lighter and more colourful. [For example]... Farmer (the department store) decorated its showroom in 1918 with large bowls of arum lilies and Iceland poppies, green carpets, rich mahogany fittings and walls lined with mirrors and glass.* (Reekie 1993, pp. 88-9)

The shift to better store display seems to have been faster for womenswear than for menswear:

> *Window displays of menswear were generally less appealing. Well into the 1920s, writers in the Draper complained that the design of menswear windows lagged behind women's fashion displays...Women's windows were more aesthetically arranged than men's.* (Reekie 1993, p.15)

Other writers support Reekie's views on gender differences in merchandise display. For example, in the 1930s:

> ...*very few of the goods menswear retailer Gowings sold were on display; the stock was away in drawers and customers had to ask to be shown the merchandise. Shopping was a leisurely affair in those days* ... (Gowing 1993, p. 42)

This low-key approach to display and visual merchandising was then threatened by increasing competition from Woolworths and Coles with their high volume, self-service distribution methods in the variety store categories (Gowing 1993). The historic trend of increasing emphasis to store display observed by Reekie and Gowing has continued over recent decades. Continuing competition and the rising cost of labour seems to have motivated many retailers to put less emphasis on personal selling and more emphasis on store design and instore promotions. This is especially the case in retail categories such as supermarkets, discount department stores and hardware where self-service has been favoured since the 1960s.

Window displays are one of the first opportunities for retailers to interact physically with potential customers. Research by the author indicates that window displays are particularly important as a retail marketing tool in Australia, on a par with Britain, and more so than in the United States. Window displays are a creative process, so it is not surprising that some display consultants have a theatrical background. One Sydney consultant interviewed was preparing windows for a 'retro clothing' – that is vintage clothing – retailer and said that she drew inspiration for her work from Noel Coward plays. And, a Melbourne theatre company has diversified their services into retail set productions for animated Christmas window displays.

Some retailers seem to set up their window displays from inside the store – only focusing on what the customer will see within the store. A quick look from the outside would reveal less than inviting backs of products or packaging. The retailers should try to 'stand in the shoes' of the customer by rehearsing the customer's approach to the outside of the store, and entering through the doorway. Next, the retailer 'imagineers' what the customer will see and experience as they enter into the shopping space. By taking the customer's perspective, the retailer can assess the potential impact of the store design – and especially the window displays.

For a practical guide to window display, see the checklist in Table 5.2 developed by Banks (1993). This is part of a great number of useful guides to visual merchandising included in Banks (1993).

The designs of entranceways and doors can influence consumer attitudes, and they form part of store infrastructure. **Interior displays** take over from window displays in developing the retailer's **visual merchandising** function. Such displays are more effective if the principles noted in Table 5.3 are used.

Table 5.2 Your window display checklist

- ☐ Do my windows convey my store image?
- ☐ Do my windows advertise the merchandise I sell?
- ☐ Have I used human interest in the displays?
- ☐ Do I suggest how articles displayed can be used?
- ☐ Are all prices marked clearly?
- ☐ Have I displayed related items together?
- ☐ Are seasonal goods displayed?
- ☐ Do I tie in with local events and needs?
- ☐ Have I grouped merchandise and not scattered it?
- ☐ Do I gather everything I need before starting?
- ☐ Have I used harmonious colour combinations?
- ☐ Do I expose merchandise that will fade or melt?
- ☐ Do I inspect all merchandise before setting up in the window?
- ☐ Are my displays changed frequently?
- ☐ Do I keep window interiors and exteriors clean at all times?
- ☐ Do I make the display sell merchandise?
- ☐ Do I check the lighting?
- ☐ Is the background suitable?
- ☐ Are the props suitable to the image and merchandise?
- ☐ Do I make the window the centre of my current scheme?

Source: Banks 1993, p. 26.

Before finalising store displays, study Table 5.3 carefully. A common need of most retailers is to use displays and other aspects of visual merchandising in ways that help to differentiate their store. The importance of the need for distinctiveness cannot be underestimated. Retailing is not simply about selling merchandise. Rather, it is selling a total shopping experience, only one part of which is the actual purchase of merchandise, and the store environment through store design can add significantly to that total shopping experience.

The store design *per se* has to communicate directly with the customer. Hence, the author has coined the expression **customer-merchandise interaction (CMI)**. This concept elevates the need for the retailer to configure store design carefully so that it enhances its communication role and meets store design objectives. CMI builds on merchandise (*Chapter 4 - Merchandising*), visual displays, information, signage and **allied concepts**.

The Ken Done stores illustrate the use of allied concepts by using colourful paintings which tone in with the product styles and colours. The stores at times also use displays of fish tanks with colourful fish to the same end.

Retailers can use **training** and other support systems to develop effective CMI. Some retailers provide their store managers with merchandising and display manuals to ensure that displays reflect the correct image. There seems to be an opportunity for retailers to develop more comprehensive policies and programs for CMI. These policies and programs could include not only current merchandising manuals, but also all other key aspects of the customer-merchandise interaction including staff activities in 'tying-up the advertisement', that is promotion, and staff involvement and training in all aspects of store design such as maintaining a clean, uncluttered, well-organised, safe and healthy store environment. The policies and programs should also clarify the relative roles of each party in the retailer-supplier interface. The desired level of support from consultants and suppliers should be specified, particularly in terms of: the supply of point of sale materials, the installation of displays, the objectives of displays, and the training of staff in product knowledge and merchandising techniques.

Table 5.3 Ten principles for good displays

1. The tone, texture and colours should suit the target market.
2. There should be consistency and coherence across displays, including window displays which reinforce the retailer's brand.
3. This consistency can be enhanced by the use of a common **theme**, which in turn should be consistent with any mass media or instore promotions.
4. The use of themes can add vitality as well as consistency to displays. These themes can be varied according to seasonal or festival periods or take on idiosyncratic lines which help to differentiate the retailer.
5. Colour and lighting are essential to an effective display. **Kinetic** effects, that is movement, can be achieved through actual movement or through the use of patterns and shapes.
6. A popular method of displaying stock is by the style and size of the merchandise, and sometimes by the colour of the merchandise.
7. **Signage** is very important and can assist in guiding consumers to the right areas. It can also enhance the image of the merchandise through visual impact and product knowledge. Signs can be vertically located, on shelves, in pamphlets or as tags.
8. **Ensemble displays**, where use-related items are displayed together, can add a lifestyle impact. Furniture shops such as Freedom, Oz Design and IKEA use this method to good effect, as do antique shops and department stores with tableware.
9. **Price lining**, where retailers arrange their merchandise into price segments, is another display device that facilitates customer interaction.
10. **Vertical displays** can also be used, partly to take advantage of space but also to give different images and perhaps break up an otherwise monotonous sight line.

How can a retailer make the **total shopping experience** more interesting and exciting? Samples and demonstrations – as do specials and competitions and other sales promotions – relate to this approach. Instore promotions, sales promotions and customer services can add various dimensions to the shopping offer and experience. Some retailers use the notion of building a market atmosphere into selected store front situations. The use of themes can be particularly important, as can the use of allied concepts such as the paintings and fish tanks in the Ken Done example. Lighting, colour, music and movement are also central factors. Some of the excitement comes about because of retailers triggering other senses such as smell, sight, sound or touch. A good example of a retailer making use of colour and lighting is the annual David Jones spring flower festivals, usually in flagship stores. For such displays, creative talents are called for, and retailers may need to engage consultants.

It would be remiss to think that only visual merchandising contributes to shopping excitement. In some cases it is the entire store design that contributes, as is evident in the Woolworths supermarket format. Some of these ideas have also been applied to toy retailing. The Kid 'n Action store in Pleasanton, California invites children to touch and play with the merchandise. The entire store is modelled after a small village, with extra wide aisles to accommodate strollers and random toy testers (Retail Design International 1991). The village concept, designed by Gensler and Associates, is akin to what is referred to as the store-within-a-store, boutique layout concept.

Store design for flagship stores

A **flagship store** is a retailer's leading store and demonstrates distinctive store design, a unique retail concept, and a differentiated retail brand. The store exemplifies the retail brand, and thus brings together the retail strategy and every element of the retail mix. Just as the flagship of a navy leads the fleet, so too does the flagship store lead the retailer's 'fleet' of outlets.

The idea of **flagship stores** is not new. Early entrepreneurial department store owners pioneered the concept of an outstanding store that became a statement about the firm itself. Enduring examples are Selfridges (1909) and Harrods in London, Macy's in New York, and David Jones 1927 in Sydney (Elizabeth Street).

The flagship store may be one of only a few outlets, and usually houses the firm's headquarters. An extension to the flagship concept is where the retailer has a 'flagship' store in the capital city of a state or province, and thus in any one country may have several flagship stores.

As the department stores dispersed to the malls in the past fifty years, some flagship stores diminished in grandeur as retailers invested little money in maintenance or makeovers. At that time, too, CBDs were experiencing downturns and intensifying competition, and rather than taking a lead to reverse the trend, CBD retailers seemed to focus on the malls.

 For example, see Wilcox & O'Callaghan 2001.

More recently, department store retailers have recognised the trends to urban renewal and the reintroduction of city living, and in response some are embarking on very significant makeovers of their flagship stores.

Myer, one of Australia's two major department store retailers, announced on 21 June 2007 that the firm was embarking on "a bold and inspiring vision for its iconic Bourke Street store ... Myer Melbourne is the flagship store of our company, and an icon in Melbourne". See Myer <www.myer.com.au> Media Releases.

However, in dramatic and tragic contrast, Myer's Hobart flagship store – in a building dating back to 1836 – was destroyed by fire in September 2007. The damage was such that the building had to be demolished.

Some specialist retailers, such as jewellers and designer fashion houses adopted the flagship format long ago. These retailers are typically upmarket and often iconic. They usually bring together their heritage and contemporary branding and innovation. For some like Tiffany, every store is arguably a flagship, because of store design, distinctiveness and scarcity (and value) of store locations.

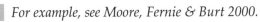

For example, see Moore, Fernie & Burt 2000.

It is mainly over the past decade that specialist retailers – many of whom are also manufacturers – have recognised the branding opportunities created by establishing distinctive flagship stores. Nike and Sony were two of the earlier venturers into flagship stores.

Apple has a significant flagship store in New York. A recent report suggests that Apple is planning its first southern hemisphere flagship store for Sydney, Australia. (See Moses, A. 2007, Revealed: Apple's Sydney Shopfront, Sydney Morning Herald, Oct. 11 (www.smh.com.au/new/technology).)

Generic store design issues

There are two generic store design issues that warrant some discussion here: **makeovers**, **refurbishments** and **new generation formats**; and **self-service formats**.

Makeovers, refurbishments and new generation formats

About every five to ten years, many stores undertake a major refit which they refer to variously as **refurbishment** or **new generation format**. For example, Kmart over the years has introduced various new generation formats based on such features as wider aisles, new sound and vision areas, scanning stations throughout the store for price checks complete with customer service telephones, Pixi Photo Studios instore, and at one time Holly's Café – an American-style diner.

The Fresh Food format introduced by Woolworths in 1986 is a good example of a major store redesign which particularly affects store layout and merchandise spatial planning, as well as affecting store infrastructure and visual merchandising. In terms of the underlying objectives of store design, the new Woolworths format particularly defined a new image and competitive position for the retailer, which included a fresh food emphasis and a more exciting visual presentation and interaction with the customer. The new format was also predicated on both stimulating store traffic – for example through a greater range of choice and more shopping excitement, and on contributing to convenience – for example through one-stop shopping, better identification of merchandise location and improved checkout facilities.

Note that it can take years before all existing stores are re-formatted. In all cases, it is important that the new format changes be properly communicated to staff who may require some training, including adaptations to selling techniques and updated buying skills and plans. Retailers must actively manage the implementation issues associated with refurbishments and new retail store formats.

The initial introduction of Big Fresh in Australia in 1992 was a major design change for Franklins, with other formats such as No Frills and Fresh continuing to co-exist. As with the Woolworths change, all four components of store design were affected. Similarly, the same objectives appeared to be driving the change, except that the more limited introduction of the Big Fresh format suggested that it had less of an impact on the central image and competitive position of Franklins. In New Zealand in 1995, the Big Fresh Format moved on to a second generation format. The new bakery section was redesigned so that the entire operation was carried out within sight of customers. There was new 'soft-cooling' equipment, which keeps produce in a fresh state overnight. The new format also included an expanded fish market with a self-selection whole fish cabinet and an extended delicatessen (Supermarketing 1995).

A **makeover** is much more than merely a new coat of paint or just a 'new and improved' store. The aim is to **reinvent** or **revitalise** the retail brand so that there is a sharper personality, image or theme. This is vital for success. With makeovers, the retailer needs to reassess the retail strategy and the desired retailer brand, review the target market, and then design the upgrade of the retail mix. Visual merchandising and promotion will be critical. However, there must be substance to the selection too, for example wider aisles and revamped store layout. The result should be a refreshed retail brand which delivers a new retail experience for customers – and indeed for staff and suppliers. The implementation of the planned makeover will likely require a project management approach to minimise disruptions.

A special example of the need for a makeover can occur in the situation where the retailer is a tenant in a planned shopping centre (mall). The property manager may decide on a makeover or rebranding of the entire centre, and require that tenants refurbish their shops accordingly. For some retailers this will be the stimulus they need to makeover their store. Conversely, , rather than comply, some retailers will chose to leave the centre,

(leasing arrangements permitting) if the proposed image is substantially inconsistent with their unique retailer brand.

Self-service formats

An increasing number of retail categories are using the **self-service** format. Common objectives of this format include: the reduction of labour costs and greater involvement of the consumer in the service encounter. Perhaps ironically, customers may get more satisfaction – in some cases – by doing some of the work themselves, such as at Sizzlers Restaurants. Perhaps it is a matter of the power and control that consumers gain over the process, although arguably they are co-opted into service roles such as collecting and packing goods in the supermarket context.

However, it is not enough for retailers to declare simply that the service is 'self-service'. It would be a mistake for retailers to interpret self-service as *no* service. Retailers using the self-service format need to design their stores and present their merchandise and information in ways that facilitate good customer service. Self-service needs to be managed by providing appropriate service delivery systems which assist the customer. How can retailers do this? Let's begin by looking at a few stores which have a best practice approach to the self-service format – namely IKEA, Toys 'R' Us, and the British chemist Boots – and then drawing some general conclusions.

IKEA, the furniture retailer, is a good example of the self-service format because it has developed user-friendly facilities for its customers including clear product information, signage, pencils and paper (to help draw up home floor plans), and easy logistics to move merchandise around the store and to the car.

Toys 'R' Us dominates the Australian toy retailing market with the new generation self-service format. This company essentially uses the grid system of layout – and uses it more effectively than most smaller toy retailers. There are numerous customer services, including scanners for customer use, information sheets and maps.

The written material at Toys 'R' Us is helpful given that the format differs from smaller competitors. The **packaging** of the products is also put to good use as instore promotion, reflecting the need for manufacturers to adapt to the retailer's needs in this respect.

This is a good example of where several retail mix components – in this case store design, instore promotion and merchandise selection – are strongly interconnected to help support the retailer's brand. The retailer must be proactive both in the merchandise assortment planning stage and in negotiations with suppliers to achieve this outcome successfully.

For larger items in some cases, customers take a ticket rather than the product to the checkout to pay for it, and then move to a collection point after payment. This arrangement has advantages to the retailer in terms of displaying and maintaining stocks, as well as minimising damage to stock. Some United Kingdom retailers, such as Argos, have made extensive use of this type of customer involvement. As with the other changes to the Australian toy retailing format, it is important that retailers educate consumers on how to make the best use of the new self-service format as well as ensure that staff training is consistent with the superstore format.

The British chemist Boots is worth examining as it applies a sophisticated self-service format to a retail category that has only had a relatively recent application of self-service. Some of the key features of the Boots approach to self-service include: a grid system, bright lighting, clear signage, lots of information sheets, and user-friendly flip-books which help identify and track health problems such as vitamin deficiency and their treatment. The packaging of certain products has also been redesigned to meet environmental objectives.

These examples all emphasise store layout, user-friendly customer-merchandise interaction, educative information sheets, consumer guide sheets to the store layout, good signage and product packaging redesigned for the new format (see Vignette 5.4).

Vignette 5.4

Integration and innovation in store design
'Self-service does not mean *no* service': The case of IKEA

IKEA offers a commendable case of innovative and well-integrated store design. Essentially a self-service homewares superstore with instore facilities including childminding and a restaurant, IKEA exemplifies the maxim that '*self-service does not mean no service*'. The author has developed this phrase as a rebuttal of what often occurs in practice where retailers, perhaps trying to cut costs, reduce the level of personal service, that is personal selling, and make no compensating adjustment in store design or promotion. A visit to IKEA will quickly reward the astute observer which an understanding of the spectrum of retail activities that can enhance customer self-service.

The façade of IKEA stores incorporates their signature colours of blue and yellow and these Swedish national colours reflect the firm's country of origin. Entrances to the store are clearly marked, convey a vibrant energy, and build a sense of expectation of what is to come upon entering the store. Extensive explicit signage helps the first time visitor, and aids such as pencils, shopping lists, tape measures and catalogues are available throughout the store, as are the signature yellow bags and trolleys for instore use.

The **infrastructure** is 'big box' and hence somewhat industrial, but this is managed with lightness so that the effect is energising and exciting rather than overwhelming. Many IKEA stores are multilevel, so vertical transport is important. Safety issues are an important consideration, especially when customers are moving trolleys loaded with purchases.

The **layout** of IKEA stores is very structured. McGoldrick (2002, p. 468) uses the term 'guided shopper flows' to describe the IKEA layout. Cleverly, the layout provides a comprehensive route through the entire store for the customer who is inclined to browse. However, for those more focused or more time-pressed, short cuts are clearly signposted so that any potential frustration can be forestalled.

Merchandise spatial planning is achieved in two ways. The merchandise is located in specific departments, for example sofas and bedding, and grouped in areas like the Market Place and Children's IKEA. The other method is through ensemble settings such as mock-ups of different sized apartments or homes, or dining areas, kitchens, offices and bedrooms – all displaying items for purchase that are 'in use'.

Visual displays in IKEA also incorporate many of the tactics discussed in this chapter. As well as ensemble displays, products are grouped in a variety of ways featuring common or contrasting colours and textures. A novel addition to the recently opened Logan store in Queensland is the mock-up of a hairdressing salon, suggesting that small businesses may well be able to furnish their outlets from IKEA. Most products have explanatory labels, and the displays show synergies between products which can assist customers with self-selection.

Overall, innovation in all the facets of store design coupled with strong attention to store organisation has delivered an excellent example of how – rather than ignoring customers' service needs – '*service*' can be put back into 'self-service'.

Store design and temporary retailing

The principles of store design apply to both permanent and temporary selling spaces. Temporary retailing occurs for many reasons. Retailers set up additional selling spaces for special events or seasonal selling.

Calendar Club has used seasonality and store design to create a unique retail offer. Starting with three stores in Australia, the business "operated 168 stores in 2006/2007". They usually operate the stores from October to January. In their own words, "Our

stores turn vacant areas into big seasonal money makers, and thanks to thoughtful design, fixtures, signage and store graphics, our stores have the appeal and credibility of permanent tenants. Yet our flexible configurations and store graphics packages – from kiosk to inline stores - can be implemented in a matter of days". See <www.calendarclub.com.au/companyprofile.html>.

Retailers create other temporary retailing outlets at festivals, fairs, and various shows (e.g. agricultural, rural, home shows). Such outlets are often extensions to their usual locations. In contrast, temporary retailing is associated, for example, with performance entertainment such as concerts, plays and special film events where merchandise such as T-shirts, DVDs and posters is offered for sale, which patrons are often keen to purchase as a means of 'tangiblising' their experience. At art galleries and museums, special exhibits often have associated additional selling spaces for catalogues, books, artefacts and memorabilia.

Other forms of temporary retailing include mobile retailing, movable kiosks and stalls, for example, set up in shopping malls on a short-term basis. Whatever the form, the principles of store design apply, so retailers using temporary retailing are well advised to treat this type of outlet seriously, as shown by the Calendar Club example above.

 ## Conclusions

Store design is an important area of retailing and has become more so over the past century. The store environment provides the retailer with a direct means of injecting convenience and excitement into the shopper's total shopping experience. To assist the retailer in making the best possible use of store design, the discussion in this chapter was divided into the four main components of store design, namely: store infrastructure, store layout, merchandise spatial planning and visual merchandising. Store design makes a fundamental contribution to the retailer's brand and must be supported by effective store organisation.

Although the four components of store design are linked through common design considerations – especially the link to store design objectives and retail strategy – and in obvious practical ways, retailers need to study each of them in detail and with reference to the vignettes chosen to indicate the better practices in these areas.

The four components have been integrated through the examination of some important generic formats, namely refurbishments or new generation formats and the almost ubiquitous self-service format, using best practice cases.

Throughout the chapter a number of new concepts have been introduced which readers can use to enhance their understanding of store design. The more important of these are:

- the four-tier method of looking at store design, that is the structure of the chapter;

- the CRTW concept of retail store traffic flow;

- highlighting the relevance of the boutique or shop-within-a-shop concept to supermarkets;

- the importance of integrating staff and customer needs into store design;

- the concept of customer-merchandise interaction (CMI);

- the need for policies and programs to support CMI;

- highlighting the relationships between store design and consumer behaviour, customer service, instore promotion, human resource management, security and risk management;

- developing the conceptual basis of two generic store design formats as a way of demonstrating the integration of the components of store design; and

- consideration of flagship stores and temporary retailing.

Despite the importance of store design, many retailers still fall well short of the best practice standards set by the case study examples. These cases should be studied by all retailers, as should the principles and concepts noted throughout the chapter. In many cases, retailers will need to draw on assistance from retail support services including construction companies, carpenters, lighting specialists, plumbers, fixtures suppliers, point of sale merchandisers and display consultants.

The achievement of best practice in store design is generally closely correlated with a retailer's understanding of the key concepts, having well-defined objectives and programs, and managing excellent alliances with retail support services providers.

Review and applications

1. Review the four components of store design. Are some components more important than others are? Explain your response.

2. Some retail texts and certain retailers refer to some retail space as a 'dead area'. What does this term mean? Why does this thinking detract from the retail service provided to the consumer?

3. Select a store that has strong co-ordination and coherence across the four components of store design. Indicate how that coordination is achieved.

4. Select a store that does not have strong coordination and coherence across the four components of store design. Indicate the aspects which the retailer has failed to coordinate.

5.   Why do you think visual merchandising has become more important over the past hundred years?

6.   Why is it that hardware stores and chemists have not used the grid store layout system as successfully as supermarkets?

7.   Discuss the relationship between store design, customer service, consumer behaviour, human resource management and risk management.

8.   Advise a small retailer on how to evaluate its store design.

9.   What is meant by the concept of customer-merchandise interaction (CMI)? How can retailers use this concept to improve their store design?

10. Select a particular retailer. How would you change their visual merchandising to make it more interesting and exciting, and to contribute more to store design objectives?

11. Explain why retailers must consider store design and merchandise selection together for effective development and implementation of the retailer's strategy. (See also *Chapter 4 - Merchandising*.)

12. 'Self-service does not mean *no* service.' Discuss the various means that retailers can use to assist customers in a self-service – or at least self-selection – environment.

13. Discuss why 'makeovers' are critical to rejuvenating retailer brands. Find examples of successful makeovers.

14. Retailers have a corporate social responsibility to reduce physical accessibility barriers to and around their stores. Explain how retailers can work to achieve this responsibility.

15. Develop a store design checklist to help retailers reduce the environmental impact of their store, and to contribute to suitability.

16. Discuss how retailers in older buildings can integrate heritage and modern features into their store designs. How can you relate this to retailer brand?

17. Explain what retailers should consider regarding staff needs when designing or redesigning a store.

18. Investigate security measures, occupational health and safety factors, and environmental hazards that retailers should manage within an effective store design.

Website references

Brazin: <www.bnt.com.au>.

Bunnings: <www.bunnings.com.au>.

Clive Peeters: <www.clivepeeters.com.au>.

Country Road: <www.countryroad.com.au>.

David Jones Ltd: <www.davidjones.com.au>.

Foodworks: <www.foodworks.com.au>.

Freedom: <www.freedom.com.au>.

IKEA: <www.ikea.com.au>.

Just Group: <www.justgroup.com.au>.

Karpati Corporation Pty Ltd: <www.karpati.com.au>.

OZ Design Furniture: <www.ozdesignfurniture.com.au>.

Sizzler: <www.sizzler.com.au>.

Toys 'R' Us: <www.toysrus.com.au>.

References

Australian Bureau of Statistics (ABS) 1993, *Retailing in Australia 1991-92*, Canberra, ABS Catalogue no. 8613.0.

Baker, J, Grewal, D & Parasuraman, A 1994, 'The Influence of Store Environment on Quality Inferences and Store Image', *Journal of Academy of Marketing Science*, vol. 22, no. 4, pp. 328-39.

Banks, K 1993, *Merchandising Guide For Australian Retailers*, Prosperity Press, Ashgrove, Queensland, PO Box 244, Ashgrove QLD 4060.

Burbury, R 1993, 'Little knowledge went a long way in lingerie', *Sydney Morning Herald*, 19 August.

Brunner, G 1990, 'Music, mood and marketing', *Journal of Marketing*, vol. 54, no. 4, October, pp. 94-104.

Dawson, S, Bloch, P & Ridgeway, M 1990, 'Shopping motives, emotional states, and retail outcomes', *Journal of Retailing*, vol. 66, no. 4, Winter, pp. 408-27.

Donovan, R, Rossiter, J, Marcoolyn, G & Nesdale, A 1994, 'Store atmosphere and purchasing behaviour', *Journal of Retailing*, vol. 70, no. 3, pp. 283-94.

Dunleavy, M 1995, 'Melbourne start to a new state of grace', the *Weekend Australian*, Property section, 12-13 August, p. 1.

Gowing, S 1993, *Gone To Gowings: A History of Gowing Bros.*, State Library of New South Wales Press, Sydney.

Greenland, S & McGoldrick, P 1994, 'Atmospherics, attitudes and behaviour: Modelling the impact of designed space', *International Review of Retail*, Distribution and Consumer Research, vol. 4, no. 1, pp. 1-15.

Hart, C 1994, *A Study Of Merchandise Assortment Strategies Within Major Multiple Retailers*, Paper presented to the Joint European Institute of Retailing and Services Studies (EIRASS) and Canadian Institute of Retailing and Services Studies (CIRASS) Conference, Recent Advances in Retailing and Services Science, Banff, Alberta, Canada, May.

Latchford, P 1992, *The Principles Of Successful Retailing*, The Business Library, Melbourne.

Larson, E 1994, 'Attention shoppers: You're being tailed', *Reader's Digest*, March, pp. 77-81.

McGoldrick, P 2002, *Retail Marketing*, McGraw-Hill, London.

Milliman, R 1982, 'Using background music to affect the behaviour of supermarket shoppers', *Journal of Marketing*, vol. 46, pp. 86-91.

Milliman, R 1986, 'The influence of back-ground music on the behaviour of restaurant patrons', *Journal of Consumer Research*, vol. 13, September, pp. 286-9.

Moore, C, Fernie, J & Burt, S 2000, 'Brands without boundaries: the internationalisation of the designer retailer's brand', *European Journal of Marketing*, vol. 34, no. 6, pp. 919-937.

Retail Design International 1991, 'Gensler Associates: The games people play', the Official Journal of the International Shopfitting Organisation based in Zurich, February/March, p. 29.

Reekie, G 1993, *Temptations: Sex, Selling and the Department Store*, Allen & Unwin, Sydney, Australia.

Shoebridge, N 1990, 'Daimaru looks beyond Australia's retailing woes', *Business Review Weekly*, 26 October, pp. 82-5.

Supermarketing 1995, 'Second Big Fresh refurbishment complete', a National Business Review Publication, 27 March, Auckland, pp. 1-2.

Swinyard, W 1993, 'The effects of mood, involvement, and quality of store experience on shopping intentions', *Journal of Consumer Research*, vol. 20, September, pp. 271-9.

Vinovich, G 1975, 'The communicative significance of musical affect in eliciting differential perceptions, cognition, and emotion in sound-motion media messages', unpublished doctoral dissertation, University of Southern California.

Ward, J & Eaton, J 1994, *Service Environments: The Effect of Quality and Decorative Style on Emotions, Expectations, and Attributions*, Paper presented to the Joint EIRASS and CIRASS conference, Recent Advances in Retailing and Services Science, Banff, Alberta, Canada, May.

Wheatley, J 1992, 'All over the shop', the *Australian Magazine*, 10-11 October, pp. 16-20.

Wilcox. M & O'Callaghan, E 2001, 'The strategic response of Dublin's traditional department store to intensifying competition', *Journal of Retailing and Consumer Services*, vol. 8, no. 4, pp. 213-225.

Advanced reading

Alexander, A 2006, 'Retailers study inner city', *Drug Store News*.

Baldwin, G 1998, 'Design effects of retail floor space in Hong Kong', *Academic Papers, Facilities*, vol. 16, no. 5/6, pp. 150-154.

Brown, R 2006, 'Best visual merchandising team: Barneys New York', *Display & Design Ideas*, vol. 18, no. 9, p. 60.

Carpenter, JM & Moore, M 2006, 'Consumer demographics, store attributes, and retail format choice in the US grocery market', *International Journal of Retail & Distribution Management*, vol. 34, no. 6, pp. 434-452.

Corsten, D & Gruen T 2003, 'Desperately seeking shelf availability: an examination of the extent, the causes, and the efforts to address retail out-of-stocks', *International Journal of Retail & Distribution Management*, vol. 31, no. 12, pp. 605-607.

de Moerloose, C Antioco, M, Lindgreen, A & Palmer, P 2005, 'Information kiosks: the case of the Belgian retail sector', *International Journal of Retail & Distribution Management*, vol. 33, no. 6, pp. 472-490.

Ericson, M 2006, 'Exploring the future exploiting the past', *Journal of Management History,* vol. 12, no. 2, pp. 121-136.

Hu, H & Jasper, CR 2006, 'Social cues in the store environment and their impact on store image', *International Journal of Retail & Distribution Management*, vol. 34, no. 1, pp. 25-48.

Jeacle, I 2004, 'Emporium of glamour and sanctum of scientific management', *Journal of Management History*, vol. 42, no. 9, pp. 1162-1177.

Jones, K & Doucet, M 2000, 'Big-box retailing and the urban retail structure: the case of the Toronto area', *Journal of Retail and Consumer Services*, no. 7, pp. 233-247.

Joyce, ML & Lambert DR 1996, 'Memories of the way stores were and retail store image', *International Journal of Retail & Distribution Management*, vol. 24, no. 1, pp. 24-33.

Kaufman-Scarborough, C 1999, 'Reasonable Access for Mobility-Disabled Persons is More Than Widening the Door', *Journal of Retailing*, vol. 75, no. 4, pp. 479-508.

Kent, T 2003, '2D23D: Management and design perspectives on retail branding', *International Journal of Retail & Distribution Management,* vol. 31, no. 3, pp. 131-142.

Ko, E & Kincade, DH 1997, 'The impact of quick response technologies on retail store attributes', *International Journal of Retail & Distribution Management*, vol. 25, no. 2, pp. 90-98.

Kozinets, RV, Sherry, JF, DeBerry-Spence, B, Duhacheck, A, Nuttavuthisit, K & Storm, D 2002, 'Themed flagship brand stores in the new millennium: theory, practice, prospects', *Journal of Retailing*, vol. 78, pp. 17-29.

Laing, A & Royle, J 2006, 'Marketing and the bookselling brand', *International Journal of Retail & Distribution Management*, vol. 34, no. 3, pp. 198-211.

Lea-Greenwood, G 1998, 'Visual merchandising: a neglected area in UK fashion marketing?', *International Journal of Retail & Distribution Management*, vol. 26, no. 8, pp. 324-329.

Li, J, Wang, Y & Cassill, NL 2004, 'A comparative study on new retailing outlets in the Shanghai apparel market', *Journal of Fashion Marketing and Management*, vol. 8, no. 2, pp. 166-175.

Merrilees, B & Miller, D 2001, 'Superstore interactivity: a new self-service paradigm of retail service?', *International Journal of Retail & Distribution Management,* vol. 29, no. 8, pp. 379-389.

Nogales, AF & Suarez, MG 2005, 'Shelf space management of private labels: a case study in Spanish retailing', *Journal of Retailing and Consumer Services*, vol. 12, pp. 205-216.

Richardson P, Jain, AK & Dick, A 1996, 'The influence of store aesthetics on evaluation of private label brands', *Journal of Product & Brand Management*, vol. 5, no. 1, pp. 19-28.

Serpkenci, RR & Tigert, DJ 2006, 'Wal-Mart's new normal is here: is everyone ready to accept the future', *International Journal of Retail & Distribution Management,* vol. 34, no. 1, pp. 85-100.

Stanton, JL & Herbst, KC 2006, 'Slotting allowances: short-term gains and long-term negative effects on retailers and consumers', *International Journal of Retail & Distribution Management,* vol. 34, no. 3, pp. 187-197.

Wong, CY & Johansen, J 2006, 'Making JIT retail a success: the coordination journey', *International Journal of Physical Distribution & Logistics Management*, vol. 36, no. 2, pp. 112-126.

Vazquez, D & Bruce, M 2002, 'Design management – the unexplored retail marketing competence', *International Journal of Retail & Distribution Management*, vol. 30, no. 4, pp. 202-210.

Vazquez, D & Bruce, M 2002, 'Exploring the retail design management process within the UK food retailer', *The International Review of Retail, Distribution and Consumer Research,* vol. 12, no. 4, pp. 437-448.

Vonderschmidt, G 2002, 'Planning User-Friendly Layouts', *Chain Store Age.*

Location

Introduction

'New Store … Opening Soon'. Advertisements such as this send a dramatic signal to potential customers, and often create immense curiosity and expectations of opening specials. Some openings are more dramatic than others. At a personal level, when calmly walking past a soon-to-be-opened shoe retailer in the West Edmonton Mall in Canada, North America's – and at one time the world's – largest indoor shopping mall, the owner besieged the author with gifts of jumpers bearing the store's name and an invitation to the opening the next day. It is not unusual for owners to create as much colour and excitement as possible when opening a new store. At a broader level, Anaconda opening on the Gold Coast or a new IKEA superstore opening in Logan (in 2006), or an entire planned shopping centre such as Westfield Helensvale (in 2005) can be front page news, whereas lesser stores may have to be content with simple advertisements or even letterbox drops. A new store opening is simply the end point of a complex process which is explained later in this chapter. Why did the retailer move into this particular region? Why did they choose this particular site? What were their objectives?

Location decisions correspond to the **distribution** component of the marketing mix, and are instrumental in **facilitating exchange** between storefront retailers and consumers. As with marketing distribution, location decisions are considered an important *long-term commitment* and are not easily reversed. Therefore, they need to be carefully addressed at an early stage in retail planning.

Most textbooks go further and argue that location is the most important retail mix component, leading to the adage 'location, location, location' – in other words, location is so important that it is the first, second and third most important retail decision. While agreeing that location is vitally important to retailers, the author would rather argue that location is one of a group of three key retail mix components which are of special significance. In terms of cost, the three most important components are first the **merchandise**, second the **labour**, and third the **property** – either through depreciation or leasing it. Strategically, location will vary across retail categories and across firms within each retail category.

A study of Australian clothing retailers by Merrilees and Miller (1994) found that location was rated as the third most important retail mix component behind customer service and quality merchandise.

Thus, it makes more sense to group location as one of the three key retail mix components without claiming more than that. Additionally, non-store retail formats such as direct marketing have less relevance for locational decisions, although tools such as trading area analysis can still be useful for these formats as well.

This chapter explores the possible objectives which underpin location decisions. It then explains the four basic location decisions of **regional choice**, **trading area analysis**, **macro site decisions** and **micro site decisions**. The first of these includes the choice of which countries, states, regions or cities to operate in. The second location decision is an analysis of geographic demand around various sub-city areas. The third location decision is the choice of a central business district (CBD), shopping centre or free-standing site – a decision allied to the second location decision. The fourth location decision is a more detailed specification of which exact site a retailer should occupy within a given shopping area.

Up to this point, the explanations of the four basic location decisions are conventional and assume that the location decision is essentially the free choice of the retailer – subject to the usual government regulations such as zoning. However, in practice the world is more complex. Simultaneously with retailers searching for suitable sites, there is a powerful group of developers and property managers who are seeking out suitable retailers. Not all retailers are welcome into the fiefdom of planned shopping centres (shopping malls) and other shopping areas, so access may become difficult if not impossible. This constraint has long been acknowledged as a problem for Australian and New Zealand retailers seeking to set up stores in Japan and Europe.

However, there can also be major constraints on some retailers even within their own countries. This situation leads to a departure from traditional retailing texts and to the proposition that the location decision is essentially an *interactive* one between retailers on one hand and property developers and property managers on the other hand. The model is presented in Figure 6.2 later in the chapter and illustrates what the author calls the **interactive model of location choice (IMLC)**. At this point, the reader should bear in mind that location is not necessarily the free choice of the retailer. A desire to establish a new business in a particular location – especially where the retailer will be a tenant – is insufficient. The retailer will need to build a convincing business proposition to present to the owner or property manager. Conversely, planned shopping centre developers, owners or property managers may not necessarily be able to attract the retailers they desire as tenants. The implications of the model are that there is some uncertainty about access to sites, an issue that is particularly pertinent for small independent retailers.

Objectives of location decisions

It is general practice to present location principles as if the retailer is seeking new premises in an area not previously adopted by the retailer. However, the same principles apply to **takeover decisions**.

An existing store may be purchased as a going concern or be rebadged to reflect the new owner's retailer brand.

In such a case, the attractiveness or otherwise of the existing retail site which may be taken over is the relevant focus. Similarly, the same principles apply in terms of renewal of leases - the decision to stay or leave an existing site is the relevant focus. For that matter, retailers may review their **location portfolio** profile at any time, leading to some sites being closed and others opened. The same location principles apply to these cases. Indeed, in some retail categories – such as petrol stations, hotels and banks – the strategy has been to rationalise numbers. Therefore, as Clarke (1995) notes, in these circumstances there is more emphasis on **relocation**, **refit/extension** or **closure** rather than on new acquisitions.

Generate traffic

Location is important not for its own sake but because it contributes to the overall retail strategy. Often the location objectives are expressed in simple terms because the overall retail objectives are simple.

A common location objective is to generate traffic.

In these cases, sites are chosen on the basis of the volume of passing trade on the assumption that a certain percentage of it will become shoppers and lead to dollar sales. This approach explains the popularity of many shopping centres in the CBD areas of Sydney, Melbourne, Brisbane, Perth, Adelaide, Hobart and Auckland as prime site choices for many retailers. Sometimes the expression 'passing traffic' is literally used as a basis for **strip shopping** or **ribbon shopping**, including fast food outlets, retail petrol stations and convenience stores. Note that many scholars inadvertently simplify the retailer's location objective by equating it with population. Estimates of population are at best a proxy for expected demand. Retailers do not want population *per se*, rather they want **store traffic**. It may often be the case that areas of greater population help generate greater store traffic, although central business districts (CBDs) – known in some countries as downtown – may be one of several exceptions to this rule unless population is defined by employment rather than residence, or as a combination of the two. Another exception is the CBDs that have experienced urban regeneration with the reintroduction of extensive residential developments that are often aimed at urban professionals. In some of these high-rise city developments, we are seeing the introduction of a new phenomenon – the **micro mall** – which is a collection of retail and service outlets aimed at a specific and often localised market.

Contribute to overall retailer image

Although site evaluations can be based on expected retail traffic, another important objective of location is its ability to contribute to the overall brand image of the retailer. Retailers with an upmarket, high status image should be looking for locations which match this image such as Double Bay in Sydney, South Yarra in Melbourne, or Parnell in Auckland. Retailers with a discount position in the market are more likely to look for low rent, less prestigious sites but which nonetheless are high traffic areas. Still other retailers may be positioned as 'alternative lifestyle' and be attracted to areas like Glebe in Sydney. Brand image is an important criterion in location decisions.

What these examples indicate is a fundamental tenet in retailing – namely, that most shopping areas tend to be somewhat internally homogeneous in terms of the style and image of the retailers. 'Like' seems to group with 'like', a tendency which is sometimes controlled directly by the shopping centre itself, or sometimes controlled indirectly by the level of rents payable. It is fairly difficult to go against these trends, for example, by being an upmarket restaurant in a less affluent suburb. Nor does it make sense to do so. On the other hand, the strong sense of identity of most shopping areas – whether they are planned shopping centres or concentrations of retailers in individual premises – facilitates the choice as to whether it is a suitable site for a particular retailer.

Contribute to overall convenience of shopping

A third major objective of location is that it has to contribute to the convenience of shopping. Convenience is critical for certain retail categories, including convenience stores such as petrol stations and fast food outlets. However, convenience is of at least some importance to most retail categories and will be influenced by the specific configuration of the site.

What may appear to be a good site could be inappropriate if it is difficult to enter or requires crossing a busy divided highway.

The objective of convenience will be less important to shops catering to either shopping goods or to specialty goods as consumers of those goods are prepared to travel further. Yet even for these retailers there are other important locational considerations, such as whether to locate in a freestanding site or with other similar retailers in a bulk goods specialty shopping centre. Convenience also requires consideration of the *appropriateness* and not simply the *nearness* of a site.

A duty free shop is usually associated with either an airport or a downtown CBD location.

In summary, the three main objectives of location are:

- to generate traffic;
- to enhance the overall image of the retailer; and
- to contribute to the convenience of shopping.

Drawing power and anchor stores

The combination of these three objectives leads to the concept of **drawing power**, that is, the strength of a location site to draw appropriate traffic to an area. The drawing power varies by area, but there is scope for quality retailers – particularly **anchor stores** such as major supermarkets, department stores, discount department stores and category killers/superstores – to enhance existing drawing power. As well as meeting these three objectives, the location decision needs to be coordinated with all other aspects of the retail mix. For instance, it has been argued that choosing a good location may save the retailer some of the expense of spending promotional dollars to attract customers to the store. This pattern is borne out in a study of Australian shoe retailers by Fam & Merrilees (1996). Its effect can be factored into the location decision.

Operationalising location objectives

In practical terms, the full set of location objectives could be met in the following way. First, a short-list of *possible* sites could be drawn up based on the **image and convenience criteria**. In any city there will be only a limited number of sites which clearly meet these criteria. Second, from this short-list the retailer could choose a location based on **economic criteria**, including:

- potential store traffic;
- leasing costs;
- the potential savings on promotional expenditures;
- access to quality suppliers; and
- the availability of adequately trained staff.

Location analysis 1: Regional location decisions

How does a retailer choose which country, state or city to operate in? Davies (1995) identified that many analyses are superficial. Retailing has been a relatively parochial industry, with most retailers being homespun within the particular country. International entry – other than retail petrol stations – has been fairly limited until recently. Some major retailers have even questioned whether retailing is appropriate for international replication. Nonetheless, major retailers overseas – including K-mart (USA), Toys 'R' Us and The Body Shop as well as certain franchisors such as McDonalds and Pizza Hut – have accelerated the pace of multinational activity.

Australian and New Zealand retailers have been slower, other than for the trans-Tasman migration of store formats, for example Foodland New Zealand planning to operate Freedom stores on a franchised basis. New Zealand retailers moving into Australia include Michael Hill (Hill 1994) and Hallensteins (see the Michael Hill and Hallensteins websites). Interestingly, Michael Hill has also opened in various Canadian cities. In terms of Australian retailers operating in other countries, some of the few exceptions include Country Road and Nutrimetics (now part of the Tupperware Brands Corporation – see the Country Road and Nutrimetics websites). In addition, a growing number of Australian-based **franchisors** – including Barbeques Galore, Snap Printing, Eagle Boys pizza, Lenards Poultry and Donut King – have extended operations to other countries. In general, it is important for retailers to check the culture, shopping habits and government restrictions as well as economic data such as income levels for each country being considered in order to validate whether a particular retail format is appropriate for that country. Market research would be extremely useful for this type of decision. A study by Fam and Merrilees (1995) shows that Hong Kong and Australian retailers share many – though not all – of the same perceptions about clothing retailing promotion tools.

Within a country, the choice of which state to operate in seems to be a sequential process, with most retailers starting in their home state and then branching out to nearby states gradually over time. The sports superstore chain Rebel Sport adopted this approach by locating its first stores in New South Wales and Victoria, with the company exhausting this potential before moving into other states (except Tasmania) and the territories (see the Rebel Sport website). ALDI followed a similar pattern by developing a major distribution centre in western Sydney and then opening Sydney suburban stores before launching interstate. In other words, logistic convenience seems to be a major consideration. Interestingly, the first Rebel Sport superstore was in Bankstown and the first ALDI was adjacent in Yagoona – both in suburban Sydney. Most retailers will pilot their new retail offering before expanding. This approach highlights the importance of a well-developed distribution system and well-developed links to both manufacturers and wholesalers. In the Australian case, there are only relatively minor differences in per capita income across states, so this does not represent a major consideration.

Within an Australian state, there are only a limited number of cities with a population of 70,000 or more. High volume category killers such as Toys 'R' Us have appropriately concentrated initially on the capital cities in Australia before they expanded into the larger country cities. It would be interesting to speculate the smallest size city that could support a category killer or superstore format (Merrilees & Miller 1997).

When comparing cities, the most useful sources of data are official government statistics. The Australian Bureau of Statistics (ABS) and Statistics New Zealand are the central agencies concerned. The Australian Census is particularly useful for generating a wide range of demographic data about each city – or even each suburb – including total population, gender and age breakdown, household income, and number and ages of children. Similar data is produced regularly by Statistics New Zealand.

Different retailers, such as the toy category and the retirement village category, will be interested in different demographic segments. There are now a number of specialist companies that use sophisticated software packages to generate maps which shade in areas of greatest potential demand – subject to the location criteria that a retailer specifies. The location criteria, for example, for a fast food outlet may be those areas with a high concentration of two income households with one or more children under the age of 16.

Retailers can draw on the services of geographic information specialists such as Maplnfo and Apasco, as well as the ABS itself which use sophisticated mapping programs based on census statistics. The former State Bank of NSW linked their internal customer databases with demographic databases developed by these geographic information specialists. The bank had previously assumed that customers who lived near a branch would do most of their business there. According to the demographic mapping, hardly any of them did (Hogan 1994). The **demographic mapping technique** was used as the basis of rationalising the branch network.

It should be kept in mind that the minimum size city for any retailer will be determined not just by market demand considerations but also by labour force considerations. This means the retailer must assess the availability of a pool of people either who have suitable skills and experience or who can acquire the necessary skills with training. Larger retailers are labour-intensive operations and may need several hundred employees to operate a store across several shifts. Retailers therefore need to investigate whether the labour is available at the times required in the proposed area.

This problem may be less severe when there is a high rate of unemployment.

Another consideration in choosing across cities is the extent of competition. Cities with less competition will generally be more attractive, and this underpins the initial success of America's largest retailer – Wal-Mart. Wal-Mart (see the Wal-Mart website) initially focused on middle-sized American cities where there was only room for one major firm - theirs! As the company became larger, it became necessary to expand into larger cities. In general, retailers should assess the extent of competition across cities before choosing a city. This stipulation is less applicable for the major chains such as Woolworths, Coles and Katies, which – by necessity – are likely to be present in all medium-sized and major cities regardless of competition. Indeed, they would see themselves as leading the competition. Extensive retail chains such as these are already in most existing shopping areas, and their location priority is to be well placed for future shopping areas. As for smaller chains and independent retailers, one should not presume that they will try to avoid competition. Some of these retailers rely on customers undertaking **comparison shopping,** and therefore the retailers actually *prefer* to be located close to competitors – for example furniture and homewares shops at Bennetts Green in Newcastle, or in Bundall on the Gold Coast.

Location analysis 2: Trading area analysis

A **trading area** is a subset of a city. It is defined as a geographic area of customers or potential customers centred on a particular shopping area or retailer. This area is often divided into three **zones**, as shown in Figure 6.1. The **primary zone** is where the majority of customers – for example 60 to 70 per cent – come from, using the shopping area or retailer as the centre. The next geographic outer layer is referred to as the **secondary zone**, and may comprise another 20 per cent of customers. The remaining customers are said to be in the **tertiary zone**.

Figure 6.1 Three indicative trading area zones

It is very important to note that, in practice, trading areas are not always the simple shape of concentric circles as indicated by Figure 6.1. Natural and manufactured barriers can sometimes force more elongated shapes for the trade area.

The Jewellstown Plaza shopping centre in Newcastle is bounded by the coast, a national highway and wetlands. And, this definition has become more pronounced as other shopping centres have located on the other side of the highway.

The size of the trading area is likely to vary depending on the natural and manufactured barriers noted above as well as on the type of store. Convenience retail categories such as supermarkets and newsagents are likely to have a small, well-defined trading area. More exclusive retail categories such as department stores, superstores or exclusive car dealers are likely to have a large trading area.

The critical size of a trading area may change over time. Wendy's, the soft-serve ice cream franchise, initially believed that each store had to be supported by a 30,000 population. In the late 1980s, the retailer changed that belief and started locating outlets in more remote areas that drew on smaller populations. This new assessment worked successfully and facilitated planning for a six year doubling in the number of outlets by the mid 1990s (Stirling 1988). McDonalds also adapted to small area locations by launching a new format – McDonalds Express – which is also relevant for their McCafe format, first introduced in Swanston Street Melbourne in 1996.

Trading areas can be analysed using the ABS data described above. Most shopping centres commission market research studies to more precisely define their trading areas. This can be done on the basis of ABS data, but may only pick upon those people *living* in the area and not necessarily those who just *shop* in the area. A simpler and more accurate method is to identify the area codes of customers who enter competitions – or perhaps using more elaborate telephone surveys of households in surrounding suburbs – until a clear pattern emerges. These methods are indicative of what Applebaum (1966) calls 'customer spotting'. A simple example of the application of this method relates to the Pen Shop operating in Sydney and Melbourne. The proprietor, Mr Charles Wolf, simply counted people traffic in potential sites as the key basis for selected new sites. He stood on street corners and counted people. Although Mr Wolf's third Sydney outlet in O'Connell Street was in the 'shopless' end of town, it was nonetheless in the corporate heart of the CBD. In other words, it was a good location to find customers "who might want to hand their clients a nice pen to sign a $50,000 contract" (Robertson 1995). The O'Connell Street site is now the flagship store supported by online sales (see The Pen Shop of Sydney website).

Apart from collecting information on trading areas, retailers operating across multiple sites can use a number of models to help them select the ideal location. The basic rationale is to identify those sites which are doing well in terms of sales or some other measure of business performance, and then to indicate the characteristics of successful sites. One such model is referred to as the **analogue approach.** Desirable future sites are analogous to existing successful sites. There should be broad comparability between the two sites in terms of target markets, merchandise mix and range, store size and other retail mix characteristics. For example, the most successful retail petrol stations may be best positioned at strategic points along commuter routes. If confirmed, this can help petrol companies rationalise the number of outlets.

However, the formulae would need to be changed in areas like the Australian Capital Territory (ACT) because planning restrictions prevent commercial locations along commuter routes. Or, as an actual example of a retailer using the analogue method, consider the opening of Red Rooster's Waratah Newcastle store in December 1994. The store manager, Mr Simon Coutts-Smith, said that "the site had been chosen on the basis of demographic studies, which showed that it offered potential in many ways better than that enjoyed by a Red Rooster store in Penrith in the heart of Sydney's western suburbs" (Red Rooster 1994).

Statistical techniques such as **multiple regression** can be used to help identify the characteristics of successful sites provided the retailer has a reasonable number of sites – for example 30 to 35 or more – to validate the technique. This method involves regressing, for example, sales per site against a number of possible determinants of successful location such as population density, traffic flow and per capita income of the area. The extra advantage of this method compared to the pure analogue approach described above is that the differential impact of alternative determinants can be evaluated. For instance, it may be that traffic flow is more important than per capita income and this information can be factored into the location decision.

Another group of models are the **gravity models** which attempt to explain the probability that a customer living in a specific area will shop at a particular shopping area. One of the better known models was developed by Huff (1964) who suggested that the probability of an individual from area 'i' shopping at another area 'j':

- is greater if the size of the shopping centre 'j' is larger than the centre at 'i';

- is greater if travel time is less;

- depends on the type of shopping trip; and

- is more likely if the merchandise sought are shopping goods and specialty rather than convenience and preference goods.

Huff's model is very plausible. First, the larger shopping centres are generally preferred by shoppers because they offer a wider range and assortment of goods. Additionally, larger shopping centres have been adding elements of entertainment and excitement to the shopping experience. Second, although larger shopping centres offer additional benefits, travel time needs to be considered. If the larger, more exciting shopping centre is too far away, consumers may prefer the local shopping centre. Third, the nature of the shopping trip needs to be considered. Much shopping can be thought of as regular events, with closeness and convenience being major considerations.

However if a special, irregular shopping trip is planned – to Melbourne, to the Gold Coast, to Hong Kong, or with an organised bus tour to factory outlets – then the extra distance is not a problem and may even enhance the excitement of the trip. Fourth, the type of merchandise sought can influence the willingness to travel. Consumers are willing to travel further for shopping and specialty goods than for convenience and preference goods. Convenience stores therefore need to be located along commuter routes or near population centres while bulk goods retailers can be more remotely located.

A special application of Huff's model relates to outshopping behaviour. **Outshopping** is defined as people travelling in order to shop *away* from their closest shopping centre or town in another shopping centre or town. An Australian study of outshopping between two rural towns by Jarratt and Polonsky (1993) identified the main characteristics of outshoppers. They found that outshoppers tend to be socially interactive, tend to be innovative in terms of their retail purchases, tend to have one or two children living at home, and tend to use radio as an information source for shopping. Outshoppers seek both variety of merchandise and shopping excitement. These findings can be used by any shopping centre to prevent a loss to outshopping or to attract outshoppers from other areas.

Another method is to compare the actual mix of retail categories in a particular area against a norm such as the state or national pattern. This may lead to the conclusion that a particular city or suburb is over-shopped in certain retail categories, for example supermarkets, and under-shopped in other retail categories, for example butcher shops. The method is useful for compiling an initial picture of the current pattern of shopping and hence the potential for new sites. However, caution is needed. One problem with the mix method is that the norms may need to be adjusted for factors such as per capita income. It is possible that, after adjustment, the extent of over- and under-shopping may be less than first thought. Another problem is that there may be sound reasons why these patterns occur. In our above hypothetical example, the suburb under review could be leading the way in preferring to buy meat at a supermarket rather than a butcher shop. Therefore, while *appearing* to be under-shopped in the butcher shop category, this suburb may be a particularly bad choice for a new butcher shop site.

There are many benefits to the planned shopping centres (malls) in knowing their trading areas. The information could clarify the impact of competition from nearby shopping centres. Additionally, the information is useful for targeting promotional media more cost effectively.

The Jewellstown shopping centre mentioned above only advertises in the East Lake side distribution of a local weekly newspaper because virtually none of the people in its trading area live on the West Lake side. This specification enables the shopping centre to get a reduced advertising rate.

Location analysis 3: Macro site analysis

By **macro site decisions** we mean the choice between the CBD, various types of shopping centres, or freestanding locations in a given city. Each type of macro location area has different essential features which contribute to the desired site decision.

The **central business district (CBD)** is often the **hub** of big cities due to the presence of civic buildings, financial and commercial headquarters, transport interchanges, historical buildings and major department stores. A number of CBDs suffered from intense competition from suburban planned shopping centres over the 1965-1985 period. However, most CBDs have since countered this competition. For example, Brisbane's City Heart Association was reconstituted in the early 1980s, giving it access to relevant rate levies. This helped fund a number of initiatives including the Queen Street Mall in 1982 and related promotions. This momentum has continued, reinforced by the Commonwealth Games in 1982, Expo in 1988, new hotels, and a new convention centre followed by the opening of the casino, the extensive redevelopment of the adjacent Southbank precinct, and the opening of new shopping centres within the CBD including Macarthur Central and Queens Plaza. Melbourne CBD has also thrived with the development of Federation Square, though it has had less competition from regional shopping centres which are less prevalent in Victoria. The Newcastle CBD has some similarities with a number of other CBD refurbishments, including improved physical infrastructure such as malls, more emphasis on leisure and entertainment as a means of differentiating the CBD from regional shopping centres, and the use of plazas as a means of creating self-contained segments – like mini-CBDs – within the CBD. The mall and plaza approach is particularly evident in the Sydney CBD as well.

Notwithstanding the efforts of various groups to vitalise CBD areas, much of the retail growth in the past two decades or so has been in shopping centres, particularly the **large regional shopping centre**. Note that regional shopping centres include major centres within metropolitan areas and not simply country areas. The Shopping Centre Council of Australia website indicates that there are 1338 shopping centres in Australia, although this may be a conservative estimate. Dominant groups such as Westfield, LendLease, Centro or Stockland generally develop the major planned shopping centres (see their respective websites). The concept proves to be very popular with retailers, with vacancy rates very low at about 1 per cent.

The original Australian regional enclosed shopping centres were Top Ryde in Sydney and Chermside in Brisbane – both in 1957 – followed by Chadstone in Melbourne in 1960 and other major centres such as Roselands Shopping Centre in suburban Sydney in 1965. The basic concept of an Australian regional shopping centre is that it comprises a major supermarket and discount department store, a large number of specialty shops, often a department store, and vast dedicated parking areas. In contrast, such shopping centres in Canada and the USA do not have supermarkets as these are more likely to be in stand alone premises or in a small open mall which may have two or more supermarkets.

In addition to regional shopping centres, most major cities also have several **community shopping centres** and an even larger number of **neighbourhood shopping centres.** Community shopping centres such as the Arndale shopping centre at Springwood Brisbane are unlikely to include a department store but may include a discount department store, a major supermarket and 20 to 30 specialty stores. The Arndale shopping centre is anchored by Coles and Franklins supermarkets and has 30 specialty stores. The Cabramatta Mall in Sydney reflects its local socio-demographic character by including an Asian supermarket and 24 specialty shops. Neighbourhood shopping centres are smaller than community shopping centres and generally have a supermarket – though not necessarily a major chain – and about ten specialty stores. The Civic Parade, Altona in Melbourne's western suburbs has just seven ground level shops.

The main differences between regional, community and neighbourhood shopping centres are the overall **scale** and **size** of the trading area. The sheer scale of regional shopping centres provides scope for **support retailers** who provide food, drink, coffee and entertainment for hungry and tired shoppers. Regional shopping centres have a higher status and more shopping excitement than either community or neighbourhood shopping centres. In particular, they will be preferred by national chains of specialty clothing, shoes and accessory stores. Moreover, retailers requiring a large trading area are more likely to prefer a regional to a community or neighbourhood shopping centre. Additionally, if a retailer were in a shopping good category, for example fashion goods, they would also prefer to be in a regional shopping centre.

Australian shopping centre trends seem to be following North American trends in that competition between shopping centres is increasing and shopping centres are looking for ways of differentiating their shopping centre offer. Entertainment and leisure activities are key ways of doing this. Examples of shopping centres which have given more prominence to these methods include Brisbane's suburban Grand Plaza and Westfield's Tuggerah centre on the Central Coast of New South Wales. However, Australian shopping centres have not yet gone as far as the West Edmonton Mall in Alberta Canada which includes an underwater submarine ride and an artificial wave pool as attractions.

An alternative approach to differentiating planned shopping centres is to specialise in the type of merchandise offered. This is self-evident with resort-based shopping centres (see Parker 1994) and airport shopping centres (see Dodd 1994). Two other major ways of differentiating shopping centres are factory outlet centres and power centres (see below).

Factory outlet stores have become more common in Australia and can be seen in most major cities, with a large number in retailing strips in Redfern in Sydney and Richmond in Melbourne. However, until recently it was comparatively rare to have a shopping centre dedicated to factory outlet stores in Australia. The first such centre was Birkenhead Point in Sydney. Recent entrants to this niche include the Harbour Town Shopping Centres in Perth, Adelaide and Gold Coast, and the DFO (Direct Factory Outlets) centres whose locations include Homebush NSW, Brisbane Airport, and Melbourne (see the Harbour Town and DFO websites). Note that it is important for stores such as David Jones to distance the siting of their discount outlets, for example David Jones Warehouse, from their full-price outlets, otherwise their entire market positioning strategy could be jeopardised. This locational condition is likely to be prominent in the minds of those designing and locating factory outlet centres. Although they have begun slowly, factory outlet centres are expected to become more numerous in Australia over time.

Power centres are specialised shopping centres which almost exclusively focus on superstore outlets of major chains as tenants. Moore Park in Sydney was one of the first such centres in Australia and includes Toys 'R' Us, Harvey Norman Computers, Freedom Furniture, Capt'n Snooze and Sleeping Giant. Other power centres opened at Tuggerah on the Central Coast of New South Wales and Glendale near Newcastle. Again, Australia has begun slowly compared to the North American experience, but the growth of power centres is likely to accelerate.

Locating in factory outlet centres or power centres is only relevant to certain types of retailers, namely those with manufacturing or designer connections or those using a superstore format. If a retailer possesses one or other of these characteristics, they still need to decide whether to locate in such a specialised shopping centre compared to some other shopping area. Retail chains will most likely decide to have a portfolio of locations, including some presence in these specialised shopping centres. The specialised shopping centres are likely to provide a critical mass of 'value conscious' buyers. The more successful these initial centres are, the more likely we will see more such centres developed in the future.

The issue of **differentiation of shopping centres** – through peripheral services such as entertainment and leisure or specialisation of merchandise via factory outlet centres or power centres – is part of a broader concern for mall design, location and promotion.

Freestanding stores are often associated with **ribbon** or **strip shopping** areas along major roads and highways. These would include, for example, many of the inner suburbs in Sydney, Melbourne, Brisbane and Perth. These areas have always been popular for car traffic-related retail trade categories such as fast food and petrol/food convenience stores. However, these areas also have some attraction for other retail categories. The former Woolworths chairman Mr Paul

Simons argued that "in free-standing stores, in convenient locations with convenient parking, we are picking up more dollars per square metre than we do in major centres" (Burbury 1995, p. 23). Other retailers such as Harvey Norman's Gerry Harvey have persisted with favouring freestanding sites compared to shopping centres both because of convenient access by customers and because of low rents (Burbury 1995).

Sometimes, more than one shopping centre or more than one freestanding site may meet the location objectives of a retailer. This necessitates a closer comparison of important attributes, including traffic conditions, the visibility of the area, parking space availability, and amenities including rest rooms and logistic access provided by the shopping area. Importantly, it is also necessary to compare leasing and maintenance costs. There may be special rental deals which could help with the final location decision. Rents are a common source of agitation for most retailers. In general, rents are a balancing force, meaning that more attractive sites in terms of higher store traffic have to pay higher rent which reduces – but does not eliminate – their initial attractiveness.

Location analysis 4: Micro site decisions

The macro site decisions depend on the extent to which the CBD, shopping centre or freestanding site meets the store traffic, image and convenience objectives of the retailer – subject of course to leasing costs. After the macro site decision is made, it is necessary to choose a site within the shopping area. This decision is a **microcosm** of the macro site decision already made. Within the shopping area, some specific sites will be more attractive than others in terms of people traffic, proximity to parking, image, proximity to other retailers, and leasing costs.

The **centre of gravity** of a shopping area is the anchor store which is generally a department store, discount department store, supermarket or sometimes a category killer. In power shopping centres, the anchor store would be an outlet of a national superstore chain, for example Rebel Sport, Freedom, or Harvey Norman. In contrast, in a more upmarket shopping area such as Sydney's Chifley Plaza, a store like Tiffany's could be the anchor. The anchor store is often the main reason most shoppers come to the shopping area. Anchors also generate the most people traffic. The anchors themselves generally get first choice as to the prime sites, and they may indicate this when the property is being developed. The prime site for supermarkets and discount department stores is often the ground floor as this is closer to parking. Department stores, however, are more prepared to be – and may even desire to be – on the second or higher floors and do not necessarily need to be as close to parking.

The remaining retailers must then decide how close to the various anchors they wish to be. Specialist clothing stores prefer to be some distance from the supermarket but much closer to the department store. Other retailers, for example liquor stores, florists and newsagents, like to locate near the supermarket to pick up either impulse or residual shopping requirements. Collectively, these last examples represent the convenience good segment of the shopping area. However, the same retailers must be prepared to pay the higher rents for the privilege of a good location.

The **convenience good retailers** within a shopping area rely on store traffic for their profitability. In contrast, **shopping good retailers** – such as sporting goods, sporting wear, fabrics, shoe shops, fashion shops, gifts and furniture – will attract purpose-driven shoppers in their own right. These retailers will therefore be prepared to occupy the middle and back sections of a shopping area, thus giving themselves **rent benefits**.

The above examples represent general patterns. Individual retailers may position themselves slightly differently if their strategy so dictates. For example, a chain of superstore stationers may decide that, despite being a convenience good retailer, they may be better served by a low rent, middle location rather than paying to be immediately near the anchor supermarket. Additionally, a superstore will have its own drawing power to attract customers.

A further consideration in micro site decisions is the compatibility of a retailer with nearby stores. Shopping good retailers, such as furniture, clothing or shoe categories, prefer to be located *near* competitors. In contrast, most convenience good retailers prefer to be located *away* from competitors. This may also be reinforced by shopping centre management which may, for example, restrict the number of competing newsagents and chemists.

Some stores are **complementary** with other stores and therefore prefer to be located nearby. For example, clothing accessory stores complement clothing stores; paint stores complement hardware stores; chemists complement medical practices; and fast food stores complement all merchandise retail stores.

Both **competitive clusters** and **complementary clusters** represent synergies that benefit all related retailers. Some retailers have taken this a step further and tied their site decisions explicitly to the site decisions of a specific, key cluster member. In the fast food category, a number of competitors have acknowledged McDonalds as the leader and tend to follow it into new areas. In the American motel industry, a budget motel chain – La Quinta – targets travelling salespeople and keeps its restaurant costs to a minimum, that is zero, by locating near to Denny's restaurants. In these cases, a **symbiotic locational relationship** or **alliance** is created which benefits both parties and simplifies some aspects of the location decision process.

Interactive model of location decisions

The discussion to this point assumes that the location decision is essentially the free choice of the retailer. In other words, the retailer selects location objectives and then chooses between regions, trade areas, types of shopping areas and specific sites on the basis of their own criteria. As foreshadowed, simultaneous with retailers seeking the best sites are developers and property managers seeking the best retailers. A simultaneous or interactive approach is called for, rather than either party operating regardless of the other (Figure 6.2).

Figure 6.2 Interactive model of location choice

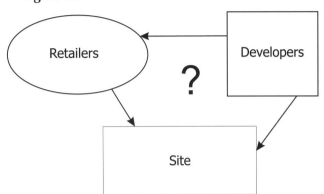

An important implication of this interactive model of location choice is that retailers cannot be sure that they will gain access to the area they desire. Shopping centre managers in particular are believed to favour large chains and franchised retailers over small independent retailers. This decision is partly based on economic considerations – the national chains are likely to generate higher sales turnover and therefore more rent for the shopping centre. Indeed, the presence of many national chains will add to the overall 'drawing power' of the centre. Related to this is an image consideration, with chains often rating higher in terms of status and store appearance. Moreover, chains may be easier to deal with in terms of day-to-day conduct and participation in centre-wide promotions. In contrast, small independent retailers are often discouraged from locating in many shopping centres. Indeed, there are cases where small independent retailers have been unable to renew leases because shopping centres have wanted to enlarge premises to make way for superstore tenants (Thomas 1994). In a similar vein, a Brisbane-based Toyworld store in a Westfield centre in Indooroopilly heard that a Toys 'R' Us store had leased space, and asked for a larger store at the same rent as Toys 'R' Us. Westfield refused and the Toyworld store subsequently closed (Shoebridge 1994). In general, shopping centre managers have their own formulae for the right tenant mix so that, for example, an excellent lingerie retailer could still have difficulty gaining access to a particular centre if that centre already has its 'quota' of lingerie shops.

The interactive nature of the location decision is not well publicised, but it is much more widespread than many researchers acknowledge. Most developers of retail shopping complexes negotiate with prospective retail tenants before developing a property. In particular, anchor tenants such as supermarkets and discount department stores are initially subscribed, paving the way for specialist retailers to be signed up as well. This process is so elaborate that it leaves little room for small independent retailers to access new shopping complexes. There is such a shortage of prospective sites that most developers have waiting lists of prospective retail tenants.

The Gandel Retail Trust had a tenant list of 800 retailers waiting to get into its centres (Corrigan 1994).

This statistic, which relates to just *one* middle level retail property developer, underlines the relevance of the interactive model.

In some cases, the party representing the property owner may in fact be a government body, such as a council or planning authority, which may impose restrictions on the type of retail outlets allowed. Nightclubs, sex aid shops and long-hours takeaway stores are not allowed to operate in certain areas as they do not fit the desired brand image of these areas. Chemist shops may not be allowed within a certain radius of an existing chemist shop. These types of restrictions have a similar effect to that of the property manager who decides what type of retailer they want in their precinct.

Conclusions

This chapter confirms the importance of location as a component of the retail mix for delivering the retailer's strategy and brand. Location is one of the three key decisions that retailers must make. Unlike other retailing texts, the need to clarify the retail strategy, retailer brand, and the objectives of location are emphasised before analysing the key dimensions of location, namely: regional, trading area, macro site and micro site decisions. The main objectives of location are: the generation of potential store traffic, appropriate store image, and shopping convenience. It is very important that the location decision be coordinated with other components of the retail mix – particularly store image and promotion – to ensure that the correct retail positioning is achieved.

In this chapter, a wide range of factors which need to be taken into account when deciding regional, trading area, macro site and micro site decisions have been put forward. Many of these factors are common to each of the four dimensions of location. Potential demand, image and cost considerations are common issues which impact differently on different retail categories. Department stores draw from a wide trading area and favour high status, high rent locations. Supermarkets draw from a narrow trading area, emphasise convenience and favour middle level rentals. Superstores generally combine: a wide trading area, parking convenience, less status and low rents. Specialist stores attached to national chains generally combine: a medium trading area, high status and high rents.

The proposed **interactive model of location choice** links retailers with developers, centre managers and regulatory authorities. The desired location profile of the retailer needs to be compatible with the desired retailer profile of developers and centre managers. At a minimum, this stipulation requires a long-term planning approach by retailers as well as greater negotiation skills. It also requires even greater clarification to ensure that the needs of retailers and developers are consistent and that their brands will be coherent.

The interactive model of location choice can also be seen in the wider context of rivalry between shopping areas. Some rivalry is the traditional conflict between CBDs and shopping centres. However, equally important is the rivalry *between* shopping centres, and this has helped spawn more specialised shopping centres such as factory outlet centres and power centres. Similarly, conventional shopping centres are being redesigned to have features which contribute to their differentiation vis-à-vis other conventional shopping centres. Leisure and entertainment are key means of differentiation, for example Brisbane's Grand Plaza shopping centre, the electronic 'intencity' concept at Westfield Hurstville and Tuggerah, and Melbourne's Jam Factory. Retailers can enhance their own differentiation and brand image by being aligned with – if not actually contributing to – particular centre differentiations.

In summary, a best practice approach to location needs to be strategic rather than a simple geographic exercise. Retail strategy and locational objectives must be more explicitly considered in locational decisions. In most cases, the optimal location is not independent of the image of the area, the image of the shopping centre, and the image of competitors and complementary retailers. All of these forces need to be **synergistic** if the total shopping experience is to be rich, exciting and convenient. These considerations suggest that best practice locational decisions need to include well-developed relationships with the other stakeholders, and that retailers must actively manage their property portfolios.

Review and applications

1. Do you agree that location is the most important component of the retail mix? Explain your response.

2. Why do you think retailers put so much effort into promoting a new store opening?

3. Why has there been only limited international activity of retailers until recently? Do you think the activity will accelerate in the future? Why?

4. What is the role of location objectives in making location decisions? How does knowledge of the location objective help a retailer in a specific retail category? (Please indicate two distinct retail categories.) Choose from a CBD site, a regional shopping centre, some other type of shopping centre, or a freestanding site to illustrate your answer.

5. How successful has the CBD near or closest to you been in combating the trend by consumers to shop at regional shopping centres? What measures have been used by the CBD to counter this? Is there anything else the CBD area could do to further improve its relative standing as a shopping destination?

6. What are the attractions of more specialised shopping centres such as power centres or factory outlet centres? What type of retailer do these centres attract? Do you expect many more of these centres to be developed in the future? Why?

7. Discuss the importance of the interactive model of location choice. What is the practical significance of this model to a large national retail chain? What is the practical significance of the model to a small independent retailer contemplating opening up another outlet?

8. What factors should a bookstore take into account in deciding a specific micro site in a particular shopping centre?

9. Discuss the role and operation of 'models' in assisting regional and site decisions. Illustrate some cases where a model may or may not be useful to the retailer.

10. Many shopping areas tend to be internally homogeneous in terms of the style and image of the retailers. Give examples which support this notion. How would you explain this phenomenon? How does it affect the location decision?

11. Some writers such as Blaxland (1994) and Ketchell (1995) have suggested that shopping centres need to be refurbished approximately every five years. What are the implications for retailers with such possible changes? Select a particular regional or community shopping centre. What changes would you recommend they undertake as part of a refurbishment? Indicate possible design changes as well as possible changes in tenant mix.

12. How would you apply best practice principles to the location decision?

Website references

Country Road: <www.countryroad.com.au>.

David Jones: <www.davidjones.com.au>.

Direct Factory Outlets (DFO): <www.dfo.com.au>.

Hallensteins: <www.hallensteins.co.nz> and <www.hallensteinglasson.co.nz>.

Harbour Town: <www.harbourtown.com.au>.

Michael Hill: <www.michaelhill.com.au>.

Nutrimetics: <www.nutrimetics.com.au>.

Rebel Sport: <www.rebelsport.com.au>.

The Shopping Centre Council of Australia: <www.propertyoz.com.au/scca>.

Sportsgirl: <www.sportsgirl.com.au>.

Stockland: <www.stockland.com.au>.

The Pen Shop of Sydney: <www.penshop.com.au>.

Wal-Mart: <www.walmartstores.com>.

Westfield: <www.westfield.com>.

References

Australian Marketing Institute (AMI) 1994, `Award-winning marketing strategies', published as a supplement to *Australian Professional Marketing*.

Applebaum, W 1966, `Methods for determining store trade areas, market penetration and potential sales', *Journal of Market Research*, vol. 3, pp. 127-41.

Blaxland, S 1994, `Shop centres need refurbishments to remain competitive', the *Australian Financial Review*, 21 September, p. 35.

Burbury, R 1995, `Trading places: Shoppers check out their hates', *Sydney Morning Herald*, 15 April, p. 23.

Clarke, I 1995, 'Deconstructing Retail Location Decisions', paper presented to the Second Recent Advances in Retailing and Services Science Conference, Gold Coast, Australia, July.

Corrigan, M 1994, `Gandel: the centres of retailer attention', the *Australian Financial Review*, 1 September, p. 52.

Davies, G 1995, 'Bringing stores to shoppers – not shoppers to stores', *International Journal of Retail and Distribution Management*, vol. 23, no.1, pp. 18-23.

Dodd, T 1994, `Airport shopping centres get ready for takeoff', the *Australian Financial Review*, 9 December, p. 17.

Este, J 1994, `First GB discount store opens up in Maroubra', *Weekend Australian*, property section, September, p. 7.

Fam, K & Merrilees, B 1995, 'A Cross National Comparison of Retailers' Perception of Promotion Tools', paper for the Fifth Symposium on Cross Cultural Consumer and Business Studies, Hong Kong, December.

Fam, K & Merrilees, B 1996, `Determinants of Shoe Retailer's Perceptions of Promotion Tools', *Journal of Retailing and Consumer Services*, vol. 3, no. 30, pp. 155-162.

Hill, M 1994, *Hello – Michael Hill Jeweller*, Penguin, Auckland.

Hogan, R 1994, `Demographic mapping plots a new course for branch networks', *Financial Review*, 23 December, p. 26.

Huff, D 1964, `Defining and estimating a trade area', *Journal of Marketing*, vol. 28 (July), pp. 34-8.

Jarratt, D & Polonsky, M 1993, `Causal linkages between psychographic and demographic determinants of outshopping behaviour', the *International Review of Retail Distribution and Consumer Research*, vol. 3, no. 3 (July), pp. 303-19.

Ketchell, M 1995, `Shopping centres need a substantial renovation every five years', *Weekend Australian*, property section, 25-26 March, p. 9

MacDermott, K 1994, `Brisbane's $102 million grand plaza opens its doors today', the *Australian Financial Review*, October, p. 42.

McDonalds 1994, Promotional feature, *Newcastle Star*, December p. 20

Newcastle Citycentre 1994, `Citycentre Newcastle - more than a shopping centre', *Newcastle City Centre News*, May, p. 1.

Merrilees, B & Miller, D 1997, 'The Superstore Format in Australia: Opportunities and Limitation', *Long Range Planning*, vol. 30, no. 6, pp. 899-905.

Parker, S 1994, `Steamer Wharf set to change retail patterns in Queenstown', the *Australian Financial Review*, 22 September, p. 46.

Red Rooster 1994, Promotional feature, *Newcastle Star*, 20 December, p. 26.

Robertson, R 1994, `New-style, low-cost motel gets a trial in Sydney's west', the *Australian Financial Review*, 29 December, p. 19.

Robertson, R 1995, `The Pen Shop gets it write', the *Australian Financial Review*, 14 February, p. 24.

Shoebridge, N 1994, `Toy retailers play a tough game', *Business Review Weekly*, 24 October, pp. 33-4.

Smith, A 1995, `Robbing shops to rival Pacific Fair', the *Courier-Mail*, 14 July, p. 33.

Smith, F 1995, `Complex time for shopping centres', the *Australian Financial Review*, commercial property survey, 6 April.

Stirling, P 1988, `Wendy's franchises a soft-serve idea', *Business Review Weekly*, 3 June, pp. 60-1.

Thomas, K 1994, `Shop reshuffle ruffles feathers', *Newcastle Star*, 13 December, p. 3.

Advanced reading

Arentze, T, Borgers, A & Timmermans, H 2000, 'A knowledge-based system for developing retail location strategies', *Computers, Environment and Urban Systems,* vol. 24, pp. 489-508.

Charney, I 2005, 'Property developers and the robust downtown: the case of four major Canadian downtowns', *The Canadian Geographer*, vol. 49, no. 3, pp. 301-312.

Dennis, C, Marsland, D & Cockett, T 2002, 'Central place practice: shopping centre attractiveness measures, hinterland boundaries and the UK Retail hierarchy', *Journal of Retailing and Consumer Services*, no. 9, pp. 185-199.

Erwin, D, Harding, E & Bhogal, I 2006, 'Which locations offer the best potential returns for UK retail investors?', *Journal of Retail & Leisure Property*, vol. 5, no. 2, pp. 104-116.

Fernie, J & Hallsworth, A 1998, 'England's Potteries: past and present pioneers of factory shopping', *International Journal of Retail & Distribution Management,* vol. 26, no. 11, pp. 439-443.

Finn, A & Louviere, J 1996, 'Shopping Centre Image, Consideration, and Choice: Anchor Store Contribution', *Journal of Business Research*, vol. 35, pp. 241-251.

Heaps, P 2005, 'Retail warehousing, shopping parks and leisure', *Journal of Retail & Leisure Property,* vol. 4, no. 2, pp. 174-180.

Hernandez, T 2005, 'Visual decisions: Geovisualisation techniques within retail decision support', *Journal of Targeting, Measurement and Analysis for Marketing,* vol. 13, no. 3, pp. 209-219.

Jones, K & Doucet, M 2000, 'Big-box retailing and the urban retail structure: the case of the Toronto area', *Journal of Retailing and Consumer Services*, vol. 7, pp. 233-247.

Langston, P, Clarke, GP & Clarke, DB 1997, 'Retail saturation, retail locations, and retail competition: an analysis of British grocery retailing', *Environment and Planning A,* vol. 29, pp. 77-104.

Lavin, M 2003, 'Not in my neighbourhood: resistance to chain drug-stores', *International Journal of Retail & Distribution Management*, vol. 31, no. 6, pp. 321-328.

Nolan, J 2005, 'The application of government data in retail business location planning', *Journal of Retail and Leisure Property*, vol. 4, no. 4, pp. 289-294.

Pioch, E & Byrom, J 2004, 'Small independent retail firms and locational decision-making: outdoor leisure retailing by the crags', *Journal of Small Business and Enterprise Development,* vol. 11, no. 2, pp. 222-232.

Porter, I 1995, `Retailers need to put closed sign up on shopping centre rents', the *Australian Financial Review,* 26 April, p. 21.

Prendergast, G, Marr, N & Jarratt, B 1998, 'Retailers' views of shopping centres: A comparison of tenants and non-tenants' *International Journal of Retail & Distribution Management,* vol. 6, no. 4, pp. 162-171.

Reimers, V & Clulow, V 2003, 'Retail Concentration: a Comparison of Spatial Convenience in Shopping Strips and Shopping Centres', *Journal of Retail and Consumer Services,* vol. 11, pp. 207-221.

Reynolds, J 2005, 'Retail location analysis: An annotated bibliography', *Journal of Targeting, Measurement and Analysis for Marketing,* vol. 13, no. 3, pp. 258-266.

Rogers, DS 2005, 'Developing a location research methodology', *Journal of Targeting, Measurement and Analysis for Marketing,* vol. 13, no. 3, pp. 201-208.

Rogers, D 2006 'Location Research Planning: The need for less hype', *European Retail Digest,* Iss. 49 (Spring), pp. 63-64.

Weltevreden, J, Atzema, O & Frenken, K 2005, 'Evolution in city centre retailing: the case of Utrecht (1974-2003)', *International Journal of Retail & Distribution Management,* vol. 33, no. 11, pp. 824-841.

Retail promotion

Introduction

Retail promotion is the component of the retail mix that represents the various forms by which retailers communicate with their customers. The early modern retailers were acutely aware of the need to be in touch with their customers (see Vignette 7.1). They had fewer means than today's retailers do, but their use of print media was most impressive and serves as an exemplar for 21st century retailers.

As Table 7.1 illustrates, promotional activities are diverse – so much so, that not all retailers have a comprehensive understanding of their own promotional strategy. For some retailers, certain components of promotion – for example personal selling – are taken for granted, and promotion is then perceived in very narrow terms such as mass media advertising only. This chapter argues that there are demonstrable benefits in taking a comprehensive view of promotion from the beginning, ensuring that all options are considered and that each component is well-integrated into the overall promotion strategy and that the promotion strategy is consistent with the retailer's vision, business strategy and brand image.

A cost-effective promotions strategy – including instore promotions – requires a performance management orientation to promotion overall.

The largest retailers spend many hundreds of millions of dollars on mass media advertising alone. In recent years, the top 20 retail **mass media** advertisers have included Coles Myer Group (until the break-up of the group in 2006), Woolworths, David Jones, Harvey Norman, Just Jeans, Retravision, Mitre 10, Katies, Big W, Safeway, Jeans West, Freedom Furniture, Strathfield Car Radio and Roger David Menswear. Less information is available about the top 20 *total* retail promotion spenders, although it would include many from the same list.

Vignette 7.1

Retail promotion: The power of print media
New lessons from old retailers

Some retailers – such as Sears Roebuck and Montgomery Ward in the US – commenced their businesses as catalogue retailers. Many other renowned shopfront retail firms added catalogues as a means of communicating with customers, wherever they were located.

In Australia, David Jones was a well-established department store when it expanded its business by starting catalogue distribution in the late 1800s. The catalogue was a very powerful medium for conveying extensive information and for reaching customers in remote rural areas and regional cities as well as reaching urban and suburban customers. The design of the catalogues, the merchandise offerings, the pricing and special promotions all contributed to reinforcing the retailer's image at the time. The catalogues also introduced fashion trends, branded merchandise and launched various product innovations such as 'ready-to-make' fashion (see Miller & Merrilees 2004).

Contemporary retailers can learn many lessons from the old catalogues. The level of detail about products and services, the inclusion of fabric swatches and tape measures, a respectful approach to customers, ordering procedures, methods available for seeking further information, and returns policies and other means of building customer reassurance were all emphasised, and have significant relevance for modern online and print catalogues.

For your deliberation:

How can modern retailers use catalogues to promote their retailer brand and innovations?

This chapter begins by identifying key objectives of promotion in general and their link to retail strategy in particular. It then reviews the various approaches for determining a total budget for promotion and allocating this budget across various promotion tools includes the special case of small retailers. To reinforce and provide insight to these budgeting decisions, this chapter then outlines various approaches to creative design in promotion, and the pros and cons of various media. Separate sections also elaborate on the key promotional media tools as outlined in Table 7.1. *Chapter 9 – Retail selling and customer service* discusses personal selling in more detail. Finally, the importance of an integrated or coordinated communications strategy is emphasised, as is the role of evaluation of promotion.

Table 7.1 A classification of promotion media and types

Mass media advertising	Print Radio Television Cinema Billboards Internet
Instore promotions	Demonstrations Sampling Visual merchandising displays Note also the contributions of store design, merchandise, packaging, the customer merchandise interaction (CMI) and the 'silent salesperson'
Price markdowns	See also *Chapter 8 – Retail pricing*
Personal selling	Including direct selling (see *Chapter 9 – Retail selling and customer service*)
Sales promotions	Special events Competitions
Direct marketing	Direct mail Catalogues Telemarketing Email
Public relations and publicity	Note the special case of product recalls
Sponsorships	Individual Partnerships Creation of foundations
Word-of-mouth advertising	Includes viral marketing and guerrilla marketing

Objectives for promotion

Perhaps more than other components of the retail mix, the broadest purpose of promotion is to make the other components of the retail marketing mix – including product, price, distribution, physical facilities and people – work better. That is, promotion assists **product** by providing information about the attributes and image of the store and its merchandise. Promotion assists **price** by informing the consumer about the overall price level of the store's merchandise or the prices of specific merchandise. Promotion assists **distribution** by telling the customer where to find the store. Promotion assists **physical facilities** by highlighting a particular brand image and store atmosphere. Promotion assists **people** by making customers better informed about the merchandise when they approach the salesperson, and reinforces for staff the corporate brand image of their employer. Thus, the broad objective for promotion is to support and enhance *all* other components of the retail mix as well as the overall retail strategy.

More specifically, promotion can impact greatly on the desired brand image of the retailer. Promotion generally is a powerful branding tool.

 Note, for example, that a luxury fashion store with an untidy hand-written sign on the door sends the wrong message to potential customers.

Budgeting decisions for promotion

How much should a retailer spend on promotion? This is not an easy question to answer. In practice there are a number of different methods to choose from, including the **marginal method**, the **percentage of sales method**, the **competitive parity method**, and the **objective and task method**.

Leading academics (see Rossiter and Percy 1987) regard the **marginal method** as the theoretically correct method. The marginal method is essentially finding the level of promotion expenditure which maximises profits. This seems reasonable, but in practice requires a number of major assumptions which are difficult to control for. For example, it is necessary to estimate an advertising sales-response function – that is, a relationship which expresses sales as a function of advertising – and to assume that the quality of promotions does not change over time.

For most retailers it would be too complex to accurately use this method. However, it may be possible for some retailers to approximate the marginal method through experimentation. This can be done by varying the promotion expenditure level both upwards and downwards, and then evaluating what happens to sales turnover.

One of the most commonly-used methods is the simple promotion to sales percentage (Aaker and Myers 1987). At the individual retailer level, this method works by retailers seeking to maintain a steady **promotion to sales ratio**. The main benefit of this method is that it is a simple rule of thumb and can be fully understood by management. It is seen as a useful starting point, although it begs the question: 'Which percentage figure is desirable?' This problem is greatest for new retailers and for existing retailers if there is a major change in their merchandise mix, since some products require more promotion than others. In general, retailers should adjust their promotion to sales percentage upwards:

- if new products are being introduced;
- if there is an increase in competition; or

- if the retailer is a challenger rather than a market leader.

If retailers adopt an experimental approach to their promotion to sales percentage, then this method approximates the marginal method, providing the percentage is reviewed at regular intervals. The more dynamic the marketing environment, the less reliable is a static promotion to sales percentage method.

Related to the promotion to sales percentage method is the **competitive parity method**. In this case, retailers set their promotion levels by closely aligning them with those of their competitors. This method is easily applied because it is readily apparent where and when competitors are promoting. If everyone keeps to industry norms, then the threat of 'warfare' is minimised. An obvious problem with this method is that the retailer's circumstances may change compared to their competitors. For example, a retailer may introduce new product lines which require additional promotion.

A fourth method of determining promotion budgets is the **objective and task method**. Essentially this method works by setting a specific objective and then ascertaining the level of promotion needed to achieve this objective. A special case of this approach is when the retailer's objective is to maximise profit, and then the objective and task method becomes the marginal method. More commonly, the objective and task method is used very specifically, for example how much promotion is needed to sell a hundred units of merchandise.

The objective and task method is a commonly-used method. The strength of this method is that it demands clear promotion objectives and therefore forces retailers to clarify what it is that they want to achieve from the promotion. This method is also a favourite among advertising agencies because the clarity of objectives makes their work easier. One of the biggest unstated benefits of the objective and task method is that it helps eliminate unwanted expenditures on promotion.

For example, if a car dealer has three unsold demonstration cars, there is no point creating enough demand through promotion for 20 cars as the dealer cannot sell more than three of these cars. The dealer would only disappoint the other 17 buyers by not satisfying them and would have spent more on promotion than necessary. In this example, it would have been particularly useless to try to get a volume discount or to maximise promotion reach. Rather, a more limited promotion reach with a lower budget would be required to achieve the specific objective.

Although each of the four main methods of determining the promotion budget has its own merits, we advocate the **objective and task method** as offering the most insight and discipline to the retailer at a practical level. As discussed, the main benefits of this approach are both a more explicit articulation of the objectives of promotion and more scope to eliminate unnecessary promotional expenditures.

Allocating the promotion budget across different promotional tools

Having discussed how a retailer would determine a total budget for promotion, the next stage is to allocate this budget across the various components of the promotion mix including print advertising, direct mail and the other media noted in Table 7.1. The different promotional tools vary in their effectiveness and cost. Television is known to be very effective for reaching mass audiences, but is also very expensive. Research shows that retail managers' perceptions of the importance of different promotion tools is the most important influence on allocating the promotion budget across different promotion media (Fam & Merrilees 1995a). These perceptions are influenced by the way managers weigh up the pros and cons of different media.

Moreover, retail strategy has an impact on the percentage of the budget allocated to each promotion medium (Fam & Merrilees 1995a). For example, retail stores emphasising store design as an important component of their retail strategy allocated more promotion budget to instore displays and less to print advertising, publicity and broadcast advertising. This suggests a degree of competition between external and internal forms of promotion. Other retail strategies led to different promotion mixes; retail stores which emphasised high sales growth typically allocated more of their budget to sales promotion.

 *As an example of actual budget allocation, refer to the findings of Fam and Merrilees (1995a) for both Australian capital city clothing retailing stores and shoe retailing stores. Table 7.2 shows these findings. There is a similar pattern for both clothing and shoe retailers. In both cases, **personal selling** is by far the largest component of the promotion budget with more than 40 per cent of the budget. 'Instore displays' is the second largest component with about 20 per cent of the budget. Print advertising is the third largest component of the budget, followed by direct mail. The final three components – broadcast advertising, publicity and sales promotion – each have about 5 per cent of the budget and were the least important in the sample of retailers.*

Table 7.2 Budget promotion mix allocation in Australian clothing and shoe retailing 1994

Type of promotion	Clothing retailers %	Shoe retailers %
Personal selling	44.0	44.2
Instore displays	19.9	19.1
Print advertising	12.9	12.4
Direct mail	9.9	8.8
Broadcast advertising	4.1	6.5
Publicity	5.4	4.5
Sales promotion	3.8	4.4

Source: Fam & Merrilees 1995a.

Specific promotion media are discussed below, providing a more in-depth understanding as to why specific media might be used by retailers. Equally, the sections provide a brief introduction into the steps that retailers can use to put these tools into practice.

Advertising options for small retailers

The main issue here is the low budget available to small retailers for promotional purposes. Some promotion types – for example instore promotion, direct marketing and public relations – are particularly suited to low budgets. Not only do these specific promotional types have a low threshold of expenditure to get coverage, the small retailers often have scope to do some of the creative design work themselves and therefore can save on that aspect as well.

The first step for small retailers to economise on their promotion budget is to ensure they have a good overall comprehension of the nature and role of promotion. The second step is for small retailers to ensure they have a good grasp of the principles of creative design. The third step is that they should have a good understanding of some of the potentially more economical forms of promotion.

The three steps provide a framework for small retailers to economise on their promotion budget. Small retailers should be wary of apparently appealing shortcuts which have not been fully assessed. Many retailers subscribe to calendars listing business names and to other various teletext types of listings only to be disappointed later because these media are inappropriate or ineffective. It is important to get some hard facts – if not guarantees – about costs and audience numbers before subscribing to these services. Similarly, the retailer should think through their total needs. If a retailer needs to reach an audience three times before they respond, then the deal of a lifetime which gives one television placement could be next to useless. Thus, instead of saving money, the retailer may have lost money because their spending failed to exceed the threshold needed to get a positive customer response.

Creative promotion design for retailers

What are the principles for creative promotion? There are many approaches to this question. Some advertising agencies advocate their own version of 'universal rules'. Some rules are more publicised than others and might therefore be seen as broadly accepted within the advertising industry. It should be noted that some of these agencies are very conscious of the exceptions to these rules (see Benn 1978). Another approach is to focus on the behavioural characteristics of goods, whether low or high involvement and low or high clarity of function (see Rossiter & Percy 1987). A third approach is to develop rules which are specific to particular media, that is radio, print, television and direct mail. A fourth approach is to develop rules which are specific to particular industries, that is consumer, industrial, services and retailing. A fifth approach is a more intensive focus on specific stimuli to the creative process, for example music, humour, and the personality or reputation of the presenter. These five approaches are not mutually exclusive.

In the search for universal rules, the simplicity and clarity of Bryce Courtney's rules are highlighted in Table 7.3. The first and third rules are very important when you consider how cluttered the media is. The average consumer is subjected to hundreds of advertising communications each day, and if the advertisement itself does not stand out (Rule 3), then it will not be noticed. If it is not simple (Rule 1), then it will not be understood by the audience. And if it does not answer the question 'What's in it for me?' by spelling out the benefits for the consumer (Rule 2), then no action will be forthcoming even by the consumer who has noticed and understood the advertisement.

Table 7.3 Some rules for creative promotion

Courtney's KISS rules for creative promotion are:	
Rule 1	KISS – 'keep it simple stupid'
Rule 2	What's in it for me?
Rule 3	Present it creatively

Source: Courtney c1990.

As an adjunct to the universal rule approach, consider the simple four part approach by Cameron, Rushton and Carson (1988). The questions they propose are:

- Who is the intended audience for the advertisement?

- What message is being conveyed?

- What is the promotional objective behind the communication?

- What is the rationale for using the specific channel of communication?

This adjunct has the additional virtue of putting the *evaluation* of the message into the wider context of what is the purpose of the communication and what is an appropriate medium.

The main advantage of the Courtney (c1990) and Cameron, Rushton and Carson (1988) rules is that they can quickly be used by managers as a starting position for evaluating creative advertising. Hence, it is possible to formulate rules for good advertising design, just as there are design rules for graphic design, industrial design and architecture. The creative world of design and advertising is partly spontaneous, but it also can benefit from adhering to a broad set of design rules.

Equally important, managers need to evaluate whether advertising designed by advertising specialists broadly meets their retail business needs in terms of profitability and/or generating awareness of the store.

Managers can use advertising design rules as a broad check on whether advertising created on their behalf is appropriate. Table 7.4 provides further suggestions for particular media.

Table 7.4 Adapting the creative promotion rules to particular media

The universal rules can be tailored to each of the media. For example, Benn (1978, p. 78) offers the following five sound copy principles which are mainly relevant for the print media:

- put a benefit in the headline;

- use short, concrete and familiar words;

- put the brand name in the headline;

- what you say is more important than how you say it; and

- put a time limit on the offer.

Each of the specialist media groups offer their own creative rules for radio, newspapers, etc, such as the Radio Marketing Bureau's video entitled *Retailers on Radio* that includes excerpts from Harvey Norman, Angus & Coote, and Bob Jane T-Marts. Their general suggestions for more effective radio advertisements including:

- Tell your customers on radio what they need to know about your product in order to make a purchasing decision. Tell them what you want them to do: buy, phone, call in, inspect, etc.

- Your radio advertising should talk about benefits that will attract people to your merchandise. Look at the product from their point of view. Avoid superlatives that waste valuable advertising time.

- When you mention specific items, you will do better if you use no more than three in a 30-second radio commercial. Try to use related items or merchandise at the same price or discount to avoid confusion.

- To be effective, all advertising needs repetition.

The pros and cons of different media

Each medium has different features which can be emphasised depending on the type of product or message that the retailer is promoting. Table 7.5 summarises these features.

Newspapers continue to be highly credible, with good local coverage. These characteristics make them ideal for the weekly specials which the major supermarkets run. Newspapers are also ideal for public relations-type promotion. However, newspapers are a static medium and are less suited to action-oriented products.

Television is most costly, but it is ideal for action-type advertisements such as new cars, running shoes or swimming pools. Radio tries to do the same thing without pictures but, being cheaper, greater frequency of placement is more feasible.

Direct mail, telemarketing and personal selling are all forms of direct marketing, with a different one favoured depending on the type of product being sold. Direct mail, like newspapers, is a static medium, while the other two are more inter-active.

Table 7.5 Media types classified by effective features

Television	• Strong, active sensory features • Caters for a large, diffused audience
Radio	• Mobile, immediate • 'Sells with frequency' (Radio Marketing Bureau)
Newspapers	• Credibility, local coverage • Short lead time
Magazines	• Colour, demographic selective • Measurable
Direct mail	• Scope to be highly selective • Measurable
Telemarketing	• Speedy interaction with simple products
Personal selling	• Slower interaction with complex products
Point of sale	• Suitable for simple products • Role of impulse buying

Each of these media is strongly represented by their respective industry. There is a radio industry, a television industry, a newspaper industry, a telemarketing industry (which includes Telstra and Optus as well as other specialist providers), and a point of sale industry. Each industry markets its products to the retailers by emphasising the virtues of their particular media or **vehicle**.

A vehicle is a specific channel, such as a specific television channel, radio station, specific newspaper, magazine or catalogue within a particular medium.

Media industry representatives can generally advise about their target audiences, which may help retailers to target their promotions. Some newspapers run several editions of their paper with region-specific distributions to save on advertising costs.

It pays to get to know each media industry. For example, in Newcastle there are three major letter-box distributors, two of them connected to major newspaper chains. They claim to have better quality control systems compared to the many smaller, possibly less well-organised operators, who could be cheaper but may be less reliable.

Instore promotion

Instore promotion includes signage, displays, samples, tastings, demonstrations, recipes and other types of information sheets, aromas, trolley advertisements and specials advertised over the store's public address system. The product packaging in terms of shape, colour, size, tags, brand name and information can also be considered part of instore promotion, as can the *en masse* stacks of packaged products. All forms of instore promotion provide the customer with information, and this helps promote the merchandise. The Body Shop makes effective use of this promotional method by making available numerous educational leaflets and posters.

In supermarkets, instore promotion adds excitement to the information function by using flashing light specials, gondola ends and freestanding displays, banners, signage, samples and tastings, and even public address announcements of specials – often called 'red light specials'. Some of this excitement comes about by the retailers triggering other senses, for example smell, sight, sound or touch.

One of the national banks uses **captive audience networks (CANs)** with an audio-visual screening of a couple seeking a home loan that plays while customers wait in the queue inside the bank's branch.

Hairdressers sometimes have audio-visual displays featuring products and hairstyles. Butcher shops and pastry shops throughout regional towns – in Scotland in particular – frequently have animated characters in window displays.

Furthermore, planned shopping centres or malls, for example, make extensive use of **captive audience networks (CANs)** for promotions for both the mall overall and for individual retailers.

Kingsmill's Department Store is a successful and enduring independent retailer with one outlet in London, Ontario. With more than 150 years of history, the firm creates synergies between its heritage values and contemporary upscale retailing. The store effectively promotes its well-developed online retailing on CANs within the store (see Kingsmill's website: <www.kingsmills.ca>).

Much of the promotion marketing literature gives little prominence to this aspect of promotion, and more or less relegates it to a role of stimulating impulse purchases. This position is inappropriate and underestimates the potential impact of this medium (see Vignette 7.2). In some retailing categories, instore promotion is extremely important, as is indicated in Table 7.2. Instore promotion links in with the discussion of visual merchandising in *Chapter 5 –*

Store design. These two areas of retailing should be looked at jointly, as each supports the other. The same activity essentially relates to two functions of retailing in the same way that personal selling relates both to promotion and selling (discussed further in *Chapter 9 – Retail selling and customer service*).

> ## Vignette 7.2
>
> ### Innovative promotion: quick response to seasonal changes
>
> Tim Hortons ®, a prominent Canadian food and beverage retailer, changes the promotions on **captive audience networks** to respond to changes in the weather. This quick response meets customers' needs and reinforces the comfort aspects of the retailer's offerings.
>
> For example, during an unexpected warm spell, cool drinks will be promoted instore. Note the importance of integrating product availability, staff knowledge and this quick response approach.
>
> See Tim Hortons <www.timhortons.com>.
>
> ### For your reflection:
>
> How can modern retailers use captive audience networks to promote their retailer brand and innovations?

The traditional role of instore promotion is to encourage impulse buying of low-involvement purchases. This makes it particularly important for supermarket promotion. However, instore promotion can trigger **latent** or **postponed** purchases (see Engel, Warshaw & Kinnear 1987). This could of course apply to high involvement shopping goods such as furniture or fashion merchandise. Often the instore promotion creates a feeling that the item is on sale – a feeling that could apply to both low-involvement and high-involvement merchandise.

Instore promotion has played an important role in a number of Australian promotional campaigns including butchers, shoe care products, snack foods, perfumes and petrol stations (see Williams 1994).

Price markdowns

Price markdowns, like personal selling, can appear under more than one heading of the retail mix. **Price markdowns** are a very important part of promotion, though it is equally an important part of pricing. Price markdowns are discussed in considerable detail in *Chapter 8 – Retail pricing.*

In terms of budgets, it is very difficult for retailers to 'cost' price markdowns because the cost is a complicated calculation of the number of units on special multiplied by the average percentage price markdown. Price markdowns are more important for clothing retailers than for shoe retailers. As an estimate, price markdowns represent about 8 per cent of sales turnover for Australian clothing retailers and about 6 per cent of sales turnover for Australian shoe retailers. In terms of Table 7.2, price markdowns are not included because of the difficulty in costing them. If price markdowns could be included, they would be the second most important form of promotion (based on retailers' perception data rather than budget data).

The fact that it is difficult to cost the budget allocated to price markdowns means that there is a risk that the item might not be incorporated in a retailer's promotion mix decision, which could lead to sub-optimal promotion decisions. The better retailers will make some estimate of the percentage of stock that may need to be marked down in price and the average percentage of price reduction. These figures can be controlled for through merchandise planning techniques and by monitoring the actual percentages attained over the season or year.

Sales promotion

Retail sales promotions are defined as **short-term incentives** for the customer. They are designed to increase sales. They may take the form of money refund offers, money back or discount coupons, samples, contests or sweepstakes.

There is only a subtle difference between the final two listed above. **Contests** *are seen to involve skills, while* **sweepstakes** *are usually more of a lottery.*

The same competition is sometimes tailored to suit the particular gaming laws of different states of Australia. South Australia has somewhat stricter gaming regulations than other states.

All forms of sales promotion share a common dimension, namely that they add interest and excitement to the shopping process. This excitement is particularly strong with contests and sweepstakes.

Each form of sales promotion has its own advantages. **Sampling,** either through the mail or through instore demonstrations, is attractive when it is difficult to smell or judge the performance of a product without using it, and includes perfumes and household cleaners. The **'show bags'** (also known as sample bags) at annual shows such as the Gold Coast Show were historically – and to a lesser extent still are – major opportunities for companies to promote their products through **sample-size offerings**.

All forms of sales promotion share a common disadvantage, namely that excessive use of sales promotions may undermine the long-term, quality image of the retailer. Another disadvantage of unplanned sales promotion is that there may be little profit associated with a large increase in sales. This outcome means that the retailer is trading off future profits for short-term sales and cash flow. If this is the objective, then everything is fine. If this is not the objective, then the appropriate constraints need to be built in.

Some companies, including the former Australian airline Compass, suffered financial losses because they underestimated the number of people who might respond to discount deals. On a smaller scale, a single butcher in a small shopping centre used unlimited quantities of '50 cents a kilogram' sausages as a sales promotion technique. Within two hours they were sold out, and the butcher spent the rest of the day making sausages – including using more costly, higher grade meat ingredients.

In general, it is important that the sales promotions be properly planned. This requirement means clear objectives, clear target markets and a well-structured program that includes:

- clear conditions to participation, including quantities;

- incentives which are big enough to arouse interest but not too large to induce large losses;

- appropriate duration, frequency and timing, keeping in mind the possible side effect on brand image;

- consideration of which type of sales promotion is needed;

- arranging necessary support from other promotional tools, such as point of sale material, sales force and advertising; and

- recognition of any relevant legislation.

Retailers often use sales promotion as much as manufacturers. However, most retailers are reluctant to get too involved in the sales promotion activities of manufacturers if this deal requires the troublesome 'cashing in' of small value coupons on behalf of the manufacturer. The overall power of retailers has 'encouraged' manufacturers, when using sales promotions, to invite consumers to send coupons directly back to them rather than through retailers. This arrangement is unlikely to change in the foreseeable future.

Some studies such as Dawes (2004, p. 303) suggest that, although there may be an immediate increase in sales over time, the "longer-term negative effect on category volume cancelled out two thirds of the gains of the price promotion", which may be explained by customers accelerating purchases or stockpiling.

Thus, a major issue for retailers is to evaluate the short- and long-term impacts of any price promotions.

Direct marketing and database marketing

Direct marketing is the process of communicating offers directly to individuals – through the post, by telephone (e.g. landline, mobile phone, SMS, facsimile), by television or via email.

Compared to other types of promotion, direct marketing has the advantage of being reasonably economical – which partly explains its rapid growth in recent years. There is a wide variation in the response rates of consumers to direct mail offers. These variations can often be explained by the following success criteria:

- the quality of the mailing list;

- the value of the offer;

- the quality of the graphics or presentation; and

- the quality of the copy.

Some mailing lists are of suspect quality and fail to distinguish among potential customers. Consequently, the response rate can be as low as one per cent. A regional Port Stephens pizza store sent out over 1,000 letter box offers only to get 11 back – and some of these included regulars who would have bought regardless of the discount offer.

One solution to this type of problem is to ensure that a better quality list is used. These can be obtained from list brokers. The best lists, however, are often the ones created internally using the retailer's own customers, or people who request or even pay to receive their catalogue. Many retailers have catalogue memberships or email newsletters.

Research has shown that the quality of the list is the most important criterion for a good response rate to a direct mail offer (see Vignette 7.3).

The offer itself is also important and should highlight benefits such as a discount, a competition or a new product which would appeal to a specified target market. The graphics and copy are not as important, but should not be so bland or cluttered as to detract from the offer. Timing is also important, especially when the product is seasonal in nature.

The importance of direct marketing can be seen from the daily flood of letterbox material that we all receive, and which spans all types of retailers. Much of this material is targeted loosely and is less effective than customer **database marketing**, as shown in Merrilees (1994) and Merrilees & Miller (1997).

Retailer websites

A major shift over the past decade has been the increasing use of retailer websites as promotional tools. Some retailers go further and use the website for a selling channel as well. Oliver and Shor (2003, p. 212) suggest that "the advent of the internet has resulted in a new form of sales promotion", and they discuss the merits of the use of promotion codes during the checkout process for online shopping.

Where a retailer chooses to use the website for promotional offers at the 'bricks and mortar' store, it is critical that the website is designed and maintained so that, firstly, it is consistent with and reinforces the retailer's brand image and, secondly, that the promotion is part of the retailer's promotion portfolio and integrated marketing communications.

Vignette 7.3

Innovative approach to buying the right list

Canadian Tire Corporation – the Canadian icon and unique retailer of auto, homewares, leisure and outwear – was in its infancy in the late 1920s. At the time, the focus was on tyres, some accessories, and maintenance of automobiles. As well, automobile ownership was a relatively recent phenomenon and the customers would generally be price sensitive because of economic conditions. Following some success with press advertising, Canadian Tire purchased a list of registered car owners in Ontario and mailed out their catalogue featuring a road map and price list. The size of the catalogue was similar to a double-sided broadsheet. Within a decade the catalogue was more than 100 pages (of about A5 size).

Here is a good example of well-targeted direct mail. Obviously the recipients of the catalogue were keenly interested in maintaining their vehicles, and given the state of both the roads and product development at the time, they would need new tires more often than today's car owner.

See Canadian Tire Corporation: <www.canadiantire.ca> and McBride (1997).

For your reflection:

How can small retailers create or acquire lists? Explore the current implications of privacy legislation in this matter.

Customer loyalty programs

Clubs and loyalty programs can be thought of as a specific service or a special combination of other customer services. Clubs, such as registered clubs and groups with common interests like hobby groups, have long been popular both in Australia and abroad. Many fashion retailers such as Katies have developed clubs, as have pharmacists (in relation to baby clubs). Airlines offer club memberships which offer enhanced bookings and exclusive waiting areas and facilities. Airlines also promote frequent flyer loyalty programs which offer benefits such as rewards based on usage for regular travellers. The common objective of clubs is to promote common interest, fun and **customer loyalty**.

Other loyalty programs are based on an alliance of companies, for example the FlyBuys program (see FlyBuys website). Interestingly, FlyBuys promotes special offers on their website. **Co-branded credit cards** have also become popular because they link a major retailer, a bank and a credit card company, offering a more flexible type of loyalty program.

Some of the criticisms from consumers about some loyalty programs include a perceived excessive time lag between purchases and accruing enough points to actually make a meaningful redemption. One more immediate way of rewarding customers is with a cash discount on the current transaction. In between these polar positions, the major supermarkets – through their associated petrol outlets – offer very aggressive petrol discounting subject to minimum purchases in the supermarket. For example, until Christmas 2006, with a minimum purchase of $80 in a single transaction at a Coles or Bi-Lo supermarket or Coles Online, customers could get 10 cents per litre discount, with an additional two cents per litre discount if they also made a minimum purchase of two dollars instore at the Coles Express attached to the petrol outlet. Woolworths and Big W had similar offerings during the same period.

Public relations, publicity and sponsorships

Public relations has been defined as the two-way communication between an organisation and its public. Public relations are construed as the most factual and credible of the various forms of promotion. Advertising and sales promotion often reflect the self-endorsement of the company *by* the company. In contrast, public relations are often statements about the company or their products by a third party, or at least strongly endorsed by a third party, and this dimension adds credibility to the message. To achieve this third party endorsement, companies generally use **media releases** which contain key information about the company. The media releases are sent to journalists for consideration for inclusion in both printed and electronic media.

Public relations is sometimes considered as free publicity because it is not paid for in the way commercial advertisements are. However, the company does not have ultimate control over whether the media runs with or does not run with the story, nor over the exact way the story will be presented. It therefore would be unwise to be overly dependent on public relations as the main form of promotion for a company. Moreover, public relations is not quite as free as it seems.

*There are **internal costs** in compiling, editing and communicating public relations stories. Also, many media companies expect the organisation to place advertisements elsewhere – in the paper, for example, if it is a newspaper – before they are 'disposed' to accepting the public relations story.*

In retailing, there are many public relations opportunities including announcing plans to expand the number of outlets, increased employment opportunities, selection of particular sites for new outlets, new marketing strategies, new merchandise, new methods of retailing, and new services to customers. All of these are 'good news' stories which are likely to be well received by print and electronic media.

Some retailers only see public relations in terms of dealing with short-term crises such as sabotaged products, product recalls, poor reported profits, or dealing with pressure groups. Some other retailers also have a short-term focus, but put more emphasis on positive situations such as expansion plans or profit turnaround. There are a number of techniques that one can use to improve short-term public relations activities. One technique is good targeting of the relevant media and media contacts who can be thought of as the front line audience or market, and whose needs have to be met before they run with the story. Usually the needs of media personnel are closely aligned with the needs and interests of their readers or viewers. Another technique is a well-constructed media release, as shown in Table 7.6.

Table 7.6 Suggested structure for media release

Do your homework: Make sure you know what would be of interest to the readers or viewers of this particular media.

- The company's logo and identification should appear on the top and a contact person and telephone number should appear at the bottom, along with a website if appropriate.

- There should be a prominent heading in upper case letter along with a date.

- The first paragraph is critical and should indicate **what**, **where**, **when**, and **who** - that is, what are the key facts, where and when did the story take place, and who was involved. This is descriptive material.

- The middle of the media release contains information which assumes that the attention of the reader has been gained. It is more analytical and deals with the **why** and **how**.

- The end of the media release is least important and is not vital to having the story accepted. It contains other secondary information such as: **THE END**, a contact name, telephone and fax numbers, and email and website addresses.

The big challenge in public relations is to develop a sustainable long-term program. The program can vary depending on which stakeholder the company is trying to target. Investors or shareholders may be very important, making investor relations a priority area. In this respect Lend Lease pioneered **investor relations** in the 1960s by going to great lengths to encourage shareholders to attend the Annual General Meeting (AGM) of the company. More recently, we have seen companies such as the Coles Group and David Jones giving their shareholders shopping discounts at their own outlets. Employee relations can also be targeted, noting that the former State Bank of NSW won an award for its video communication network which transmitted messages from the chief executive officer to all employees. Retailers can also target suppliers, financiers and franchisees.

A special case of strategic, long-term public relations programs is the development of the organisation's corporate image. Corporate image advertising is aimed at creating an image of a specific corporate personality in the minds of the public and seeking a favourable image among selected audiences. In effect, the company is treated as a product which seems particularly relevant for service providers such as retailers. Retailers generally build their reputation by selling a range of merchandise and services, rather than on the associated reputation of just one or two particular products.

Vignette 7.4

Effective public relations and the retailer's brand - the case of the product recall

Some retailers consider product recalls the problem of the manufacturer or supplier. Nevertheless, it is at the store level that the retailer must pull stock from the shelves, advise any known customers, and arrange for returns and refunds.

Best practice dictates that the most senior person in the business should lead the public relations initiative. Behind the scenes, the public relations team will be working internally in the firm – gathering information and establishing processes such as free call telephone numbers staffed by competent and reassuring representatives of the firm, and updating information on the firm's website – and externally with suppliers and the media. The aim is to create transparency in customers' eyes, build confidence in the measures taken and the prospects of prevention of similar occurrences.

Measures in addition to media releases include have the senior manager available to the press for interviews, and placing large scale advertising to explain what has happened, who is affected, what readdress they have, measures for prevention, where customers can obtain further information, and preparing instore signage. Once the crisis has been resolved, the public relations and the retailer's brand should be re-evaluated and action taken as needed.

For your reflection:

How can small retailers manage public relations overall for positive stories? What can they do when the news is 'bad'?

As indicated, the focus of public relations is usually on 'good news' stories. However, the retailer must also be prepared to manage contrary stories quickly and effectively. The retailer should have in place an emergency response plan for crisis management. Whether the 'bad news' is a store fire, robbery, accidents, or complaints, the retailer must be able to pull together a response team very quickly. Woolworths experienced extensive community resistance when it proposed opening a store in Maleny, Queensland. Wal-Mart, the world's largest retailer regularly experiences similar resistance especially in small towns. A special case for public relations is the **product recall** (Vignette 7.4).

Retailers need to develop their corporate image through well-developed plans, and by ensuring that employees have a clear sense of the organisation and the appropriate culture. Here is a role for **internal relationship marketing**. Among other things, employees may require a sense of employment security. Providing that the company's behaviour in terms of values, culture and actual business conduct is really supported, external communication can contribute to corporate image. This **external communication** can take the form of corporate advertising, store advertising, product advertising, public relations, logos, brochures, staff-customer interactions and marketing strategies. The key is to have a clear and distinctive image to project, and to be consistent across outlets and over time.

To conclude, it is worth reiterating that all of the above also applies to small retailers. Good news stories can be generated in local newspapers – including free-to-the-public weeklies – and radio stations. While it may seem hard for smaller retailers to sustain these efforts, take a leaf from one Newcastle hairdresser, Sandy Chong, who wrote a regular column about hair health and salon services including childcare, hairdressing competitions and visiting hair product celebrities for the *Newcastle Herald* during the 1990s.

Towards an integrated retail communications strategy

Ideally, retailers should assess their promotion needs in a unified and co-ordinated way which is clearly aimed at the chosen retail strategy. This can be applied to each promotion medium separately, but the links between the various media need to be recognised and incorporated. A modern way of doing this is through the **integrated marketing communication** (**IMC**) concept. IMC has been defined as:

> ... *tuning target groups, messages and means of communication in such a way that they complement and reinforce each other so that the overall effort yields more than the sum of the parts.* (Mooij 1994, p. 374)

Perhaps surprisingly, IMC does not yet dominate specialised promotions textbooks, however there is sporadic mention of the concept. Shimp notes that point-of-purchase promotion can serve as a capstone for an integrated promotion program:

> *P.O.P. by itself may have limited impact, but when used in conjunction with advertisements and sales promotions, P.O.P. can create a synergistic effect.* (Shimp 1993, p. 548)

The importance of instore promotion as a capstone of an integrated promotion program is also advocated in the Australian-focused book *Interactive Marketing* by Williams (1994).

Apart from a tighter coordination of promotion, an IMC approach is founded on the idea that communication efficiency is best achieved through a combination of media. The most successful communications are those in which the consumer receives a message from various sources (Tynan 1994). Mooij (1994) lists the advantages of IMC as:

- consistency in building a strong brand, including the retailer's corporate brand;

- a synergy of efforts and budgets;

- the possibility of greater impact;

- where the total effect is larger than the sum of the parts; and

- a more effective use of the budget that leads to lower costs.

Taking isolated examples, it is not difficult to find cases of particular retailers using some form of an IMC approach to their promotion. Retailers often feature television or sporting celebrities on television and then have cardboard mock-ups or posters of the celebrities placed as a point-of-purchase display. For example, the Sleeping Giant newspaper advertisement of a seven day sale appeared in exactly the same form as a direct mail letterbox drop. Incidentally, the advertisement was a good example of an advertisement which clearly highlighted benefits to the consumer. It also showed the importance of one or another promotional medium, for example print advertising and direct mail, being used to communicate information about another promotional medium, that is a sale or price markdown.

Sportsgirl does a good job in tightly linking the photographic medium to brochures, to print advertisements, and to instore displays. Staff at Big W spend time in 'tying up the ad' - that is, in changing shelf-talkers, price tags and other instore signage to align with current mass media advertisements. A good example of an IMC promotion campaign is that of AMP in the early 1990s when they aimed at selling financial services to women. It began with television advertising (mass media), which encouraged a direct response by women to get a pamphlet (direct telemarketing), which was then sent out by AMP (direct mail). In turn, AMP sold the contact numbers as 'leads' to its field salespeople (direct marketing), who carried out follow-up direct telemarketing and direct selling activities.

Sometimes the promotion industries themselves highlight the benefits of IMC. The Yellow Pages often promotes itself as complementing the other media, and both the White Pages Online business listing and The Yellow Pages Online have become more popular as more and more consumers have internet access. The Australian Financial Review advertisement by Visy Displays, developed by advertising agency Whybin & Partners, effectively promotes the message that point-of-sale promotion complements mass advertising promotion.

Research in the 1990s found that less than half of a sample of 327 Australian clothing retailers had actually adopted IMC (Fam & Merrilees 1995b), and that situation persists today. Therefore, overall, the benefits of IMC have yet to be fully understood by clothing retailers. This study recommended that the best way to initiate an IMC program was to begin with the co-ordination of direct mail and sales promotion. As retailers build experience with IMC, they can add other co-ordinations such as mass media and instore displays, and then web-based promotions at a later date.

Evaluation of promotion

There is considerable scope to learn more about the best creative promotion and the most appropriate media to use. Larger retailers may be in a better position to track their promotion by testing the extent to which consumers recall their promotion, and how favourable their attitudes are to the promotion. This type of evaluation is primarily concerned with how well a particular promotion is enjoyed. A greater challenge is to develop new ways of evaluating the effectiveness of promotion – that is, the impact the promotion actually had on sales.

There are different ways of monitoring the effectiveness of promotion, including recording the volume of sales before and after promotion. This gives the retailer an approximate measure of the impact of advertising, but it is necessary to 'control' for as many other influences on sales as possible. For example, a big jump of sales following a promotion may be more due to a special price offer rather than the advertisement itself. Retailers need to build up their experience with these types of evaluations before they can be more confident about what the major determinants of any sales increase are.

Meanwhile, some types of promotion are easier to assess than others. Direct marketing is somewhat easier to evaluate because you can control who receives the message and who responds to the message. Coupons and order slips assist this control for direct mail, as do specially assigned telephone numbers for telemarketing campaigns. In other words, evaluation is easier for direct marketing because the impact is more measurable. This benefit adds to both the usefulness and the use of direct marketing compared with other forms of promotion.

Word-of-mouth advertising

Word-of-mouth advertising is not readily included with the other types of promotion in Table 7.2. Most retailers have at least a vague notion of the concept, but few quantify it in the same way as the other forms of promotion. An American study of retailers concluded that the majority of retailers did not believe they could fund or control word-of-mouth advertising (Bolen 1994).

Put simply, anything which the retailer does to encourage positive word-of-mouth – particularly from an actual customer to a potential customer – can be considered word-of-mouth advertising. Anything which the retailer implements through the retail mix to increase customer satisfaction – for example offering a better range of merchandise, improving store design, or opening more easily-accessible outlets – increases the probability of positive word-of-mouth advertising.

The benefits of providing good retail service are considerable, but the benefits start to multiply when positive word-of-mouth advertising is incorporated. In some cases, up to half of the sales of a service provider have come about from positive word-of-mouth advertising. This effect is so powerful that it has the potential to swamp most of the other forms of promotion. Given the potential importance of word-of-mouth advertising, best practice retailers will attempt to measure its impact and to incorporate it in their retail strategy and promotion budgets.

Conclusions

Most retailers have an obsession about selling, and promotion plays a big part in this exercise. The purpose of this chapter has been to alert retailers to the wide variety of promotional tools and the relative merits of each in various circumstances. In other words, which promotional tool is most likely to effectively contribute to promotional objectives?

Although all of the major types of promotion are covered, this chapter particularly emphasises the growing or newly-recognised importance of both direct marketing and instore promotion. These two types are likely to become more important, perhaps at the expense of more traditional promotional tools such as television, radio and print media. Database marketing in particular is seen as the future of marketing and is particularly attractive as a low-cost medium for smaller retailers. Personal selling is another promotion tool which needs to be better recognised in the retailing context. It is important that employees are aware of the importance and purpose of promotion. This would help them to portray the right image, and to motivate them to conduct instore activities such as product demonstrations to customers or 'tying up the ad'.

Many retailers are more consciously drawing upon a wider range of promotion tools. The rapid acceptance by small retailers of database marketing has been pointed out. Also, we have large retailers like the former Coles Myer being the first company to use telemarketing to gain shareholder support for their buy back of shares from the American K-mart company. New types of promotion are coming on stream, too. These range from advertisements on the back of cash register receipts to highly-sophisticated new forms such as FlyBuys and other loyalty programs. Loyalty programs – like price mark-downs and personal selling – are really combinations of different retail mix components.

Promotion is one of the most visible and exciting components of the retail mix. It is the one which the author, and readers, can most readily access on a daily basis. The new forms of promotion make this area particularly exciting, however the better retailers will attempt not to be swamped by the flood of new opportunities, and to keep a tight rein on the direction and purpose of their overall promotion. This approach should be guided by the overall retail strategy and, at a more detailed level, by the IMC concept. Best practice promotion requires an IMC approach. Moreover, given the potential importance of word-of-mouth advertising, best practice retailers will attempt to measure its impact, incorporate it in their retail strategy and promotion budgets, and actively manage it. Overall, promotion is critical to the successful execution of the retail strategy and the development of the retailer's brand. Innovative approaches offer the retailer the possibility of distinctive campaigns which resonate with the target market and with other stakeholders.

Review and applications

1. In what sense does promotion support retail salespeople? How would this nexus between promotion and sales force effectiveness influence the way you design promotional campaigns?

2. How does promotion support store atmosphere?

3. "The key to good direct marketing is a quality mailing list." Discuss.

4. What factors increase the effectiveness of sales promotion? Discuss these in the context of both petrol station convenience stores and electrical appliance retailers.

5. Under what circumstances might a retailer give more priority to sales promotion than conventional mass media advertising?

6. Why is personal selling considered to be the most important form of promotion in retailing?

7. How do the corporate images of David Jones, Myer and Harris Scarfe differ? If one of these companies wanted to change their corporate image, what methods would they use?

8. "Sampling will eat into my profits." Discuss the advantages and disadvantages of instore sampling for a small delicatessen retailer.

9. Evaluate any two retail advertisements, or other promotions, using the Cameron, Rushton, Carson criteria (1988).

10. How can branding ideas help to achieve integrated marketing communications?

Website references

Australian Discount Retail (Trading) Pty Ltd (Crazy Clark's and Go-Lo): <www.golo.com.au>.

FlyBuys: <www.flybuys.com.au>.

References

Aaker, D & Myers, J 1987, *Advertising Management,* 3rd edn, Prentice Hall, Englewood Cliffs, NJ.

Allen, R 1992, `Direct answers on direct selling', *Sydney Morning Herald,* Money section, 3 June.

Bolen, W 1994, `The role of word-of-mouth advertising in retailing', *American Business Review,* May, pp. 11-14.

Benn, A 1978, *The 27 Most Common Mistakes In Advertising,* Amacon, New York.

Boylen, L 1989, `Hard selling by coupon', the *Australian Financial Review,* 11 April, pp. 43-4.

Burnett, J 1993, *Promotion Management,* Houghton Mifflin Co., Boston.

Buss, J & Herford, G 1994, *Personal Selling in Australia,* McGraw-Hill, Sydney.

Cameron, M, Rushton, A & Carson, D 1988, *Marketing,* Penguin, London.

Courtney, B c1990, article in the *Australian Financial Review.*

Dawes, J 2004, 'Assessing the impact of a very successful price promotion on brand, category and competitor sales', *Journal of Product and Brand Management,* vol. 13, no. 5, pp. 303-314.

Engel, J, Warshaw, M & Kinnear, T 1987, *Promotional Strategy,* 6th edn, Irwin, Homewood, Illinois.

Fam, K & Merrilees, B 1995a, `Beyond ADVISOR? A fresh look at empirical communication budget models', University of Newcastle Working Paper, July.

Fam, K & Merrilees, B 1995b, `The extent, nature and benefits of integrated marketing communications - the retail advertisers' perspective', University of Newcastle Working Paper, August.

Higie, R, Price, L & Feick, L 1987, `Types and amount of word-of-mouth communications about retailers', *Journal of Retailing,* vol. 63, Fall, pp. 260-78.

Kuczynski, A 1992, `Beyond advertising, towards integration', *Marketing,* June, pp. 50-3.

McCloy, O 1993, *Smart Selling The Consultative Approach,* Business and Professional Publishing: Sydney.

McBride, H 1997, *Our Store: 75 Years of Canadians and Canadian Tire,* Quantum, Toronto.

Merrilees, B 1994, `Database marketing in the retail clothing trade', *Database Marketing,* No. 7, December, p. 44.

Merrilees, B & Miller, D 1994, *Retail Customer Service and Organisational Capability,* Paper presented to the Joint European Institute of Retailing and Services Studies (EIRASS) and Canadian Institute of Retailing and Services Studies (CIRASS) Conference, Recent Advances in Retailing and Services Science, Banff, Alberta, Canada, May.

Merrilees, B & Miller, D 1997, 'Database Marketing by Australian Shopfront Specialist Clothing Retailers', *Journal of Database Marketing*, vol. 4, no. 3, pp. 221-235.

Miller, D & Merrilees, B 2004, 'Fashion and commerce: a historical perspective on Australian fashion retailing: 1880-1920', *International Journal of Retail and Distribution Management*, vol. 32 no. 8, pp. 394-402.

Mooij, M 1994, *Advertising Worldwide: Concepts, Theories and Practice of International, Multinational and Global Advertising,* 2nd edn, Prentice Hall, Englewood Cliffs, NJ.

Oliver, R & Shor, M 2003, 'Digital redemption of coupons: satisfying and dissatisfying effects of promotion codes', *Journal of Product and Brand Management*, vol. 12, no. 3, pp. 121-134.

Rossiter, J & Percy, L 1987, *Advertising and Promotion Management,* McGraw-Hill, NY.

Shimp, T 1993, *Promotion Management and Marketing Communications,* 3rd edn, The Dryden Press, Orlando, Florida.

Tynan, K 1994, *Multi-Channel Marketing: Maximising Market Share With An Integrated Marketing Strategy,* Probus Publishing Co., Danvers, Mass.

Williams, M 1994, *InterActive Marketing,* Prentice Hall, Sydney.

Advanced reading

Bolton, R & Shankar, V 2003, 'An empirically derived taxonomy of retailer pricing and promotions strategies', *Journal of Retailing*, vol. 79, pp. 213-324.

Ellen PS, Mohr, LA & Webb DJ 2000, 'Charitable programs and the retailer: Do they mix?', *Journal of Retailing*, vol. 76, no. 3, p. 393.

Jenkins, V 1994, *An Introduction To Direct Marketing,* Longman, Melbourne.

Kotler, P 1994, *Marketing Management: Analysis, Planning, Implementation and Control,* 8th edn, Prentice Hall, Englewood Cliffs, NJ.

Laroche, M, Pons, F, Zgolli, N, Cervellon, M-C & Kim, C 2003, 'A model of consumer response to two retail sales promotion techniques', *Journal of Business Research*, vol. 56, no. 7, pp. 513-522.

Walton, S & Huey, J 1992, *Sam Walton, made in America: my story*, Doubleday, New York.

Retail pricing

Introduction

More than three decades ago, the widespread practice of manufacturers pressuring retailers to use the compulsory recommended retail price lists – a form of resale price maintenance – became illegal in Australia. That change gave retailers greater freedom to set their own prices. However, the transition from passive to active pricing puts the responsibility for pricing squarely upon the shoulders of retailers. This chapter canvasses the key issues that retailers should understand in order to equip them for such a challenge.

The chapter begins by defining the various roles of price. Price is an important part of the retail mix and the only part that actually generates revenue for the retailer. The chapter discusses the important price/quality relationship and introduces the notion of elasticity of demand. An outline is given of the various objectives that pricing can contribute to – depending on the overall retail strategy and retailer brand. It is extremely important to link the pricing decisions to the retailer's strategy and retailer brand. The chapter then discusses the three main price setting methods which relate to costs, demand and competitors, and goes on to provide a new framework for integrating these different price setting methods. Finally, the chapter explores how the structure of prices across the product mix is determined. There is special consideration of price markdowns ('the sale') and other promotional pricing methods. A major issue that retailers need to resolve is whether to emphasise promotional pricing or everyday low prices (EDLP). The issue of price wars is also examined.

To some retailers, pricing decisions are deceptively easy. These retailers are likely to use simple mark-up methods of pricing in a way which resembles the compulsory recommended retail price schemes of yesteryear. They closely adhere to advisory – but not enforceable – recommended retail price schedules. The trouble with this approach is that it is unlikely to achieve the **optimal price** that best meets the pricing objectives of the retailer.

Other retailers understand better the different **contexts** which call for a more flexible approach to pricing. They are more likely to experiment with different prices and maybe even use different pricing methods. However, the standard theoretical literature written in most retailing texts does not integrate the various approaches very well. At times cost is emphasised, at other times demand is emphasised, and at still other times competition is emphasised. Which method is appropriate for the retailer? Rather than leave this as a problem for the student or retailer to solve, we propose an integrative framework of pricing which is basically a flexible framework depending on the pricing question asked.

The role of price

Price can be defined as the average or per unit value of a certain item of merchandise. Price can either be the **list price** which is marked on the item or the **actual price** for which it is sold. There can be a difference between the list price and the actual price if some of the items are sold on special or on sale. The **average price** can be calculated as the total value of the items sold divided by the number of units sold.

Price is the major component of the cost of merchandise to the consumer. If a consumer buys an item on credit, then any credit charges are also part of the total cost. A higher rate of interest would increase the total cost of merchandise to the consumer. Reduced financing costs can be considered a form of promotional pricing.

Apart from cost considerations, any review of a retailer's pricing policy should also consider the use of credit and other payment systems. Ideally, retailers should be taking reasonable steps to make it easier, quicker and more convenient for the consumer to buy.

Price is an important part of the retail mix. In some retail categories, such as supermarkets, price is probably the most important component of the retail mix. The importance of the retail mix emanates from the importance of price in consumer purchasing decisions. However, price is only one of several factors which influence consumer decision making. Quality, convenience and atmosphere are also important to the consumer. In clothing retailing, for instance, customer service, location and quality merchandise seem be to relatively more important than price (Merrilees & Miller 1994).

Within each retail category, price varies in importance depending on where a retailer is competitively positioned in the market. For discount retailers in any category, low pricing is probably the most important component of their retail mix. For upmarket retailers, low prices are not important although high prices assume strategic significance as a signal of high quality.

The relationship between price and quality is worth emphasising. Sometimes consumers have difficulty assessing the true value of a product and rely on cues – such as the advice of a salesperson or the listed price – to guide them.

Perfumes are a good example as there may be only a small difference in the actual quality of two brands but one brand may sell for $80 a bottle while the other sells for $30 a bottle. A major segment of customers may compare these prices and believe that there is a large difference in the quality. In other words, this segment of customers uses price – possibly backed up by considerable image advertising – as a cue for quality. One should not assume that the answer for the retailer is simply to increase the price. A high price tactic will only work if the merchandise is of higher actual quality or if the retailers and manufacturers combined can convince consumers that the merchandise is of a *perceived* higher quality. There can be severe repercussions – in terms of consumer complaints or loss of goodwill – for retailers if these claims cannot be justified. Such retailers often become the subject of current affairs programs, web logs (blogs) or consumer campaigns (see the Choice website, for example).

The possibility that price can communicate quality cues also applies for cheaper items. Retailers sometimes use odd pricing, for example $13.95, rather than even pricing, for example $14, to exaggerate the lower price and to indicate that a real bargain is in the offing. In other words, although the actual difference between the two prices is small, psychologically the difference seems greater. Petrol stations are an apt example of this practice, where prices of 102.9 or 107.9 cents per litre – or some other figure ending in nine – are the norm.

Price needs to be treated as an integral part of the retail mix, which mutually supports all other components to support the retailer's strategy and brand. For example, discount retailers will generally support low prices with less promotion, cheaper locations and store design, and less expensive merchandise. In other words, discount retailers will do everything they can to keep their costs down, which enables them to keep their prices as low as possible while portraying a coherent image to customers.

Apart from contributing to the formulation of the retail mix both across and within retail categories, price plays an important role in contributing to sales turnover through its definition of average unit price multiplied by the number of units sold. This financial role of prices contributes to profits and gives a **return on investment (ROI)**.

The definition of sales turnover as being equal to average unit price multiplied by the number of units sold warrants further comment. It sounds like a licence to print money – if one keeps raising prices then sales turnover goes up. Or does it? There are limits to this process due to a concept called the consumer demand schedule. This schedule is an inverse relationship between the price of a product and the number of units demanded by the customers. So, as the retailer raises prices they generally sell less units, and these offsetting tendencies mean that sales turnover will not necessarily rise when the price is increased.

Indeed, if consumer demand is very responsive to price changes, referred to as elastic demand, then sales turnover could actually *fall* if prices are raised too far. The **elasticity of demand** is defined as the absolute value of the percentage change in demand (that is, sales volume) divided by the percentage change in price.

Elastic demand is defined as when the elasticity of demand is greater than one. For example, if a 10 per cent cut in prices leads to a 20 per cent increase in sales volume, this means that the elasticity of demand is 2.0 (20 divided by 10) - that is, elastic.

Inelastic demand is defined as when the elasticity of demand is less than one. For example, if a 10 per cent cut in prices leads to a 5 per cent increase in sales volume, this means that the elasticity of demand is 0.5 (5 divided by 10) - that is, inelastic.

All retailers can benefit from the concept of elasticity of demand. It can help retailers to predict how price changes will affect turnover.

Retailers can anticipate what might happen to the number of units sold if prices were 5 or 10 per cent higher or 5 or 10 per cent lower. Any other percentage figures could be used by the retailer.

As shown, pricing is important and prices do not operate independently of other elements in the retail mix. Furthermore, pricing is a sensitive marketing instrument that retailers must handle carefully. Some retailers could inadvertently increase price with the intention of increasing **sales turnover**, only to find a high drop-off in units sold if demand is elastic.

Pricing objectives

It is useful to be as explicit as possible when setting the objective or goal that pricing assumes in an organisation. The most common types of pricing objectives are:

- to maximise profit;
- to earn a specific target rate of profit;
- to maximise sales turnover;
- to maximise market share;
- to project a particular image or competitive position of the firm; and
- to clear obsolete stock.

Often these objectives are mutually exclusive, that is, they cannot be simultaneously achieved. Generally, an image pricing objective would require higher prices, for example as with luxury perfume. At the other extreme, if the objective of the retailer is to clear the stock at the end of the season, this would result in a low price.

Different retail categories seem to emphasise different pricing objectives. For example, supermarkets tend – as a category – to emphasise either sales revenue or market share pricing, while department stores are more concerned with image pricing and profit maximising pricing.

Within each retail category there are likely to be some differences in pricing objectives, depending on the market positioning of the retailer. A market leader – if it is positioned on low prices – will generally have very low prices. Alternatively, if the market leader is positioned on quality, it will tend to have one of the highest prices. Other retailers will also vary their prices depending on their competitive position and the specific goals of each firm.

A special case is not-for-profit retailers such as The Smith Family Retail Stores, the Salvation Army (Salvos Stores and Family Stores), The Wilderness Society (WildShop), Scouts Australia, and Oxfam Australia (Oxfam Shops) (see respective websites). These retailers place more emphasis on sales turnover than on profit maximisation, although they do need to run efficiently and effectively to achieve their business objectives.

It is important for each retailer to clarify their price objectives before setting their price levels and before selecting a particular pricing method.

Pricing methods

There are three main types of price setting methods which relate to **costs**, **demand** and **competitors**. Within each type of pricing method there are a number of sub-types.

Cost method of pricing

The **cost method of pricing** is often used and reflects an accounting identity for price:

Price = unit variable cost + unit overhead cost + profit margin

Note that **price** refers to the average price per unit of the merchandise being sold, while **variable cost** refers to costs such as labour or the cost of materials purchased which can vary with the number of units sold.

 If a retailer sells one shirt per employee per hour and the shirt costs $12 wholesale with labour costs of $ 8 per hour, then unit variable costs are $20.

Overhead costs are costs which are fixed for lengthy periods, such as building leases or electricity. If overhead costs are $80 per day and the retailer sells eight shirts a day, then unit overhead costs are $80 divided by 8, that is $10 per shirt sold.

Finally, if the retailer wishes to make a $10 profit margin on each shirt, we can complete the price formula given above as:

Price = $20 + $10 + $10 = $40 per shirt

Thus $40 is the price the shirt would retail for, given the pricing objective of returning a particular profit margin.

The profit margin in this example can be expressed as a percentage of the final price of the shirt; that is, $10 divided by $40 equals 25 per cent. This percentage figure, or whatever the figure happens to be, is referred to as the **profit mark-up**. Retailers often think about the different mark-ups they are making on different items. Later, we explore why retailers tend to use a range of mark-ups in their shops.

The cost method of pricing is very popular. It is favoured by retailers using an optional recommended retail price approach, in which case manufacturers are setting both the mark-up and the price on behalf of the retailer. There are, however, three main limitations of the cost method of pricing.

The first limitation of the cost method is that the method itself does not determine the mark-up. It is up to the retailer to set an appropriate mark-up depending on their pricing objective. There is a risk that some retailers could use the cost method for simplicity, but could then choose a mark-up percentage which does not meet their objectives. The problem is not the mark-up method *per se*, but rather inflexibility on the part of the retailer to adjust the mark-up to suit their objectives.

A second limitation of the cost method of pricing, and partly related to the first limitation, is that even if the retailer arrives at the correct mark-up initially, changes in demand and competitive factors may call for a change in the percentage mark-up. If these changes in demand and competitive circumstances are frequent enough, it may be better for the retailer to shift to a different pricing method altogether.

A third limitation of the cost method of pricing is a technical complication. In order to calculate unit overhead costs at the start of the year, it is necessary to know future sales volume over the forthcoming year. This may not be a major problem for a well-established retailer with a fairly stable demand, however the exercise is a problem for a new retailer or for an established retailer with erratic demand. In these latter situations, it is difficult to know what sales figure to use to calculate unit overhead costs.

Demand method of pricing

The demand method of pricing is not consciously used as much as the cost method. However, demand considerations often influence price in subconscious ways. In any case, it is far better to be more explicitly aware of the role of demand on price.

The key issue here is the price that consumers are willing to pay for an item. Theoretically, the traditional way that this issue is dealt with is through the consumer demand schedule concept. This concept suggests that, after a consumer's initial needs are met, they will thereafter show more resistance to paying higher prices. In broad terms, price resistance is greatest with merchandise with an elastic demand. If a particular retailer has a high proportion of customers with an elastic demand, then any attempt to greatly increase prices could lead to large scale switching by their customers to other retailers. The elasticity of demand concept can also be used to explain the pricing structure of retailers.

Another potentially more pragmatic way of dealing with the demand method of pricing is the concept of **perceived demand**. The perceived value of a product can be seen in the first instance in terms of the consumer demand schedule. However, the consumer demand schedule generally assumes a homogeneous product and gives minimal attention to the many attributes of the product or service which, in turn, increase a buyer's perception of value. **Perceived value** is better seen as a detailed assessment of the attributes consumers value, especially in terms of the various `value-adding' activities undertaken by retailer through: convenient locations, inventories, information, salesperson advice, wrapping, delivery, special orders and an exciting shopping environment. Retailers can adapt the package of value-adding extras to suit their target markets. The pricing of the package will generally be above cost, assuming that it is based on accurate market research of the needs of the target market.

Competition method of pricing

The competition method of pricing arises when a retailer uses competitors' prices as a benchmark to set their own prices. A retailer could elect to set a price: fairly similar to competitors' prices, somewhat higher than their competitors, or even lower than their competitors. There is often a tendency for similar quality items offered by retailers to be bunched around the same price. That is, there tends to be a prevailing market rate for a particular item. If a retailer charges too much above the prevailing market rate, they may lose business very quickly. If they charge too much below the rate, they either make a loss or may sell so much that they force other retailers to match their prices. These potential repercussions mean that the favoured approach is to approximately match competitors' prices and rely on convenience or some other attribute to win sales. This is certainly a very popular method, with price discounting for airline tickets and petrol station pricing relevant examples of this approach.

Some retailers consciously set prices below those of competitors. This can be thought of as **everyday low prices (EDLP)**. To be sustained, it generally requires either a lower profit margin or a very low cost structure. Alternatively, retailers may consciously set prices above those of their competitors. To justify this strategy, these retailers need to offer perceived value to their customers through appropriate value-adding services.

Combining pricing methods

As shown by this last example, there is scope for the competition method of pricing to incorporate demand considerations and to a lesser extent cost considerations. Therefore all three pricing methods are not mutually exclusive, though their emphases are very different. The **benchmark** of good retail pricing remains – even if retailers find it convenient to use cost-plus or mark-up methods of pricing, they should do so with explicit regard to consumer demand and competition considerations.

Determining the price structure across the product mix

Most retailers sell a range of products, that is merchandise assortment, rather than just a single product, and this raises special issues for pricing. Simply, it would be unusual and probably irrational to sell every product at the same price or profit margin. There are opportunities to take advantage of differential demands by differentiating either prices or profit margins across products. An unusual exception to this rule is those shops which have positioned themselves by selling *all* products at the one price. For example, some retailers in Melbourne advertise that all items are $2. Another example, Dollars & Sense, has all items under $10. The original Coles variety store strategy from 1914 focused on all items being offered for less than a shilling, which by 1918 was revised to two shillings and six pence (McLaughlin 1991). These exceptions reflect a small number of cases where the entire retail strategy uses a single price or a specific price ceiling basis.

Across retail categories we can contrast low volume, high margin products with high volume, low margin products. The former include jewellery and furniture retailers, and the latter include supermarkets and newsagents. The high margins of jewellery and furniture stores reflect the higher value-adding functions of additional selling costs such as wages, higher inventory management costs per dollar of sales turnover, and additional customer services such as delivery or packaging. The lower margins of supermarkets and newsagents are exacerbated by intense competition, but are partly compensated by a greater volume of sales.

Within retail categories, similar forces explain the price structure. For example, in supermarkets staple products such as coffee, tea, milk, breakfast cereals, soup and sugar tend to have lower margins than slower moving items such as herbs and spices. The lower margins are justified by high volume of sales, the greater public information about price levels that in turn contributes to high inter-store demand elasticity, and the use of loss-leader pricing.

The supermarket example – where part of the store's product range has low margins and the rest have high margins – requires us to think about a pricing system linking all products. There are obvious interdependencies across products. Low margin products may well be explained in terms of the support they give to high margin products, so any contraction of the former product lines based on poor profitability could lead to a major reduction in store patronage.

Another set of product range pricing issues is that of **optional extras**, **price bundling** and **price unbundling**. How much extra should an appliance dealer charge for the delivery, installation and training in the product use of a new appliance, and the removal of the old appliance? (See Vignette 8.1.) These are optional extras for the customer and could be charged at the current market rate (e.g. $100). In fact, most retail dealers charge less than this (e.g. $50).

One Retravision dealer is known to charge nothing for these extras for dishwasher purchases.

The dealer is essentially selling a product and four services, requiring five possible pricing decisions. So why do most appliance dealers charge less than the going market price which commercial carriers and tradespeople would charge? Part of the rationale may be that dealers are selling not just an appliance, but also reassurance that the appliance will arrive on time, safely and be operational without complications. This can be communicated in various ways, but one way is telling the consumer that they will deliver, install, train and remove – in one convenient bundle – for a very reasonable fee.

An alternative strategy employed by some car manufacturers and dealers is to advertise a low and unbundled no frills base price, and then to charge higher prices for the optional extras that are then promoted during the selling encounter. Given the higher cost of cars compared to appliances, this strategy may make sense if the relevant segment of car buyers is price sensitive. If the relevant price segment is not price sensitive – for example for luxury cars or top of the range buyers – then these buyers may prefer most of the optional extras to be bundled together at the start of the selection process.

Returning to the case of appliance dealers, we can re-conceptualise their pricing strategy by inferring that some of them have effectively bundled the product together with several services into one package. Bundling products or services makes more sense when emphasising convenience, one-stop shopping advantages, or a high quality image.

Bundling can also be used to get people to buy either the merchandise in total, or through an attractive package to buy more than they would if the components were unbundled. Season tickets to the orchestra or theatre at a discount rate both encourage and enable patrons to attend more frequently than they would otherwise. For example, McDonalds has run its 'McValue meals' product promotions – which are cheaper than the sum of the individual products – for many years now because the customer might not have bought all of the component parts without the package deal. Buy a suit and get a shirt free is a similar discount package. As with the other examples, there is a sense in which part of the package – the shirt – is a **loss leader**, supporting and being supported by the suit. Bundling requires recognition of interdependencies across product lines. Delicate judgements are required to justify the cross-subsidies, but simplistic financial audits – which in this case would indicate that the shirts are not paying their way – are too superficial.

Another way of dealing with product-mix pricing is the use of **price points**, also known as **price lining**. A clothing store may price its garments – such as shirts or dresses – at three distinct levels, for example $69.95, $79.95 and $89.95, which reflect different levels of quality merchandise. Katies is an example of a retailer that has used this strategy explicitly. While the above discussion of bundling highlights the complementary nature of many retailing products and services, in contrast the use of price points highlights different segments, with consumers generally sticking to a particular segment. A slight change in the price within one segment is unlikely to induce many consumers to switch across segments.

By now, the reader will undoubtedly agree with the author's proposition that merchandise/product-mix issues add greatly to the complexity of retail pricing decisions.

Price markdowns

Promotional pricing refers to retailers pricing *below* their listed or normal prices. This begs the question as to what *are* normal prices. There have been trade practice investigations by the Australian Competition and Consumer Commission (see the ACCC website) into some retailers who advertise discounts from 'list prices' when no sales have ever occurred at that original price. In this section, our only concern is with genuine promotional pricing which presumes that a reasonable percentage of merchandise has been sold at the list or normal price. We begin by examining the most important form of promotional pricing, namely price markdowns or 'sales'. Other types of promotional pricing are then examined.

Perhaps the best known type of promotional pricing are the institutionalised 'price-off' sales, which include post-Christmas, pre-Christmas, annual, half-yearly, stocktake, opening specials, end of catalogue, clearance and end-of-season sales. These sales are highly seasonal in nature, are often connected with a festival or other special event, and are fairly predictable in their timing and frequency. In the past, some of these sales provoked stampedes of shoppers – with the smashing of front doors and crowd frenzy – leaving a number of people jolted or injured. At times, the safety precautions and crowd control techniques of retailers have been found wanting. In general, these behaviours are testament to the seriousness of these events and the importance of such sales both to shoppers and to retailers. Australians love a bargain, and 'the sale' is destined to be with us for the foreseeable future. Some emerging literature suggests that retailers risk 'training' certain customer segments who are willing to trade-off fashion against a reduced price, and who will defer purchases until items are 'on sale' rather than purchase them at full price (see Betts & McGoldrick 1996; Levy, Grewal, Kopolle & Hess 2004).

As an inventory management strategy, all types of retailers will at some time have the need for a sale. However, upmarket retailers in particular need to be careful that the conveying of the advertisement sale message *enhances* rather than detracts from the desired image. For example, upmarket stores can use signs that are simple, bold and elegantly presented along with 'tasteful' advertisements.

The end-of-season sales particularly relate to fashion products. Indeed, most fashion retailers would – or at least should – budget on the likelihood that approximately 30 per cent of their stock will have to be marked down at the end of the season, even if sales go fairly well. Research by Merrilees and Fam (1999) indicates that price markdowns are equal to about 8 per cent of clothing retailers' turnover, and about 6 per cent of shoe retailers' turnover. If the average price markdown is 20 per cent, this would mean that about a third of clothing retailers' stock and about a quarter of shoe retailers' stock is marked down. The percentage of stock marked down could be greater if the retail buyers did not accurately predict fashion trends when ordering the stock, if competition from other retailers was particularly strong, or if the weather was unseasonable, for example a short or unusually warm winter.

Some retailers have institutionalised the process of out-of-season merchandising by having dedicated outlets positioned either exclusively or very strongly for selling out-of-season stock. The recent innovation of planned shopping centres such as Harbour Town on the Gold Coast, Adelaide and Perth, and DFO (Direct Factory Outlets) in Brisbane and Melbourne supplement other examples such as Birkenhead Point which claims to be the original factory outlet shopping centre in Sydney., David Jones, for example, has 35 self-named regular department stores and two David Jones warehouse outlet stores – one at Birkenhead Point and the other at Harbour Town on the Gold Coast (see respective websites).

In addition to the mainstream or 'regular' sales conducted by retailers, some retailers also conduct one-off sales. Some of these sales have relatively non-descript names such as 'The Seven Day Sale'. Sometimes these one-off sales relate to retailers moving premises or to those who are closing down. To an outsider, some of these sales appear suspicious – how many times can the one retailer close down? In the advertising of such sales, care and thought are needed by the retailer to communicate credibility to consumers.

Ford (1995) reiterates our point about fashion goods, and provides further insight into retailers' approaches to price promotion sales. There is clearly a wide variety of approaches to sales. IKEA's end-of-catalogue sale is not held automatically, but depends on the need at the time. Many retailers use sales to clear 'de-featured' products that have been superseded or are more basic models compared with those which are currently popular. A different approach is used by Villeroy and Boch, which imports fine china and sells it predominantly through leased outlets in department stores. They approach their suppliers for a special deal on one of their popular patterns and use the sale as a drawcard.

Moreover, unlike most retailers, Villeroy and Boch freely share advice with consumers about the timing of the next sale (Ford 1995). Most retailers are concerned that such sales could cannibalise their regular sales by encouraging early purchases at a discounted price rather than regular purchases at the normal price. In other words, if the sale is too frequent or predictable, it could lead to a change in buying patterns in which sale purchases become the normal behaviour.

One-off sales could be related to the special sales promotions campaigns being conducted by retailers that were discussed more fully in *Chapter 7 – Retail promotion*. Sometimes the sales promotions relate to cash back offers instigated by manufacturers. One-off sales are not always successful or appropriate. In particular, more upmarket retailers – such as department stores – need to be cautious to ensure they do not make too much use of such sales for fear of devaluing their retailer brand status, which can jeopardise the entire positioning of the retailer in consumers' minds.

Other forms of promotional pricing

We have considered price markdowns as a major form of promotional pricing. We now consider a number of other possibly less well-known forms of promotional pricing.

Loss leader pricing is a common form of promotional pricing – particularly in supermarkets – and refers to super specials on a select group of products which are temporarily priced at cost or even at a loss in order to attract people into the store. The selected products are generally well-known national brands in staple areas such as coffee or breakfast cereals. Check for yourself the mid-weekly newspaper advertisements of supermarkets in order to see which areas are generally chosen. To a lesser extent, other categories may also use this practice. For example, McDonalds uses its 50 cents ice creams in a similar way.

A **reduced financing cost** is another promotional pricing technique which is particularly popular for car dealers, boat dealers, and retailers of appliances and furniture. Special low rates of interest can reduce the total cost of buying a consumer durable. A similar impact occurs with deferred interest or repayment schemes. Such schemes were common in 2005 and 2006 when rates of interest began to creep up again. If we consider that the total price of a durable has two components – the purchase price plus the interest cost – easy finance is akin to 'loss leading' on one component to make the total package attractive to the consumer.

Retail and manufacturer **warranties** can also be varied as a form of promotional pricing. Warranties are somewhat like insurance policies – the consumer pays a cash premium up front for cover in case something goes wrong in the future. A recent trend in Australian retailing is the extending of retailer warranties. These warranties are generally offered by the retailer and cover a longer period than the standard warranty provided by the manufacturer. They are mainly relevant for consumer good purchases and are offered by most department stores and major electrical appliance chains. About a third of customers take up this option. Typically, they are for a five-year period and cost approximately $100. Some car dealers also offer extended dealer warranties, and with some car dealers these may even be free – the only catch being that the consumer may be tied to the dealer's service department for the duration of the extended warranty rather than being allowed to seek out possibly cheaper maintenance elsewhere.

Vignette 8.1
Pricing and branding:
Using price unbundling to reinforce a price-based retailer brand

Price bundling was discussed earlier where it was pointed out that appliance retailers often bundled their services in their prices in order to create a 'convenience' retailer image. In recent years this trend has been reversed. For example, Clive Peeters (also see the Clive Peeters website), a major appliance retailer, has reinforced a low price/wide range retailer brand by unbundling the price of extra services. The retailer charges separately for each additional service, for example delivery, installation, removal and extended retailer warranty. This approach enables the equipment or product price of the appliance to have the lowest possible floor price tags with further discounts prominently featured. Sales staff emphasise that extra services are contracted out to third parties, and are therefore 'unrelated' to the total product price. Consistent with their tagline 'So e-e-easy', the retailer's sales staff 'encourage' customers to disconnect old appliances and to install appliances themselves where possible. This pricing strategy does much to reinforce a low price/wide range retailer brand image. Furthermore, the retailer supports the low price claim by offering a post-purchase 14-day guarantee of lower prices as compared to competitors.

The pricing strategy also relates well to a growing segment of potential customers who are value conscious. However, there is a risk of alienating the 'convenience' segment of customers who want a seamless service with a minimum of fuss. For example, the delivery and installation of two different appliances may require two different appointments if there are separate installers.

For your consideration:

Can you suggest how a household appliance retailer such as Clive Peeters could *concurrently* manage the two customer segments, that is value conscious customers and convenience seekers?

Everyday low prices versus promotional pricing

Sales and specials have become so common in recent years that nearly all retailers engage in the practice at some point during the year. With everyone offering a price bargain to their customers, this makes life particularly difficult for those retailers positioned in the market on the basis of low price. The incessant stream of sales muddies the waters as to where the true discounters are. One response to this problem is the concept of **everyday low prices** (**EDLP**). For example, the Big W discount department store's pricing promise 'We sell for less' can be seen as an EDLP approach as can the hardware superstore Bunnings tagline 'Lowest prices are just the beginning' (see Big W and Bunnings websites). This concept carries the message that the retailer's prices are permanently cheaper, and that consumers can economise on their shopping search time by shopping with that retailer on a regular basis. This is not to deny that occasionally other stores will be cheaper than an EDLP-based store.

EDLP, with perhaps a minor role for sales and specials, can be compared with the alternative strategy of having higher base prices but with a strong emphasis on promotional pricing. How does a discount retailer choose between these two pricing strategies? The foremost advantage of the EDLP pricing strategy is that it is a very powerful statement in relation to a low price strategy. Second, EDLP should save on advertising costs because there are fewer sales to be promoted. It is of course still necessary to continue advertising the overall EDLP policy. Third, fewer price adjustments are necessary and thus EDLP saves on staff time and reduces the potential for discrepancies between the marked shelf price and the price charged at the checkout, as such inconsistencies cause consumers some concern. Fourth, EDLP reduces stock-outs and price markdowns, and can help improve inventory management. And finally, there is greater customer loyalty because the long term rewards of single store shopping are greater.

The advantages of an EDLP policy are considerable but need to be weighed against the disadvantages. The biggest drawback of EDLP is that only a very small number of players in each retail category can effectively use the strategy. This is because a retailer needs a low cost structure to sustain EDLP. For example, the high cost structure of American retailer Sears explains why it was unable to sustain its EDLP policy introduced in 1989 (Coughlan & Vilcassim 1989). A similar problem faced Australian supermarket retailer Coles with its 1992 low price strategy. It was reversed because its cost structure prevented a sustainable low price position. A second disadvantage of EDLP is that some customers still expect regular price-off sales, which was also the case at Sears (Coughlan & Vilcassim 1989). In other words, there is a type of ritual element in sales built into the expectations of consumers and it will require time for these expectations to be altered.

A third disadvantage of EDLP is that any retailer is free to use the term EDLP, resulting in some retailers looking for a terminology to upstage the rest – such as every day *lowest* prices. This third disadvantage may be short-lived but it does further highlight the time lags inherent in sorting out which retailers are likely to end up with the true title of EDLP. Even then, competition allows for new or existing players to challenge on the price front. Ortmeyer, Quelch and Salmon (1991) suggest **everyday fair pricing plus** (**EDFP+**) as an alternative pricing position for the majority of retailers:

> *EDFP+ means three things: restoration of everyday prices to levels that represent good value to customers even though they do not purport to be the lowest in town; fewer sales events; and most importantly, excellence in other differentiating elements of the merchandising mix, such as service and assortment.*

Ortmeyer, Quelch & Salmon 1991, p. 56.

The need to weigh the pros and cons of an EDLP policy remains. In any case, the advantages of EDLP seem particularly great in supermarkets where there is an emphasis on the convenience and habitual benefit of choosing just one or two stores for regular shopping rather than regularly comparing and chasing the weekly specials. However, in the American context Ortmeyer, Quelch and Salmon (1991) note that at least nine major supermarket chains adopted EDLP, implying that they all cannot use EDLP as their sole point of difference. Some chains have consequently added assortment or checkout speed as a further source of differentiation. Moreover, fashion retailers may see EDLP as less relevant because they must give prominence to end-of-season sales as an inevitable part of the fashion business cycle (Ortmeyer, Quelch & Salmon 1991).

Changing price and the risk of price wars

Price changes are fairly frequent in retailing, especially when temporary price cuts in the form of price markdowns and sales are included. The prime motivator of price cuts is the prospect of rapid extra sales, perhaps driven by excess stock or current sales moving too slowly. This anticipation of brisk extra sales corresponds to the concept of elastic demand for the retailer, that is, high sensitivity of customers' purchase levels to changes in price. **Elastic demand** is more likely:

- if the item requires medium to large dollars of expenditure, for example salt and matches would not qualify;

- if there are alternative outlets for comparison shopping, for example a single outlet in a remote country town would not qualify;

- if customers have a high awareness of normal price levels, for example infrequently purchased items like maple syrup would not qualify – who knows the normal price of maple syrup?; and

- if the brands can be compared easily, for example designer dresses would not qualify.

As the exceptions above indicate, these conditions do not always apply, so each retailer must assess how responsive their customers are to price changes.

While a change in price may seem like a good idea at the time, it is crucial that the retailer take into account likely price responses by competitors. Will competitors respond or not? If they do respond, for example, to a price cut by matching the lower price, then the original benefit to the initiating retailer could be undone. It then might have been better not to have cut prices in the first place.

How can retailers know in advance whether or not competitors will respond to any price change that they may initiate? This is a delicate game of psychology. It partly depends on how aggressively a retailer communicates their price cuts – more aggressive moves generally elicit more reaction. While some reaction patterns can be learnt over time, the actual reaction also depends on the business intelligence activities of the retailer's competitors. Retailers gain various levels of business intelligence – which includes competitive intelligence – by monitoring the actions of competitors. A study of Australian clothing retailers (Merrilees & Miller 1994) found that about one third of their sample of clothing retailers both closely monitored the prices of their competitors and responded to any change in their competitors' prices. This fraction could vary across regions and across retail categories depending on how competitive they were. Nonetheless, at least some retailers do not closely monitor competitors' prices, perhaps because of specialised product lines or because they focus more on customer service than on price.

The greatest problem with price cuts is the risk that they may escalate into a price war. Many of the classic price wars in Australia, for example margarine and newspapers, have been between manufacturers, but retailers have played a part in the conduct of the price wars. Vignette 8.2 summarises some of the lessons of one of the better documented price wars, namely the Sydney newspaper price war between Fairfax and Rupert Murdoch's News Limited. Newsagents were among the losers in this war as they received a constant 25 per cent mark-up off a discounted newspaper cover price.

More explicitly in the retailing area, there has been intense competition in most retail categories, with prices being one of the key weapons in these battles. These retailing price wars have three notable features: firstly, they are often associated with excessive use of sales; secondly, they are pushed by one or more established players trying to aggressively increase their market share – in some cases fuelled by new retail formats such as with toys; and finally, in some cases they are provoked by the entry of a major new player, for example Toys 'R' Us and for a short time World 4 Kids – a Coles-Myer Ltd business in the 1990s. Table 8.1 summarises these features.

Toward an integrated pricing framework

There is a lot of information to absorb about pricing decisions, and it may be somewhat confusing to stop at this point. Instead, we propose a straight-forward framework to integrate the material covered. So far, this chapter has covered a range of pricing methods for determining the overall price level, a wide variety of issues for determining the price structure across the product mix, as well as the dynamic issues of *when* to change price.

Vignette 8.2

The Sydney newspaper price war

The seminal study by Merrilees (1983) of the price war between Sydney publishers News Limited and John Fairfax presents a classic example of different pricing strategies being used in a price war and their differential impacts on business performance. The study reveals the difficulty of identifying who starts a price war. In this case, the cause was attributed to News Limited. At the time, each company published both morning and afternoon newspapers.

News Limited kept the price of its afternoon paper low, while Fairfax resisted discounting and kept is price high. The study shows that – given that afternoon papers have an *elastic* demand – the decision by Fairfax not to match the price discount cost it dearly in terms of profitability. Instead, Fairfax chose to retaliate by initiating a price discount on its morning newspapers.

As it turns out, the two morning papers were not as close substitutes as the two afternoon newspapers. That is, they had relatively *inelastic* demand. If you have inelastic demand, it is better to keep prices higher rather than lower. Therefore, this action also cost Fairfax in terms of profitability.

An elementary knowledge of pricing principles would have indicated to Fairfax that they were using the wrong pricing strategies in both markets, in contrast to News Limited who used the correct but different pricing strategies in both markets.

Contributed by Professor Bill Merrilees

A two-step **method of integrating pricing** issues begins first with a recognition of the unifying roles of retail strategy, market positioning and pricing objectives. Second, another step to integrate these pricing issues is to realise that they are asking different questions. Different pricing questions call for a different emphasis on particular pricing methods. There is no one pricing method which effectively deals with all types of pricing decisions. The most relevant pricing method depends on the type of pricing decision that a retailer wishes to make. In some cases, it may even be appropriate to use a combination of pricing methods.

This integrated framework is implemented through Table 8.1 which deals with generic questions about price. A versatile approach is needed in terms of which pricing method is relevant to the question. The recognition of a variety of pricing questions is a key aspect of the integrated pricing framework. The other key aspect is the realisation that some pricing methods – or selected combinations of them – are more relevant to certain pricing questions (see Table 8.2).

Table 8.1 Features of Australian price wars

Feature 1: Often retail prices wars may seem different because they take the form of 'sales'. However, these sales are becoming more and more frequent and are offering larger discounts which make them as 'lethal' as any manufacturing price war. The price wars – in a less overt way – have even extended to department stores, with David Jones instructing buyers to purchase more merchandise at lower price points, Myer offering up to 30 per cent off in Summer Savings (2006 Catalogue), and discount department stores having random one day sales. Across retail categories, price wars are more intense if one or more of the established players is seeking aggressively to increase their market share, which is certainly the case with supermarkets.

Feature 2: The new competition can be sparked by rejuvenation across existing retail forms or by new retail formats. In clothing retailing, both of these factors have occurred in recent years. Mail order and open markets have been revitalised and are taking more of the apparel dollar away from traditional storefront outlets. Newer retail formats include factory outlets and planned factory outlet centres – supported in part by organised shopping trips to a series of individual factory outlets or to centres such as Harbour Town, DFO or Birkenhead Point.

A very significant relatively new retail format is *e-retailing* or *e-tailing* which epitomises the new competition (see Dennis, Fenech & Merrilees 2004). In hardware, toys and office stationery, the superstore format – which emphasises low prices and deep product assortment – has emerged (Merrilees & Miller 1997).

Many smaller independents are being squeezed out of business in the same way that the national supermarket chains have been squeezing out independent stores of the past four decades. Sometimes even the bigger players cannot deal effectively with competition, with prominent examples over the past 15 years including Venture (budget clothing and manchester), Brash's (music), Daimaru (department store), and Franklins (low price supermarket).

> **Feature 3**: In some cases, the new competition is fuelled by the entry of new players who 'do not understand the learnt rules of orderly conduct'. This is particularly the case in toy retailing with the entry of American retailer Toys 'R' Us to Australia in 1993 (Merrilees & Miller 1997) and in supermarkets with the entry of ALDI in 2001 (Merrilees & Miller 2001).
>
> *Contributed by Professor Bill Merrilees*

Table 8.2 A framework for integrating pricing decisions

The following are generic types of pricing questions with the most relevant pricing method(s) given in the right column.

1.	Will a given price allow a target mark-up to be attained?	**Cost orientation**
2.	What price is appropriate if there are special selling or delivery costs?	**Cost orientation** and **Demand orientation**
3.	What price levels are competitors charging?	**Competitive orientation**
4.	If prices are varied, how much will sales change?	**Demand orientation**
5.	Should different prices be charged for different merchandise categories and by season?	**Demand orientation**
6.	Can higher prices than competitors be charged if based on image and reputation?	**All orientations**

The retailer can use this table as a guide to whether a **cost**, **demand** or **competition** approach is relevant. The first step is to recognise the interactions between retail strategy, retailer brand, market positioning and pricing objectives. The second step is to articulate the essence of the pricing issue. This can be expressed as a question. The main types of questions are shown. To illustrate, if a retailer is concerned about whether a selected price level will enable a target rate of profit, then a cost orientation is appropriate. What if a retailer is concerned about what price is appropriate if there are special selling or delivery costs? A cost orientation could be used in the first instance, although perceived value is also a factor and may enable a price to be charged which is greater than the additional costs.

Conclusions

This chapter demonstrates the importance of price in the retail mix and the need to be explicit about which pricing objectives a retailer wishes to achieve. Pricing strategies need to be linked tightly to the retail strategy, retailer brand and the overall market positioning of the retailer. The chapter has also discussed a variety of pricing methods including cost, demand and competition bases. The reader needs to understand the nuances of each method, including how to determine price when there is a range of products being sold. The price structure section included a discussion on why some supermarket items have low profit margins while others have high profit margins. The chapter explained the considerations necessary to price optional extras, drawing on the concepts of price bundling and price unbundling.

Australians love a bargain, so an essential topic that had to be discussed in this chapter was 'the sale' – that is, all forms of price mark-downs. The diversity of sales may surprise some readers, with new types such as 'end of catalogue' and 'seven day sale' continually being added to the more familiar seasonal, clearance, stocktaking, Christmas and other festival sales. The chapter also discussed other forms of promotional pricing including loss leaders and reduced financing charges.

To assist the reader in dealing with the complexity of which pricing method to use, the chapter developed a framework for integrating pricing decisions. The framework highlights the fact that there are a variety of different pricing questions, and that particular pricing methods are more relevant to particular questions.

The chapter has discussed the broader issue of retail price wars, which seemed to reach an all-time high in the 1991-93 recession, but the tempo has continued into the 21st century. Some of this competition is healthy – especially that relating to new retail formats. However, price wars are a challenge to retailers if they wish to survive the price wars and remain in a competitive position. We advocate the need for a strategic business intelligence analysis of the retail environment to gain an understanding of the causes of any price wars. Finally, retailers should recognise that the chapter advocates a systematic best practice review across all aspects of the retail mix to support the retailer's brand.

Review and applications

1. 'Price is very important for discount retailers, but it is also important for upmarket retailers.' Discuss.

2. Think about two retailers in a retail category of your choice. Can you infer that these retailers have similar or different pricing objectives? If they are different, how does this predict different price levels between the retailers?

3. 'The usefulness of a particular pricing method depends on the pricing question that you ask.' Discuss.

4. As a retailer of appliances, how would you price optional extras such as delivery, or extended warranty and installation? Should these extras be bundled or unbundled?

5. Why do you think optional recommended retail prices and competitive pricing are two of the most popular pricing methods? Are there any limitations or dangers in either or both of these methods?

6. What causes retail price wars? What role do new retail formats play in retail price wars? What advice would you give to a small independent retailer caught in the middle of a toy price war?

7. Discuss the proposition that the over abundance of price promotions that is 'sales' – has 'trained' customers not to pay full price.

8. Develop a pricing portfolio for a fashion retailer. Explain your findings.

Website references

Australian Competition and Consumer Commission (ACCC): <www.accc.gov.au>.

Big W: <www.bigw.com.au>.

Birkenhead Point Shopping Centre: <www.birkenheadpoint.com.au>.

Bunnings Warehouse: <www.bunnings.com.au>.

Choice: <www.choice.com.au>.

Clive Peeters Ltd: <www.clivepeeters.com.au>.

David Jones Ltd: <www.davidjones.com.au>.

DFO (Direct Factory Outlets): <www.dfo.com.au>.

Harbour Town: <www.harbourtown.com.au>.

Myer Ltd: <www.myer.com.au>.

Oxfam Australia: <www.oxfam.org.au/shop>.

The Salvation Army: Salvos Stores: <www.salvosstores.salvos.org.au>.

Woolworths Ltd: <www.woolworths.com.au>.

References

Betts, EJ & McGoldrick, PJ 1996, 'Consumer behaviour and the retail "sales": Modelling the development of an "attitude problem"', *European Journal of Marketing,* vol. 30, no. 8, pp. 40-58.

Corrigan, M & Ellis, S 1994, `Winter of our discount ends: Why retailers are sweating', the *Australian Financial Review,* 3 June, pp. 1, 4.

Coughlan, A & Vilcassim, N 1989, `Retail marketing strategies: An investigation of everyday low pricing vs promotional pricing policies', Working paper, Graduate School of Management, Northwestern University, December.

Dennis, C, Fenech, T & Merrilees, B 2004, *e-Retailing,* Routledge, London.

Ford, C 1995, `Shopping in the war zone', *NRMA Open Road,* May-June, pp. 6-8.

Levy, M, Grewal, D, Kopalle, PK & Hess, JD 2004, 'Emerging trends in retail pricing practice: implications for research', *Journal of Retailing,* vol. 80, pp. xiii-xxi.

McIlwraith, I 1993, `Coles in struggle to meet targets', the *Sydney Morning Herald,* 29 November, p. 21.

McLaughlin, J 1991, *Nothing Over Half a Crown: A Personal History of the Founder of the G. J. Coles Stores*, Loch Haven Books, Main Ridge, Victoria.

Merrilees, B 1983, `Anatomy of a price leadership challenge: An evaluation of pricing strategies in the Australian newspaper industry', the *Journal of Industrial Economics*, vol. XXXI, no. 3 (March), pp. 291-311.

Merrilees, B & Fam, KS 1999, `Effective methods of managing retail "sales"', *International Review of Retail, Distribution and Consumer Research*, vol. 9, no. 1, pp. 81-92.

Merrilees, B & Miller, D 1994, *Retail Customer Service and Organizational Capability*, Paper presented to the Joint European Institute of Retailing and Services Studies (EIRASS) and Canadian Institute of Retailing and Services Studies (CIRASS) Conference, Recent Advances in Retailing and Services Science, Banff, Alberta, Canada, May.

Merrilees, B & Miller, D 1997, 'The Superstore Format in Australia: Opportunities and Limitations', *Long Range Planning*, vol. 30, no. 6, pp. 899-905.

Merrilees, B & Miller, D 2001, 'Innovation and Strategy in the Australian Supermarket Industry', *Journal of Food Products Marketing*, vol. 7, no. 4, pp. 3-18.

Ortmeyer, G, Quelch, J & Salmon, W 1991, `Restoring credibility to retail pricing', *Sloan Management Review*, Fall, pp. 55-66.

Advanced reading

Binkley, JK & Connor, JM 1998, 'Grocery Market Pricing and the New Competitive Environment', *Journal of Retailing*, vol. 74, no. 2, pp. 273-294.

Biswas, A, Dutta, S & Pullig, C 2006, 'Low price guarantees as signals of lowest price: The moderating role of perceived price dispersion', *Journal of Retailing*, vol. 82, no. 3, pp. 245-257.

Bolton, RN & Shankar, V 2003, 'An empirically derived taxonomy of retailer pricing and promotion strategies', *Journal of Retailing*, vol. 79, pp. 213-224.

Cataluna, FJ, Franco, MJ & Ramos, AV 2005, 'Are hypermarket prices different from discount store prices?', *Journal of Product & Brand Management*, vol. 14, no. 5, pp. 330-337.

Cox, JL 2001, 'Can differential prices be fair?', *Journal of Product & Brand Management*, vol. 10, no. 5, pp. 264-275.

Desmet, P & Le Nagard, E 2005, 'Differential effects of price-beating versus price-matching guarantee on retailers' price image', *Journal of Product & Brand Management*, vol. 14, no. 6, pp. 393-399.

Evanschitzky, H, Kenning, P & Vogel, V 2004, 'Consumer price knowledge in the German retail market', *Journal of Product & Brand Management*, vol. 13, no. 6, pp. 390-405.

Fratto, G, Jones, MR & Cassill, NL 2006, 'An investigation of competitive pricing among apparel retailers and brands', *Journal of Fashion Marketing and Management*, vol. 10, no. 4, pp. 387-404.

Gendall, P, Fox, MF & Wilton, P 1998, 'Estimating the effect of odd pricing', *Journal of Product & Brand Management*, vol. 7, no. 5, pp. 421-432.

Gendall, P, Holdershaw, J & Garland, R 1997, 'The effect of odd pricing on demand', *European Journal of Marketing*, vol. 31, no. 11/12, pp. 799-813.

Halepete, J, Hathcote, J & Peters, C 2005, 'A qualitative study of micromarketing merchandising in the US apparel retail industry', *Journal of Fashion Marketing and Management*, vol. 9, no. 1, pp. 71-82.

Hardesty, DM & Suter, TA 2005, 'E-tail and retail reference price effects', *Journal of Product & Brand Management*, vol. 14, no. 2, pp. 129-136.

Kalita, JK, Jagpal, S & Lehmann, DR 2004, 'Do high prices signal high quality? A theoretical model and empirical results', *Journal of Product & Brand Management,* vol. 13, no. 4, pp. 279-288.

Kopalle, PK & Lindsey-Mullikin, J 2003, 'The impact of external reference price on consumer price expectations', *Journal of Retailing*, vol. 79, pp. 225-236.

McWilliams, B & Gerstner, E 2006, 'Offering low price guarantees to improve customer retention', *Journal of Retailing*, vol. 82, no. 2, pp. 105-113.

Moon, S, Russell, GJ & Duvvuri, SD 2006, 'Profiling the reference price consumer' *Journal of Retailing*, vol. 82, no. 1, pp. 1-11.

Moore, M & Carpenter, J 2006, 'The effect of price as a marketplace cue on retail patronage', *Journal of Product & Brand Management*, vol. 15, no. 4, pp. 265-271.

Park, EJ, Kim, EY & Forney, JC 2006, 'A structural model of fashion-oriented impulse buying behavior', *Journal of Fashion Marketing and Management*, vol. 10, no. 4, pp. 433-446.

Schindler, RM 2006, 'The 99 price ending as a signal of low-price appeal', *Journal of Retailing,* vol. 82, no. 1, pp. 71-77.

Schindler, RM & Chandrashekaran, R 2004, 'Influence of price endings on price recall: a by-digit analysis', *Journal of Product & Brand Management,* vol. 13, no. 7, pp. 514-524.

Sheinin, DA & Wagner, J 2003, 'Pricing store brands across categories and retailers', *Journal of Product & Brand Management*, vol. 12, no. 4, pp. 201-219.

Srivastava, J & Lurie, NH 2004, 'Price-matching guarantees as signals of low store prices: survey and experimental evidence', *Journal of Retailing*, vol. 80, pp. 117-128.

Walker, J 1999, 'A model for determining price markdowns of seasonal merchandise', *Journal of Product & Brand Management*, vol. 8, no. 4, pp. 352-361.

Wagner, R & Beinke, KS 2006, 'Identifying patterns of customer response to price endings', *Journal of Product & Brand Management*, vol. 15, no. 5, pp. 341-351.

Wood, CM, Alford, BL, Jackson, RW & Gilley, OW 2005, 'Can retailers get higher prices for "end-of-life" inventory through online auctions?', *Journal of Retailing*, vol. 81, no. 3, pp. 181-190.

Zhao, H & Cao, Y 2004, 'The role of e-tailer inventory policy on e-tailer pricing and profitability', *Journal of Retailing,* vol. 80, pp. 207-219.

Zielke, S 2006, 'Measurement of Retailers' Price Images with a Multiple-item Scale', *International Review of Retail Distribution and Consumer Research*, vol. 16, no. 3, pp. 297-316.

Retail selling and customer service

Introduction

Retailers and the media discuss customer service widely. Often, the media and some business consultants concentrate on customer service failures (see Newlin 2006; Plant 2007) and retailers tend to emphasise examples of how they 'delight' customers (Michelli 2007). In retailing, the customer is central to the successful completion of the retail exchange, yet the introduction of self-service, the mediocre execution of merchandise management and store design, poorly planned cost cutting and insufficient staff training all tend to diminish effective and efficient customer service. Industry leaders like Nordstrom's, the North American department store (Spector and McCarthy 2000), stand out and yet both industry and academic researchers have scope for much more significant research into customer service.

The focus of this chapter is on the customer service component of the retail mix and on one of its most significant expressions – personal selling. The basic intent of **customer service** is to help customers to complete their shopping encounters satisfactorily. **Customer satisfaction**, an overall indication of how satisfied the customer is with the retailer overall, is the desired outcome of all retail marketing activities. It has an especially unifying force when it comes to retail services. The simplicity of that statement masks the complexity of customer service and the opportunities for retailers of all sizes to tailor their customer service offerings to achieve **service quality**, that is an overall indication of customer attitudes to the retailer.

This chapter suggests that **customer care** is critical for successful retail performance. **Customer contact** occurs in many ways. Face-to-face encounters for sales (**personal selling**), refunds or information, and telephone, email and other e-communications are all potential points of customer contact. However, total customer service is broader than just customer contact, as this chapter shows by discussing the complexity of customer service, its nature and scope, as well as service failure recovery systems. In addition, concepts such as **customers**

as co-opted staff, the roles of **frontline staff**, and **service measurement** point to areas where retailers could create distinctive customer service portfolios.

Critical questions to note are: (1) do retailers actively choose the service mix which is required to implement their retail and brand strategy? And (2) do retailers have in-place service management and measurement systems?

Customer service cannot be *ad hoc*. It must be buttressed by **customer service systems**. Normann (1984) emphasised the **service management system**, which includes a service vision, target market and service strategy as well as a **service delivery system** analogous to manufacturing operations. Davidow and Uttal (1989, p. 160) explain that: "The infrastructure of consultation, more effective application of technology, better training and exemplary support...underpins customer service...which is whatever helps the customer get the benefits he expects from a product". This is the essence and strength of service – that it encompasses the networks of people, physical facilities and information that support the production of customer service.

The idea of 'manufacturing services', if adopted by retailers, means that they can exert more control over their service operations. Added to the 'manufacturing' or systems approach is the need for the retailer to **evaluate** customer service performance. Other approaches build on the service management framework and particularly emphasise methods of **measurement**, which are discussed later in this chapter. Another approach is the organisational capability approach which Ulrich and Lake (1990) pioneered. They underscore the importance of human resources (especially recruitment and selection, training and development, recognition of staff and remuneration) as the most important of organisational capabilities, together with internal communications and organisational flexibility. The connection between these organisational capabilities and the delivery of excellent customer services, including personal selling and resulting in customer satisfaction, is inescapable.

The idea of customer service and its special relationship with retail selling is not new. As Burnham (1955) noted,

> *In store organization charts of the 1920s and 1930s such titles appeared as 'superintendent in charge of customer service'. These executives, aided by floor managers and section supervisors, were primarily concerned with the relationships between the store, as represented by the salespeople, and the many individuals who made up the store's clientele. It is noteworthy that customer service rather than sales management was stressed in the titles of such operating executives.*

This chapter explores the nature of customer service, presents a taxonomy of customer service, and discusses how retailers select customer service objectives and an appropriate mix of customer services to suit their specific retail strategy and retailer brand. The chapter then discusses a strategic approach to retail selling which favours the development of explicit selling objectives, codes of conduct for staff to interact with customers, and recognition of other necessary selling support systems including staff training. When these factors are synergistic, they strengthen the retail selling process.

The nature and scope of customer service

Designing and delivering excellent customer service appropriate to the retailer's strategy and brand can create a sustainable competitive advantage for the retailer. At the broadest level, **retail customer service** can be defined as any retail activity that increases customer satisfaction (Levy & Weitz 1992). It is useful to take a broad view of customer service which can be adapted to particular studies and retail categories. Customer service is a multi-faceted concept, and should be understood in terms of recognising *each* of the many components. Alternatively, it is more useful to classify and group various types of customer services, as shown in Table 9.1. The benefits of the taxonomy are that it helps the retailer to consider the full range of customer service dimensions, and to cluster the components appropriately.

Table 9.1 A taxonomy of customer services groups

Personal service: staff interactions with customers

Add-on services: alterations, delivery, installation, gift vouchers, gift wrapping, gift registries.

Special customer orders

Measures to address customer risk aversion

Payment options: credit and debit cards, cash, cheques, EFTPOS.

After-sales service

Value for money: including low or discounted price.

Shop atmosphere

Physical services

Appropriate speed of service

Convenience

Clubs and loyalty programs

Service failure recovery systems

Personal service

Traditionally personal service has been and still is very important in some retail categories, and is discussed in more detail later in this chapter. The point here is that customers often have high expectations of personal service which retailers can develop into a competitive advantage. If mismanaged, however, those unmet expectations can lead to a loss of store patronage. The trend to *depersonalise* services was prominent, for example, in banking with the widespread introduction of automated teller machines (ATMs). However, even in that sector there has been a shift back to more face-to-face services such as home visits by home loan advisors.

Some retailers, such as department stores, combine forces with manufacturers to bring in consultants to advise customers on fit and style, for example in shoes or intimate apparel. Co-operative advertising between the retailer and the manufacturer/ supplier notifies customers about these services. Retailers must ascertain the optimal level of personal service, and then develop training and other systems to support these services.

Add-on services

Add-on services such as alterations, delivery or installation were once commonplace. The cost of these services has meant that retailers either no longer offer these services, or offer them on a 'user pays' basis.

Some retailers are offering delivery and installation 'packages' for white goods with individual pricing for the packages. Customers selecting the standard package are informed about the specific day of delivery; those choosing the 'silver package' are given a five hour 'window' for the time of delivery; for the premium package, customers receive a guaranteed two hour delivery 'window'.

Alterations to clothing are less often directly available from the retailer generally, although some retailers have formed alliances with other firms which carry the alteration function. Fashion retailers have much scope to improve this service offer so that the customer leaves the store assured that the garment will fit well.

Many food and grocery retailers no longer provide delivery services. Yet, as the demographic profile of the market changes, retailers will need to reconsider their customers' needs. In the e-retailing domain, delivery of purchases remains one of the areas that would benefit from innovative alternatives.

The proliferation of gift vouchers for products and services such as spa treatments, entertainment and travel experiences, gift-wrapping and gift registries suggests scope for retailers to add value for customers. Many shopping malls offer gift vouchers that are redeemable centre wide. From a customer's perspective, it is important that the vouchers do not have expiry dates. In some jurisdictions, expiry dates are illegal.

Surprisingly, in the 'Christmas Store', a dedicated section of a department store, staff explained that gift wrapping was not available because of the pre-Christmas sale that resulted in the staff being busy – and for the same reason price tags could not be removed. How frustrating for customers seeking the extra convenience of finalising a gift, complete with wrapping. In contrast, some stores develop alliances with local service groups or charities so that volunteers provide the wrapping service and customers either make a donation or pay for the wrapping materials. An added benefit of this for the retailer is the contribution to community relations.

Special customer orders

These orders arise when the retailer is prepared to order something for the customer which is not immediately available in the store or which may require some degree of customisation. This is common in furniture stores and bookstores, however it has become less common in clothing stores. Generally, many shoe stores are reluctant to try to track down a particular style or even the right size and colour. Apart from trying to source products from other branches of the same retailer, store managers may not have the authority to deal directly with the supplier. Another constraint on special orders is that small retailers often have to meet a supplier's order threshold before the request will be acceptable. For retailers, nurturing relationships with suppliers could help in trying to meet special orders for customers and thus in strengthening the retailer's brand.

Measures to address customer risk aversion

Measures to address risk aversion include services such as lay-bys, refunds and exchanges which reduce the risk of mistakes when initially buying merchandise. Stores are usually more likely to have a flexible exchange policy than a flexible refund policy. In fact it is quite common for retailers to display signs which indicate that no refunds will be given. Sometimes the signs are roughly handwritten, which of itself communicates a store with a low level of service.

Note that it is contrary to trade practices legislation not to give a refund for damaged or faulty goods. Despite this legal requirement, some retailers are less than forthcoming in meeting their obligations.

Retailers need to determine the extent of their refund and exchange policy, and communicate this policy and its related procedures very clearly to customers as well as to staff. Some stores have very tasteful signs which indicate their policy. Catalogue and direct mail retailers and e-retailers need to give higher weight to return and exchange policies to reassure customers who cannot trial goods before ordering.

Warranties and guarantees are additional customer service options that reduce consumer risks. Many consumer durable retailers now offer extended warranties, that is, beyond the period offered by the manufacturer. However, the consumer needs to balance the likelihood of the risk against the increased cost, as the sale of these extended warranties is often very profitable for retailers.

Payment options

Credit and debit card payment options are very important because consumers have more choices about how to pay for their merchandise with the introduction of advanced technologies. The introduction of **EFTPOS** – electronic funds transfer at point of sale – and of credit card facilities meant that retailers had to re-engineer their payment processes. Store credit cards and other informal credit facilities have long been popular, and many co-branded credit cards are available in addition to store credit cards.

In contrast in the early days of modern retailing, many retail entrepreneurs resisted offering credit facilities because of their personal views and values regarding the possibility of customers incurring debt, or perhaps more pragmatically because of concerns about creating bad debts for the business.

Smart cards include pre-paid phone cards, multi-use electronic purses (still yet to find much general acceptance), and pre-paid cards for small frequent purchases. Some retailers have resisted these innovations, placed unreasonable restrictions on their use in terms of which cards are acceptable, or required high minimum values for purchases by credit cards.

After-sales service

After-sales service represents another group of services that can be important to some customers. They are very relevant when the customer wants additional information (such as how to assemble the unit that came as a flat pack) or when something goes wrong, or when the customer wants to complain or get help. The use of 1800 telephone numbers can be an effective tool for retailers to use to implement this service, but they must back it up with appropriate staff training. One trend has been to download this responsibility to the manufacturer.

Arguably the manufacturer is the expert, however the retailer must be assured that the customer will receive excellent after-sales service, or else the retailer's reputation will suffer. Moreover, the retailer needs the information from the customer calls in order to be able to evaluate the issues raised.

Some retailers seem to be referring customers primarily to their websites rather than dealing with them directly by telephone. The other issue here is that the retailer is assuming that every customer has easy access to the internet.

Value for money

Low or discounted price is an important part of the offer to a segment of the retail market. If this is a fundamental part of the retailer's strategy, then it tends to dominate other service offerings. Indeed, it may be necessary to curtail offering high levels of other types of customer service in order to keep costs down and to therefore support the low-cost strategy. See *Chapter 8 – Retail pricing* for discussion of **every day low prices** (EDLP) and other discount strategies.

In other cases, value for money will be important, and the extent of other service offerings will depend on where the retailer is positioned on the value for money continuum. Even customers for premium priced products will expect value for the money they invest in their purchases.

Shop atmosphere

Shop atmosphere is another important service that customers receive. The collective of mood, displays and information are major supplements to personal service. **Point of purchase** (POP) displays have been referred to as the 'silent salesperson', given the roles they play in communicating with the customer. Retailers using the self-service format need to present their merchandise and information in ways that facilitate good customer service. As discussed earlier, self-service does not mean *no* service. It would be a serious mistake for retailers to interpret self-service as 'no service'. Rather, self-service must be managed by providing effective and efficient service systems which assist the customer.

Physical services

Physical services such as fitting rooms and rest rooms can be very important to certain customers, and yet are often omitted or poorly maintained by retailers. The physical design of fitting rooms seems to be particularly important for many customers. Thus, for example, sufficient space makes access easy for people with prams, wheelchairs, shopping trolleys or parcels. Also, many less mobile shoppers need to have a companion to help them in a fitting room, which is another reason to have adequate space. Good lighting, mirrors, clothes hooks, shelves for bags, and even a bell or a buzzer to request additional service are all integral to fitting room design and fit out.

Other physical services may include child-minding facilities, children's play areas, and areas for feeding children. Many big box retailers have also introduced cafés, echoing the department stores and variety stores of the past which provided refreshment facilities in a safe environment. In warmer climates, some stores provide iced water dispensers and undercover car parking. In Canada, many stores and shopping malls provide well-located hand sanitizer liquid dispensers – often adjacent to escalators and stairways or near food courts.

The push for greater environmental awareness – including a reduction in the use of plastic bags – has led some retailers to provide plastic bag recycling facilities and the availability for purchase of bags manufactured from more environmentally friendly materials.

Appropriate speed of service

Speedy service seems to be particularly important to the younger and higher income customers. Supermarkets are continuously redesigning checkout facilities to speed up the process, partly by using scanners, bar coding and improving the ergonomic handling and packing of merchandise by staff, and partly by offering express checkouts. Whether customers will embrace the self-checkout facilities that various supermarkets are trialling remains an open question.

The desired speed of service is context specific for many customers. For example, in pharmacies some customers want much more detailed and deliberate service so that they fully understand the administration of prescribed medications.

Various banks, supermarkets and fast food outlets have tried to feature speedy service by offering rewards to customers if their wait exceeds a certain standard. In most cases, the standard is abandoned quickly when the retailer cannot meet its promise.

Retailers have significant scope to develop innovative queuing systems which customers would find more equitable.

Convenience

Convenience in all its facets is extremely important to the consumer. These services include location, parking, easy accessibility by public transport, bicycle paths and walking, hours of operation, layout of the shopping centre and the store, travel within a shopping precinct, and sense of security. Convenience also embraces the adjacent retail facilities so that one destination may provide the opportunity to make multiple purchases from different stores. Apart from longer shopping hours – usually regulated by governments – other convenience tactics include free home delivery and pick up services by pharmacists for example. Valet parking at shopping centres or restaurants is another approach to convenience.

Clubs and loyalty programs

Clubs and loyalty programs can be thought of as a specific service or a special combination of other customer services. Clubs, such as registered clubs and groups with common interests like hobby groups, have long been popular both in Australia and abroad. Retailers such as Katies have developed clubs, as have pharmacists (in relation to baby clubs). Airlines offer club memberships which offer enhanced bookings and exclusive waiting areas and facilities. Airlines also promote frequent flyer loyalty programs which offer benefits such as rewards based on usage for regular travellers. The common objective of clubs is to promote common interest, fun and **customer loyalty**.

Other loyalty programs are based on an alliance of companies, for example the FlyBuys program (see the FlyBuys website). Interestingly, FlyBuys promotes special offers on their website. **Co-branded credit cards** have also become popular because they link a major retailer, a bank and a credit card company together, offering a more flexible type of loyalty program.

Some of the criticisms from consumers about some loyalty programs include a perceived excessive time lag between purchases and accruing enough points to make a meaningful redemption. One more immediate way of rewarding customers is with a cash discount on the current transaction. In between these polar positions, the major supermarkets – through their associated petrol outlets – offer very aggressive petrol discounting subject to minimum purchases in the supermarket. For example, until Christmas 2006, with a minimum purchase of $80.00 in a single transaction at a Coles or Bi-Lo supermarket or Coles Online, customers could get 10 cents per litre discount, with an additional two cents per litre discount if they also made a minimum purchase of two dollars instore at the Coles Express attached to the petrol outlet. Woolworths and Big W had similar offerings during the same period.

Service failure recovery systems

Service failure recovery systems is the final customer service group in the proposed taxonomy. This group differs from the others as it arises because the **retail service encounter** is incomplete – either because of the service provider, because of their suppliers or even the customer. For example, an air flight for a particular customer could be aborted because of a scheduling error, because of a shortage of aviation fuel or the passenger being ill. In one sense, it does not matter what caused the termination of the service. It is still an incomplete service and thus lowers the customer's satisfaction. On the other hand, retailers have a wide variety of options to deal with these service failures, and they should proactively increase strengths and capabilities in developing and implementing systems. Higher quality recovery systems represent a higher level of customer service, which will be a necessity for retailers in the future.

Setting customer service objectives and determining the appropriate customer services mix

Once the retailer understands the wide variety of customer services groups and the options within each, the retailer has to select an appropriate **customer service mix**: which meets the needs of the target customers; which is compatible with the retailer's strategy, brand and capabilities; and which meets profitability goals and market positioning objectives. Generally, more upmarket customers will be in a position to demand higher levels of customer service. However, there are exceptions. For example, many high income customers shop at discount supermarkets, apparently happy to trade-off a 'no-frills' service approach for considerable price savings. This apparent paradox might explain one source of their wealth – more prudent shopping for staples and other everyday products.

Retailers can chose core and peripheral services, and shape a mix of customer services to suit their specific customers. **Market research** will play a valuable role here. Customer surveys will help retailers to understand customer priorities, however the retailer should match the customers' needs and wants with the organisation's capabilities. Some retailers have insufficient budgets or are otherwise unwilling to spend large amounts redesigning store layout, installing computerised transactions or training staff. These situations narrow the options available to the retailer, who could benefit by seeking outside advice from a consultant to ensure that they have scrutinised the major possibilities.

The customer service mix will vary by retail category and by the retailer's strategy and brand. Creating a distinctive customer service offering will strengthen the retailer's unique brand and contribute to differentiation from competitors.

The service management system

The major aspects of a service management system are: (1) *selection* of an appropriate service strategy to suit a specific target market; and (2) the *development* of a service delivery system to deliver the actual service. The idea of development is important because these systems usually require some time to build up, nurture and mature. They may require refitting of the store or the ongoing training of staff. The key components of a service management system are: the role of customers in the service delivery system; the role of front line staff; customer service programs critical to the system; and measurement support systems.

Customers as co-opted staff

One of the great revelations of Normann's (1984) work was that customers could be considered as a part of the retailer's service delivery system. This is a powerful concept. Retailers can use this notion together with continuous improvement and total management tools to inspire and re-engineer – that is, reshape – the ways that they offer services.

The idea that customers as well as staff are part of the production of services is more obvious in services retailing such as hairdressing where it is impossible to have a haircut without the customer being involved. Some customers are very involved with specifying length, style and colour, and in conversation with the service provider. The concept of **co-production** is gradually attracting scholarly research and more interest from retailers.

The same principles apply to merchandise retailing. The introduction of self-service has brought about a major shift in the relative contributions of customers to the provision of retailing services. Retailers must decide the degree of self-service to be offered, because in practice there is a wide spectrum between 'total' self-service and full service models. As discussed in *Chapter 5 – Store design*, IKEA is a good example of a retailer developing the self-service components by having easy store layout, effective arrangement of stock, and clear informative signage.

It is not simply a one-dimensional choice of how far to go along the self-service to full-service spectrum. Retailers can add other qualities to the shopping experience.

For example, retailers can increase the involvement of customers by providing printed educational materials about the products. Oxfam, IKEA and The Body Shop all provide useful materials and signage. Other retailers involve customers by providing price scanners, in-house information kiosks, scales for weighing produce, or 'smart' shopping carts that advertise directly to the customer. Some retailers require customers to be involved in former staff functions such as packing groceries in supermarkets, while other retailers enlist customers to help deter shoplifting.

There is considerable scope for creative thinking and innovation to involve customers in the service process. However, retailers should check that customers do not resent being co-opted, but rather that they welcome and value their roles in the co-production of services.

Customer service programs: frontline staff

Much of the customer service literature deals with customer objections in the buying process and with customer complaints. The usual suggestions focus on how to train front line staff to respond to objections and complaints. In both situations, the sales personnel have to understand the customer's needs and to deal with them as objectively as possible.

For example, during the buying process the salesperson may become aware that the customer is only willing to spend a limited amount of money on an item. The next step is to check this perception with the customer and then focus more closely on items in the particular price band. The salesperson should then emphasise the positive, quality attributes of the merchandise.

Customer complaints must be handled sensitively. The situations are real to the customer even if they seem trivial to the sales associate or customer service staff. If the retailer has clear policies about refunds and exchanges, the sales staff can act expeditiously and with confidence and truly represent the retailer's brand. Staff need to be trained or briefed about how to deal with difficult or unusual situations, including those where they suspect **deshopping** behaviour or other possible deceptions, and with specific complaints. If dealt with effectively, the retailer may be able to forestall negative word-of-mouth.

Equally, complaints offer a valuable source of information as a symptom or barometer of other concerns or dysfunctions in the retail mix. If the complaint data is properly analysed, it may reveal patterns such as some of the following:

- poor quality merchandise;
- poor delivery by either the supplier or the retailer;
- poor advice by the salesperson;
- poor integration between promotions and sales staff product knowledge; or
- or vague store policies.

In general, front line staff have very important roles to play in delivering customer service. Vignette 9.1 indicates some actual problems, all of which are preventable. Whatever retail category and wherever the retailer is placed on the customer service spectrum, there is no latitude for complacency.

Vignette 9.1

Trouble in store – when the front line staff aren't living the brand

Despite all the effort put into developing strategies and into designing the retail mix, including the customer service portfolio, many customers receive poor service.

Pratt (2007) discusses a mystery shopping exercise visiting 14 well-known retailers in Toronto, Canada. However, similar outcomes would eventuate in many shopping environments in many countries. Not unexpectedly, the findings revealed examples spanning very poor service to excellent.

Poor service included: the ineffective answer to a request for information about a gift registry; an off-hand referral to a catalogue; the electronics 'expert' who had poor product knowledge; and perhaps worst of all, in a pet shop a woman cradled a boxer pup in her arms for half an hour after being given the animal to hold.

On the other hand, excellent service was judged to have taken place where, although there was no final sale, the sales associate gave her business card to the customer. And in another situation, excellent technical product knowledge was conveyed.

For your consideration:

How can retailers develop strong employee commitment to customer service and to the retailer's strategy and brand?

How can customers contribute to improving customer service?

Other customer service programs

Once the desired customer service mix is identified, the retailer develops the appropriate systems or programs to deliver the desired customer service levels. As a general principle, each type of customer service strategy requires different types of systems and support programs, and therefore suggests the need for active management in the local context, taking into account any cultural factors and nuances.

For example, when developing measures to reduce the perceived financial risk to customers, aspects including lay-by policy, exchange policy, refund policy and policy about the acceptance of credit cards require a policy to be worked out by the retailer.

Support systems for measuring customer service

Measurement systems help to ensure that the retail mix is appropriate to customer needs and that all available information is utilised to monitor, evaluate and modify the delivery of service to the customers. Measurement should be used as a positive tool to improve customer service rather than as a tool to 'punish' staff. As indicated, various authors highlight the importance of the measurement of customer service and satisfaction. The emphasis should be on timely, accurate information that is cost effective. There are five key areas of measurement.

First, market research can help to ascertain customers' needs. The research can be conducted by inhouse researchers or commissioned from external providers, and can be of a very simple nature designed to highlight basic requirements of the target market.

Second, retailers can measure ongoing service quality. The **gap model** has often been used as a basis, with the delivery gap in particular being related to organisational quality (Parasuraman, Zeithaml & Berry 1985). The SERVQUAL survey instrument has been common and compares customer perceptions of a service with expectations. This survey instrument is lengthy and complex, and is usually more suited to larger retail chains, however a single outlet retailer can also use it successfully to identify a specific service gap in customer service.

Other approaches to measurement include: developing and monitoring **key performance indicators** or **KPIs** (see *Chapter 10 – Retail operations, performance management and support systems*), and alternatives such as customers surveys, customer focus groups and the use of mystery shoppers (people paid to buy products from the firm anonymously in order to assess service), and the use of the retail audit. Without a sophisticated approach to managing and measuring service encounters, there are likely to be many dissatisfied customers, lost sales and a potential diminution of the retailer brand.

Third, retailers can continually monitor and evaluate their organisational capabilities, which can be done *directly* though checklists of technological, financial, human resource, physical and intangible capabilities, and through surveys of employees, and *indirectly* though service quality studies. The retail audit protocol will be useful for this (see *Chapter 10 – Retail operations, performance management and support systems*).

Fourth, related to service quality, retailers can also measure the overall level of customer satisfaction.

A sophisticated approach to managing customer satisfaction is to model the various drivers of customer satisfaction. The Merrilees Model of Customer Satisfaction (1995) links process variables controlled by the retailer – such as delivery – to the experience of the customer with respect to negative critical incidents (happenings such as the wrong product being delivered), to customers' perceptions of overall service quality, and finally to the level of overall customer satisfaction received by customers (see Figure 9.1). To operationalise the model for a particular retailer, it is necessary to survey a sample of customers.

Fifth, in addition to customer satisfaction retailers can track any emerging customer dissatisfaction, for example, by analysing complaints or by consulting with staff about incomplete sales or increasing returns.

Figure 9.1 Model of customer satisfaction

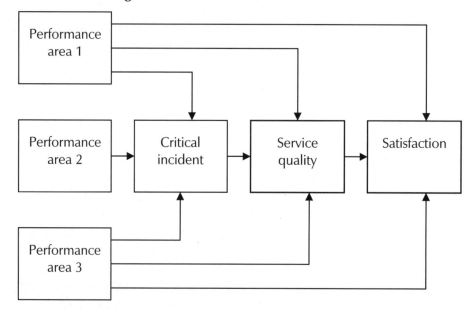

Source: Adapted from Merrilees (1995).

Personal selling

In some marketing environments, for example business-to-business (B2B) marketing, **personal selling** is clearly the most important form of promotion. The same idea applies to retailing, as *Chapter 7 – Retail promotion* shows. For some types of retailing, for example direct selling by firms such as Avon or Tupperware, personal selling is an extremely important component. Nonetheless, not all retailers explicitly associate personal selling with their promotions budgets. Most firms have separate budgets for personal selling, which is grouped under salaries and wages, and for other promotional tools and activities. In retailing, personal selling – that is selling by sales people – is an important means of promoting merchandise and services. Sales staff are available to indicate the availability of certain merchandise, to show where it is, and to advise on the quality, price and use of merchandise and its suitability for specific customers. As with B2B marketing, in **business-to-consumer** (B2C) marketing the product knowledge of staff is a very important part of the promotion process. In some cases, personal selling becomes a reference point for other types of promotion such as point-of-sale material, which is sometimes referred to as the **silent salesperson**.

Despite the importance of the selling function to shop front retailers, only a minority seem to have a well-planned and well-structured approach to selling. Many texts focus on a descriptive outline of the selling process without firstly linking selling tactics to the overall retail strategy and retailer brand; and without secondly explicitly choosing a particularly retail selling system. To be strategic, retailers should develop explicit selling objectives, codes for conduct for staff interacting with customers, and other necessary selling support systems including staff training. When these factors are synergistic, they strengthen the retail selling process and support the retail brand image.

This chapter defines a **retail selling system** as:

> ... the expression of the retail selling objectives. Retailers achieve this expression by the integration of a purpose driven, specific selling style with explicit selling support systems. The retailer implements the retail selling system through the retail selling process and, like any system, it must be evaluated.

Figure 9.2 demonstrates the components of the system and some of the notional linkages.

It is useful for retailers to keep reminding themselves that personal selling is not only a form of customer service but also a potent form of promotion, especially when determining the promotion budget and the promotion mix. Moreover, the retail selling system ought to support and reinforce the retailer's brand image. Retailers can use the model shown in Figure 9.2 to build an actual retail selling system; they can uniquely configure the core elements of the retail selling systems by designing them to meet the personal selling needs of the retail firm.

Retail selling objectives

The first core component of the retail selling system is the formation of **retail selling objectives**, which broadly include but are not limited to:

1. generating current sales;

2. generating future sales;

3. building long-term relationships with customers;

4. generating more informed choice for potential customers;

5. enhancing the overall convenience of the shopper; and

6. contributing to the desired retail brand image and marketing position of the retailer.

Objectives 4, 5 and 6 all contribute to positive customer satisfaction and hence to customer loyalty and positive word-of-mouth promotion. By being explicit about the retail selling objectives, retailers help to increase staff satisfaction through performance management.

The retailer should develop the objectives in consultation with stakeholders including staff and customers. The objectives are the basis for key performance indicators which are a prerequisite for performance management and evaluation.

Figure 9.2 Integrated retail selling systems: The core components

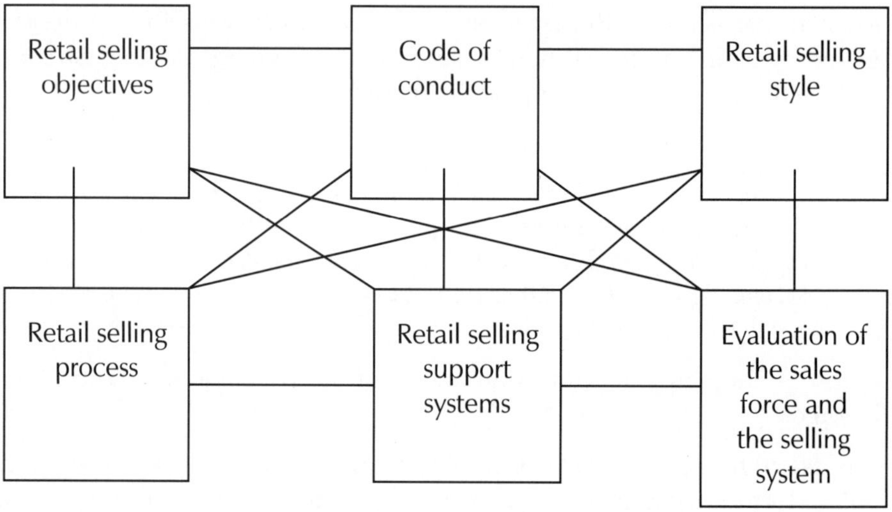

Note: The connecting lines in Figure 9.2 are indicative of the dynamic nature of the relationships between the components of the system, and are intended to show some but not all of the potential linkages.

Retail selling style

The practices that retailers use are summarised in Table 9.2.

The first two styles – point-of-sale and low-key sales assistance – are **low cost** selling styles. They are also **low quality** in terms of assisting customers. Conversely, the last two styles – hard selling and interactive selling – are **higher cost** and **higher quality** in terms of customer assistance. Retailers need to analyse the cost-quality trade-off and match it to their overall retail strategy and retailer brand image. Beyond this there are considerable differences in the selling *approach* between the two high sales service styles.

Although we cannot prejudge what cost-quality trade-off any particular retailer would prefer, the discussions in this chapter continue on the assumption that the

interactive selling style is the ideal benchmark. However, retailers can use this framework in a modified way to suit both the point-of-sale selling style and the hard sell style. It is even possible to use the framework for the low-key selling style, although arguably this inferior variant evolved for reactionary reasons.

Another way to describe the interactive selling style is as the **consultative selling style**. Earlier proponents of consultative selling were mainly involved in industrial (business-to-business or B2B) rather than retail (business to consumer or B2C) selling. Consultative selling has been defined as "an approach to creating long-term, mutually beneficial sales relationships with customers by helping them improve their profit through use of the salesman's (sic) products and service" (Hann, Cribbin & Heiser 1973, p. 5).

Table 9.2 Alternative retail selling styles

Point-of-sales emphasis approach

This style gives almost sole emphasis to an efficient point-of-sale, order taking approach to selling. Most service is self-service by the customer, and the main interaction will be at the checkout, pay-point or cash desk. Discount retailers such as Kmart and Crazy Clarks (see their websites) commonly use this style.

Low-key sales assistance approach

This style offers minimal salesperson assistance because of a deliberate low-key approach to selling. These retailers are conscious that the hard sell approach is inappropriate for their business, and they react by deliberately minimising aggressive selling. Sometimes, however, salespeople may overreact against strong approaches and in the process offer minimal sales service of any description.

Hard sell approach

This style involves a highly active salesperson who is primed to pursue customers aggressively and, where feasible, sell as much as possible including any relevant add-ons such as warranties. Some might see this as a more or less one-way relationship from the salesperson to the retail customer.

Interactive selling

This style emphasises the two-way relationship between the salesperson and the retail customer. Usually some form of contact is made initially by the salesperson with the customer, who is later followed up to discover their needs. This approach draws upon the listening skills of the salesperson and their product knowledge. It focuses on meeting customers' needs and adding relevant additional information where appropriate.

This business-to-business selling emphasis can be adapted to a retailing context by substituting *customer satisfaction* for the term *profit*. The consultative selling approach is superior to a more traditional approach (Buss & Herford 1994), being described as a "paradigm of co-operative and honest relationships between sellers and buyers, in which the seller achieves their goals and successes by helping its customers to achieve their goals" (McCloy 1993, p. xiii).

The common feature of these consultative selling models is an emphasis on identifying and satisfying customer needs through the facilitating role of the salesperson. The term **interactive selling** suggests a balanced relationship between the need of the salesperson to complete a sale and the need of the customer to make an informed choice. Therefore, interactive selling constitutes an explicit but subtle refinement of consultative selling.

Codes of conduct

Retailers can support staff by providing them with codes of conduct for dealing with customers. These codes might take the form, for example, of rules for customer communication. Most codes seem to be clear, simple and easy to action. A code used by the St Vincent de Paul Society in their stores was based on the 'principle of courtesy', that is, making people feel comfortable and welcome (Table 9.3). Interestingly, charity stores have both employed and volunteer staff, and codes of conduct can help to guide everyone on how to approach customers.

Table 9.3 Code of conduct for retailing staff

The image of the Society depends of you. So follow these golden rules:

1. Greet people warmly – a smile can work wonders.

2. Use the magic phases: 'Please', 'Thank you', 'You're welcome', 'I'm sorry'.

3. Be aware of every action – maintain steady eye contact and avoid distracting gestures.

4. Do a little bit extra whenever possible – show you really care.

5. Always keep promises and ensure your good-bye has a smile and is pleasant.

Source: St Vincent de Paul Society, 1990s, communications with Professor Bill Merrilees.

The code of conduct may include company policy on when and how to greet customers, whether to use a soft sell or hard sell style, the importance of product knowledge, and general ethical principles. The main advantage of developing a code of conduct for use by employees is that it makes explicit – and therefore reinforces – the desired selling style of the retailer. It facilitates a more consistent use of the selling style across all employees – whether they are sales staff or other staff – who have contact with customers.

A code of conduct should be developed in consultation with the affected staff, and should take into account customer feedback. Separate focus groups of staff and customers can contribute to developing a responsive code of conduct consistent with the retailer's strategy and brand image. Implementation will be ineffective if the code of conduct is presented to staff as a *fait accompli*. Rather, senior managers must lead the development process and encourage staff 'buy-in'. One concern that staff sometimes have is that the firm imposes required scripts for interaction with customers, reducing flexibility and initiative, and worse still applies penalties for non-compliance.

Having developed a code of conduct, the retailer must ensure they communicate the code and its purposes and practice to both staff and customers. Staff, including part-time, casual staff and volunteers in not-for-profit retailing – for example Oxfam shops – should be trained in relation to the code. They must understand what it means and how the retailer expects them to enact the code. For new staff, understanding the code and its behavioural implications will be a crucial part of the employee orientation program, which should be the first training activity for new employees.

Despite the advantages of using a code of conduct, a regional study by the author revealed that only 40 per cent of clothing retailers actually used such a code. The study demonstrated that simply developing a suitable code may move retailers closer to best practice retail selling and help to give them a competitive advantage in personal selling.

With suitable supervision and performance feedback, employees will improve their learning about how to sell effectively and efficiently to customers. All sales staff should have clear performance goals that they have developed in consultation with their supervisors, and that are consistent with the retail selling objectives. Sales staff should be encouraged to be reflective about their performance and about the processes and systems that contribute to retail success.

Codes of conduct present a convenient opportunity for retailers to emphasise **ethical standards**. Importantly, codes of conduct can help accelerate this learning among the staff. Some of the more important ethical standards are summarised in Table 9.4. While the first three principles may seem fairly obvious, they are not always practised by all retailers.

Ensuring informed customer choice, the fourth principle, has included as a direct challenge to retailers to extend their horizon of ethical practices. Some retailers might argue that the medical ethical principal of informed consent is too expensive to adopt in retailing. The author disagrees. Informed consent is a **benchmark** that retailers can aspire to. It places a premium on retailers explaining the relative merits of different merchandise in light of the identified needs of customers. Mass merchandise retailers would rely more on pre-tested labelling and signage to achieve this objective. Throughout this text, a fundamental tenet of retailing best practice is the concept of **informed customer choice**. Retailers subscribing to this approach can incorporate it as part of their retailer brand image.

For codes of conduct to be effective, they must be translated into action through leadership (i.e. leading by example), training, supervision, retail selling support systems, and the retail selling process. Finally, they have to be linked to the retail performance management system. The codes can be reviewed using tools such as the retail audit protocol which could show the extent to which they contribute to better customer service and to greater customer satisfaction and loyalty.

Table 9.4 A hierarchy of ethical principles for retail selling

1.	Not causing malice to customers	Not being misleading, for example knowingly selling inferior goods at inflated prices.
2.	Being courteous and honest	See the Code of Conduct in Table 9.3 for example.
3.	Doing some good for the customer	Whereas the first principle is based on *not* causing financial or other harm to the customer, this principle is based on *doing* some good for the customer. In the retailing context, this is most likely to eventuate from providing attentive service, for example not talking to fellow staff about social or personal matters when potential customers are left unattended and inconvenienced.
4.	Ensuring informed choice by the customer about the retail offer	This ethical principle is similar to that in medical practice where a patient contemplating an operation or particular investigation or treatment makes a decision based on full and open information about the various options and their potential consequences.
5.	Incorporating environmental considerations into retail choices	These considerations are initially included in the type of merchandise available and in the way retailers conduct their operations, and can be reinforced during the selling process.

Retail selling process

Selling, like any other business activity, is best thought of as a *process* or a series of processes. Slightly different processes are involved in different selling contexts, such as industrial, retail or some other type of selling focus. In the retail selling of both merchandise and services, the main stages or sub-processes in retail selling are:

- the pre-approach;

- the greeting;

- identifying customer needs;

- helping customers to make an informed choice;

- closing the sale;

- following up the sale; and

- evaluating sales staff and retail selling systems.

These seven stages readily indicate that there is much more to selling than just making a sale. By taking a broader perspective, retailers can understand the essential elements of selling.

Stage 1: The pre-approach

The pre-approach stage of selling refers to all those activities that precede and are relevant to the selling encounter, and ensures that the sales person is well prepared for the various selling situations. Therefore, the salesperson must be familiar with the store layout, merchandise spatial planning, the attributes and uses of the merchandise, and the code of conduct through being trained to the required level.

Stage 2: The greeting

The greeting is the first personal contact – either verbal or non-verbal – between the customer and the salesperson. It is particularly important in the retail selling process because, unlike the B2B setting, the salesperson and the customer are unlikely to know each other. In some cases, the customer may not want to know the salesperson at all and may wish to browse in anonymity. The scene is set for potentially embarrassing situations if there are conflicting expectations. Retailers deal with this predicament by developing rituals or greetings which tend to be culture specific. The most popular greeting is 'Can I help you?'. This is a closed question and invites the typical customer response of 'No thanks' or 'I'm just looking'. Simply varying or deliberately differentiating this greeting could have a sales impact. 'Can I help you?' and its frequent variant 'May I help you?' fit into what is called the **service approach** or **service greeting** (see Table 9.5).

Guidelines for improving retail greeting practices include first using the two-stage greeting, which offers the advantage of acknowledging the consumer in a non-threatening way while still being ready to offer service later (Type 5, Variant 2). The problem with those retailers who adopt a single stage *welcome* or *browse* greeting is that they are not actively contributing to the informed choice of their customers. Second, as part of a two-stage greeting process the retailer may further be able to improve service by differentiating the service offer. Third, there is scope to differentiate the welcome part of the two-stage greeting. Sales staff can use extra non-verbal communication, for example name badges or welcome badges, along with genuine interactive body language. Finally, the greeting can be elevated in importance through enriched, contextual retail selling support systems which could comprise an integrated selling strategy with explicit selling objectives, appropriate employee and management training, and a code of conduct for employee-customer interaction.

Table 9.5 The retail greeting: a typology

Type 0 **The Browse**	■ a *de facto* greeting; ■ there is a deliberate decision to allow the customer to browse, made in the light of the customer segment; ■ coupled with informal non-verbal communication; or ■ can be supported by the physical environment, store image, customer information and education material.
Type 1 **The Welcome Approach**	■ also characterised as **the salutation**; ■ includes social conversation; and ■ can be deliberate but non-verbal such as smiling or nodding, or other friendly acknowledgement.
Type 2 **The Merchandise approach**	■ also characterised as **the hard sell**; and ■ uses more direct questions about merchandise alternatives.
Type 3 **The Classic Service Approach**	■ characterised as 'Can I help you?'
Type 4 **The Differentiated Service Approach**	Variant 1: 'How can I help you?' or similar open-ended variant of the classic service greeting. Variant 2: The interactive service greeting.
Type 5 **The Multiple Greeting Approach**	More than one stage to the greeting of a single customer: Variant 1: Multiple greetings of the same type. Variant 2: Multiple greetings of different types, that is, combinations of types including the multiple use of the same type together with other types.

Note that the *order* of greetings may change. The most common combination, in one study by the author, was an initial welcome greeting followed by an offer to help, where 75 per cent of clothing retailers used a two-stage greeting. The second most common combination was the deliberate decision to allow the customer to browse first and then to offer help.

Source: Original research with Professor Bill Merrilees.

Stage 3: Identifying customer needs

Some customers have a clear idea about what they want, while others are less certain. The sales staff should use all of their skills to help sort out which customers actually want sales assistance. Non-verbal cues can help the salesperson deal with the situation, although it is important for the salesperson to be aware of and to respect cultural differences in communication – both verbal and non-verbal. When the salesperson and the customer are verbally communicating, the salesperson should attempt to ascertain the key features and benefits that the customer may be seeking. Willingness to pay a certain price is a related aspect that also requires clarification.

The retailer's pre-approach measures make the process of identifying customer needs easier. The advertising, window display and the store brand image will have helped already to 'qualify' or screen customers into the various market segments. This makes the job of the salesperson clearer, though there is still the important task of identifying the needs of individuals within the market segment. The salesperson can also identify any associated needs and how to meet them. For example, the customer may want to buy accessories to match the clothing purchase that they are considering. The sales staff need to be supported in this endeavour through systems that facilitate inter-departmental sales – which is a form of **cross selling**. Too often a customer is merely told that the required products are elsewhere is the store, and is left to find the actual department or display as well as make separate payments. Once the sales person has identified the needs of a particular customer, they can assist the customer to make an **informed choice**.

Stage 4: Helping customers make an informed choice

This is the essence of the selling process. Based on an understanding of the customer's needs, the salesperson interacts with the customer to assist in evaluating the pros and cons of alternative merchandise and services. Such **consultative selling** is an interactive process that works best when the salesperson:

- is more informed about the customer's needs;

- is more informed about the pros and cons of alternative merchandise or services; and

- is able to match the customer's needs to the alternative merchandise or services.

As part of the selling interaction, salespeople may encounter what are traditionally referred to as **customer objections**, and these arise when the customer raises some negative aspect of the merchandise or retail offer. The salesperson tends to interpret this legitimate concern as resistance to the sale. Arguably, objections are simply information questions *en route* to making an informed choice. Therefore, objections are equal in status and nature to any question asked by the customer, and should be integrated into the usual consultative process without undue fuss or fanfare.

Occasionally, the salesperson needs to raise the 'objection' if they think that the proposed use of the product is inappropriate or even dangerous. The ethical principles discussed can help here.

Price objections are a special case. Usually pre-approach measures, including store advertising and retailer brand image, will have qualified those customers who want to pay in a certain price range, or will have filtered out those who do not. Some remaining customers may still think a particular item is too highly priced. Salespeople are usually advised to focus then on the quality and benefits of the merchandise and their relationship to the customer's other identifiable needs.

What will happen if a customer only has a limited budget for such an item? Customers are ultimately interested in value, which is a trade-off between quality and price. Some of the benefits are intangible, which complicates the matter and makes it difficult for the customer – not to mention the salesperson – to see the full picture. The role of the salesperson is not to *sell* a particular item of merchandise; rather, it is to *help* the customer compare the value of two or more alternative brands. The best value brand is not necessarily the most expensive.

Stage 5: Closing the sale

If the salesperson has developed the appropriate *rapport* with the customer, it will become clear from customer cues when the customer is ready to buy. At that point, there is no need for the salesperson to be reticent. Assuming the selected merchandise fits the customer needs, then part of the sales service is to complete the sale. A simple clear question from the salesperson to the customer should suffice. Depending on the context, it may be appropriate to check if any add-on merchandise or services are required if this has not already be established while helping the customer make an informed choice. The challenge is to be able to offer additional products or services without turning the offer into a hard sell, and the principles of interactive selling should continue to guide these behaviours.

In Pratt's (2007) mystery shopping case studies, sales staff at each of the fourteen stores failed to close the sale. The quote from co-researcher Andrij Brygidyr demonstrates the problem:

> *"There's one thing that every single person did wrong ...They never asked for the order. They never said, 'Want to take a suit home with you today? Perhaps a tie?' You're there to sell. You cannot forget that." (Pratt 2007, p.37).*

Stage 6: Following up the sale

Although the close of a sale is the end of a specific selling encounter, it can also be the beginning of a future selling encounter. This idea is consistent with the objective of retail selling being to build long-term relationships with customers, and is part of the total shopping experience. If all aspects of the current selling encounter go well, this will build goodwill for the future. Informed choice rather than 'selling for selling's sake' is a major building block to this end. Sales staff can use explicit activities, for example remembering customer names, to help develop long-term relationships, although this may be difficult with longer shopping hours and irregular shifts for casual or part-time staff. The retailer can use various systems – including direct marketing based on customer databases, in-house charge accounts or special memberships – to maintain ongoing relationships with customers.

Stage 7: Evaluating sales staff and retail selling systems

Retailers must distinguish between two inter-related evaluations – those of the sales staff as individuals and those of the retail selling system as a whole. Most texts concentrate on the former type of evaluation, namely: 'How successful is a particular employee as a salesperson?'

Individual evaluation can occur using a range of activities. Retail trainees or newly-appointed sales staff are evaluated during their probationary period to determine if they are suitable for the position. Their manager or supervisor may assess other sales staff, and give constructive feedback in relation to previously agreed goals. Staff can only be accountable for those goals over which they have control. Rewards for retail staff for improved performance may include bonuses, prizes (subject to Fringe Benefits Tax), and greater job security. Usually these rewards are based on individual or store performance. Generally, they include the overall sales of the salesperson or the retailer. There is a growing trend in insurance, for example, to reward repeat business and not simply initial sales. If all the stages of the selling process are conducted effectively and efficiently, the result should be greater customer satisfaction and increased repeat business. Retailers need to be innovative in developing broader performance indicators to reflect these selling objectives. An extension of the individual evaluation is the combined individual and work team evaluation. The benefits of this composite evaluation are that the individual is still accountable, and is still recognised and rewarded for individual excellence.

Although the evaluation of individual sales staff is important, storeowners and managers must also look at the big picture. Individual sales staff are a vital part of a wider retail selling system. Additional components include hiring staff, training and reward systems, and the adequacy of management, advertising, merchandise and credit policies, and the performance of backstage employees. The responsibility is with the retailer to review the entire retail selling system periodically, including objectives, selling style, code of conduct, the selling encounter and evaluation.

Retail selling support systems

Retail salespeople do not sell in a vacuum. The code of conduct is an example of one support system that guides employee-customer interactions. Other selling support systems include: appropriate and sufficiently-stocked merchandise, advertising, sufficient staff to do the job, training, performance feedback to staff, equitable reward systems, store organisation, suitable store design and visual displays, an attractive store atmosphere, and effective and efficient technology such as EFTPOS and barcode scanning. Lack of investment in these systems creates both dissatisfied, inefficient staff and poorly served customers (see Vignette 9.2).

*The indirect or **non-selling** tasks of the salesperson are further important aspects of the retail selling support systems. These tasks constitute the **selling infrastructure**, and take two forms. The first is **routine tasks**, which refers to predictable and regular non-selling tasks such as 'tying up the ad', pricing and tagging merchandise, labelling goods, stacking shelves, displaying merchandise, checking stock and tidying displays. The second is **non-routine tasks**, which refers to tasks that may be less regular or predictable, including seasonal changeover of stock, stocktaking, handling customer complaints or concerns, and customer surveys.*

Overall, apart from selling skills, sales staff require **training and development** in various skills including time management skills. The salesperson must be able to fit in the non-selling tasks without wasting time or deferring tasks such as tidying stock to the next shift. Sales staff have to learn to set priorities among the overall range of activities performed in non-selling time. The onus is on the retailer to ensure that the optimal selling support systems are provided to sales staff. The better retailers adapt their support systems to suit the particular needs to the retail strategy, or, where necessary, adapt their strategy to suit their system's capabilities.

Other forms of retail selling

Retailers using other forms of retail selling including direct selling, direct marketing, catalogue retailing, vending machines, unattended kiosks and e-retailing should extrapolate the principles of customer service and selling presented in this chapter. These forms of retail selling should be part of the retailer's explicit strategy, and their relationship to the retail brand should be soundly established and managed. Each of these forms will need specific investment as well as the allocation of organisational resources, dedicated support systems and performance management systems that link to the other aspects of the retailer's business.

Vignette 9.2

Moving from mediocrity to excellence

Reflect on your own experiences as a customer, talk with family and friends, - it seems that almost everyone has a 'horror' story about poor customer service. Many people have stressful experiences with employees being rude or confronting. For some people the extent of poor service is so widespread that they have developed personal 'form letters' to send to retailers and service providers. Worse still, a customer may take the time to fill in a customer feedback form, but receive no feedback in turn. No one wins in these situations.

The risks for retail chains are high because one underperforming outlet may tarnish the reputation of the entire chain or franchise network.

Customers may retaliate by shopping elsewhere, using negative word-of-mouth, blogging, or complaining to the media or consumer organisations. If the retailer is fortunate, the customer will take the time to complain directly by mail, email, in person or by telephone. Retailers should welcome such feedback because they have the opportunity to try to rectify the problem or make amends in some way that is agreeable to the customers. While the retailer may feel some customers are unreasonable, investment in training, motivating, supporting and rewarding staff will help them to respond proactively to churlish customers or to customers with a legitimate concern.

Portsmouth (2007, p. 9) recently encapsulated the situation:

Fortunately for many retailers, they can survive simply by being less bad than the competition. Those who'd prefer to thrive, however, should offer the training and remuneration that underpin great service – a valuable point of differentiation in today's retail world. Given how much a great shopping experience sticks in the minds of consumers, stores would not only notch up the first sale, but also repeat and referral business. And that would be a happy ending for retailers and shoppers alike.

Lack of investment will lead to poor implementation. Too often, the person dealing with the customer's concern is not authorised to take action to resolve the situation effectively and efficiently. Retailers need to design and invest in their customer service mix so that it supports the retail strategy and the retailer's brand.

For your consideration:

- Should retailer executives be mystery shoppers in their own firms? (Assuming they are not known by sight; if they are, should they try telephoning or emailing to test customer service?)

- What lessons could fashion retailers learn from this example? Are the lessons similar or different for supermarkets and big box retailers?

Conclusions

One of the exciting and challenging opportunities for modern retailers is to create distinctive customer service systems that result in well-satisfied repeat customers who happily refer others. To achieve that result, retailers have to design the customer service component of the retail mix so that it is consistent with and supports the overall strategy and retailer brand, and they have to invest in the customer service mix. The chapter developed a taxonomy of customer service groups, rather than simply presenting a long list of customer services. The taxonomy enables retailers to comprehend the full range of customer services, and additionally to cluster the relevant components. Some of the novel groupings include measures to reduce risk financial aversion, such as a refund policy, and service failure recovery systems aimed at minimising customer dissatisfaction with incomplete transaction or service encounters. In some retail categories, the offering of some types of customer services, such as add-on service and personal service, has waned with retailers allocating lower priority to these types of services. In contrast, other types of customer services such as new payment options and customer loyalty programs have higher priority.

For some retailers, customer service levels seem to be accidental, that is 'something somehow happens'. Within the firm, this approach is unlikely to lead to high levels of consistent and co-ordinated customer service quality. In other cases, the support systems are too superficial, for example instructing staff to smile at each customer, or minimalist. Conversely, retailers with sophisticated levels of customer service are likely to have planned which components they emphasise in the customer service mix. They will also have invested in clear priorities, managing the customer service systems, providing integrated support systems, and introducing effective and efficient measurement systems.

Retail selling is one aspect of the customer service mix that retailers too often treat with an *ad hoc*, perfunctory approach. Mimicking another retailer's selling approach is poor practice. Benchmarking can be a useful start to developing a distinctive retail selling system, but skilled retailers understand the differences between thoughtless imitation and the deliberate benchmarking of processes. The concept of the retail selling system suggests the complexity of service and selling. Only the tip of the iceberg, some aspects of the selling style can be simply observed. The casual observer does not readily discern the more subtle aspects of style such as the deliberate use of multiple greetings, or the often-elaborate selling support systems that can be fundamental to the retailer's success. An observer only sees the impacts of those support systems. The retailer who actually designs and uses a *unique* retail selling system can measure its performance against KPIs for individual, group, function and store performance.

Good customer service does not simply happen. It is staged, managed and evaluated continuously. The aim is to ensure its consistency with the retail strategy and the retailer brand, and its responsiveness to the competitive environment and customer needs and wants. The customer service component of the retail mix presents the retailer with the scope to develop a unique customer service profile and offer, and to leverage it into a competitive advantage.

Review and applications

1. Evaluate the taxonomy of customer service groups. Can you identify the need for any additional groupings?

2. 'The growth of the self service format will eliminate the need for personal service'. Discuss this claim.

3. 'Self-service is a cynical attempt by retailers to exploit customers. It gives the shopper – frequently women – more unpaid work to do.' Debate this proposition.

4. Explain how small retailers can establish innovative customer loyalty programs.

5. Discuss how retailers can evaluate their customer service portfolios.

6. Explain how the customer service component of the retail mix can be designed to give a retailer a sustainable competitive advantage.

7. Discuss what customer services a retailer could offer to enhance environmental sustainability.

8. Discuss how far retailers should go in incorporating ethical principles into their business in general, and their code of conduct for employee-customer interaction in particular.

9. Explain the relationships between customer service, organisational capabilities, organisational learning and corporate memory.

10. Develop an orientation program for part-time sales staff (associates). How would you evaluate the effectiveness of such a program?

11. 'Selling is more than sales'. Discuss this statement by exploring the role of the salesperson in customer relations.

12. Explain how retailers can manage customers' concerns positively. Is there a difference between customer complaints and customer objections? What should happen with compliments from customers?

13. The concept of customer resistance is well known. How should the retailer deal with staff resistance to certain customers?

14. 'The role of the salesperson is not to sell a particular item of merchandise, but instead to help the customer compare the value of, for example, two alternative brands'. Debate this proposition. Consider also the ethics of manufacturers offering incentives to selling staff (as opposed to customers) for the sale of certain products.

15. Explain the backstage functions that support the selling process. Consider how incentives and rewards systems can recognise backstage employees.

Website references

Check specific retailers' websites to see what they say generally about customer service. Next, consider how those retailers who sell online integrate the principles of effective customer service, how they personalise retail selling, and how they have built their retail selling systems.

References and reading

Anderson, J, Jolly, L & Fairhurst, A 2007, 'Customer relationship management in retailing: a content analysis of retail trade journals', *Journal of Retailing and Consumer Services*, vol. 14, pp. 394–399.

Burnham, E 1955, 'Key problem of retail store selling: It is time to explode the view that employment in department stores is the last resort of people with no special skills', *Harvard Business Review*, pp. 103-118.

Buss, J & Herford, G 1994, *Personal Selling in Australia*, McGraw-Hill, Sydney.

Carlson, C & Wilmot, W, 2006, *Innovation: The Five Disciplines for Creating What Customers Want*, Crown Business, New York.

Dabholkar, P, Thorpe D & Rentz J 1996 'A measure of service quality for retail stores: scale development and validation', *Journal of the Academy of Marketing Science*, vol. 24, no. 1, pp. 3-16.

Davidow, W & Uttal, B 1989, *Total Customer Service: the Ultimate Weapon*, Harper, Perennial, NY.

Delgado-Ballester, E & Munuera-Aleman, J 2001, 'Brand trust in the context of consumer loyalty', *European Journal of Marketing*, vol. 35, no. 11/12, pp. 1238-1258.

Hann, M, Cribben, J & Heiser, J 1986, *Consultative Selling*, Amacom, New York.

Keeling, K, McGoldrick, P & Macaulay, L 2006, 'Electronic kiosks in retail service delivery: modeling customer acceptance', *Journal of Marketing Channels*, vol. 14, no. 1/2, pp. 49-76.

Kim, S & Jin, B 2002, 'Validating the retail service quality scale for US and Korean customers of discount stores: an exploratory study', *The Journal of Services Marketing*, vol. 16 no. 2/3, pp. 223-237.

Laroche, M, Pons, F, Zgolli, N, Cervellon, M-C & Kim, C 2003, 'A model of consumer response to two retail sales promotion techniques', *Journal of Business Research*, vol. 56, no. 7, pp. 513-522.

Laroche, M, Ueltschy, L, Abe, S, Cleveland, M & Yannopoulos, P 2004, 'Service quality perceptions and customer satisfaction: evaluating the role of culture', *Journal of International Marketing*, vol. 12, no. 3 (Fall), pp. 58-85.

Lee, Y-I 2004 'Customer service and organizational learning in the context of strategic marketing', *Marketing Intelligence & Planning*, vol. 22, no. 6 pp. 652–662.

Levy, M & Weitz, B 1992, *Retailing Management*, Irwin, Homewood, IL.

McCloy, P 1993, *Smart Selling: the Consultative Approach*, Business & Professional Publishing, Sydney.

Merrilees, B 1995, 'What drives customer satisfaction? Linking process performance, critical incidents, service quality and customer satisfaction', *Australian Journal of Market Research*, vol. 3, no. 2 (July), pp. 39-43.

Merrilees, B & Miller D 1997, 'The nexus between human resource capabilities and a competitive advantage in retail personal service', *Journal of Customer Service in Marketing & Management*, vol. 3, no. 1, pp. 19-29.

Merrilees, B & Miller, D 2001, 'Superstore interactivity: a new self-service paradigm of retail service?', *International Journal of Retail & Distribution Management*, vol. 29, no. 8, pp. 379-389.

Merrilees, B, Miller, D, & McKenzie, B 2001, 'Cross-cultural retailing research: a comparison of shopping experiences in Estonia and Canada', *Journal of East-West Business* vol. 7, no. 1, pp. 83-100.

Michelli, J 2007, *The Starbucks Experience: 5 Principles for Turning Ordinary into Extraordinary*, McGraw-Hill, New York.

Mittal, V, Kamakura, W & Govind, R 2004, 'Geographic patterns in customer service and satisfaction: an empirical investigation', *Journal of Marketing*, vol. 68, no. 3, pp. 48-62.

Newlin, K 2006, *Shopportunity! How to be a Retail Revolutionary*, Collins, New York.

Normann, R 1984, *Service Management*, John Wiley & Sons, New York.

Parasuraman, A, Zeithaml, V & Berry, L 1985, 'A conceptual model of service quality and implications for future research', *Journal of Marketing*, vol. 49 (Fall), pp. 41-50.

Plant, A 2007, *The Retail Game: Playing to Win – a Guide to the Profitable Sale of Goods and Services*, Douglas & McIntyre, Vancouver.

Portsmouth, I (ed) 2007, 'Who's minding the stores?', *Profit: Your Guide to Business Success*, vol. 26, no. 5 (November), p.9.

Pratt, L 2007, 'Retail report card', *Profit: Your Guide to Business Success*, vol. 26, no. 5 (November), Section: Customer Service, pp. 31-37.

Roberts, E 2003, '"Don't sell things, sell effects": Overseas influences in New Zealand department stores, 1909-1956', *Business History Review*, vol. 77, no. 2, pp. 265-289.

Rust, R & Oliver, R (eds) 1994, *Service Quality*, Sage, Thousand Oaks, CA.

Selnes, F 1993, 'An examination of the effect of product performance on brand reputation, satisfaction and loyalty', *European Journal of Marketing*, vol. 27, no. 9, pp. 19-35.

Spector, R & McCarthy 2000, *The Nordstrom way: the inside story of America's $1 customer service company*, Wiley, New York.

Ulrich, D & Lake, D 1990, *Organizational Capability: Competing from the Inside Out*, Wiley, New York.

Walton, S & Huey, J 1992, *Sam Walton, Made in America: My Story*, Doubleday, New York.

Wong, A & Sohal, A 2003, 'Service quality and customer loyalty perspectives on two levels of retail relationships,' Journal *of Services Marketing* vol. 17 no. 5 pp. 495 – 513.

Zhao, X Bai, B & Hui, Y-V 2002, 'An empirical assessment and application of SERVQUAL in a Mainland Chinese department store', *Total Quality Management and Business Excellence*, vol. 13, no. 2, pp. 241-254.

Implementation

Retail operations, performance management and support systems

Introduction

The formulation of the retail strategy, the retail concept, the retail personality and the retailer brand image, and the detailed specification of the retail mix guide the overall day-to-day operations of the retail business. Moreover, the retailer must put in place effective, efficient and integrated performance management systems to monitor and evaluate performance.

Translating retail strategy into action

How do we implement retail strategy? We achieve this through the use of **retail operations**, that is, through the people, technologies and systems that translate the retail strategy into action. Implementation must be well planned and systematic. Many strategic plans end up proving worthless because they did not have a sound implementation process. When developing the implementation processes, the retailer should continually review the external influences and the internal context of the firm. Any changes will suggest a review to ensure that the strategy and the firm's organisational capabilities are consistent. That way the retailer remains proactive and responsive rather than adopting a reactive or defensive stance.

The purpose of retail operations is to support and operationalise the retail brand. We can think of retail operations as having two types or stages. Stage 1 is translating the retail strategy into retail practice. Examples include implementing a new strategy, a major strategy revision, or managing a major change in the retail mix. Stage 2 is the ongoing management of the current retail mix. The aims of stage 2 cover maintaining equilibrium, adjusting tactics in the retail mix, continual fine-tuning, continued performance improvement, and continued learning. Generally, retailers achieve the day-to-day management of the retail mix by managing people, technologies and systems.

Retail performance management systems

The leaders of the retail firm must be committed to managing performance. This commitment needs to be supported by a performance management strategy and by performance management systems, which incorporate **key performance indicators** (**KPIs**) (see Figure 10.1). The shift has occurred from performance *measurement* to performance *management*. That shift suggests that it is insufficient to simply *measure* performance. Rather, we must develop suitable systems, measure appropriate key performance indicators using suitable tools, and then take the necessary management action to adjust performance-to-date in line with the current retail strategy, or, if necessary, adjust the strategy so that it is more closely aligned with organisational capabilities.

Figure 10.1 Organisational performance management

Performance management strategy

Performance management systems		
Processes	Functions	Outcomes/results

Key performance indicators		
Macro Performance indicators	**Financial** Organisational performance indicators	**Non-financial** Organisational performance indicators

This chapter presents a framework for contemporary performance management, and discusses the application of a range of tools as well as the support systems which can be used in conjunction with these tools. The development and implementation of a performance management strategy must be underpinned by an appropriate organisational structure and culture, as well as by support systems including staff development and training. The chapter examines some retail management issues such as stock shrinkage, stockouts, occupational health and safety matters, fire safety, bomb threats, and natural disasters such as earthquakes and floods. No matter how successfully the retail strategy is implemented, that success can only be identified by effective performance management systems (see Figure 10.2 and Figure 10.3 following).

Figure 10.2 Retail performance management systems: process approach

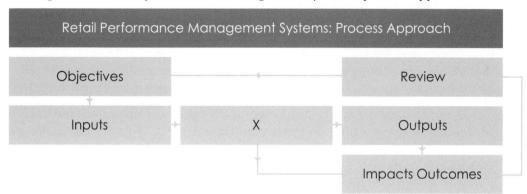

Figure 10.3 Retail marketing performance management

Evaluation and curiosity as a way of life

How can we know how the firm is fairing if we don't evaluate performance? How can we identify what the value-added activities are? How can we comprehend the position of the firm in relation to best practices? In simple terms, we must measure, monitor and evaluate performance – that is the performance of functions, processes and people. The success of evaluation will depend in part on the match between the measures used and their purpose. Generally, measurement is some combination of time, cost, quality and quantity (Fitz-Enz 1984).

A particular type of leadership and organisational culture is required to encourage an organisation and its members to welcome and to appreciate evaluation. Hence evaluation must have underpinning values of organisational learning and continuing improvement, rather than being motivated by a punitive approach. This means that the performance management strategy should be clearly communicated within the organisation. Where there are multiple outlets, the performance management strategies in one outlet should be consistent with – though not necessarily identical to – those of other outlets as well as with the organisation's overall retail strategy. This argument does not negate the need for performance standards, for example with fast food franchises like McDonalds where the consumer has an expectation of identical product and service quality. Indeed, multi-outlet retailers have the opportunity both to improve standards and for extensive organisational learning based on the performance outcomes of each of the various outlets or head office departments.

The Q-Factor manager has been mooted as the type of manager needed to take organisations successfully into the future (Gilbert 1991). **Q-Factor** managers are enquiring, driven by curiosity rather than unthinking adherence to a rules and compliance mentality. Such Q-Factor managers can harness and focus their curiosity by using environmental scanning, business intelligence, benchmarking and a best practice approach, and so contribute to the retailer's competitive advantage.

A framework for retail performance systems

What are performance management systems? The key features of the basic framework of a **performance management system** are:

- performance goals and objectives;

- performance indicators;

- performance measurement systems data collection and analysis;

- monitoring and review processes; and

- management action.

Using this simple schema, any aspect of an organisation can be subjected to performance management. The critical notion is that performance management must be planned and then managed by a system, which includes measurement, but which is not *only* measurement. The key element is the idea of **management action**, otherwise the mere measuring of performance is wasted. Importantly, any aspect of the retail strategy can be subjected to performance management.

Typically, the first performance management system used in many organisations is in the financial area. However, it is insufficient to use financial measures and to only focus only on the bottom line – that is, financial results (Bogan and English 1994). A more comprehensive approach is to examine both processes *and* results. While choices are often made between either a functional approach or an outcomes-based approach, a valuable way for retailing is to use the **I-T-O approach** or **inputs-transaction/transformation-outcomes approach** – which is sometimes termed the **process component approach** (Figure 10.4) using both financial and non-financial performance indicators (see also Table 10.1).

Figure 10.4 The process component approach showing the selling process

Facilitators[*]:
> Performance management strategy and systems
> Management information systems
> Macro key performance indicators, business intelligence
> Benchmarking, best practice

The process[†]:

Inputs	Transformation	Outcomes
Input components: • Capable well-trained staff • Relationship with suppliers • Store location and fittings	Transformation components: • Customer service • Merchandise These are catalysts to sales	Outcomes components[o]: • Satisfied customers • Lower levels of inventory • Increased job satisfaction • Increased profitability

[*] The retail performance management system can be facilitated by having a performance management strategy, supported by suitable systems for data collection and analysis related to each aspect of the retailing process.

[†] The generic retailing process can be thought of as I-T-O. This idea can be applied to retailing overall and to specific retailing processes, including any aspect of the retail strategy.

[o] Unexpected outcomes could include the rate of stock turnover, or the number of associated special orders. Performance should be identified for each component.

The benefits are that this approach helps to recognise the links between various components and any process. That is, within any process each component will influence other components; and further, each process can potentially influence other processes. If the focus is only on results, there will be inadequate understanding of the *processes* leading to those results. This means that it would not be immediately obvious where the retailer should intervene to achieve different results. However, by linking processes, components and outcomes, the retailer will benefit from a more comprehensive view.

Put simply, a process comprises **inputs** (materials, services) to a **transaction** (exchange, transformation) which results in **outputs**. So, in manufacturing, the process of car manufacturing requires multiple parts and labour (inputs), which are then assembled (transformed), producing a car (output). The range of this process can be extended by considering the impacts or outcomes that result from the outputs. Thus, in the car example, some of the impacts could be in additional advertising if it is a new model car, and in increased motor vehicle sales. Some of the outcomes may be unintended, such as greater accident rates because of poor design.

In retailing, the most obvious process is selling – the goods, that is the inputs, are sold, that is the transaction. The output is a completed sale. Nevertheless, if the process component approach is used, there is greater appreciation of the components that contribute to the process. The benefit of this approach is that the retailer can better comprehend that inputs to the process are not just goods, but rather all of those components which prepare for the sale or transaction. Customer service and the merchandise are in fact catalysts to the transformation. This is where the extended idea of outcomes is important. What are the impacts or outcomes of completing a sale? They include customer satisfaction and therefore positive word-of-mouth advertising, reduced inventory, increased sales, and staff satisfaction. As shown in Figure 10.2, the retail process is complex because it is both merchandise-based and service-based. Thus, the outcomes are very important.

Corporate and functional objective setting

The first stage of the suggested performance management system is to identify the objective of performance improvement. In other words, what is the retailer striving to achieve? The target for improvement would ideally be in an area vital to the retailer's strategy.

For example, the retailer may be striving to improve the level of customer satisfaction in order to build up a more loyal group of customers. This might be seen as a corporate level objective. Alternatively, the objective could be at a functional level, for example, the desire to reduce staff turnover or to have more cost-effective advertising.

In broad terms, the objective is to improve an identifiable gap in performance which can arise either from a perceived deficiency in performance or a desire to do even better than an existing satisfactory performance. The latter will be relevant if the retailer is trying to lift an average performance into best practice.

Corporate objectives are dynamic and may need to be adjusted if there are major changes in the retailing macro environment.

It is therefore essential that retailers monitor the macro environment to ensure that the current retail strategy is appropriate.

Corporate and functional performance indicators

The basic purpose of performance indicators is to substantiate that progress has been made towards achieving the objective as identified in the previous section. The first indicators are what we term **macro indicators**, and include GDP growth, the rate of unemployment, total national retail sales, retail sales by major category, regional data, competitor activity, and social indicators such as changes in population, marriages or labour force participation. It is important for retailers to monitor changes in these macro indicators to ensure that their current strategy is appropriate. Many smaller retailers tend to neglect the importance of macro indictors.

The remaining organisational indicators can be classified as either financial or non-financial. Most **financial indicators** are at a corporate level, although financial indicators can also be used to compare the performance of product categories, inventory levels, departments, or products within and between stores.

Table 10.1 Non-financial organisational performance indicators

Aspect	Types of KPIs
Supply	• Timeliness • Accuracy
Merchandise	• Stock turnover • Stock requested but unavailable

Support services
  Legal
  Accounting
  Marketing
  Public relations
  Facilities management
  Information systems
	• Internal customer satisfaction based on quality, timeliness and responsiveness

Human resource management Human resource services	• Internal customer satisfaction based on quality, timeliness and responsiveness • Job satisfaction • Turnover • Staff orientation and training • Communication • Performance feedback • Training effectiveness • Absenteeism • Staff grievances • EEO/AA complaints
Selling	• Complaints • Goods returned
Marketing	• Timeliness • Understanding customer needs • Understanding customer satisfaction

Non-financial indicators can be applied to various functional areas such as marketing, human resource management, selling, internal support services, outsourced support services and supply. Table 10.1 gives some examples of the types of non-financial performance indicators which can be used in these areas. In some cases, there may be additional benefit from aggregating or sub-totalling some of these indicators into **composite indicators**, notably **customer satisfaction**, **staff satisfaction**, **supplier satisfaction** and **service quality**.

Data collection and analysis

For successful measurement in performance management, suitable data collection and analysis systems and tools are necessary. Their scope includes data collection systems such as retail information management systems, and tools such as benchmarking. Depending on the size of the retailing organisation, the system may be very sophisticated in the ways in which information is gathered, manipulated, analysed and disseminated. Larger retailers will generally have well-developed information technology systems and services. While smaller retailers usually have simpler information needs, the same principles apply.

Many of the systems that retailers have in place will yield valuable performance information. Systems such as point of sale, EFTPOS, inventory and distribution systems, human resource management information systems, and space management systems can all provide relevant performance information.

In addition, retailers can commission particular studies and market research, or conduct in-house research of analysis depending on the internal capabilities of the retail business. Specific studies could focus, for example, on customer satisfaction, staff satisfaction or internal communication. Research tools should gather both quantitative and qualitative data. Suitable tools include surveys, interviews and observations. Staff surveys, customer surveys, mystery shoppers, focus groups, trading area studies and official data – for example Australian Bureau of Statistics or Statistics New Zealand – can all be used to great advantage in a carefully designed and executed study.

When considering data collection and analysis, it is imperative for the retailer to balance the benefits and costs of acquiring the information. The expected benefits should include improved information for decision-making, and thus contribute to the firm's competitive advantage. The anticipated benefits should outweigh the initial costs, which include time, money and other resources. It would be wasteful, for example, to conduct a customer satisfaction survey and then not act on its results.

The choice of targeted data must take into account the timeliness and accuracy of the information. The data must be timely, and this implies two things. The first is that if it is only available *after* the relevant critical decision must be made, then it cannot be useful for informed decision-making when needed. The second is that the 'age' of the data must be put into context before extrapolating from it. If, for example, data about parking patterns contributes to decision-making, it is essential to identify when the data was gathered, if parking regulations are still the same, and what other changes are occurring in the area, for example changes in shopping hours. By balancing timeliness, accuracy, and the cost effectiveness of data collection and analysis, the retailer will ensure that a judgement is made which supports the retailer's performance management strategy, and which is consistent with organisational capability.

Monitoring and review processes

The outputs from data collection and analysis are the key inputs to the monitoring and review processes. When the retailer decides to implement monitoring and review processes, various questions must be answered, including:

- Who is responsible?

- What resources are available? and

- When will reviews be done?

As part of the development of the performance management plan, responsibilities must be agreed and allocated. A **schedule of reviews** should be prepared, and non-programmed reviews should occur when monitoring reveals exceptions to anticipated results. Not all indicators will need to be monitored and reviewed at the same time. The preferred approach is a critical indicator/ time method. This means that the retailer identifies critical performance indicators as well as the most suitable timeframe for review. For example, staff turnover may be reviewed annually, customer satisfaction six-monthly, occupational health and safety three-monthly, and other indicators such as financial indicators weekly or monthly.

In addition to scheduled performance monitoring and review, the retailer should respond quickly to **critical incidents**, which can be categorised in two ways. The first could be called an **identified potential critical incident**, that is, an event which it is reasonable to suggest *may* occur, for example 'near misses', whether they relate to 'almost' accidents or 'almost' running out of essential stock, for example a café running out of milk. A procedure can be introduced so that when near misses are recognised, they are reported to a nominated manager and a review process is set in train. The second type of critical incident could be termed an **unpredictable critical incident**, that is, an event or episode of which there was little or no likelihood of it ever occurring such as a power supply shutdown for more than a few hours – such as unexpectedly happens in urban areas affected by bushfires or cyclones from time to time. Indeed, there may be strong supportive evidence that specific phenomena would never occur – such as the 1989 Newcastle earthquake which happened in the lowest-rated earthquake zone in Australia.

Figure 10.5 The retail audit protocol

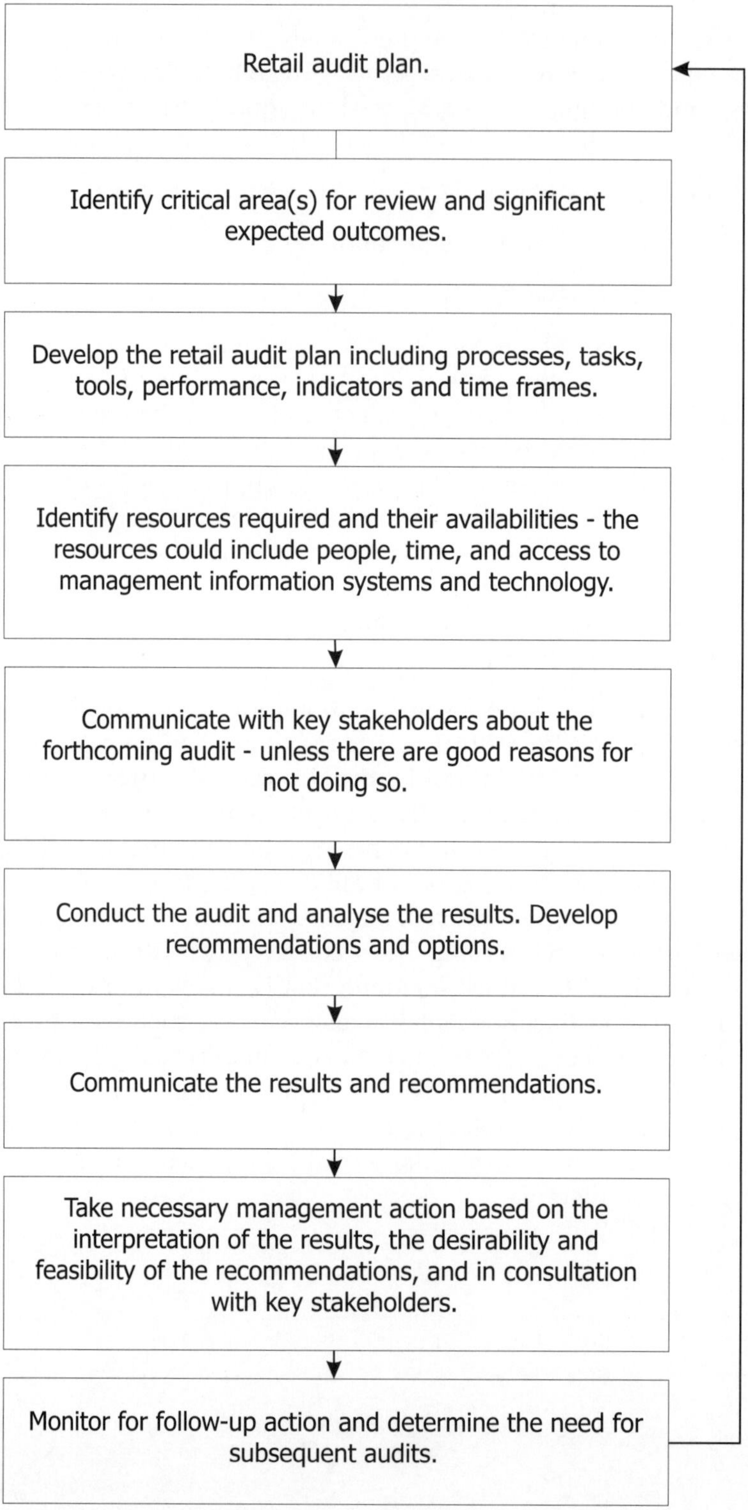

```
┌─────────────────────────────────────────────────┐
│                                                   │
│              Retail audit plan.                   │◄──┐
│                                                   │   │
└─────────────────────────────────────────────────┘   │
                                                        │
┌─────────────────────────────────────────────────┐   │
│   Identify critical area(s) for review and        │   │
│   significant expected outcomes.                  │   │
└─────────────────────────────────────────────────┘   │
                          ▼                             │
┌─────────────────────────────────────────────────┐   │
│   Develop the retail audit plan including         │   │
│   processes, tasks, tools, performance,           │   │
│   indicators and time frames.                     │   │
└─────────────────────────────────────────────────┘   │
                          ▼                             │
┌─────────────────────────────────────────────────┐   │
│   Identify resources required and their           │   │
│   availabilities - the resources could include    │   │
│   people, time, and access to management          │   │
│   information systems and technology.             │   │
└─────────────────────────────────────────────────┘   │
                          ▼                             │
┌─────────────────────────────────────────────────┐   │
│   Communicate with key stakeholders about the     │   │
│   forthcoming audit - unless there are good       │   │
│   reasons for not doing so.                       │   │
└─────────────────────────────────────────────────┘   │
                          ▼                             │
┌─────────────────────────────────────────────────┐   │
│   Conduct the audit and analyse the results.      │   │
│   Develop recommendations and options.            │   │
└─────────────────────────────────────────────────┘   │
                          ▼                             │
┌─────────────────────────────────────────────────┐   │
│   Communicate the results and recommendations.    │   │
└─────────────────────────────────────────────────┘   │
                          ▼                             │
┌─────────────────────────────────────────────────┐   │
│   Take necessary management action based on the   │   │
│   interpretation of the results, the desirability │   │
│   and feasibility of the recommendations, and in  │   │
│   consultation with key stakeholders.             │   │
└─────────────────────────────────────────────────┘   │
                          ▼                             │
┌─────────────────────────────────────────────────┐   │
│   Monitor for follow-up action and determine the  │   │
│   need for subsequent audits.                     │───┘
└─────────────────────────────────────────────────┘
```

One way of organising the monitoring and review process is to use the **retail audit protocol** (see Figure 10.5). The protocol is designed on the principles of performance management systems. This means that the review process is treated systematically so that the process is integrated and action-orientated. The protocol gives the retailer a blueprint which can be adapted to the retailer's particular circumstances.

The application of the retail audit protocol can be shown using 'goods returned' as the critical area for review (see Table 10.2). In this example, the retailer must identify expected review outcomes, that is, what do we want to know and what is reasonable to expect from the review. The retailer must next develop a plan, noting what processes, performance indicators and time frames will apply and what resources will be required. A vital decision must be made – who will be the retail audit coordinator for this audit? The key to success in terms of staff relations and continuous improvement is to communicate with key stakeholders which includes staff and suppliers. Thus, the audit is conducted, the results analysed, and, importantly, options for action developed and recommendations made. The process, however, must not stop at this point. Staff should be briefed on the results, along with other stakeholders who have been explicitly involved. Yet the process is still not complete. The necessary management action must then be taken, based in part on consultations with staff. The final step is then to monitor the follow-up action and assess the need for subsequent audits.

Table 10.2 Applying the retail audit model to the example of goods returned

Component	Application
Identify critical area(s) for review and significant expected outcomes.	Areas for review: goods returned. Expected outcomes: 1. Data about frequency, volume and types of goods returned. 2. Understanding of reasons for returns, whether product or service based, for example staff gave insufficient information about products. 3. Options for reducing returns.
Develop the retail audit plan including processes, tasks, tools, performance indicators and timeframes.	Processes will include: 1. Reviewing any existing data, including subsequent returns to the supplier. 2. Monitoring returns over a four week period, for example in July.
Identify resources required and their availability – the resources could include people, time and access to management information systems and technology.	Resources required: • Allocate the role of retail audit-coordinator. • Goods returned data forms. • Staff briefed on how to keep records and the importance of ascertaining reasons for

Component	Application
	return, for example wrong size or poor performance, and what follow-up action was taken. • Survey of sample customers who have returned goods in the past, if known, and of those who return goods in the four week period.
Communicate with key stakeholders about the forthcoming audit – unless there are good reasons for not doing so.	Brief staff and suppliers.
Conduct the audit and analyse the results. Develop recommendations and options.	Retail audit co-ordinator supervises the retail audit, analyses the results and develops options. The results could show that returns are mostly related to product deficiencies, which means that options must be developed in relation to suppliers. In contrast, the returns may be related to staff giving poor information about product features, in which case options will focus on staff training and product knowledge. Customers may report dissatisfaction with any follow-up action, which means options can focus on management policy about returns and the skills of the staff to implement the policy.
Communicate the results and recommendations.	Staff should be briefed on the results and recommendations. If suppliers or customers have been explicitly involved, the retail audit co-ordinator may recommend briefing them too. The suppliers, for example, may have been unaware of product quality problems, or they may have comparable data from other retail customers.
Take necessary management action based on the interpretation of the results, the desirability and feasibility of the recommendations and in consultation with key stakeholders.	The ideas from the staff should contribute to plans for management action – this can be achieved through focus groups or staff meetings. If the key difficulty is with product quality, consultations with key stakeholders about remedial action must include both the staff and the suppliers.

Component	Application
Monitor the follow-up action and determine the need for subsequent audits.	The nominated retail audit co-ordinator monitors the follow-up action to ensure not only that it occurs, but also that any outcomes are analysed and acted upon.
	A subsequent audit on goods returned could be planned for a different month to see if the same or different factors are significant.

For larger organisations, a well co-ordinated project management approach will assist in developing integrated monitoring and review processes. For smaller retailers, it is equally important to plan the monitoring and review of performance. Rather than approach performance review on an *ad hoc* or crisis basis, smaller retailers need to be pro-active – even if the indicators selected are simple and readily obtained. Smaller retailers can use effective performance management systems to great advantage. It is important to reinforce here that all three types of indicators – **macro, financial organisational and non-financial organisational** – are pertinent to smaller as well as to larger retailers, and that the process of review, reflection and management action can lead to enhanced performance for all retailers. Unfortunately, smaller retailers frequently rely solely on financial organisational indicators. Indeed, some larger retailers give scant attention to the other types either, as is often reflected in annual reports. The process of review, reflection and management can lead to enhanced performance for all retailers.

Performance gaps and options for management action

Identified performance gaps demand immediate management action. How that management action is determined will depend on the type of performance gap and the availability of organisational capabilities to respond to that gap. With significant gaps, it is generally advisable to consult with key stakeholders as to the possible causes and possible remedial actions.

The stakeholders may include staff, customers or suppliers. As shown in Figure 10.3, options for action must be developed. In general, a consultative approach is preferable as it enables the retailer to give leadership while involving the key players. Consultative processes generate many ideas and help to gain commitment to the recommendations made. This approach is in line with quality improvement programs and the best practice movement. Seeking external advice may complement this consultative approach to developing options.

If the gap is financial, external advice may be sought from government agencies such as the Australian Taxation Office, accountants, financial advisors, business investment advisors or bankers. If the gap is in customer satisfaction, advice may be canvassed from business consultants, consumer organisations or industry groups. Regardless of whether the identified gap is financial or non-financial, it must be remembered that the solutions – as in any change process – will probably be in more than one area. So, a solution which suggests a new financial reporting structure must also be supplemented with internal communications, staff training, and other staff support systems. As shown in the retail audit protocol, any changes must be subjected to further monitoring and review. The management action which is determined may mean that there should be adjustments to goals. Therefore, the performance management cycle is not complete until the next iteration is in place. Vignette 10.1 relates the performance management cycle to the retailer's brand.

Vignette 10.1

Performance management and the retailer brand

Publicly listed retailers generally make their annual reports and interim results available on their websites. These documents serve to inform investors and other stakeholders about the company's performance. Positive performance results reflect well on the retailer's brand and build confidence in the market place. Conversely, any reporting of negative results or failure to meet forecasts taints the retailer's brand. Interestingly, Myer Pty Ltd which is currently a private company, is also providing this information on its website.

For your reflection:

- Explain the retailer's possible motivations and identify KPIs that Myer appears to be using.

  See Myer:
  <www.myer.com.au/investors/financialresults.asp>.

- Explore how smaller retailers can benefit from using KPIs.

The special case of gaps between best practice and actual practice

Actual practice may be acceptable to the retailer. However, gaps between best practice and actual practice can be identified – often through internal and external benchmarking processes – based on a medley of critical performance indicators. The retailer must make deliberate decisions as to what extent those gaps should be addressed, and how that will be accomplished. Such decisions must relate to the overall retail performance management strategy, and to the capabilities of the organisation. The determining factor will be the extent to which the retailer will gain **competitive advantage** by addressing the gaps.

The special case of risk management systems

A very significant performance management issue for retailers is the development of comprehensive risk management systems. These systems must be able to deal with stockouts, shrinkage, natural disasters (such as earthquakes, lightning strikes and floods), bomb threats, occupational health for staff and customers, and workers' rehabilitation and compensation. Given the potential impacts of the failure of any of these systems, it is vital to have effective performance management systems.

Ideally, retailers emphasise preventative strategies. If prevention fails, then **early warning systems** are essential to control negative impacts, and to offer opportunities for immediate intervention. Early warning systems often make use of comparative data as well as reflecting key performance indicators. For example, there may be a sudden increase in the number of personal injuries through falls in a particular area of a store. That information may have been derived from comparisons with previous years and with others sections, as well as the noting of a deviation from a performance target of zero falls in the area. Action needs to be taken quickly, not only to deal with the existing injuries but to prevent further mishaps. There may also be options for change which will need to be communicated to other parts of the store or to other stores, or there may be a need for policy changes about the frequency of cleaning and the placement of merchandise.

Conversely, early warning systems may show a significant improvement in a particular area. This may in turn lead to management action aimed at understanding the improvement, and making any changes which are desirable. Those changes may need to be communicated throughout the organisation and all its outlets. Smaller retailers must seek to understand performance variations, either positive or negative. They must then actively communicate any changes to key players. For example, there may be a significant decrease in complaints about unavailable stock, which invites the question of what has brought about the change? Is it better training, greater staff initiative in dealing with complaints, or better product delivery schedules? Or is it that the complaints have not been recorded, rather than not received?

Effective risk management systems benefit the retailer, the staff and the customer – regardless of the size of the retailing business. The varied areas of risk require distinctly different approaches as far as specifics are concerned, however the performance management framework can still be successfully used.

Financial management tools

Retailers use an array of financial management tools to help manage and improve performance. The expected practices include budget processes and budget planning schedules, capital requirement planning, and financial statements (profit and loss, balance sheets, and statements of cash flow).

Performance analysis ratios usually require two or more key components of financial statements to show retailer's financial performance including expense classifications and budgeting.

For success, retailers need a variety of systems including inventory management. Financial tools can help with decisions on promotion, service mix, product range and staffing as well as with decisions about financial and marketing responses to unfavourable performance.

Retail support services

The term **retailing support services** refers to all those retailing functions which support the core retailing activities as defined by the retail mix. Examples of support services include the supply of fixtures and signwriting services. Often retailers, both large and small, obtain these services from third parties using a process of **outsourcing**. Retailers have to decide whether to use outsourcing 'as needed', or whether to develop in-house capabilities in some of the support services areas. Retail support services are essential for implementing a retail strategy.

The interface between retailers and support service providers is much more extensive than many readers might expect. The potential range of providers spans the retailing spectrum.

Financial retail support services may be sourced from accountants, banks, business development advisors, investment advisors, stockbrokers, government departments and agencies such as the Australian Taxation Office and insurance brokers, for example property, workers' compensation, public liability.

People management retail support services may cover recruitment and selection, performance management systems, remuneration packaging, superannuation, staff training and development, employment relations, childcare facilities and services, employee assistance programs, occupational health and safety, rehabilitation of injured workers, staff counselling, interpreting and translating, and risk management including security, fire protection and fire prevention.

Physical retail support services may cover plant and equipment hire, architects, interior design and decoration, warehousing, storage, telecommunications, and trades, for example plumbing, electrical, electronics, lighting, air conditioning, printing, signs, landscaping, painting and maintenance. Other services include environmental management, waste management, recycling, salvage and composting (supermarkets are now outsourcing their green waste management). Retailers also use support services such as cleaning services, uniform and linen services, hygiene services, and pest control services. At times, retailers may also use external meeting and conference facilities.

Intangible and other retail support services may include legal services, trademark and patent advice, marketing, marketing research, promotion, media relations, media coaching, retail industry analysis, government relations, planning, evaluation, information technology, defensive driving, performance management systems, conflict resulting and catering.

Retailers must decide if the relationship with the service providers is collaborative or advisory. A collaborative relationship is usually preferred. Mutual respect, trust, empathy, responsiveness and a gradual transfer of skills are hallmarks of effective collaborative relationships. The transfer of skills helps the retailer to maintain services support services while the service provider is absent, and to become a more discerning client.

Retailers need to develop expertise in implementing and managing outsourcing arrangements. Small retailers particularly need to follow this path, and may need independent advice to help establish suitable processes for engaging services providers. Ideally, retailers will give constructive feedback to service providers, especially regarding product safety or service efficacy and opportunities for continuous improvement.

Conclusions

Any discussion of contemporary retailing would be incomplete without discussing the role of retail operations or examining the evaluation of retail performance. We have identified two stages of retail operations to help the retailer develop relevant approaches to the task at hand. The explanation of performance management is much more comprehensive than merely measuring performance. To be effective, it must start with a performance management strategy that is consistent with the retail strategy as well as with the capabilities of the organisation. We have presented a simple model of the performance management system, and then examined each component and its use in retailing by small and large retailers.

This chapter introduced the concept of three types of performance indicators – macro, financial organisational and non-financial organisational indicators. The 'I-T-O' approach is useful because it highlights the relationships between functions, processes and outcomes. The retail audit protocol enables the retailer to organise the monitoring and review process. The protocol is enhanced by the concept of critical incidents – including the idea of 'near misses' – which, like customer complaints, require immediate recognition and action.

The emphasis on management action cannot be over-emphasised. No retailer, large or small, can ignore the importance of effective management action based on sound indicators and on timely and accurate information. Management action, in short, is the key to superior performance and to maintaining a competitive advantage.

Review and applications

1. What are the benefits to retailers of using a performance management system based on the process component approach? How would you explain the system to the owner/manager of a hardware store?

2. Critically assess the performance management schema.

3. Develop a performance management system for a retailer of your choice. How would you evaluate the effectiveness of the performance management system which you have designed?

4. What special performance management system aspects would you include in developing a performance management system for vendor relations?

5. If you were given the task of designing a performance management system particularly for customer satisfaction for a smaller retailer, how would you go about doing it? Specify a particular firm or industry segment.

6. Develop a performance management system for an aspect of risk management for a retailer of your choice. Justify why the aspect is important to the retailer.

7. Explain how a retailer could develop a best practice performance management system for store environmental management. Take into account, for example, cleaning, energy consumption and the disposal of waste. Your choice of retailer could be a florist, pharmacist, hairdresser, drycleaner, or a hardware, delicatessen or fresh seafood retailer.

8. Develop retail audit protocols, choosing from the following groups, and apply to a retailer of your choice.

Group 1: Credit policy

- Lay-by defaults
- Refunds or exchanges

Group 2: Merchandise

- Stock control
- Product and service knowledge
- Stock quality
- Private brands

Group 3: Staff

- Stress management
- Internal communication
- Staff support systems (including facilities)

Group 4: Customer service

- Special orders
- Personal services

- Staff attitudes to specific customer categories (such as children, older clients, people with communication difficulties)

- Average waiting times for service

- Telephone responsiveness

Group 5: Health and safety

- Occupational health and safety critical incidents

- First aid awareness and skills

- Emergency procedures

9. Develop a retailer brand audit.

10. Consider an early innovation in retailing. What still applies to retailing today?

References

Australian Bureau of Statistics (ABS) 1993, *Retailing in Australia 1991-1992*, ABS catalogue no. 8613.0.

Bogan, C & English, M 1994, *Benchmarking for Best Practices: Winning Through Innovation Adaptation*, McGraw-Hill, New York.

Fitz-Enz, J 1984, *How To Measure Human Resource Management*, McGraw-Hill, New York.

Fitz-Enz, J 1993, *Benchmarking Staff Performance*, Jossey-Bass, San Francisco.

Gilbert, R 1991, *Reglomania: the curse of organizational reform and how to cure it*, Prentice Hall, Sydney.

Levy, M & Weitz, B 1995, *Retailing Management*, 2nd edn, Irwin, Chicago.

Merrilees, B & Miller, D 1994, *Retail Customer Service and Organizational Capability*, Paper presented to the Joint European Institute of Retailing and Services Studies (EIRASS) and Canadian Institute of Retailing and Services Studies (CIRASS) Conference, Recent Advances in Retailing and Services Science, Banff, Alberta, Canada, May.

Ulrich, D & Lake, D 1990, *Organizational Capability: Competing from the Inside Out*, John Wiley, New York.

Advanced reading

Fernie, J, Fernie, S & Moore, C 2003, *Principles of Retailing*, Butterworth-Heinemann, Burlington.

Ou, W-M, Abratt, R & Dion, P 2006, 'The influence of retailer reputation on store patronage', *Journal of Retailing and Consumer Services*, vol. 13, pp. 221-230.

Reynolds, J & Cuthbertson, C 2004, *Retail strategy the view from the bridge*, Elsevier Butterworth-Heinemann, Burlington.

Retail Opportunities and Challenges

Retail innovation and sustainable retailing

Introduction

People are at the heart of retailing. They include owners, customers, staff, suppliers, shareholders, other stakeholders and the community. Many retailers have understood this tenet and used innovative methods to involve people in developing and maintaining enduring businesses (see Vignette 11.1). Other retailers, however, fail because they do not understood or apply this fundamental premise of business. This book's retail journey has moved through identifying retail opportunities, understanding the dynamics of the market, developing retail strategy and unique brand positioning, designing and implementing the retail mix, and ensuring cost effective performance. What are the continuing challenges and opportunities for retailers? How can retailers foster retail innovation and develop sustainable retailing? This chapter discusses industry trends and proposes some approaches that proactive retailers can take to ensure they maintain their sustainable competitive advantage. The most successful retailers, large or small, will be those who actively create the future in all its richness and diversity.

Trends: Macro context and retail industry

In earlier chapters the importance of knowing the broader context for retailing was emphasised, and is reiterated here. Some of the macro trends that will affect retailers are listed below:

- **Corporate social responsibility (CSR).** Consumers will become even more discerning, and they will gradually expect retailers to act as responsible corporate citizens. Large retailers exercise incredible power in the supply chain, and some large corporations have budgets larger than many countries.

Vignette 11.1

Sustainable retailing, innovation and respect for staff

Can modern day retailers develop and implement strategies that use innovation and deliver sustainable retailing while at the same time valuing individual staff? Yes. Two examples are IKEA and Tesco.

In many countries, the competition for suitable employees is high. Therefore potential employees may be able to choose which employer they will work with, and that choice will depend on more than just remuneration. In Canada, IKEA offers "on-site day care at head office; flexible work programs... [and] career opportunities in over 35 other countries" (Yerema 2007, p. 43). A notable innovation, which partially addresses the issue of non-recognition of foreign credentials, is the introduction of programs to assist recent immigrants – and in some instances their families – to adapt to their new home (Kirby 2007, p. 43). This recent study "reveals just how fast and dramatically the modern workplace is changing" (Kirby 2007, pp. 41-42).

The international retailer Tesco has opened an innovative new format to meet specific customers' needs in California. The company researched what potential employees wanted, and found that respect was essential. Tesco displays that respect by paying good wages and providing benefits such as health care plans to **all** employees (Inside Retailing 2007). The issue of health care plans is often context specific and is, for example, a major concern for part-time and causal employees in the US.

Furthermore, in two 'green' initiatives Tesco has introduced product innovations into their private label merchandise, and in their distribution centre they have installed a solar panelled roof.

As Kirby (2007) points out, "it takes *creativity*, more than big budgets, to be the best" (p. 42) (emphasis added). Retailers of any scale can bring together innovation, sustainable retailing and respect for staff.

Sources:
Inside Retailing 2007, 'Tesco opens first 6 Fresh and Easy California stores', available at <www.insideretailing.com.au/articles>, 02 Dec 2007.
Kirby, J 2007, 'Canada's top 100 employers', *Maclean's*, Special Report, 15 Oct., pp. 41-42.
Yerema, R 2007, 'The top 100', *Maclean's*, Special Report, 15 Oct., pp. 43-46.

Vignette 11.2

'Green' bags do not have to be green-coloured: One retailer's black bag innovation.

In Australia, the acceptance of green coloured shopping bags by consumers has a fascinating side effect, where people use the bags almost cult-like for many purposes other than their supermarket shopping. In some situations it seems that people use them for everything *except* for shopping.

From the retailer's perspective, Woolworths aims to comply with voluntary codes by offering recyclable bags for sale, by not offering a bag for three items or fewer unless requested, and by teaching staff how to pack bags effectively and efficiently.

Loblaw's, the largest supermarket retailer in Canada, claims that their stylish "little black number [which] became the summer's hottest accessory" is itself recyclable. "Customers are encouraged to return them to the retailer when they're worn out so they can be used to make more bags". (Fielding 2007) Moreover, Loblaw's has applied for the trademark to 'Canada's greenest shopping bag' to protect Loblaw's from other stores that might challenge the claim. The claim to be the greenest is based on the 85% amount of post-consumer recycled material present in the President's Choice brand (Loblaw's private brand). They have also trademarked: "Something must be done" (Fielding 2007), and "Green bag – better than any other reusable shopping bag on the market" (Fielding 2007). In summary, Fielding (2007) suggests "that Canada's greenest bag may also be the country's greatest marketing strategy".

For your reflection:

What related measures can you recommend to retailers? What specific advice can you give to small retailers?

Sources:
Fielding, D. 2007, 'Everyone's gone green', The Globe and Mail: Report on Business, September, p. 26.
Woolworth Ltd, 2007: <www.woolworthslimited.com.au>.
Woolworths Supermarkets, 2007: <www.woolworths.com.au>.

- **The greening of retailing.** Governments are striving to develop policies that either regulate or encourage businesses and individuals to behave more responsibly in terms of energy creation and consumption, greenhouse gas emissions, and environmental friendliness (such as the reduction of plastic bag usage – see Vignette 11.2).

- **The divide between rich and poor.** The divide between rich and poor countries has not narrowed significantly. Poverty, inadequate housing, disease, lack of educational opportunities and the exploitation of workers remain intransigent issues, and meetings of representatives of rich nations in forums such as the G8 summit, the International Monetary Fund or the World Trade Organisation continue to attract protestors who argue that developed nations and large corporations can do much more to assist poor countries.

- **Strength of economies.** The strength of both local and global economies affects retailers and consumers alike. Probable features of the economy over the next decade include continuing economic growth at a moderate rate, a continuation of a relatively low rate of unemployment, and a steadfast growth in the service sector. Services retailing will, as a consequence, also continue to grow faster than merchandise retailing.

- **Transition economies.** Some transition economy countries have benefited from joining blocs such as the European Union. They are shifting, rapidly in some cases, towards modern retailing, and in particular in those countries aiming for full membership of the European Union.

- **Government policy.** Changing government policies influence the retail industry and include further business deregulation, simplified taxation arrangements, and alterations in the emphases of secondary, tertiary and continuing education. Reforms in the labour market and in employment relations policies and practices will continue. These trends will set the scene for a conspicuously different retailing industry environment over the next two decades.

- **Growth of the middle class.** The burgeoning middle class in countries like China and India will create opportunities for local and international retailers.

- **New market segments.** Demand for responsiveness to the needs and wants of particular market segments will occur. These segments will include dual income couples, people with special needs, the lesbian and gay communities, workers with family responsibilities, and separate age groupings of mature people such as 45 to 55 years, 56 to 65, 66 to 75, and 76 to 80 and 80 plus. Some writers refer to the latter group as the 'old old', implying that they are inactive consumers. Over the next few decades, these people will have improved health status and greater buying power, thus providing a market niche for responsive retailers. Such groupings would recognise the lifestyle, income, employment, leisure and health profiles that are significant to each discrete cluster. Many older people will continue to live in their own homes and will require – and be prepared to pay for – a changing array of retailing products and services including the delivery of purchases, the installation of domestics appliances and electronic products, housekeeping, home maintenance, dog washing and walking, automobile servicing at home, prepared meals, and computer maintenance and repairs.

- **Emergence to the 'savvy consumer'.** More consumers are becoming astute and are beginning to question the *caveat emptor* – or 'let the buyer beware' – motto. The voices of the anti-consumerism movements will insist that retailers show greater responsibility and accountability in all their activities. Existing government instrumentalities – such as the Commonwealth and state ombudsmen and consumer affairs offices and the Australian Competition and Consumer Commission – continue to parallel and support increasing consumer awareness. Consumer and community organisations such the Australian Consumers' Association, the Brotherhood of St Lawrence and the Australian Council of Social Services (ACOSS) will also continue to have a prominent role. This trend will compel retailers to renegotiate their relationships with suppliers. The recent spate of recalls of products manufactured in China speaks to a lack of vigilance by retailers. They must have greater expectations of product safety and fitness for purpose, and much more scrutiny of the quality of their suppliers' practices – for example where suppliers contract to manufacturers who in turn sub-contract to outworkers who may be employed under unfavourable terms and conditions.

- **Business ethics.** The push to address business ethics will come from governments, shareholders and consumers. This is a trend for all businesses. Business schools, too, are reintroducing either ethics courses or ethics-based course content. Arguably, both are needed. Retailers can respond proactively by developing ethical policies and practices in consultation with staff, consumers and other stakeholders. The retail audit process or other evaluation tools can measure the efficacy of those policies and practices, as with any other aspect of retailing practice.

Ethical products, green marketing, quality management, environmental resource management and social responsibility will be themes pursued in the retailing industry with more vigour. The caution – and indeed the challenge – is that such pursuits must be genuine, substantial and sustainable.

Trends: Retail formats, the retail mix and shopping hours

The previous decade's trends continue unabated. New formats will continue to augment existing offerings. Retailers and other stakeholders should be aware of the following significant trends:

- the growth of intertype competition, for example store vs. non store retailers, department stores vs. discount department stores vs. specialist stores, supermarkets vs. takeaway food retailers vs. specialist food retailers vs. cafes, bistros, family restaurants and fine dining venues;

- the growth of superstores by category killer retailers in new retail categories, and concerns about these retails not withstanding (Mitchell 2006);

- the growth in takeaway food retailing – also known as the food service industry – especially delivery services, internet ordering and drive-through services with an increasing variety of healthy food offerings over more hours each day;

- the growth of home shopping and non-store retailing using a variety of media available for longer hours than traditional shop fronts retailers;

- the growth of convenience stores in the downtown or central business districts (CBDs) serving city residents and city workers, and major arterial roads especially co-located with automobile fuel stations;

- the rejuvenation of CBDs (Hill 2007);

- the growth of low price variety stores;

- the further development of the boutique layout form by larger super-market outlets, and more 'store-within-a-store' concessions in department stores;

- the recognition of the importance of the visual dimensions of retailing;

- the recognition of the importance of the experiential dimensions of retailing;

- the growth of private merchandise brands in supermarkets, clothing retailers and home appliances;

- the spread of supermarket chains to more remote, smaller trading areas including freestanding, community shopping centres and larger neighbourhood shopping centres;

- the declining share of department stores and discount department stores;

- small retailers as a group continuing to lose market share;

- newsagents, chemists, florists, greeting card shops and confectioners continuing the development of more scrambled merchandise assortments so that they resemble specialist convenience stores;

- the reinvention of some shopping malls so that they offer unique retailing precincts (Hill 2007); and

- the demand for convenience – including shopping hours and accessibility.

Many of these trends are inevitable. For example, about sixty *superstores* opened throughout Australia over the 1993-95 period, with plans by developers and retailers to open a further one hundred outlets (Barrymore 1995). In other words, major future growth was planned – although not every specific plan has materialised. The continued growth of superstores such as Toy 'R' Us and Bunnings will exert considerable pressure on small, specialist retailers in the same category. The superstores also threaten discount department stores. Most superstores have a 'hard goods' characteristic such as hardware (Bunnings), toys (Toys 'R' Us), sporting goods (Rebel), computers (Harvey Norman), furniture (Freedom, Oz Design Furniture) and stationery (Officeworks). All of these categories are major departments in discount department stores such as Big W, Target and Kmart.

Home shopping could grow to $30 billion in Australia by the year 2010, and embraces traditional home shopping such as mail order catalogues as well as innovative electronic forms. Some industry players and retail analysts question the potential magnitude of this growth – and especially for information superhighway shopping traffic. Home shopping will undoubtedly increase for banking, film, music, hard copy books and e-books. Other entertainment and travel reservation services will be amenable to home shopping. **Auction websites** will continue to create an arena for exchange by individual consumers and retailers.

However many shoppers will seek a **multi-sensory shopping experience** - smelling, touching, hearing, visualising and contextualising the merchandise as well as some services. The challenge for storefront retailers is to *provide* this enhanced shopping experience – perhaps in collaboration with better-designed shopping centres. The Body Shop and Lush are useful role models in this respect, as are gourmet food shops and other outlets offering tastings. Retailers will enhance the multi-sensory shopping experience through entertainment shopping.

The increasing popularity of superstores reflects a preference for convenience, range and, to a lesser extent, price or at least perceived value by shoppers. Essentially, superstores allow one-stop shopping, that is, choice through depth of product range within a restricted width of merchandise range. The same consumer preferences explain the increasing popularity of convenience stores (except for price), variety stores and more remotely located major supermarket chains. Department stores and discount department stores are part of an earlier approach to one-stop shopping, which remains valid for some segments of the market, for example working people who have significant time constraints, but they are having difficulty competing with superstores and other specialist chains. This trend is reinforced by a lack of strong focus and purpose, and by the difficulty both type of department stores are having with the delivery of service quality.

The challenges and opportunities ahead

The trends discussed suggest many challenges that can always be reframed as opportunities. Globalisation, the increasing demand for rapid availability of fashion, the pressure to drive down costs, and a significant shift towards sustainability in all aspects of business and daily life are part of the challenging context for retailers. In the past, retailers have responded to challenging situations with vigour, and there is no reason to suppose that the 21st century will be any different (see Vignette 11.1). Within the retailing industry there is increased fragmentation and specialisation as well as an increased concentration of ownership in some categories.

 Consumers have changing needs, changing desires and changing expectations. Retailers can interpret this trend as a problem, or as an opportunity to rebrand and refocus their retail strategy.

Retailers have some scope for mass customisation. Interestingly, increased individualism has meshed with universal branding, but a backlash will see some segments seeking customised uniqueness in products, services and retail experiences rather than merely being leaders or early adopters of 'the next great fad'. Instead of buying in to the rhetoric of 'the ageing population' as a catch-all phrase, some retailers will think of segments such as 'baby boomer trendsetters'.

The distribution challenges for e-retailing are still to be met. Most of the delivery problems faced by the early catalogue retailers who sold to geographically dispersed customers still exist.

Excellent conduct of resource efficient companies will be the hallmark of successful retailers. They will offer customers resource efficient products and services including opportunities for the reuse, recycling and salvage of products no longer of use to the customer. And, the better retailers will do this *ahead* of government intervention.

Individual retailer strategies

The emphasis in this book is that a number of retailers can co-exist in each retail category provided they differentiate their retail offer in a way that the consumer desires. Those retailers who are successful are more likely to have researched or clarified their market positioning and co-ordinated their retail mix accordingly. There is plenty of scope for individual retailers to create distinctive strategies by differentiating their retail offer and by developing best practices in at least some of the components of the retail mix.

Some retailers may reach excellence in store design, others in product range and others in yet some other component such as advertising. For example, Woolworths set new standards in supermarket store design. At the micro retailing level, Simply Clothing recognised a niche and developed skills in home selling to nursing homes.

Realistically, retailers have to focus on those best practices that are most germane to their retail strategy and retailer brand. The challenge for all retailers is to strive towards best practice in selected components of the retail mix *and* to ensure that they achieve a competitive advantage in the process.

Although many different strategies may compete against each other, in any given retail category there is often *a scale war* in which the large retailers find themselves in opposition to small retailer. The supermarket chains, take-away chains, department stores, discount department stores, large specialist national chains and superstores are placed at one end of the spectrum while small retailers are placed at the other. For the past forty years, the former group has been winning market share at the expense of the latter, and this trend will continue.

The challenge for small retailers is to slow down the atrophy of their market share. The essential way to do this is through a niche strategy that meets the needs of small segments of customers better than the strategies of larger retailers. The small scale retailer requires a very sophisticated approach to retail marketing and the development of relevant capabilities. In some cases the small retailers will gain advantage through franchises or some other co-operative venture. If small retailers are able to respond to take up the challenge of developing capabilities, such as human resource training and development, then the forecast becomes quite positive.

Apart from the battle between large and small retailers, there is also the battle between the giants themselves – and the contest in the supermarket stakes is particularly fierce. But the continuing superior strategies of Woolworths – and particularly their better practices in positioning ('The Fresh Food People'), staff relations, store design, target marketing and location – are likely to win them greater market share in the future. Coles continues to face a major challenge in this area, although the change of ownership may bring about repositioning and sustainable strategies. Challengers in various categories will have to reinvent themselves if they are to topple the leaders.

Retailer capabilities

If retailers are to address the future boldly, what capabilities are needed? The organisational capability model groups the significant future-oriented capabilities into four dimensions: physical, financial, human and intangible. The fifth dimension is a best practice approach to the *integration* of these dimensions that is consistent with the desired retail strategy and retailer brand, and the retail mix.

New retail formats will influence **physical retailing capabilities**, as will new technologies, be they information technologies and related equipment or transport and storage technologies, for example of perishable goods. Greater customising of clothing using both intangible capabilities and physical capabilities such as machines will produce stock items as one-off garments made to the customer's measurements, as pioneered in Australia by Levi Strauss a decade ago.

Financial capabilities must interact with individual retailer strategies so that they are mutually supportive. Not only will the capabilities relate to business finance, but also to investment strategies, inventory decisions, and to financial relationships with suppliers, financial institutions, governments, employees, customers and shareholders.

People-related capabilities would be paramount for the successful retailer of the future. Overarching all capabilities in this dimension will be a predisposition to leadership excellence demonstrated through pro-active management expertise and superlative management systems. Excellent customer services capabilities must be matched with the excellent management of employees who are respected, consulted and involved. Although self-service formats such as supermarkets, superstores and home shopping will diminish the use of personal service, for the remaining outlets we see an upsurge in the importance and quality of personal service. Indeed, such an upsurge will be vital for the competitive advantage of these outlets.

Intangible capabilities are often unacknowledged, but these capabilities will be the distinguishing characteristics of successful retailers in the future. They are not only about internal characteristics and competencies which are under the control of the retailer, but are also about capabilities which the retailer can access, such as information sources and relationships with suppliers.

The fifth dimension is a best practice approach to the *integration* of these dimensions, consistent with the desired retail strategy and retail mix. Integration will create synergies and ensure cost effective polices and processes which add value for the customer and other stakeholders.

Retail employees

Retailing continues to expand and, in Australia, more that one million people work in a variety of contractual arrangements, with a predominance of part-time and casual employees. In the last decade, enhanced career profiles for the various retail roles have emerged. Store managers, retail marketers, brand managers and others are finding their place in the dynamic world of retailing. Related roles are available in shopping malls, although centre managers at times have difficulty finding suitably qualified recruits.

All the trends in retailing have impacts on existing and potential retail employees. Retailers who are proactive will try to meet the needs, including the language needs, of the increasing numbers of international visitors, for example tourists, and business and education visitors. The trends to globalisation, migration, international tourism and international business present the opportunity to develop the language skills of employees in key customer and supplier contact positions.

Increasing retail development, especially the opening of many more large stores, will require competent staff. Changing retail formats and increasing outsourcing will alter the employment mix within retail firms. Greater recognition of the contribution of retailing to the economy – and of the need for skilled management especially – will influence the provision of traineeships and tertiary courses. Professions and trades as well will recognise that retailing is a significant component of their work. Members of such trades and professions will seek the needed requisite retailing skills themselves through outsourcing, or they will recognise the opportunity to employ graduates of retailing courses.

The spotlights will be on two areas. The first will be on sustaining the skills and loyalties of existing staff. This premise means retailers, contrary to past practice, must give significantly more attention: to staff motivation, dignity and respect; to staff consultation and participation; and to staff training and development. The need to achieve employee buy-in to the retailer brand is paramount. The second spotlight will be on acquiring – through recruitment, outsourcing or training – additional skills in anticipation of the needs of the retailing firm. There are some pivotal opportunities here to link the people aspects of the firm much more intimately to the retail strategy. Success will depend on the leadership and commitment of senior management.

Imaginative and innovative human resource specialists, who consult widely and understand the retailer's business strategy and retailer brand, can design the paths to success in people management. An exceptional opportunity exists to develop a **retailing career structure** which would not use the iniquitous and inequitable core and peripheral workers framework. Instead, a career framework would highlight **career ladder employees** who are supported by well-trained and broadly skilled, stable staff – all of whom are integral to the business.

Early development of both the concepts and supporting skills of services retailing should be encouraged by retailers, academics and training providers. The need for retailing skills in merchandising is well recognised; what needs to be explored is the acquisition of retailing skills by those in services retailing.

Many industries and organisations are addressing the need to develop performance management systems. Contemporary retailers need systems now, and they should design the systems in consultation with employees, and implement them with proper resource investment, training, support systems and evaluation processes.

Customers are not homogeneous in their needs. Therefore, innovative retailers can develop the abilities of their staff to deal with people with special needs, including: people with vision, speech and hearing problems; people with mobility restrictions (including *personal* restrictions requiring walking aids, or the *mobility* restrictions for carers pushing a wheelchair or a stroller/pram); and people for whom English is not their first language.

Smaller firms need to address the atrophy of market share by using niche strategies. The retailer must take the opportunity to identify the essential skills required and to examine the options that outsourcing presents, so that skills which are not regularly required are still available when needed. Smaller retailers should shift from a mindset of blaming larger competitors to taking responsibility for identifying niches and their supporting capabilities, and then building those capabilities. For smaller firms, the challenge and the opportunity to develop alliances for co-operative training and human resource benchmarking already exist.

One significant challenge is to integrate part-time and casual staff into the staffing profile of the firm. All staff should understand the total business of the organisation. Often, for example, in large discount department stores or supermarkets, casual staff are allocated to an area, such as the checkout, with little or no concept of the broad range of goods and services offered by the store. Understanding the total business of the store could improve customer service and employee job satisfaction, as well as employee buy-in to the retailer brand.

Further, there are distinct challenges to retailers: to build and recognise staff expertise and loyalty; to evaluate staff skills, training needs, and staff satisfaction; and to develop worker-friendly policies including occupational health and safety, equal employment opportunity and affirmative action, and policies for staff with carer responsibilities and study needs. Profit sharing schemes, incentive plans and systems are some of the mechanisms available to acknowledge and reward employees. When planning to outsource aspects of human resource management or any functional activity, a retailer should evaluate this option using specific criteria.

To ensure a continued supply of suitably prepared employees, retailers will be involved in the secondary education sector, so that prospective employees understand the potential career opportunities through displays at career markets, through work experience, and through contributions to course development by retailers. In the emerging field of retail marketing in the tertiary education sector, prospective retail managers should be aware of the skills needed and the opportunities available through careers-on-campus seminars, through retailer contributions to course development, and through liaison with local service clubs and business groups which may sponsor business-based research projects, prizes, scholarships and cadetships. In addition to action in the secondary and tertiary education sectors, there is a pressing need for well-developed short courses for existing retailing employees both at the front line and at more senior levels.

Developing best practice people management will be one of the distinguishing features of successful retailers over the next decade. The benefits of this approach will accrue to the retailer, the staff and the customer.

Retail customers

It is appropriate to start and end with the retail customer. This book takes the position that best practice retail marketing uses retail branding and innovation to both meet customer needs and add value for the customer. The most important trends in consumer preferences are the desires for convenience, product range and value for money prices. Retail formats and strategies should respond to these needs, and retailers need to have the relevant capabilities to do so. In some cases, home shopping may be the best way of meeting these needs, but frequently storefront retailing will be a more appropriate format for offering a total shopping experience.

Consumers are placing more emphasis on fresh, healthy, nutritious and pre-prepared/easily prepared meals. This trend accelerated in the mid 1980s – in part with the advent of the microwave oven – and it is likely to continue into the future. With demands for more natural and less processed foods, major novel responses in available food types, packaging and retail formats are required.

Another consumer preference growth area is the need for information. This demand reflects a more discerning market that is better educated and more socially aware. Retailers can provide information in various ways, including through packaging labels, contents, Heart Foundation endorsement ticks, store signage, store leaflets, informed salespersons, and advertising and publicity, as well as through their websites.

A further growing consumer desire is for more excitement in the shopping experience. The multi-sensory shopping experience draws on the activities of the retailer and the shopping location – especially the planned shopping centre (mall). The growth in academic research into the psyche of the retail consumer should better equip retailers to meet this challenge by helping them better understand the total shopping experience.

More generally, retailers will improve the quality of their goods and services. The buzzwords are customer satisfaction, with retailers giving more attention to both customer service and to service quality as the means of achieving this. In a related move, retailers will find better ways of managing customer complaints, and also extend this to managing supplier complaints. In tandem, the creation of customer loyalty programs is escalating significantly.

Multi channel retailing as an innovation and distribution mechanism is not new, as discussed in *Chapter 1 – An introduction to retailing*. What has changed is the range of channels that are now available to retailers. The current diversity of channels spans traditional channels such as the retail store, catalogues, direct mail marketing and direct personal selling. As well, more recent modes such as online retailing (e-retailing), email and SMS direct marketing, and CANs are prevalent. Movements have emerged such as underground marketing where, for example, only a very select customer group learns of the opening of a fashion forward retailer with 'street-cred'. This type of retailer may use only word-of-mouth, email or SMS in a viral marketing campaign to seed the information dispersion so that relevant customers will learn of the current temporary location of the store. Some retailers will probably expand the variety of channels they use as more technological innovations emerge.

Sustainable retailing – a preliminary agenda

A significant opportunity exists for retailers to develop sustainable retailing strategies and related retailer brands. Fundamental action by retailers has several aspects:

1. The first aspect of sustainable retailing is developing a business that **is** sustainable, that is has a sustainable competitive advantage (Vignette 11.3).

2. The second aspect is developing resource efficiency throughout the supply chain. Avoiding waste, working with suppliers to achieve resource efficiencies in processes, products and services, and reducing the waste of product recalls are all beneficial approaches.

3. The third aspect is to offer to customers product and service choices that are fit for purpose, environmentally friendly, and resource efficient, so that customers themselves can make environmentally friendly choices (see Vignette 11.2).

4. The fourth aspect of sustainable retailing is to design and operate stores that are built from environmentally sustainable products and that are resource efficient in their operation (see Vignette 11.3).

Vignette 11.3

Sustainability and the small retailer

Small retailers have even more cause to develop sustainable retailing than larger firms do. The abundance of small specialty retailers who fill well-defined niches *can* co-exist with large format retails. For small retailers, sustainable retailing makes sense because it is a systematic approach to efficient and effective retail marketing.

For your consideration:

What resources and networks can small retailers use to improve their potential for retail success in niche markets?

Vignette 11.4

The roles of retailers and suppliers in product reuse and recycling – scope for branding and innovation

Retailers have significant scope to follow up the sale of their products with processes for product reuse and recycling. In the past, 'trade-ins' were a popular way to attract customers – especially in the whitegoods area. One benefit to the customer was the ease of disposal of the product being replaced. Similarly, current retailers who deliver new products will arrange to take away the old product, usually for a fee. However, the drawback in both cases to the community is that the retailer usually just dumps the products rather than reconditioning them for further sale as second hand goods or for donation to charities.

The end use of textiles is also attracting attention but most retailers, suppliers or governments have done little to encourage the consumer to dispose of clothing and textiles in responsible and environmentally sound ways. Older methods exist such as donations of clothing to charities, and newer methods such as online auctions offer the seller some financial return for disposing of clothing and textiles. With the ever increasing predominance of 'fast fashion', more and more clothing is purchased and rapidly disposed of – either because it is quickly unfashionable or because it has been made to last only a short time. However, overall, little research has examined the end use of clothing and textiles. The aim of some recent research has been to examine current practices from the consumer perspective, and to endeavour to develop an understanding of potential innovations and interventions that could contribute to the sustainable consumption of fashion.

For your reflection:

- Explore strategies that retailers could introduce to contribute more to sustainability.

- What actions could government take?

- What should consumers do?

5. The fifth aspect is that retailers have the opportunity for leadership in promoting recycling and the reuse of product components (Vignette 11.4). For success, retailers will need to develop internal processes and their relationships with suppliers to create strategies that emphasise and enable reuse, recycling or salvage. A simple example is the collection and recycling of engine oil when a car is serviced.

Computers, mobile phones and electronic games are also examples of potential e-waste.

6. The sixth aspect is that innovation will be at the centre of sustainable retailing in all its forms. Retailers must work with many stakeholders to achieve resource sustainability and be net contributors to the community.

Increasing demands for sustainable retailing are coming from all stakeholders, albeit with fairly quiet voices at present. Many public retail companies are now producing statements on corporate governance, environmental issues and fair-trading. The term sustainable retailing can incorporate all these dimensions and more. The business itself must be sustainable, so that customers, suppliers, employees and other stakeholders can depend on the continuity of the business. Proactive retailers – both large and small – can aim for sustainable retailing by:

- *creating a sustainable competitive advantage;*

- *using ethical practices;*

- *exercising corporate social responsibility;*

- *minimising the firm's environmental footprint; and*

- *introducing innovative practices that enable customers to co-produce aspects of sustainable retailing.*

The contribution of retail innovation

Retail innovation can be both market *driven* and market *driving*. The concept of retail innovation has been woven through out this book, and robustly related to retailer strategy and branding. Much of the literature focuses on product and service innovations which are very informative and useful. However, more extensive searching shows many additional initiatives and innovative processes and practices that retailers are using. As is often the case, practice precedes theory, so we can look forward to stronger conceptualisations of retailer innovation as the research proceeds the results, and the literature reports on the findings.

One of the issues for retailer who are trying to foster innovation is creating the right internal environment as well as strong relationships with supplies so that co-operative innovations can be developed to meet specific needs. As illustrated in Vignette 11.5, uncritically following marketing and management fads may not be the best approach. Coherence with the retailer's strategy and brand will govern which management tools and techniques are suited to the firm.

Vignette 11.5

Strategies for success or inhibitors to innovation?
Views from the business press

Quality improvement programs such as Six Sigma have received negative press recently, with one reporting arguing that such programs could "undermine individual contributions to the company ... Some major proponents have begun to scale back their involvement [including] 3M and Home Depot. ... The program ... was not compatible with the spirit of innovation that had once made 3M great" (Globe & Mail 2007, p. 22). The caution here, as with any innovation or business development process, is for retailers to *adapt* such programs to their specific needs rather than to *adopt* them outright.

For your deliberation:

How should retailers evaluate management improvements tools?

Source:
The Globe and Mail [G & M] 2007, 'Six stigma: for two decades, one program designed to quantify quality was all the rage. Get ready for the backlash', Report on Business, September, p. 22.

Conclusions

This book commenced by highlight the ubiquity of retailing. Now, having reached the end of the book, you the reader may be aware of the complexity of retailing, and that the frontstage is just that. Like a theatre, the performance and interaction with the audience are frontstage, but no performance goes ahead without a strong concept, extensive planning, resource investment, training, and a sophisticated backstage which supports the frontstage. Success is measured in part by audience response, and in many other ways including sales and the cost-effectiveness of operations.

Performance must respond to trends, and Vignette 11.6 encapsulates some issues that planners face.

Strategies and performance must also respond to opportunity. Vignette 11.7 shows that retailers can be proactive. By applying the approaches developed in this book, they have the scope to develop and invest in distinctive strategies and unique retailer brands to create sustainable competitive advantage.

Vignette 11.6

Retail development and redevelopment - a planner's perspective

Retailers need to work with architects, planners, property developers and governments when planning stand-alone shopping sites, or indeed entire shopping centres. An Australian success story is Westfield which is now strongly represented in New Zealand, the US and the UK. An emerging issue for consumers is the apparent homogeneity of many planned shopping malls – a situation at odds with the shift to increasing multi-sensory shopping experiences which also surprise and please consumers.

More broadly, Hill (2007) encapsulates the current issues:

... developers are clearly watching global trends. Like North America, we [in New Zealand] are already experiencing the return to the shopping centres much more like those of the past either by renovating our older centres or by designing new ones using traditional urban design concepts. There continues to be demand for large carparks close to storefronts, but retail developers are experimenting with landscape and design elements that create places 'to be' in a community. And, in some cases developers are even building the housing and offices to create communities within their shopping centres.

As planners we need to be aware of new trends changing market. We need to be proactive and forward thinking, and the emerging trends in retail development (and redevelopment) provide the opportunity we have long sought to create better and more sustainable retail precincts in our communities. Most importantly, we should recognise that our plans and regulations may need to evolve to allow what will inevitably take place while encouraging the best planning and design approaches.' Hall 2007, p. 23.

Source:
Hall, K 2007, 'North American retail development trend: a planner's perspective', *Planning Quarterly: New Zealand Planning Institute Quarterly*, vol. 166 (Sept.), pp. 10-11, 23.

Vignette 11.7

Strategies for growth – views from the business press

Retailing is a business, even in the not-for-profit sector. Many of the specifics of retailing – such as the retail mix – are unique. Conversely, retailing has much in common with any business, so knowledgeable and experienced retailers will benchmark processes and concepts widely. As Shiffman (2007) recommends, "social change, demographic trends, economic shifts and rapidly evolving technologies are creating countless new challenges and opportunities".

Shiffman's advice covers seven areas:

1. "Turn a shade of green" by investing in sustainability;

2. "Adopt CRM software" as a means to developing positive customer relationships;

3. "Harness your corporate brain." This can also be thought of as developing corporate memory and organisational learning. Recall that high staff turnover can result in the 'loss' of corporate memory, experience and skills.

4. "Open up your business for the world to see." The idea is that greater transparency attracts greater feedback from employees, customers and other stakeholders.

5. "Sell more with search engines." Shiffman suggests that search-engine marketing is one of today's essential sales boosters. For some retailers this will not be the case, but it should be deliberately rejected rather than just neglected.

6. "Create employee shareholders." This concept is not new – being introduced over a hundred years ago in some department stores. It is finding favour again as firms try to develops trust and commitment, as well as reward and incentive schemes. Some staff may be concerned about being tied to the firm, so arrangements should be flexible.

7. "Put social media in your mix." For smaller, less techno-savvy retailers this will be a 'scary' strategy, but one that Shiffman argues will be worth the effort. The caution is that skills are needed, as are monitoring and consistency.

Source:
Shiffman, K 2007, 'The 7 best ways to build your business now', *Profit: Your Guide to Business Success*, vol. 26, no. 5 (November), Section: Growth Strategies, pp. 22-28.

A final word on the excitement of retail marketing

Two assumptions underpin discussions about retailing in this book. The first is that retailing is here to stay, though not necessarily in the forms that we currently experience and understand. The second assumption is that there is always another way to manage – and often a better way. Therefore, retailers need to embark on an exciting journey, discovering the best ways and the best practices in retail marketing and management. The rewards of such a journey are perhaps analogous to the discoveries on the silk road in the Orient so long ago – new products, new ways of doing things, new ideas – *nova* retailing! Retail branding and retail innovation have always be relevant to successful retailers.

We urge you, the reader, to add your own enquiry, ideas and contributions to the retailing future of Australasia and wherever you find yourself in the retail value chain. Search for fresh ideas, unique approaches and innovation – develop an entrepreneurial spirit. Learning is an iterative process; try to learn from each retailing experience. Please learn to celebrate discoveries and successes. We remind you that the future is *now!*

Carpe Diem

Review and applications

1. Explore how retailers can recognise the lifestyle, income, employment, leisure and health profiles that are significant to each discrete consumer cluster.

2. Explain how retailers can be more responsive to the 'baby boomer' generation who will continue to live in their own homes. For instance, they may require and be prepared to pay for a changing array of retailing products and services including: the delivery of purchases, the installation and maintenance of domestic appliances and electronic products, housekeeping, home maintenance, dog washing and walking, automobile servicing at home, prepared meals, computer maintenance and repairs, and specialised travel packages.

3. Discuss how retailers can develop and introduce much more employee-friendly policies.

4. Choose any retailer – large or small – and design a green retailing strategy.

5. Explain how small retailers can develop retailer brands that embrace corporate social responsibility strategies.

6. Consider how a retailer can integrated its heritage values and a contemporary retailer brand.

7. Discuss the risks and opportunities inherent of introducing blogs and other 'social media'.

8.   Design a campaign to attract excellent candidates for retailing careers.

9.   Explore the concept that shopping centres are community hubs.

10. Reflect on your earliest retailing memories. What has changed? Why?

Website references

Inside Retailing: <www.insideretaling.com.au>.

Inside Retailing 2007, 'Tesco opens first 6 Fresh and Easy California stores', available at <www.insideretailing.com.au/articles>, 02 Dec 2007.

Woolworth Ltd, 2007: <www.woolworthslimited.com.au>.

Woolworths Supermarkets, 2007: <www.woolworths.com.au>.

References and reading

Barrymore, K 1995, 'BBC Hardware store sells to investors for $8.7 million', *The Australian Financial; Review*, Feb., p. 55.

Blanchard, T, 2007, *Green is the new black: How to change the world with style*, Hodder & Stoughton, London.

Carlson, C & Wilmot, W, 2006, *Innovation: The Five Disciplines for Creating What Customers Want*, Crown Business, New York.

Danziger, P 2006, *Shopping: Why We Love It and How Retailers Can Create the Ultimate Experience*, Kaplan, Chicago.

Dennis, C, Fenech, T, Merrilees, B 2004, *e-Retailing*, Routledge, London.

Fielding, D 2007, 'Everyone's gone green', *The Globe and Mail: Report on Business*, September, p. 26.

Grewal, D & Levy, M 2007, 'Retailing research: past, present and future', *Journal of Retailing*, vol. 83, no. 4, pp. 447-464.

Hall, K 2007, 'North American retail development trend: a planner's perspective', *Planning Quarterly: New Zealand Planning Institute Quarterly*, vol. 166 (Sept.), pp. 10-11, 23.

Kirby, J 2007, 'Canada's top 100 employers', *Maclean's*, Special Report, 15 Oct., pp. 41-42.

Koehn, N 2001, *Brand New: How Entrepreneurs Earned Consumers' Trust from Wedgwood to Dell*, Harvard Business School Press, Boston.

Merrilees, B & Miller, D 2001, 'Innovation and Strategy in the Australian Supermarket Industry', *Journal of Food Products Marketing*, vol. 7, no. 4, pp. 3-18.

Mitchell, S 2006, *Big-Box Swindle: the True Cost of Mega-Retailers and the Fight for America's Independent Businesses*, Beacon Press, Boston.

Plant, A 2007, *The Retail Game: Playing to Win – a Guide to the Profitable Sale of Goods and Services*, Douglas & McIntyre, Vancouver.

Rapaille, C 2007, *The Culture Code: an Ingenious Way to Understand Why People Around the World Buy and Live As They Do*, Broadway books, New York.

Sartain, L & Schumann, M 2006, *Brand from the Inside Out: Eight Essentials to Emotionally Connect Employees to Your Business*, Jossey-Bass, San Francisco.

Schor, J, 2005, *Born to Buy*, Scribner, New York.

Shiffman, K 2007, 'The 7 best ways to build your business now', *Profit: Your Guide to Business Success*, vol. 26, no. 5 (November), Section: Growth Strategies, pp. 22-28.

The Globe and Mail 2007, 'Six stigma: for two decades, one program designed to quantify quality was all the rage. Get ready for the backlash', *Report on Business*, September, p. 22.

Yerema, R 2007, 'The top 100', *Maclean's*, Special Report, 15 October, pp. 43-46.

Index

420729

T

tools
    business intelligence, 36
    forecasting, 83
    positioning statement, 39
    promotion, 177
    retail audit, 37
    retail audit protocol, 240
    statistical, 158
    total quality management (TQM), 101
    trading area analysis, 150
total shopping experience, 122, 135
training
    needs analysis, 35

    skills audit, 35
trends, 282
    environmentalism, 21
    flexible shopping hours, 22
    megatrends, 19, 21
    professionalising, 20
    training, 21

V

value chain analysis, 4
visual merchandising, 132
    customer-merchandise interaction
        (CMI), 134
    instore promotion, 132

420729